Victorian Military Campaigns

Victorian Military Campaigns

Edited by Professor Brian Bond
King's College, London

The Sikh Wars, 1845-49
The Third China War, 1860
The Expedition to Abyssinia, 1867-68
The Ashanti Campaign, 1873-74
The South African War, 1880-81
The Egyptian Campaign, 1882
The Reconquest of the Sudan, 1896-99

Tom Donovan
London

First published in 1967 by Hutchinson & Co (Publishers)
Ltd.
© Hutchinson & Co (Publishers) Ltd. 1967

This edition published in 1994 by

Tom Donovan Publishing Ltd.
52 Willow Road
Hampstead
London NW3 1TP

ISBN: 1-871085-21-7

Printed in Great Britain by
Antony Rowe Ltd., Chippenham, Wiltshire

Contents

Maps

Illustrations

Convention was signed there after the war.
(*'With the Flag to Pretoria'*, vol. 1)

Major-General Hector Macdonald, a photograph taken at the time of the Second South African War. 'Fighting Mac' was one of the few Victorian generals who rose from the ranks.
(*'With the Flag to Pretoria'*, vol. 1)

The Egyptian War. Fort Pharos after the British Naval bombardment. Note the ancient cannon and mortars.
(*'Royal Engineers' Operations in Egypt, 1882.' War Office Library*)

Ibid. Battery W at Tel-el-Kebir. This photograph taken soon after the battle gives some idea of the desert terrain which provided the greatest obstacle to Wolseley's advance. (*British Museum*)

The Egyptian War. (a) Colonel Arabi in exile in Ceylon.
(*'British Battles on Land and Sea'*, vol. 1)

(b) Sir Drury Lowe, who commanded the spectacular cavalry dash to Cairo which speedily ended the war after the Battle of Tel-el-Kebir. (*'Navy and Army Illustrated'*, vol. 1)

The Sudan. (a) Sir Horatio Herbert Kitchener as Commander-in-Chief of the Egyptian Army in 1896. (*'Navy and Army Illustrated'*, vol. 1)

(b) The Mahdi. (*'British Battles on Land and Sea'*, vol. 1)

Acknowledgements

I would like to thank Major B. M. Hamilton for his kindness in lending me the papers of his great-uncle General Sir Bruce Meade Hamilton, brother-in-law of Major-General Sir George Colley; Colonel P. R. Butler, D.S.O., for lending me the manuscript of his father's biography of Colley; and Brigadier B. W. Webb-Carter, D.S.O., O.B.E., for lending the manuscript of Ensign Wynter's account of the Abyssinian Campaign to David Chandler.

The Editor and contributors are especially grateful for assistance and advice to Mr D. W. King, O.B.E., the War Office Librarian, and his Staff, particularly Mr C. A. Potts and Mr N. B. Leslie; and also to Brigadier John Stephenson, O.B.E., Director of the Royal United Service Institution, and Mr David Erskine, the Librarian. Mr Jack Dove and his assistants at Hove Public Library were unfailingly helpful to those of us who studied the Wolseley papers there. I should also like to acknowledge the help we have received from Mr Alan Bell of the National Register of Archives, and from the staff of the British Museum, the Public Record Office, the Library of the Royal Commonwealth Society, and the Old India Office Library.

Acknowledgement for the illustrations has been made on another page, but a special word of thanks is due to the War Office Library for allowing books to be borrowed for photographing; and to Lieutenant-Colonel E. E. N. Sandeman, O.B.E. (Retd), Librarian of the Royal Engineer Corps Library at Chatham, and Mr W. Y. Carman, Acting Director of the National Army Museum, and his

Staff at Camberley for permission to use previously unpublished photographs.

I would like to acknowledge with thanks permission to quote given by the following publishers: Edward Arnold Ltd, for *Field Marshal Lord Napier of Magdala* by Lieutenant–Colonel H. D. Napier; Macmillan and Co. Ltd, for *Africa and the Victorians* by R. Robinson and J. Gallagher with A. Denny; and *The Imperial Idea and its Enemies* by A. P. Thornton; and John Murray Ltd, for *Kitchener: Portrait of an Imperialist* by Philip Magnus. Acknowledgement of the many other publications which have been drawn on only slightly less heavily than these has been made in the references at the end of each campaign and in the *Notes on Sources* at the end of the volume.

I should like to take this opportunity to thank Captain Sir Basil Liddell Hart for his generosity and patience which have allowed me to create yawning gaps on his bookshelves. His serious illness early in 1966 caused me to refrain from asking him to read the book in its early stages, but any historical merit that my own chapter may possess is to a large extent due to his influence over the past seven years. I am also grateful to Professor Michael Howard for encouraging me initially to undertake the project, though he too is entirely free from responsibility for the book's shortcomings. I am very grateful to Mr Richard Morse for weeding out many errors and solecisms at the page-proof stage, but he is likewise blameless for those that remain. Lastly I should like to thank my wife Madeleine for her invaluable secretarial help at a time when I was handicapped by ill-health.

BRIAN BOND

Medmenham, Bucks.

Editor's Introduction

This book has been written in the conviction that much of interest remains to be said about those small campaigns and expeditions from which the British Empire was seldom free during Victoria's long reign. Certainly there have been many detailed accounts of these minor wars, notably in Sir John Fortescue's thirteen-volume *History of the British Army*, but these all had their shortcomings: the range of sources consulted was often narrow; imperialist assumptions imposed their own limitations; and above all the military chroniclers usually failed to place the wars in their political context. In recent years the opening of public archives has prompted the publication of several scholarly studies of the political and administrative aspects of imperial defence, but these works are only marginally concerned with military campaigns.[1] On the other hand the revival of popular interest in the Victorian Age has led to the publication of some vivid accounts of particular campaigns, or of a series of wars in one region. Excellent though the best of these are they can only hint at the variety of Victorian campaigning, at recurrent difficulties and—not least interesting and important—at the effects of these wars in imperial and domestic politics.

Thus, while each contributor has been free to develop the aspects of his campaign which seemed to him most interesting or significant, all have been primarily concerned to put the military events into their political context. These are the kind of questions they have asked themselves: how and why particular wars occurred and how firmly were they controlled politically; what degree of military competence was shown in their execution; and how effective were they as instruments of policy.

A selection such as this is obviously open to criticism. The number of campaigns studied was determined by the need to provide a fair sample, both in terms of the world-wide theatre and the length of the reign, and yet to allow space for detailed scholarly essays which could be included in a single volume. For this reason, as well as the fact that they have already been much written about, Britain's large-scale wars during the period—the Crimean War, the Indian Mutiny and the Second South African War—have been omitted. As for the actual choice, certain campaigns seemed to me to have been surprisingly neglected considering their intrinsic interest. These included the Abyssinian Expedition, the First South African War, and the Egyptian campaign. The remaining subjects, equally fascinating and little better known, were then chosen to provide the maximum variety. The Sikh Wars marked the end of British armed conquest within India's frontiers, and represent the early years of Victoria's reign. The China War exemplifies the many punitive expeditions against supposedly inferior nations, in this case undertaken in uneasy collaboration with the French; and also demonstrates India's immense value as a military base. The Ashanti War was chosen in part to illustrate Wolseley's administrative genius, but also for the peculiar problems encountered in campaigning in tropical Africa. The Gordon Relief Expedition of 1884–5 might seem a strange omission but since it has recently been the subject of an admirable book, *England's Pride* by Julian Symons, and as Wolseley was already the dominant figure in two preceding chapters, it seemed more appropriate to conclude with Kitchener's reconquest of the Sudan.

Quite possibly another volume could be produced with an entirely different selection. It would do well to include the Afghan Wars, the Maori Wars, the Red River Expedition in Canada, the conquest of Burma, and several of the Indian frontier wars, such as the Chitral Relief Expedition. This book, however, makes no claim to have said the last word about Victorian small wars; its purpose is to arouse interest in the campaigns themselves, to throw new light on their political background, and perhaps to provoke a reconsideration of some much-maligned Victorian generals.

The object of the Introduction which follows is threefold. First to outline the evolution of British colonial policy through the nineteenth century, stressing the gradual withdrawal of British troops from the self-governing colonies and the closely associated evolvement of the concept of 'imperial defence'. Next the Army is portrayed, first in its pre-Crimean complacency and then under the reinvigorating impact of the Cardwell reforms. Lastly, an attempt is made to isolate some of the special characteristics of minor warfare in the nineteenth century.

(i) VICTORIAN COLONIAL POLICY AND THE BEGINNINGS OF IMPERIAL DEFENCE

It is a truism to describe the Victorian era as one of expansion, for, to the early Victorians especially, the export of British civilisation seemed not only necessary but irreproachably right. It would be a serious mistake, however, to believe that Victorian statesmen in general regarded territorial expansion as an end in itself, or looked upon the armed forces primarily as instruments for such expansion. On the contrary, although 'exertions of power and colonial rule might be needed in some places to provide opportunity and to protect [settlers] ... the empire tended to be thought of as an auxiliary'.[2] The chief means of expansion were industrial and maritime supremacy operating on the basis of free trade. Moreover it was well understood that trade did not generally follow the flag: in the 1850's, for example, the average value of British trade to foreign countries was £209 million, as compared with £76 million for the trade to the Empire.[3] Thus under the policy of 'indirect imperialism' through free trade annexations were as a rule carefully avoided. British influence was extended through more subtle means—by threats, cajolery or tempting loans reinforced occasionally by naval bombardment or military expedition. By such means 'foreign tariffs and monopolies were broken down, the gouty empires of China and Turkey opened to British influence, and innumerable lesser sheikdoms, sultanates and chieftancies were drawn into the invisible empire of informal sway'.[4]

By about 1870 certain expectations of the Victorian liberals and free traders had been disappointed by the response of non-Europeans, particularly the Chinese and Africans, to this indirect imperialism. These peoples showed no sign of developing liberal Western institutions, nor did they prove congenial or valuable trading partners. Hence

B

in the later decades of the century British business interests were concentrated increasingly in the Americas and Europe, with India and Australia next in priority.

The implications of this trend for Britain's overseas military commitments were clear: as British governments became tired of endless frontier wars and the costly and thankless task of trying to enforce justice between settlers and natives, so too the white settlers grew increasingly restless and bitter against control from Whitehall. The solution seemed to be colonial self-government, carrying with it the burden of responsibility for at least internal self-defence. In this sense British imperial strategy in the second half of the century was defensive. In practice, however, Britain could not entirely divest herself of responsibility for the defence of her self-governing colonies and India against hostile tribes; while external protection against potentially hostile European powers took on an increasingly urgent aspect. But, apart from South Africa, the 1860's saw virtually the end of imperial military activity inside the white colonies.

India was not a colony of European settlement and for this and other reasons it did not follow the common trend towards self-government and responsibility for self-defence. In short, despite the moral misgivings it aroused and the burdens it entailed, the retention of British India was held to be essential. This could be justified on economic terms alone. India was the great entrepôt of eastern trade; it absorbed some 20 per cent of Britain's exports and no less than one-fifth of her overseas investments. Yet India was of even greater value as the hub of British power in the East; or as Lord Salisbury called it disparagingly in 1867 'an English barrack in the oriental seas'. After the suppression of the Mutiny the creation of a unified Imperial Army in India provided a powerful weapon for overawing or crushing Asiatic rulers who obstructed Britain's interests. The enormous advantages of this Army to Britain were summarised by Lord Hartington in 1878: 'The Indian Army is not limited in numbers by an annual vote of Parliament. It is not voted by Parliament at all; its numbers are not enumerated in the Mutiny Act; and the native portion ... is not even subject to the Mutiny Act. In fact it may be described as a non-Parliamentary Army, as compared with the Army which is maintained at home and in the other dependencies of the Crown.'[5] What this quotation does not make explicit is that the Indian taxpayer not only bore the cost of his country's occupation but also paid for about 70,000 British troops—roughly a third of the regular army. Though of doubtful constitutional legality, it will not surprise us to find that British colonial campaigns—even outside the Indian continent—were fought to a remarkable extent by British and native troops of the Indian Army.[6]

India was of unique military importance in quite another sense. From the 1870's to the end of the century it is no exaggeration to say that Britain's statesmen and soldiers were obsessed with the problem of how best to defend the North West Frontier of India against Russian encroachment. This, easily the dominant issue of military policy in the 1870's and 1880's, shaped not only the organisation and distribution of the armed forces in India, but also goes far to explain the deterioration of the army at home which was virtually reduced to the role of supplying drafts to India. Edward Crawford explains how and why the frontier of British India was extended to the Indus in the 1840's after the humiliation of the First Afghan War. The Second Afghan War was simply an incident—albeit a dramatic one—in this protracted 'confrontation' between Britain and Russia.

In the period preceding the Crimean War it is difficult to discern any coherent British naval and military policy. Partly in the attempt to preserve a nucleus of the regular army in face of constant demands for reductions after 1815, units were dispersed into 'the obscure recesses of empire' and troops were stationed, as Sydney Smith put it, 'on every rock in the ocean where a cormorant can perch'. But this failure to develop a comprehensive colonial strategy was not very astonishing or dangerous so long as no rival existed with sufficient sea power to menace British possessions. Thus apart from the garrison at the Cape, designed to protect the colonists against the natives, and those in Canada for defence against the United States, the task of the numerous outposts remained the traditional one of 'defending bases from which the navy could control trade routes, intercept attack on British territory, and in company with the army, act offensively against enemy territory'.[7] In the 1840's and 1850's the Radicals' hope that overseas military commitments would soon be eliminated seemed quite realistic.

Then in the 1850's something approaching a strategic crisis resulted from the fact that 'technical achievement had outstripped strategic thought'. In brief the revolutionary technical changes which in some twenty years transformed navies of wooden sailing ships into steam-powered ironclads and simultaneously transformed naval gunnery, led to the exaggerated fear that 'steam had bridged the Channel' and hence that Britain—as the Duke of Wellington had warned in 1847—was in imminent danger of invasion. This invasion scare gave the Colonial Office a genuine strategic reason—as distinct from the Radicals' persistent demands for reduced expenditure—for speeding up the withdrawal of overseas garrisons. Despite the danger to Canada posed by the American Civil War, a recrudescence of the Maori Wars in a fiercer form, and disturbances in Australia, South Africa and Jamaica, the decade 1860–70 witnessed the culmination of the 'withdrawal of the legions' from the partially or wholly self-governing colonies, and the substitution of colonial self-help in defence. This significant change in military distribution followed the recommendations of a Select Parliamentary Committee ('The Mills Committee') set up in 1861 which characteristically contained not a single expert on defence. 'Their outlook', as W. C. B. Tunstall has written, 'was so dominated by the idea of self-reliance that it is difficult in some cases to distinguish the desire for imperial co-operation from the desire for imperial disintegration.'[8]

By 1870 Edward Cardwell had carried the policy of withdrawal from the self-governing colonies almost to completion: all British troops had quitted Australia, New Zealand and Tasmania, and the last were soon due to leave Canada except for the garrison at the naval base of Halifax. Since this concentration of troops at home was speedily followed by reductions there can be no question that financial retrenchment rather than increased military efficiency was uppermost in the minds of Gladstone and his Cabinet.

What is perhaps more surprising is the failure of successive governments in the 1860's and 1870's to overhaul British naval strategy. In fact excessive faith continued to be placed on local defence, fixed fortifications and floating batteries, while the vastly more important guarantee of colonial security—the Royal Navy—was allowed to deteriorate for lack of money and attention. Colonial defence continued to mean simply British piecemeal arrangements to defend individual colonies and other possessions. 'The War Office, the Colonial Office and the Treasury continued to work in co-operation in order to secure economy and reform, but made no attempt to secure the co-operation of the Admiralty in working out a general strategic policy.'[9]

Only in 1878 were the first tentative movements made towards the systematic study—as a prelude to practical measures—of imperial defence as a whole. Not merely was that year marked by the seemingly serious Russian threat to British interests in the Mediterranean and in Afghanistan; it also saw the reappearance of France as an imperialist rival. These powers, singly or in alliance, had henceforth to be considered as potential enemies. With the rapid increase in the speed and range of modern steamships individual British bases and coaling stations were now considered vulnerable to sudden attack. The immediate consequence of this new uneasiness was the creation of a Colonial Defence Committee in 1878, and the appointment of a Royal Commission the following year 'to enquire into the defences of British possessions and commerce abroad'. Though both bodies took an insular view of imperial problems they did at least raise the question of colonial participation in a general scheme for imperial defence.[10]

The general complacency regarding Britain's naval supremacy was rudely shattered in the late 1880's when Admiral Lord Charles Beresford gave support to civilian critics of the service such as Sir Charles Dilke. In the past decade the French Navy had made rapid progress; Russia, Italy and the U.S.A. were all building modern warships; while Germany, though not as yet a naval power, had become a colonial competitor. Numerical superiority could no longer ensure Britain of victory against France and Russia together and, more to the point, Britain was becoming increasingly vulnerable to naval blockade and commerce destruction through dependence on imported food. The Royal Navy's inefficiency may be charitably explained by the fact that it had not engaged in a major action since the Napoleonic Wars. Smokeless powder was not introduced until the turn of the century, and armour-piercing shells were issued only in 1902. Practice firing in the 1880's was described as 'merely farcical'. Worst of all the lack of a Naval Staff or of any organisation for war practically reduced the Navy to 'an agglomeration of vessels'.

A decisive improvement was made by the Naval Defence Act of 1889, which authorised the construction of 8 large and 2 small battleships and other auxiliary vessels by 1894. The Franco-Russian alliance in the latter year underlined the need for a sustained effort to preserve the 'Two Power Standard', and by the end of the decade the beginning of the German naval challenge ensured that there would be no further slackening on Britain's part.

This period of hectic naval construction and reforms also saw the development of a more informed study at government level of the problems of imperial defence, due largely to the labours of the Colonial Defence Committee. Useful as this Committee was however as a permanent body for the collection of data and preparation of plans for overseas operations, it suffered from severe limitations; particularly in its lack of powers of decision and the absence of any colonial representatives. The Colonial Conferences of 1887 and 1897 revealed how far the British Government was from achieving voluntary colonial collaboration in a genuine imperial plan for both land and sea operations. At both conferences the colonial delegates generally held firm to the view that it was England's duty to control foreign affairs of her empire and bear the full responsibility for its external defence. By the 1890's the movement for imperial federation in the colonies was declining; a severe depression turned their thoughts away from defence; and, perhaps most important, each was developing regional interests and its own national pride. It was far from clear to Canada and Australia especially that England's future wars would necessarily be theirs. Even in South Africa, where there clearly was a great likelihood of war, no effort was made to reach co-operation in military relations between the British and the colonial governments. Thus to the end of the century Britain continued to formulate, execute and pay for the defence of her empire with virtually no support from the self-governing colonies.

Much confusion has resulted from the historical myth that a 'New Imperialism' of territorial expansion—inspired by Disraeli—began in Britain around 1870. In fact there was no dramatic change, but rather a realistic adaptation to Britain's gradual loss of dominance in the world.[11] Until the last quarter of the century Britain had enjoyed an almost effortless supremacy outside Europe, thanks to her unrivalled combination of industrial strength and maritime power. In Palmerston's era therefore there was no need to acquire economically valueless territory for the sake of strategic security; indeed Britain could concentrate her power and interests in areas most suited to contribute to her wealth and strength—notably in India rather than Africa. The late Victorians, by contrast, became increasingly aware of the ephemeral nature of Britain's supremacy overseas. Their outlook became more defensive, especially as regards the Russian threat to India; desiring to preserve and protect an unwieldy empire against new dangers in an increasingly unstable world. These apprehensions go far to explain Britain's participation in the 'scramble for Africa' from the mid-1880's, and her efforts to persuade the self-governing colonies to share the burdens of imperial defence.

The South African War of 1899-1902 cruelly exposed the limitations of British power, and caused the beginning of a reorientation of her foreign policy towards a closer involvement in European affairs. Even with colonial assistance the British Army had a hard struggle to defeat the Boers, and only did so at the risk of leaving the homeland almost militarily defenceless. If isolation from Europe had ever been 'splendid' it was clearly no longer so. By 1904 the long colonial rivalry with France had been converted into an Entente, and in the following year Russia's defeat by Japan convinced most statesmen that India was no longer in serious danger of an overland invasion. Most significant of all, after nearly a century of pre-occupation with her overseas Empire, Britain began to prepare in earnest for a European war.

(ii) MILITARY ORGANISATION IN RELATION TO OVERSEAS CAMPAIGNS

In the period between Waterloo and the Crimean War Britain's military organisation declined alarmingly. At the close of the Napoleonic wars the regular army numbered about 220,000 men; by 1820 the lowest total of 80,000 was reached, and twenty years later the number had risen to just over 100,000 with about 46,000 of these stationed in Britain and Ireland. So persistent was the clamour for reductions of the military budget that the Duke of Wellington only managed to preserve a token fighting force at the cost of the non-combatant departments. Thus even the small number of troops available gave no true indication of the nation's unpreparedness for war. It took the Crimean débâcle to reveal the disastrous consequences of the lack of land transport, and of civil departments with clear responsibility to supply and maintain an army in the field. Several of the chapters in this book demonstrate the fantastic commissariat and transport problems with which Victorian generals had to grapple.

The pre-Crimean army cried out for reform from every point of view. Recruits were still mostly drawn from the lowest social class and were treated 'alternately as a criminal to be punished with flogging and as a child whose every action should be watched and guarded'. Until 1847 soldiers were enlisted for life service (21 years); flogging was not completely abolished until 1881; and pay and living conditions remained inexcusably low through most of Victoria's reign.

The officers' attitude to their men was at best paternalistic. Until 1871 the majority obtained their commissions and promotion up to the rank of lieutenant-colonel by purchase, and consequently had little inducement to regard their temporary occupation as a profession. Indeed their approach to warfare differed little from that to hunting, for as Wolseley remarked, 'They knew how to lead their men as straight under fire as their fathers and grandfathers had done before them, and what more was necessary or should be required of them?'[12] Unfortunately the drill movements that had proved adequate in the Napoleonic Wars were no longer so by 1855; and in any case years of concentration on display had transformed the British Army's drill into 'a complicated puzzle'. Peace-time manœuvres were completely unknown until a first experimental camp was set up at Chobham shortly before the outbreak of the Crimean War.

The general incompetence displayed by the civil and military authorities, and the suffering of the troops in the Crimea—vividly reported for the first time by a 'war correspondent' at the front, W. H. Russell of *The Times*—at last brought home to the British public the disgraceful condition of the army (henceforth, incidentally, journalists were usually to accompany and report in full even the smallest military campaigns). Under the prompting of such dissimilar reformers as the Radical M.P. J. A. Roebuck, Florence Nightingale and Sidney Herbert various improvements were made, though progress remained slow until the Cardwell Ministry of 1868–74.[13]

Administrative chaos lay at the root of the muddle in the Crimea and affected all military operations in that era. Army affairs were in hands of no less than thirteen departments with ill-defined or overlapping responsibilities. A brief summary can only hint at the confusion. Operations overseas were under the control of the Secretary of State for War and the Colonies at the Colonial Office, who acted in conjunction with the Secretary at War at the War Office, who was the chief link between Parliament and the army on all financial matters. The Commander-in-Chief, at the Horse Guards, representing the personal authority of the Sovereign, was responsible for discipline, command and patronage. The Master-General of the Ordnance provided all stores for cavalry and infantry, and was also (confusingly) responsible for the discipline, pay and allowances of the engineers and artillery. The Commissariat department was run by civilians at the Treasury, while the Militia was controlled by the Home Secretary. It was not surprising that even energetic officials were frustrated by this tangled undergrowth.

Great improvements were made as a result of the Crimean experience. The offices of Secretary at War and Master-General of the Ordnance were abolished, and their political responsibilities were absorbed by the Secretary of State for War—who became independent of the Colonial Office. The Commander-in-Chief took over the military command of the artillery and engineers from the Master-General of the Ordnance; while the War Office took over the Commissariat from the Treasury and the Militia from the Home Office. The major unsolved problem, the relationship between the Secretary of State for War and the Commander-in-Chief, was settled—theoretically at least—by the War Office Act of 1870. The latter was subordinated to the former as his chief military adviser, and the Commander-in-Chief, in the person of the Queen's cousin, George, Duke of Cambridge, was obliged to quit his personal eyrie in the Horse Guards and enter the War Office, then situated in Pall Mall. The essence of these organisational reforms between 1855 and 1870 was that the armed forces ceased to be a mere aggregation of regiments and semi-independent corps, and began to resemble a unified army under a single politically responsible minister.

Thus after 1870 it was clear—at least in principle—that the Secretary of State for War was politically responsible for the control of all military operations except those organised entirely from India. In practice, however, the picture is not so clear. Colonial officials naturally corresponded with the Colonial Office and local military commanders with the War Office. When hostilities threatened, or during a war, these offices, and usually the India Office and the Admiralty too, had obviously to work closely together, yet no institution existed to make co-ordination easier.

In the absence of a permanent Defence Committee of the Cabinet until 1895 the efficiency with which particular wars were politically managed depended very much on the vigour of individual ministers and personal relationships between the Secretary of State for War, the Colonial Secretary, the First Lord of the Admiralty and the Secretary of State for India. Victorian Prime Ministers, as this book shows, seldom took a direct interest in the management of imperial campaigns, except of course where the political issues were so important—as for instance in the decision to invade Egypt in 1882—that the matter was discussed by the whole cabinet. Indeed until the twentieth century there existed no organ short of the cabinet which could consider all aspects of defence and recommend a policy for all departments. 'The service and all other departments would have resisted any serious effort to introduce such a body as an invasion of their traditional independence of each other.'[14]

Cardwell's period at the War Office from 1868 to 1874 certainly constituted the watershed in the nineteenth century history of the British Army, and he is rightly regarded as one of the most successful tenants of the office. The great merit of Cardwell's approach was that he worked out a logical scheme for the complete reorganisation of the service. His basic aim was to solve the chronic recruiting problem, which was largely due to the army's deservedly low public reputation. The recall of battalions from the colonies was partly designed to end the unpopular practice whereby the majority of troops passed their service in exile from their country and families. By linking the infantry battalions in pairs he hoped to equalise the periods of home and foreign service, and also to reduce the period of full-time enlistment to six years. Localisation of units was also expected to assist recruiting by associating regiments of the line with particular areas, and with the Militia and Volunteers.

Cardwell's reforms, particularly the abolition of purchase, the introduction of short service enlistment, and the reorganisation of the War Office, paved the way for a modern professional army; and in this they were analogous to contemporary reform of the civil service and higher education. Nevertheless Cardwell and his successors either overlooked, or were powerless to change, many of the old anomalies and defects, outstanding among which was the survival of a Royal Commander-in-Chief until 1895. This strengthened the forces of military conservatism and caused a constant tug of war between the military and civilian heads of the army.

The Queen took a proprietary interest in army affairs and the making of military policy, while the Commander-in-Chief grew increasingly opposed to change and deplored—with some justice—the unfortunate effects of party politics on the service, particularly in financial matters. Among many overdue reforms the Duke of Cambridge stubbornly opposed the creation of a General Staff and none appeared until 1904. This was largely the explanation as to why no comprehensive military policy was ever worked out to determine the functions of those heterogeneous bodies comprising the armed forces of the Crown.

Also, for a variety of reasons, Cardwell's reforms in organisation fell far short of his expectations in practice. This was partly his own fault in that, being preoccupied with retrenchment, he left a dangerously narrow margin in the number of battalions at home necessary to work the linked battalion system, and in the establishment of those battalions if military efficiency was to be preserved. His successors continued his schemes with unequal enthusiasm, allowing further reductions to be made in the strength of the units at home. Above all there was the public and parliamentary apathy towards military reform which was not to receive another jolt until the South African War.

From the viewpoint of a general given command of an overseas expedition after 1870 the effects of Cardwell's reforms were by no means wholly beneficial. In some cases the young, inexperienced short-service soldiers proved physically incapable of enduring the rigours of a campaign. Lacking military experience they were blamed, sometimes unfairly, for disasters such as Isandhlwana and Majuba.[15] These accusations may have been exaggerated, but the defects in the system for a country almost continuously engaged in small and distant wars were undeniable. What happened, in brief, was that in practice a balance in the linked battalion system was never achieved; consequently the home battalions were increasingly hard put to supply drafts to the larger number of units abroad. Short service exacerbated the problem not only because of the greater turnover of men than formerly, but also because it did not pay—either in terms of finance or physical fitness—to send men to distant stations if they had only a year or two to serve. This constant demand for drafts from the home battalions, already at far too low establishments, plus the failure of Cardwell's humanitarian reforms to achieve sufficient improvement in recruiting, meant that in the long run the home army was ruined as a fighting force. Thus Wolseley described the home battalions in 1890 as 'squeezed lemons', and Colonel Henderson describing the army before the South African War remarked that 'a man must have been east of Malta before he is qualified to sit in judgement on the regular army of Great Britain. The beardless regiments of Aldershot or the Curragh can no more compare with the masses of strong men . . . who hold India and Egypt, than the lazy routine of English quarters can compare with the vigilance and stir of the restless East.'[16]

It is unfortunate that neither Cardwell nor his successors created an élite expeditionary force—possibly by expanding the Royal Marines—or even a special reserve, to meet the recurrent crises necessitating the despatch of a few battalions to distant theatres. Hence the reinforcements sent to Zululand in 1879 and South Africa in 1881 threw the home army into confusion while, as Dr Williams shows (pp. 250–3), the Egyptian Expedition of 1882 was only manned by calling out the Reserve. Wolseley was much-criticised for his habit of picking out the best men from various units, but it appears he had no alternative.[17]

Surprisingly little attention was given by military theorists to the problems of combined operations, despite the fact that a joint services committee in 1875 revealed the absence even of a permanent secretariat to draw up such war schemes. In fact the War Office and Admiralty continued to go their own independent ways until shortly before the First World War.

In the last quarter of the nineteenth century, then, Britain's military organisation was so defective that out of a regular army of some 200,000 men, nearly half of them stationed at home, it proved difficult to embark an expeditionary force of even 20,000 men. Cardwell and his successors (until the advent of Haldane to the War Office in 1905) never attempted a precise definition of the purposes in order of priority for which the armed forces existed; but relied instead on improvisation and 'muddling through'.[18] This book shows how successfully generals such as Napier, Wolseley and Kitchener overcame, perhaps even flourished on, these organisational weaknesses, but even they could not have prevailed against sterner opposition. Among many other timely lessons, the South African War revealed to what a dangerous extent Britain had come to depend on her Indian Army and on colonial volunteers to offset the inefficiency of the home forces and the appalling weaknesses in military organisation.

(III) VICTORIAN MILITARY CAMPAIGNS:
SOME PRINCIPLES AND PROBLEMS

It is characteristic of the Victorians' pragmatic approach to colonial warfare that no systematic study of the subject was published until 1896, when Captain C. E. (later Major-General Sir Charles) Callwell, R.A., produced his valuable work *Small Wars: Their Principles and Practice*. Callwell clearly hoped that his text-book would be of lasting practical importance to his profession, but in fact its chief interest has probably been historical; for although the type of operations Callwell discussed never entirely disappeared, the reorientation of British foreign policy in the 1900's raised a host of more vital issues of training and organisation for a major European war.

Callwell's starting point was the distinction between regular warfare and 'small wars'. For the former, he believed, there existed broad agreement on the principles of tactics and strategy, but in the latter 'conditions are so diversified, the enemy's mode of fighting is often so peculiar, the theatres of operations present such singular features, that irregular warfare must be carried out on a method totally different from the stereotyped system'.

As in major wars, however, military problems were largely determined by the political objectives. These fell into three broad classes: campaigns of conquest or annexation, campaigns for the suppression of insurrection and lawlessness, and punitive expeditions designed to avenge a wrong or wipe out an insult. The first type necessarily involves fighting on foreign soil and usually entails overthrowing a government with an organised military system, even if it is only a primitive one such as Burma's under King Thebaw. The second more often involves fighting on British territory and the opponents are usually guerrillas or banditti. Callwell appreciated what modern governments have had to re-learn painfully since 1945, that 'the crushing of a populace in arms, the stamping out of widespread disaffection by military methods, is a harassing form of warfare even in a civilised country with a settled social system. In remote regions peopled by half-civilised races or wholly savage tribes such campaigns are most difficult to bring to a satisfactory conclusion.' Neither here nor in the book generally, however, does he note that ideological fervour is harder to conquer militarily than the wildest terrain. The third type—punitive campaigns—are analogous to the first in that they are usually conducted on enemy territory and against organised government. Often punitive campaigns resulted in annexation, as in the extension of British rule over much of India, and French rule in Indo-China; but where they did not the military role could be comparatively limited in duration and effort. Most of the campaigns studied here were at least partly punitive in origin: the China War and the Abyssinian Expedition show that permanent entanglements could be avoided, whereas the Ashanti war was only temporarily effective and led to eventual annexation, and the occupation of Egypt became permanent despite the British Government's genuine desire to withdraw.

Callwell emphasised, and this book underlines, a point which has only been fully assimilated since the recent world-wide upsurge of nationalist movements. Condescending—or at best uninformed—references to conquering 'natives', 'fuzzy-wuzzies' or 'wogs' obscured the fact that Victorian campaigns were conducted against a bewildering variety of enemies, many of whom were far from primitive in the popular sense or contemptible as military opponents.[19] No two enemies were alike in their weapons, tactics or military discipline. At one extreme the Egyptian forces led by Colonel Arabi in 1882 closely followed the methods of European armies, which was hardly surprising since they had been trained and armed by European officers; and the Indian mutineers too had to be dealt with by more or less orthodox tactics. At the other extreme were the primitively armed and tactically unsophisticated savages encountered by the British and French in West Africa. Between these extremes the Zulus, for example, presented unique tactics—which Lord Chelmsford ignored to his cost in 1879. Their impis were well-disciplined armies with a complex organisation and an astonishing capacity to manœuvre with speed and precision on the open veldt. Yet their weapons were those of savages and their fighting methods (though devastating against other tribes), were too inflexibly offensive. Quite different again were the Maoris in the North Island of New Zealand. They were inferior in organisation and discipline to the Zulus but were better armed, and were formidable defensive fighters behind their earthen strongholds or pahs. Moreover until the final war waged by the fanatic Hauhaus the Maoris were extremely chivalrous opponents, sometimes, we may feel, putting the Europeans to shame.[20] The Dervish followers of the Mahdi in the Sudan were true fanatics. Though a few possessed assorted firearms by 1885 they relied essentially on spears and knives, and though—as at Abu Klea—they occasionally showed capacity for disciplined manœuvre, their forte remained the reckless massed charge. The Boers, lastly, were a law unto themselves, and the peculiar difficulties the British encountered in fighting them both in 1881 and 1899 illustrate the Victorian army's problem in developing suitable training for small wars. The Boers of 1881 possessed excellent rifles (though they were virtually without artillery) and were ably led, tactically at least. Yet they had no real military organisation, being merely 'bodies of determined men ("commandos"), acknowledging certain leaders, drawn together to confront a common danger'. Such a loosely controlled force might have been expected to adopt guerrilla tactics but, quite the contrary, they boldly sought pitched battle. Their remarkable success must cause us to look critically at their regular opponents' tactics.

In the First South African War and, it will be suggested, in some of the other campaigns studied here, the Army's poor military performance is inexplicable without some understanding of the political situation, both in the theatre of war and in Britain. Perhaps the supreme example of government wrangling before a campaign in this period was that surrounding the belated decision to send Wolseley to try to relieve Gordon in Khartoum. No two Cabinet ministers thought alike or even remembered what they had decided from one meeting to the next. Furthermore the War Office and Admiralty were independently at loggerheads over the route a relief expedition should take.[21] Michael Williams shows that the political situation was equally confused—and confounded by the possibility of French collaboration—in 1882.

Wolseley at least seems always to have been given a free hand to conduct the expedition once it had been decided on, and he was not the kind of commander who was continually looking homeward for advice. David Chandler shows what a struggle Sir Robert Napier had in 1867 before finally cutting himself free from the Indian government's 'red tape'. Three of our campaigns suggest the various forms political interference could take: General Gough in the Sikh Wars was probably worst off with the Governor-General Lord Hardinge at his elbow in the field; Sir George Colley was hampered by secret government communications with the enemy; while Lord Kitchener in the Sudan in 1898 received his orders from the Foreign Office via Lord Cromer, the Governor-General of Egypt, who constantly urged on him the need for economy. Nevertheless, despite these exceptions, the majority of nineteenth century field commanders were blissfully free from political interference by comparison with our own times, for the obvious reason that the home government simply could not communicate with them. A new era begins in the 1870's with the extension of the telegraph to India, Australasia and the Far East. Conditions of communication in the colonies before these innovations may be briefly suggested from the case of New Zealand. The Governor might have to wait eight months for the two-way journey of an enquiry to Whitehall, while communications inside New Zealand were so poor that the quickest way to get a letter from Auckland to Wellington was often to send it via Australia. The news of the outbreak of each new phase of the Maori Wars took weeks to reach London, so it had to be a long war if reinforcements were to play a part: when the 2nd battalion 14th regiment was 'rushed out' from the Curragh in 1860 it took 82 days and this was considered a fast trip![22] Facts such as these suggest that the pre-Crimean scattering of small detachments throughout the Empire may have had sound military as well as financial motives.

Perhaps the characteristic which most distinguishes small wars from those of regular armies is that the former are in the main 'campaigns against nature', a factor that surely helps to explain their continuing fascination. In addition to natural obstacles and hazards few Victorian generals possessed adequate maps; indeed this was the case in the South African War of 1899–1902 even though the theatre of war had been under British influence for half a century. Inadequate or erroneous topographical information partially accounts for some of the worst defeats of the century. The annihilation of Hicks Pasha and his Egyptian troops in 1883 occurred when he became lost in the Sudanese jungle on his march from the Nile towards El Obeid. Two years later in the same area Sir Herbert Stewart's detachment lost its way—admittedly in a night march—from the Abu Klea wells to the Nile and had to fight a battle with its square formation disorganised by dense scrub. Sir George Colley was greatly handicapped for want of a good map of the Majuba Mountain, and though he went to great lengths to gather information before advancing, his ignorance of the configuration of the summit and the amount of 'dead ground' on the slopes played a significant part in his defeat. Thus lack of maps or of reliable local guides provides one illustration of the fact that in matters of military intelligence the native enemies often held a considerable advantage over regular troops.

As well as topographical intelligence it is obviously of equal importance for European armies to have the means of subsistence on enemy territory. The advent of railways, motor transport and—in the Second World War—supply from the air, should serve to remind us of the fantastic natural obstacles which Victorian armies had to overcome when not even the first of these means of transport was generally available. Thus there are examples of campaigns where strategy or tactics were determined by the water supply. In 1882 Wolseley's tactics before the decisive battle of Tel-el-Kebir were conditioned by his need to secure his water supply by seizing the lock at Kassassin: a small detachment had therefore to be risked against the whole Egyptian army, until the main British force and its supplies could be brought up from Ismailia. Two years later the shorter land route to Khartoum was judged impracticable from lack of water. In the Abyssinian Expedition of 1868, as David Chandler shows, the provision of food and water raised more difficulties than the enemy army.

Supply and transport are of course intimately bound up in all military operations, and breakdowns along the line have not seldom accounted for British military disasters, most notoriously in the Crimea. The problem is less the pushing forward of troops, guns and horses—difficult though this may be—than providing necessaries of life at 'the front' which may lie in jungles, deserts or mountains. In these conditions, and especially if the local population is hostile or the enemy resorts to guerrilla attacks against the line of communications, a large army can be reduced to little more than an escort for its food. This was practically the case during the First South African War and on the last stages of the Abyssinian Expedition. The most spectacular example from this period however is surely the Second South African War, when over 400,000 troops were employed to enable perhaps ten per cent to engage in actual operations against the Boers, who never put more than 40,000 men into the field. In sum there were few nineteenth century colonial wars where transport and supply did not present enormous difficulties or seriously affect the proportion between 'teeth' and 'tail'.

Limited time was another factor which was frequently superimposed on natural obstacles and climate, and which provided a dramatic element to several Victorian campaigns. Sir Robert Napier in 1868

c

had not only to cross a desert and then nearly 400 miles of roadless mountains to reach Magdala; he had to accomplish all this and return before the spring monsoon made the innumerable river gorges across his route completely impassable. Sir Garnet Wolseley had a similar problem, though in quite different physical conditions, in 1873–4 when he had to reach Kumasi and extricate his army before the rains thickened the jungle barrier and decimated his troops with fever. Shortness of time presented the same general with a truly agonising problem in 1884 in his heroic effort to relieve Khartoum; the cataracts had to be passed while the Nile waters were still high, and of course Khartoum had to be reached before it was stormed by the Mahdi. Here, incidentally, is another example of deficient information, for all the experts proved to be wrong in their assessment of the duration of high waters on the Nile.

A bare mention of these difficulties can only hint at the genius for foresight as well as for improvisation which was demanded of Victorian commanders, not to speak of the courage and endurance required of the troops. The more successful of these campaigns, such as Napier's in Abyssinia and Wolseley's in Canada (in 1870) and Ashanti, are worthy of association with the Victorians' outstanding civil achievements—such as Brunel's engineering feats, the laying of trans-oceanic cables, the exploration of central Africa, and the construction of railways, bridges and great irrigation works in India. Perhaps the narrowly military exploits of the 'soldiers of Empire' have been given too much acclaim, and their organisational and engineering feats too little.

*   *   *   *   *   *

Captain Callwell anticipated the essential 'discoveries' of modern students of guerrilla and counter-guerrilla warfare in perceiving that the time-honoured tactical and strategical principles of European warfare were often ineffective and sometimes even suicidal when applied to small wars. Despite the beginnings of reform at home, and the lessons available from other nations' experiences, the British army still inclined to cling to the orthodox methods of Wellington's day, irrespective of the terrain and the opposition. One explanation is that field commanders were too often selected on the principle of seniority, and consequently were physically unfit or mentally out of date. Wolseley spent a lifetime struggling against this system, but the selection of Sir Redvers Buller to command in 1899 and Sir John French in 1914 suggests that he made no lasting impression.

Just one example of tactical ineptitude may be given here since it is not discussed in the book. The inflexibility of British tactics has seldom been better illustrated than in the Maori Wars. Time and again a vast amount of effort and many lives were fruitlessly expended in storming the Maori strongholds by infantry assaults in close order. Perhaps the worst display was that of General Sir Duncan Cameron at Rangiriri on 20 November 1863. After an ineffective bombardment by three Armstrong guns Cameron, who had led the Black Watch up the heights of Alma, ordered three successive frontal assaults which resulted in nothing but a futile loss of life. It is an ironic comment on an era which placed foolhardy courage above intelligence in the assessment of high-ranking officers for rewards and promotion that on leaving New Zealand Cameron was made Governor of the Royal Military College, Sandhurst.[23] When the futility of these Crimean assaults was recognised, Cameron's successors resorted to sapping methods worthy of Vauban. This certainly saved lives but was equally ineffective since the enemy simply abandoned their pah and retired a few miles to construct another.

Two material handicaps are also worth mentioning as manifestations of a conservative tradition. First, it was largely as a result of the re-forming zeal of Sir Garnet Wolseley and his 'Ring' of supporters after 1870 that a more sensible diet was at last provided for soldiers on campaign to replace the lethal fare of salt beef or pork and biscuit, with a strong dram of rum and a pinch of tea and sugar. The money spent on such 'luxuries' as jam, pickles, cheese, bacon and above all preserved vegetables, was amply repaid in improved efficiency. A second long-overdue improvement in the last quarter of the century was the gradual substitution of khaki for the obsolete redcoat. Wolseley had long campaigned against 'the loss from sunstroke and heat apoplexy that resulted from the cruel habit of making our soldiers fight, even in the tropics, in leather stocks, tightly buttoned-up jackets, and without any effective protection from the sun on their heads'.[24] Quite apart from the suffering it imposed, it was criminal to send troops to fight in red tunics and white helmets against marksmen armed with modern rifles, as the Boers demonstrated in 1881.[25]

It might seem a truism that boldness and a vigorous offensive spirit are especially important in small wars, yet Callwell argues persuasively that against poorly armed and ill-disciplined natives a dramatic early blow will have a far more demoralising effect than against a regular opponent. Conversely a cautious advance resulting in a European check or defeat—as for example Colley's reverse at Laing's Nek, and Hicks Pasha's in the Sudan—will inspire the enemy with a fanatical confidence and make eventual victory far harder to obtain. Only when the enemy can be relied on to launch a reckless tactical offensive, as was the case with the Zulus, does it pay to stand on the defensive and let him exhaust himself against disciplined volleys—the tactics of Rorke's Drift as against Isandhlwana.

Another important thesis advanced by Callwell was that in small wars tactics usually favour regular troops and strategy the native opponent. The explanation has already been touched on: regular armies usually depend on a precarious line of communications, their local knowledge is inferior to the natives' and they are usually far less mobile. Thus their vision and movements are circumscribed while nature is also working against them; a defeat and forced retreat, as in the First Afghan War, can entail complete disaster; whereas the very looseness of the enemy's organisation is in this respect an asset. In both the Boer Wars, for example, the enemy was rarely crushed in battle (Paardeberg is an exception) since his units simply scattered if defeat threatened. The Egyptian army of 1882, by contrast, had the encumbrances of a regular army without its training and discipline, so that defeat in battle destroyed it as a fighting force. The contrast between the Boers and Egyptians however illustrates the difficulty of evolving hard and fast principles of general validity for the conduct of small wars.

Another interesting question was whether it paid in small wars, more than in wars against Europeans, to divide one's army into independent columns. If the gamble is successful native leaders may be bewildered and paralysed by being attacked from different directions, and will not have the necessary experience—or control—to strike rapidly at isolated detachments. Wolseley brilliantly demonstrated this gambit when he split his army into four columns for the advance to Kumasi. But while European generals seldom encountered the irregular equivalents of Lee and Jackson, a determined and confident enemy did occasionally exploit such divisions with crushing effect. The Boers repeatedly achieved this in the Second South African War;

and the massacre of Custer's force at Little Big Horn was basically due to the same miscalculation. Lord Chelmsford's disaster at Isandhlwana was due rather to the reckless dispersion of his force than because he advanced in separate columns.

If the conduct of small wars must differ radically in some respects from regular warfare, it follows that tactics which are obsolete among European armies may yet continue to be highly effective against non-Europeans. The classical illustration of this point perhaps is the square as a tactical formation. After Waterloo the development of firearms and artillery made it increasingly suicidal to bunch men together on the battlefield, and this was generally appreciated by the time of the Franco-Prussian War, when loose skirmishing lines were becoming normal. Against most non-European opponents however—with the exception of the Boers—some type of 'square' remained valuable right to the end of the century. It should be explained that squares had become far more sophisticated than the rigid eighteenth century formations of infantry and artillery of popular imagination. In fact the name was deceptive, for squares took on various shapes according to the terrain and the military situation, for example large loose formations for crossing open country when the enemy was distant, and small compact formations for resisting attack. Sir Herbert Stewart's advance from Korti via Abu Klea to the Nile aptly illustrates the flexible uses of the square, and its great value against a numerically superior and fanatic enemy; while in this volume John Keegan describes how Wolseley succeeded in adapting a mobile square formation even to the dense jungles of Ashanti.

Likewise volley firing, which was driven out of Europan warfare by the development of more sophisticated weapons and tactics during the nineteenth century, remained the most effective way to stop native rushes—as the British demonstrated on numerous occasions such as Abu Klea and Rorke's Drift, and indeed at Isandhlwana where the defenders exacted a fearful toll before they were eventually overwhelmed when one corner of their perimeter collapsed.

Lastly one of the few sensible justifications of the cavalry in its traditional *arme blanche* role of the charge with lance or sabre was, that although of very dubious value in European warfare, it was still potentially of decisive importance against natives. Many Victorian campaigns were conducted in countries such as Abyssinia and Burma where cavalry was practically useless, but the first and last chapters in this book—and the dash to Cairo in 1882—demonstrate its continuing effectiveness in the right conditions.

*   *   *   *   *   *

Were it not for the handicaps imposed by the great distances from the home base and by the natural obstacles of the theatres of war, Britain's military supremacy over her colonial enemies in the Victorian era might have been so overwhelming as to rob the campaigns of any lasting interest. In fact Britain's armed services were so badly organised and overstretched that they did not always triumph easily, and sometimes did not triumph at all. These campaigns, then, pose military problems of real interest even though no Austerlitz, Sadowa or Sedan be numbered among them. All were to some degree instruments of imperial policy and could affect politics in three possible ways: by inspiring early nationalist feeling against European interlopers (as in the Sudan and the Transvaal); by altering the course of British foreign policy (as did Gladstone's invasion of Egypt); and by influencing the domestic balance of power (as did the South African War of 1881). Thirdly these campaigns inevitably throw much interesting and sometimes amusing light on Victorian attitudes and behaviour; there is, for example, the rush of exalted personages to serve under Wolseley in 1882, the passion shared by Wolseley and Kitchener for collecting bric-à-brac from their foreign foes and gold plate from their domestic admirers, and the barbarous episode of the Mahdi's skull. Much remains to be written about the military aspects of Victorian society, and this book only attempts to unveil a corner of the picture.

In summing up Britain's advantages in these colonial campaigns pride of place must be given to the Royal Navy. Though there were no great sea battles for Britain between Trafalgar and the First World War, and though the most important naval action in the last quarter of the nineteenth century was the comparatively undemanding task of bombarding Alexandria in 1822, naval power was the ultimate guarantee of all British operations on land. Not merely did the navy ensure the safe passage of troopships and safeguard the bridgeheads; it also participated directly in most of the campaigns: by bombarding hostile tribes (on the Gold Coast in 1873), by sending boats up the rivers in direct support of the army (up the Peiho in 1860 and the Nile in 1885 and 1896–8), and not least by sending detachments with their own guns and rockets to co-operate with the soldiers (as in Abyssinia, South Africa and Egypt).[26] The only drawback, from the long-term view, was that these pragmatic local acts of co-operation did not lead to positive inter-service planning on a higher level. The second advantage Britain invariably enjoyed (with the possible exception of the First South African War) was vastly superior weapons. It is therefore curious to find that writing in 1896 Callwell believed that machine guns had so far proved unreliable in crises and had not yet demonstrated their value. Thirdly, with rare exceptions such as the one grimly described in Kipling's poem 'That Day', the British enjoyed much better discipline than their foes; the defence of Rorke's Drift perhaps providing the supreme example of what could be achieved by a handful of men who kept their heads against vast odds. Even after defeats like Isandhlwana and Laing's Nek discipline was maintained—and through regimental pride and tradition rather than fear of punishment. Unfortunately, I have suggested, discipline in the more rigid sense imposed its own burdens against foes like the Boers—or the Maoris—who refused to stand and fight in the accustomed manner.

Though several of the chapters in this book are concerned with well-managed campaigns that ended in inexpensive victories, there yet remains an underlying theme of slow and reluctant adjustment to new conditions of warfare. When due allowance has been made for the variety of opposition and the unpredictability of conditions in each ensuing campaign, it must still be admitted that zealous military reformers had an uphill struggle against professional conservatism and public apathy. Although the more successful Victorian generals displayed a genius for military organisation and improvisation, Buller's performance in South Africa in 1899 should remind us that Victorian military campaigning ended pathetically and almost tragically.

References

1 For example F. A. Johnson. *Defence by Committee.* London: O.U.P. 1960. N. H. Gibbs. *The Origins of Imperial Defence.* Oxford: Clarendon Press, 1955. D. C. Gordon. *The Dominion Partnership in Imperial Defence 1870–1914.* Baltimore: Johns Hopkins Press, 1965.
2 R. Robinson, J. Gallagher with A. Denny. *Africa and the Victorians.* London: Macmillan, 1961, p. 3.

3 A. P. Thornton. *The Imperial Idea and Its Enemies*. London: Macmillan, 1959, p. 6.

4 Robinson and Gallagher, op. cit., p. 5.

5 Ibid., p. 12.

6 Thornton, op. cit., p. 97. Indian troops were used outside the borders of India in the Crimea 1854–6, Persia in 1856–7, China in 1859–60, New Zealand in 1860–1, Abyssinia in 1867–8, Perak in Malaya in 1875, Malta in 1878, Afghanistan from 1878 to 1881, Egypt in 1882, the Sudan in 1885, Mombasa in 1896 and the Sudan again from 1896 to 1899.

7 W. C. B. Tunstall 'Imperial Defence 1815–1870' in *The Cambridge History of the British Empire*, vol. II. Cambridge University Press, 1940; p. 808.

8 Ibid., p. 829.

9 Ibid., p. 827.

10 Gordon, op. cit., pp. 61–71.

11 Robinson and Gallagher, op. cit., passim. See also E. Stokes. 'The Myth of Imperialism' in *History Today*, August 1960.

12 General Viscount Wolseley. 'The Army' in T. H. Ward ed. *The Reign of Queen Victoria*. London: Smith, Elder, 1887; vol. I, pp. 155–225.

13 Brian Bond. 'Prelude to the Cardwell Reforms 1856–1868' in the *R.U.S.I. Journal*, May 1961. And 'The Late Victorian Army' in *History Today*, September 1961. On 'the father' of war correspondents see Rupert Furneaux. *The First War Correspondent: William Howard Russell of the Times*. London: 1944.

14 Johnson, op. cit., p. 13.

15 Notably by Sir Ian Hamilton in *Listening for the Drums*. London: Faber, 1944; pp. 130–42.

16 G. F. R. Henderson. *The Science of War*. London: Longmans, Green, 1910; p. 405.

17 W. Verner. *The Military Life of H.R.H. George Duke of Cambridge*. London: Murray, 1905; vol. II, pp. 266–7.

18 The nearest attempt at such a definition was that of Edward Stanhope when Secretary of State for War in 1891. He put great emphasis on home defence and virtually dismissed the possibility that Britain might one day have to send an expeditionary force to the Continent. The celebrated 'Stanhope Memorandum' is printed as Appendix A in J. K. Dunlop. *The Development of the British Army 1899–1914*. London: Methuen, 1938.

19 For example among the bloodstained trophies in the royal palace of Kumasi, Wolseley's looters found Bohemian vases and Persian rugs, while on the walls were engravings of the Duke of Wellington, the Custom House on the Thames and Burns's 'Highland Mary'. See A. Lloyd. *The Drums of Kumasi*. London: Longmans, Green, 1964. Many of the Maori warriors carried English prayer books in their haversacks and were usually able to outquote their Christian opponents. See E. Holt. *The Strangest War*. London: Putnam, 1962; p. 194.

20 Ibid, p. 197.

21 J. Symons. *England's Pride: The Story of the Gordon Relief Expedition*. London: H. Hamilton, 1965, p. 60 ff. A detailed account is given by Gallagher and Robinson, op. cit., pp. 76–121.

22 Holt, op. cit., pp. 58, 148, 162.

23 Ibid., pp. 196–7, 227.

24 Wolseley, op. cit., p. 189.

25 Julian Symons, op. cit., p. 99 has pointed out that 'khaki' in the 1880's 'referred to any uniform made of drill or holland, and not to the mud-coloured clothing we now associate with the word'. In 1884 Wolseley's recommendation for khaki was not accepted so the troops on the Gordon relief expedition wore red and blue Mediterranean serge frocks.

26 A very full account is the 'Military History of the Royal Navy 1857–1900' in Sir W. L. Clowes. *The Royal Navy—a History*. London: Low, Marston, 1903; vol. VII, pp. 91–561.

The Sikh Wars
1845-9

The Sikh Wars
1845-9

E. R. Crawford

The Sikh Wars were the final struggle of the British in their conquest of India, with a state organised in the traditional style of the sub-continent; and it was also the last considerable conflict in which the old sepoy army took part. Ten years after it was over the Mutiny resulted in a complete change in the military and political organisation of British India with the supplanting of the East India Company by the Crown. Militarily the wars were old-fashioned ones fought with the techniques, and even some of the personnel, of Waterloo. The control of the Home Government through the archaic structure of the Company was, due to the great slowness of communication, far less important than it later became; and the motives for the conquest of the Punjab were a mixture of the needs of strategic and political security with some illusions about the commercial profits likely to follow the imposition of British rule.[1] A powerful state on the plains of India with no strong natural frontier between it and British territory was regarded as a far more uncomfortable neighbour than Afghanistan.

The main interest to the historian lies in the development of the Sikh state and, more particularly, its army which proved the most dynamic section in its society. The nation of the religious sect known as the Sikhs, a reform movement in Hinduism influenced by Islam, was built up by Maharajah Ranjit Singh at the beginning of the nineteenth century. When that ruler died in 1839 he had created a powerful army trained and disciplined on European lines, numbering 40,000 men. Traditional Indian armies had been composed of the levies of great noblemen and they generally consisted of cavalry, who owned their own equipment and horses—and thus were small land-owners of some means and gentle birth—together with levies of socially inferior and ill-equipped infantrymen. With them was a nucleus of mercenaries in the paid bodyguard of the ruler together

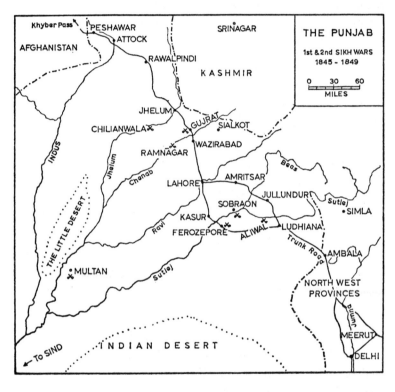

with some specialist troops such as artillerymen—the latter an inno-vation of the Moghuls. Making due allowance for different climatic and geographical conditions this military system was essentially mediaeval even if, in some respects, its weaponry was more advanced. Into this confused and inefficient milieu the introduction of eighteenth century European methods came as a tremendous shock. In particular, well-drilled infantry able to manœuvre and repulse cavalry charges in the open, was absolutely decisive. Methodical engineering and gunnery techniques also rendered nearly all Indian fortresses vulnerable, even though due to the continued successes of European-led armies these defences were, because of the low morale of their garrisons, frequently stormed out of hand.

In response to this European threat, the Indian states, Mysore, the Mahrattas and finally the Sikhs, attempted to build up countervailing forces in the shape of regular armies of their own. The Sikh army, because it was based on the last Indian state to be conquered, was the most consistent and therefore the most effective attempt to do this; but the result of these military changes was a political and social crisis which nearly destroyed the state, and which enabled the British to impose a stable settlement after they had smashed the Sikh military organisation—the Khalsa army.

Severe practical difficulties were faced by the rulers of traditional Indian states in creating a regular army. These were, in ascending order of importance, the supply of material, of personnel, of money and finally continuity of administration. War material, quite contrary to the experience of backward states today, was the least of their problems. It became far more important from 1860 onward when military technological change accelerated with the introduction of the breech-loading rifle. It was within the technical competence of an Indian state to turn out quite good muskets, gunpowder and ammunition and even to cast serviceable cannon.[2] Thus, though their weapons were not always quite equal in quality to those of the British, such inferiority in armament was a very secondary cause of Indian defeats.

A far more difficult problem lay in finding suitable officers. European mercenary officers, though extensively employed by Indian princes and very effective against other Indians, were not surprisingly unreliable against a European opponent and in fact were hardly ever trusted by their employers. Indians were equally untrustworthy, not through any lack of competence or courage on their part, but because they were mostly drawn from local noble families and their main loyalty was to their caste, religion or class, not to any concept of the nation. Essentially, therefore, the aristocratic disadvantages of eighteenth century European armies were magnified tenfold in the case of

Indian states, while by contrast the armies of the Company's European troops, being divorced from their European social origins, tended to be more cohesive and reliable.

Another aspect of an indigenous ruler's difficulty was that although an infantry force could be created outside the Indian social and military structure it was far more difficult to bring into existence a regular force of cavalry, for to do so involved a direct attack on the social position of the ruling classes of the state. Finally the difficulty of creating a stable and continuous administrative structure which could pay the army and keep it in being despite dynastic vicissitudes, was beyond the abilities of even the most capable of Indian rulers. In the Punjab it proved impossible to graft a modern European-type army on to a semi-feudal structure so that British success was greatly helped by treachery and dissent.

Within the state of the Punjab the death of Ranjit Singh in 1839 had resulted in a ferocious struggle for power in the usual manner of an oriental or mediaeval court. As a rule in Indian politics, this led eventually to the accession of a ruler lacking neither in ability nor decisiveness, but in this case a protracted struggle resulted in 1843 in the accession of a small child, Dulip Singh, who was reputedly Ranjit's son.

The army in effect retained a 'liberum veto' over the government, because any ruler who attempted to control the state had first of all to subordinate the army to himself. To control the army proved impossible, and eventually the East India Company had to destroy it and then subordinate the Sikh lords.

In the army a most interesting development took place. Because the court was unable to enforce its commands and because the senior officers were involved in the court struggles, the largely illiterate sepoys created elected regimental committees called *panchayats* after the Indian village councils. Eventually the sepoys took on a political role as well and they came to consider themselves as representatives of the embodiment of the Sikh and even the Indian nation.[3] This assertion may seem far-fetched, but there is definite evidence that in the First Sikh War agitators appealed to the racial and religious solidarity of the British sepoys with considerable success.[4]

However the *panchayats* were never able to develop a political programme or party with any appeal to civilian social groups apart

from religious ones which tended to divide the army itself. Instead the
initial aims of these nationalist and military committees were to expand
their numbers, raise their pay and to put into power a sympathetic
government. As there was a financial crisis, due to military over-
expansion, even before the death of Ranjit Singh and European
accounting and auditing methods had not been established, there was
considerable embezzlement and wastage. To make things worse all
accounts were kept in Persian, presumably to mystify the *hoi-poloi*
who might query them. The only remedy the soldiers were able to
conceive of at first was to invade Lahore, as happened in 1841, and kill
or beat up anyone who could speak Persian, as these were presumably
the *munshis*—or clerks—who cheated them of their pay.[5] At the same
time the great *sirdars* or lords had an incentive to keep back the taxes
which they owed the central government, thus further weakening the
national treasury. But by the end of 1845 it began to seem as if the
Khalsa army was taking on a less passive political role, for they formally
judged and executed the wazir Jahawar Singh on 21 September 1845,
and the Lahore *pandhayat* took over the government two days later.
There was a faction in the army which wanted war with the British,
and it was supported by the court which wanted nothing better than
the destruction of its army by the Europeans; for even if it meant
British rule the *sirdars* rashly hoped they could preserve their social and
political position.

Meanwhile on the other side of the Sutlej (see map, p. 39) the
British, well informed by their agents in Lahore, had taken certain precautions. They had wished to avoid an armed clash until late in 1845[6]
for their army was still disorganised as a result of the disastrous First
Afghan War of 1839–42 and the recent conquest of Sind from 1841 to
1843. This latter move had effectively encircled the Punjab by cutting
off the Sikh route to the sea via the Indus, although the exaggerated
hopes placed on the commercial advantages to be derived from control
of the Indus navigation had been disappointed.[7] Still, important strategic
gains had been made while the Sikhs had been quarrelling. By the
end of 1844 a pontoon train of seventy boats had been brought forward
to the Sutlej in preparation for a possible move on Lahore. The other
precautions taken were the strengthening of the garrisons of Ferozepore, Ludhiana, Ambala and Meerut.[8]

The province which was to be fought over, the Punjab, is a great

D

wide flat plain broken only by the five rivers from which it gets its name. These streams are full only in April and May when the melting snows of the Himalayas cause violent floods; otherwise they are a great width of exposed sandy channel frequently changing course and full of shifting shoals. They are only of limited use for navigation today, though before the railways reached the area small boats were important for the cheap movement of goods, but it was virtually impossible to use steamships on them. There are frequent fords except during the flood season; and therefore although the rivers cut across the path of armies marching north-west or south-east, they do not provide a real obstacle to the advance of a determined force. The areas between the rivers known as *Doabs* were once in prehistoric times lightly wooded but are now wind-eroded grasslands, scrub or waste unless irrigated. The area under irrigation has grown enormously since 1845 and that of woody scrub correspondingly shrunk. Along the edge of this great plain the foothills of the Himalayan complex begin. Chilian-wala is situated on this junction so that here ravines and inequalities of ground become more pronounced. As the hilliness increases so naturally the amount of cultivated land declines.

The whole area is characterised by great extremes of temperature. As the whole of the province is north of the tropic the seasons are well marked, the hot period being from April to September and the cool one from October to March. In the hot season temperatures will often rise to 120°F, while January nights may well fall below freezing point. Most rain falls between June and September when it is often very unhealthy, though there is often some light rain in January, particularly in the north where the ground rises. In Multan in the south it often does not rain at all for a period of years. It must be remembered that most of the fighting took place in the cool season, except around Multan, and the discomfort of the European troops was therefore considerable.

By the end of November 1845 the situation was becoming tense and the British garrisons on the Sutlej amounted to seven thousand men. The commanders were Major-General Sir John Littler at Ferozepore with one British and seven sepoy battalions and two Indian cavalry regiments; and Brigadier Wheeler at Ludhiana with the 50th Foot, one regiment of Indian cavalry and five of infantry. At the beginning of December Wheeler's force moved southward to Bassian, the chief grain depot. At Ambala were another 10,000 men and at Meerut 9,000. If the Sikhs had crossed the Sutlej they might well have defeated the isolated detachment at Ferozepore, and have dispersed the remaining British forces as they attempted to concentrate. Preparations had been taken for a concentration of British troops by collecting food supplies in magazines along the road from Meerut to Ferozepore, for otherwise the speed of march would be restricted to that of a bullock cart. Finally a considerable Sikh army crossed the Sutlej on 11 December under Lal and Tej Singh, both *sirdars* who had gained the confidence of the Khalsa

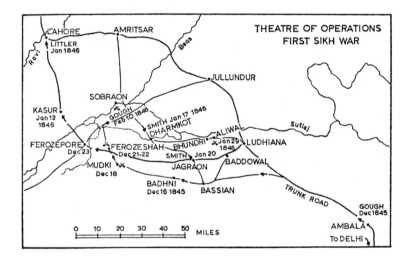

army. The court at Lahore was glad to see the last of the soldiers.

The British too were desperately anxious to concentrate before they were overwhelmed in detail, but they had several advantages on their side. The Sikh army had crossed the river and taken up a defensive position at Ferozeshah, ten miles east of Ferozepore, between it and the rapidly gathering British army. However, Lal Singh's failure to attack and gain a striking success can be accounted for, as he had, soon after his army marched, sent a messenger to Captain Nicholson, the British agent at Ferozepore, giving him details of his intentions and expressing the hope that they would remain good friends.[9]

By 17 December the British army under General Gough*, with Lord Hardinge† the Governor-General, had concentrated to a strength of between eleven and twelve thousand men at Badhni, thirteen miles west of Bassian. They comprised five regiments of horse, forty-two guns and thirteen battalions of which four were British. On the eighteenth of the month contact was made at the village of Mudki between Badhni and Ferozepore. The Sikh army had been divided into two, one part to watch Littler, the other to oppose the main relieving force under Gough. At Mudki a detachment of Sikhs was stationed. Accounts of their numbers are conflicting, but there may have been two to five thousand

*Field Marshal Sir Hugh Gough (1779–1869) came of Irish gentry stock. He was adjutant of his regiment (119th) at fifteen and served with distinction in South Africa (1795), the West Indies (1796–1803) and the Peninsular War, being badly wounded at Talavera and again at Nivelle. After a period on half-pay he went to India in 1830 as a major-general. He held the chief command in China in 1841–2 before becoming Commander-in-Chief in India in August 1843. After the First Sikh War he was made a Baron and after the Second a Viscount. He vacated the Indian Command in May 1849. Gough's courage, chivalry and racy brogue endeared him to his men, though Lord Ellenborough asserted in 1844 that 'he had not the grasp of mind and prudence essential to conduct great military operations'. 'Were his military genius as great as his heart', commented Sir Charles Napier, 'the Duke [of Wellington] would be nowhere by comparison.' Gough is said to have commanded in more general actions than any British officer of the century excepting the Duke of Wellington. D.N.B.

† Field Marshal Sir Henry Hardinge (1785–1856). An early graduate of the 'staff college' (1807) when it was still located at High Wycombe. He then served with Wellesley in Portugal (1808) and accompanied Moore on the retreat to Corunna. From 1811 he held senior staff appointments with the Portuguese army, and was rewarded with a colonelcy without purchase. In 1815 he lost his left hand at Ligny when acting as British military commissioner at Blücher's headquarters. Though retaining his commission he became a Tory M.P. in 1820, and was Secretary at War 1828–30 in Wellington's Ministry, and again in 1841–4 in Peel's. In July 1844 he reached India to replace Lord Ellenborough, his brother-in-law, as Governor-General. He waived his right to command in the field and served as second-in-command to Gough in the First Sikh War. On its successful conclusion he received the thanks of Parliament, was raised to the peerage as Viscount Hardinge of Lahore with a pension of £3,000 per annum, and received a further £5,000 from the East India Company. He left India at the end of 1847 with a very high reputation, but as successor to the Duke of Wellington as General Commanding-in-Chief at the Horse Guards (1852–6) he was blamed for the mismanagement of the Crimean War—'the least satisfactory episode in his career'. D.N.B.

To avoid confusion he is referred to as 'Lord Hardinge' throughout this chapter.

infantry and large bodies of irregular horse perhaps amounting to ten thousand men with twenty-two guns. The Sikhs were posted in a dense belt of jungle with ploughed fields in front of them. After an artillery duel in which little could be seen for dust, the Sikh cavalry, which threatened the British flanks, was driven back by the horse artillery, so the infantry—twelve battalions in two lines—stormed forward. All accounts agree on the dust and indescribable confusion. Senior officers rode frantically from place to place and the Governor-General Lord Hardinge took a prominent part. As a result the losses of the senior officers were heavy while the total casualties were 872, of which 506 were Europeans. Quite obviously the British sepoys had hung back and camp gossip states that they were firing high as well.[10] Darkness fell before the action ended, causing British troops to fire into one another. The battle could be plausibly represented by the Sikhs as a highly successful rearguard action, but they had lost seventeen guns and the British held it as a victory. The cause of the high casualties was the rapid hurrying into battle of the troops too soon before night fell—thus ensuring disorganised and unco-ordinated attacks. On the other hand Gough undoubtedly feared that the enemy would escape him, a singular miscalculation of their mood, though understandable in view of previous campaigns in India.

The following day the army secured their wounded, brought in the captured guns, destroyed the gun carriages while storing the actual cannon in Mudki fort, and awaited reinforcements. The enemy loss was estimated at about 300 killed. Few arrangements were made for wounded, which was particularly unfortunate for the British sepoys.[11] The problem now facing Gough and Hardinge, for the latter though in theory a military subordinate was consulted by the C-in-C, was to join hands with the garrison of Ferozepore and if possible overwhelm, when concentrated, one of the two Sikh armies which watched the two British detachments. The apparent risk in this plan lay in the Sikhs concentrating first, for it was easier for them to do this, but the hazard was in fact slight since their generals were in constant communication with the British and seemed only too anxious to help. They did not have to be informed of British movements for they could be guaranteed to remain passive in an emergency. The distance between the two British camps was about twenty miles and it was hoped that Littler would unite with Gough and then attack the camp at Ferozeshah where about 13,000 Sikh troops were stationed under Lal Singh—Tej Singh, the other general, having about 17,000 men. When concentrated the British would number about 18,000, but unfortunately General Gough omitted to inform Littler, whose instructions were given to him on his arrival at the battlefield by Lord Hardinge—as Littler's despatches show —while no proper directions were given to any of the divisional commanders. Thus Littler started at 8 a.m., four hours later than Gough and the latter was only stopped from attacking unsupported against entrenched superior numbers, with one hundred guns opposed to his sixty-five, by the direct orders of Lord Hardinge in his civilian capacity as Governor-General. This occurred at 11 a.m. and by the time the force was united and the attack put in it was 3.30 p.m.

The Sikh camp was entrenched in the form of an oval. The attacking army was deployed, with Gilbert's division on the right, then Wallace's in the centre and Littler's on the left. Smith's division was in reserve and the cavalry were concentrated on each wing. The entrenchments were not very formidable, providing merely shelter from artillery fire and not obstacles to an infantry advance. Even then one of Littler's brigades under Reed attacked prematurely, and was driven back with heavy loss. Then the rest of the army went forward through the scrub against a heavy artillery fire and threw back the Sikhs. A furious struggle began, while Smith on instructions from Hardinge moved swiftly into the gap caused by Littler's retreat and smashed a Sikh counter-attack, taking many guns. Finally the 3rd Light Dragoons on his left swept over the entrenchments and despite very heavy casualties attacked the enemy from the rear. By this time what with dust and gunpowder smoke the light was obscured and night was swiftly coming on. Smith pushed forward, picking up stragglers from various regiments while the Sikh camp had caught alight and ammunition was blowing up. The confusion was such that few observers make any sense out of this portion of the battle. Smith found himself with two or three thousand men in the centre of the enemy's position. After an uncomfortable time he withdrew about 3 o'clock in the morning and marched through the scene of the unsuccessful attack by Littler's division to the village of Misriwala where he found many leaderless men. Meanwhile the rest of the army under Gough and Hardinge had reformed outside the entrenchments. There Hardinge, not knowing where Smith was and having suffered heavy casualties, sent to the rear Napoleon's sword, a present to him from Wellington, together with Prince Wlademar of Prussia who was accompanying the army. He also ordered all State papers at Mudki to be burnt. Sir Hope Grant stated that 'never perhaps in the annals of Indian warfare has a British army on so large a scale been nearer to defeat which could have involved annihilation'. It was a fair assessment and the British leadership was very depressed.

Next morning, after Smith had rejoined him, Gough once more attacked the entrenchments which had been vacated by Lal Singh, meeting resistance only from a few stragglers. They captured seventy-three abandoned guns, and formed up on the other side of the captured camp where Gough and Hardinge rode down the line to their cheers. At this point Tej Singh's fresh army came in sight. Gough drew up his troops on the northern and western face of the Sikh entrenchments, but he was in a desperate position as his army was tired, his sepoys unreliable and his ammunition scarce. Tej Singh's artillery opened fire, and he threatened Gough's right with his irregular cavalry. The latter however refused to charge infantry in squares, and it is noteworthy that the few Sikh regiments of regular cavalry had deteriorated after Ranjit Singh's death. The 3rd Light Dragoons charged and threw them back. Tej Singh then began to draw off his troops and at 4 p.m. of 22 December, the battle of Ferozeshah came to the end.

The verdict on these operations must be that the Sikhs were deprived of the victory that their valour had richly deserved by the treachery of their leaders. Indeed, the rajahs had offered the British every opportunity which Gough's ineptitude had thrown away. The Sikh losses were about 3,000 while British casualties amounted to 2,415 of which 700 were killed. Since just over half of these were European, and the sepoy regiments brigaded with the British had suffered far less, the Indians seem to have fought reluctantly. The brunt of the battle had certainly fallen on the six British battalions. Tej Singh now retired across the Sutlej, thus evacuating British territory and leaving behind a trail of dying and wounded men, for whom there was of course no medical provision either by their own side or by their enemies.

Few military lessons can be learnt from these operations. Gough, whatever his shortcomings as a general, was nonetheless an exceedingly brave and attractive character. His gesture on the second day at Ferozeshah during the Sikh cannonade in riding out in a white coat to draw the enemy's fire from his soldiers illustrates both his generosity of spirit and his irresponsibility as a commander-in-chief. He was backed up though by the highly efficient Harry Smith, and his worst mistakes were covered by Lord Hardinge. It is notable that he did not send any communication to Littler but left it to Hardinge. As a result when Littler arrived late it was only Hardinge's use of his Governor-General's veto that prevented total disaster. The system of dual command which Sir John Fortescue criticises was indeed theoretically quite unworkable, but it seems for once to have been justified by results. All contemporaries liked Gough personally, and he apparently took advice from Hardinge as a fellow officer and gentleman without any resentment. The fairest assessment might be that with any other general it ought not to have been necessary, but with any other general the arrangement could not have been carried out because of personal friction. Hardinge too deserves credit for his tactful handling of Gough whom he obviously liked, and he too was sufficiently self-effacing not to insist on taking any of the credit. Indeed Gough was quite certain that he was right in ordering an immediate attack, believing a more decisive victory would be gained, but he bore no malice at being overruled, and admired Hardinge for his personal bravery which he referred to in flattering terms in his despatch. The Sikh army though equally brave was deliberately sacrificed by its leaders and given no opportunity at all.

Though the Sikhs had fallen back over the river Sutlej they were found by Gough's patrols on 27 December near Sobraon on the British side. Both sides then rested until 6 January 1846, the British being reinforced by 10,000 men, including two regiments of European cavalry, while their enemy started to construct a bridge across the river and to throw up fortifications to cover their crossing point. Both armies watched each other while the British waited for a convoy of provisions and a powerful siege train. The hard-fought battle at Ferozeshah had apparently infected even Gough with caution until the balance of forces should become more favourable to him. During the stalemate the Sikh generals sent a force of 8,000 men under Ranjodh Singh marching eastwards along the north bank of the river until opposite Ludhiana, where there was a small British force. By striking across the river to capture the siege train coming up they could hamper their enemy, and perhaps, too, could inflict a defeat on the small detachment at Ludhiana. At the same time Sikh cavalry raids across the

Sutlej had enabled them to draw supplies and plunder from British territory—helped by the fact that the villagers were their co-religionists.

To counter this Smith was detached with a force consisting of a brigade of infantry, two regiments of Indian cavalry and some artillery to escort the siege guns up to the main army, and to destroy the lodgements made by raiders south of the Sutlej. This he did, taking a small fort at Dharmkot containing mostly Muslim mercenaries, and after receiving further reinforcements, marched to Jagraon close to the siege train. There he picked up the 53rd Foot on 20 January and then turned north-east to Ludhiana where there were four native battalions under Brigadier Godby. On 21 January he came across the entire army of Ranjodh Singh encamped at Baddowal in a strong position and numbering about 8-9,000 men with 40 guns. Smith had with him only about 4,000 men and 18 guns. Faced by this disparity of force he refused battle and attempted to by-pass the enemy to the south, trusting to his superior mobility. It was undoubtedly a very risky operation but as the enemy cavalry were, as usual, quite incapable of charging home, he managed it with the loss of only 200 men and much of his baggage. The Sikh irregular cavalry killed largely the sick, wounded and stragglers, though they let the camp-followers go, saying that they had no quarrel with the people of Hindustan.[12] Smith received reinforcements so that even after leaving one battalion to look after the baggage he commanded 10,000 men. Meanwhile the Sikh army had fallen back to the river, picked up a reinforcement of 4,000 regular infantry trained by Avitabile, a mercenary of Ranjit Singh's, and were about to march south again when their scouts clashed with Smith's on 25 January. The British army marching westward from Ludhiana was led by cavalry and horse artillery who deployed on sighting the Sikhs, while the main body continued to march in column behind them, and then too opened out. Unlike the two previous mêlées, the forthcoming clash at Aliwal was an encounter battle where the British cavalry could show its superiority. In addition the Sikhs were caught by surprise and their artillery had no time to deploy.

The terrain was open and grassy, affording a clear view to the British commander and enabling him to control the movements of his soldiers. The Sikhs opened fire at 700 yards on the advancing army. Smith halted and dressed his line and then threw forward his right, Godby's brigade and the wing nearest the river, to take the village of Aliwal which was still lightly held. It was carried, along with the battery it contained, and the line swept forward. While the enemy endeavoured to form a second front, pivoting on the village of Bhundri, a small body of horsemen attempted to charge the British line but was almost annihilated.[13] This was noted by Mackinnon of the 16th Lancers as the only instance of a Sikh cavalry charge in the campaign. Around Bhundri, Cureton with the 1st Brigade of cavalry dispersed the Sikh horse and then charged the regiments of Avitabile from the rear. The latter had formed squares and though these were broken fought back furiously, inflicting heavy losses on the 16th Lancers, finally retreating in confusion to the river. On the right Smith, taking personal command, drove back the enemy line and then attacked their troops in the camp where many still were, before they could re-form. The Sikhs now attempted to rally, sheltering below the high flood banks of the river to cover their retreat, but when attacked in the flank by a battalion of sepoys they were unable to make a fresh change of front, and a battery of artillery dispersed them. A final attempt to form a line along the far side of the Sutlej was also dispersed by a furious, but brief, cannonade from every British gun.

It was a complete and masterly victory won at a cost of just over 500 casualties while those of the Sikhs were estimated at 3,000. Perhaps more important, 51 guns were captured and 16 rendered useless or sunk in the Sutlej, and the moral effect of these losses was enormous. The casualties this time were far more evenly distributed among the European and sepoy regiments. This was probably because of the tight control which Smith kept over his force and, moreover, the clear visibility did not enable any half-hearted troops to hang back, though the *sowars* certainly did not attack with the élan of the British troopers. All agree that Smith had combined his arms magnificently and had defeated a force of 13,000 or 14,000 men with one of only 10,000. The captured camp was thoroughly plundered by the Indian cavalry, and it was noted after the battle that all the corpses were stripped in the night, though the villagers appeared to have fled.[14] Certainly there was little plunder for the hardest fighting soldiers, the infantry and 16th Lancers. The wounded, however, appear to have been much better cared for than at Mudki and Ferozeshah, perhaps because there were fewer, but also because Smith took great pains to look after them.

After the battle the British army halted until the 3rd of February, disposing of the wounded and the captured guns and then rejoining Gough on 8 February. The siege train had come up, and while morale was high after this brilliant victory and the enemy's correspondingly depressed, Gough resolved to attack the strongly entrenched bridge-head at Sobraon. It is interesting to note that no more messages had been received by Major John Lawrence* from Lal Singh after the battle of Ferozeshah until ten days after Aliwal,[15] suggesting that the Sikh commanders were very unimpressed by the British generalship at the former battle.

The Sikh position south of Sobraon consisted of a semi-circle of entrenchments about 3,000 yards long, both flanks resting on the Sutlej and behind the position one pontoon bridge. Their fortifications were not uniformly formidable since their generals were half-hearted and gave little supervision to the defences. There were weaknesses on the right wing in particular, where some newly raised troops were stationed. The whole position was defended by 67 guns and an unknown number of men, largely Khalsa regular infantry. Some artillery was stationed on the far bank, and the cavalry held themselves in reserve, and watched the fords flanking the position.

Gough's plan was simple. It was to launch his main assault against the enemy's right, his weaker wing, with Dick's division of thirteen battalions, five of them European, while Smith and Gilbert's smaller divisions feinted against the enemy's left and centre respectively. Most of the heavy artillery was assigned to Dick. Gough's total force, was 15,000 men with about 70 to 80 guns. Unfortunately owing to the commander's impetuosity, the bombardment launched at dawn on 10 February was started without adequate ammunition supplies so that Gough asked Dick's division to attack when the fire slackened at 10.30 a.m. before the other supporting attacks had been developed. Despite an initial success, the Sikhs counter-attacked and drove Dick back. The other attacks came on unsupported and suffered heavily, also being beaten back. Finally, a renewed assault by Dick's rallied

* Major John Lawrence was one of the three famous Lawrence brothers. He replaced Broadfoot, the previous political officer on the frontier, after the latter was killed at Ferozeshah. He died as Commissioner for Oudh at Lucknow in 1857 in the Mutiny. He was Governor-General's agent at Lahore between the First and Second Sikh Wars and afterwards Commissioner for the Punjab.

soldiers enabled the other columns to gain a footing. The Sikhs then fell back fighting savagely. Little quarter was given, for the Sikhs were reported to have killed the British wounded in their successful counter-attacks. The sappers cleared a way through the less formidable entrenchment on the enemy's right, and the 3rd Light Dragoons were passed through in single file. Then they charged with effect.

Two things were fatal for the Sikh army: first the Sutlej had risen seven feet in the night; and second, Tej Singh had, it seems, considerately removed the centre pontoons of the bridge, cutting off their retreat. Some of the Sikhs entered the water as formed bodies of men but were scattered by the impact of the current and by the British fire. The river was soon choked with dying, wounded and drowning men and the Sikh losses were estimated at from 8,000 to 10,000 men. In the words of Mackinnon, the British fire 'soon converted the greater part of the Sikh army into a hideous and struggling wreck of humanity' while 'the sluggish waters of the Sutlej were clogged with human carcases'. The British loss was nearly 2,300 men, of whom over 300 were killed. The arrangements for the wounded were the best in the campaign, as they were removed to Ferozepore where the cantonments had been turned into a hospital. The sepoys had fought better than before, judging by the comparative casualty rate, but it must be remembered that the British regiments had not been reinforced by drafts and so were numerically weak. The battle itself had been poorly managed, particularly the artillery side of it, this being Gough's fault as the artillery officers concerned had complained of insufficient time for preparations.

The war was now at an end, for though Gough crossed the Sutlej on 13 February and occupied Kasur, he and Hardinge were met there by Ghulab Singh, a chief who had not participated in the fighting, and who subsequently as a reward for his diplomacy was to be made Maharajah of Kashmir. Ghulab Singh accepted the terms laid down by Hardinge. In fact the situation was by no means entirely favourable to the British despite Sobraon, for nearly one half of the European soldiers had fallen in four fierce battles, and the Indian troops were still by no means completely reliable. In the days before steam-driven troopships, drafts and reinforcements took over three months to arrive in India, while the Sikhs could still field an army of nearly 40,000 men even though much of it was of inferior quality to the soldiers lost at Sobraon and it lacked the support of powerful artillery.

Still, the moral effect of the Sikh casualties, the loss of 226 guns and the further threat to the Sikhs of 12,000 men of the Bombay army under General Sir Charles Napier concentrated in Bahawalpur to the south meant that these weaknesses had to be concealed—at least from the rank and file of the Khalsas.

The terms of the Treaty of Kasure were severe. The most immediately important was the restriction of the Sikh army to 25 battalions and 12,000 horse, and the surrender of 25 guns. The most significant for the future of the sub-continent was the indemnity placed on the Sikh state of half a million pounds, failing the payment of which the area now known as Kashmir* would be handed over to Ghulab Singh. As expected the indemnity was not paid and Ghulab Singh gained his reward. The other terms involved the cession of the Jullundur Doab—the area between the rivers Beas and Sutlej—the stationing of a British army at Lahore until the end of 1846, a promise not to employ European mercenaries or make war or peace without British permission, and to provide free passage through the country for the latter's armies whenever they wished.

*　　*　　*　　*　　*　　*

Thus at the end of the first war the terms inflicted on the Sikh state were designed to cripple it militarily and to control its external political relations while leaving its internal government in the hands of its old rulers. Or so it seemed. In fact the British administration in India contemplated eventual direct annexation and of thoroughly controlling the sub-continent up to the Indus. Certainly this interim frontier was very unsatisfactory and far inferior for defensive purposes to the line eventually reached in the Indus valley. Apart from these strategic considerations there were certain economic ones; namely that the revenues from the conquered Punjab were expected to exceed the expenses of a garrison there.

Within the state of Lahore important changes quickly followed the war. To begin with the vale of Kashmir had to be detached from the

* The Jammu province of present-day Kashmir, which is largely Hindu, was a feudatory state controlled by Ghulab Singh and his Dogras. To it was now added the vale of Kashmir, an area inhabited by Muslims, while Ghulab was made a Maharajah, released from his feudal burdens and had his status guaranteed by the British.

old domain of Ranjit and handed over to Ghulab Singh; and in the second place the Sikh soldiery in some dozens of forts and strongplaces had to be persuaded or intimidated, either into disbanding or joining the permitted regular force of twenty-five battalions. In Kashmir, the *de facto* government rested with Shaik-Iman-ud-din, the previous Muslim governor. Lord Hardinge considered it quite impracticable to send a British army into that province with a possibly hostile Punjab behind it. His object was to detach the territory from the Punjab, and to employ Lahore's resources as far as possible. The actual submission of Kashmir to Ghulab Singh took from March 1846, when the Treaty of Kasur was signed at Lahore, to November of the same year. A Sikh army was being collected with British advisers when in September the Shaikh informed Lieutenant Edwardes* that he had secret orders from Lal Singh, the wazir at Lahore, to the government. Lal Singh's motives were jealousy of Ghulab and family rivalry. The Shaikh was promptly told that proof of these allegations would mean his personal safety and a free pardon in the event of his submission.[16] As the British army was being held in reserve while the Sikh one advanced, the Kashmiris submitted promptly and on 9 January 1847 a court composed of British officers found the Sikh wazir guilty of duplicity. He was immediately deposed and exiled, and his departure strengthened British control. At the same time he was hated by the Sikhs for his inglorious part in the war. The resistance of Kashmir to Ghulab Singh was not primarily based on religious passion, but was simply the struggle between feudal lords and would-be lords. Once Kashmir had submitted, however, Ghulab Singh was under an even heavier obligation to the British.

Most of the Khalsa troops submitted, not surprisingly, since their arrears of pay were to be settled. Nevertheless there was a crisis con-

* Sir Herbert Edwardes (1819–68). In 1837 he attended classes at King's College, London, but on failure to gain entrance to Oxford went to India instead as a cadet in 1841. He qualified as an interpreter after only three years, passing examinations in Urdu, Hindi and Persian. In the First Sikh War he was A.D.C. to Gough. The high-water mark of his career was reached in 1847–9 when he re-formed the civil administration of Bannu province and gained a great reputation in the Second Sikh War. He was promoted major and awarded the C.B. His negotiating powers, as Commissioner at Peshawar, were responsible for the non-intervention of Dost Mohammed, ruler of Afghanistan, during the Indian Mutiny. Edwardes' brilliant career in India was cut short by ill-health in 1865.

cerning the fort of Kangra in the Himalayan foothills which had been annexed by Britain. Here, in May 1846, the commandant was still holding out and refusing to submit. It was considered necessary to take the fortress, or face the consequences of a spread of the rebellion throughout the Punjab, which might draw in thousands of unemployed soldiers and lead, even if crushed, to uncontrollable banditry. By the end of 1846 the British had to leave the Punjab under the terms of the treaty, though Lord Hardinge, as early as September, was considering various ways of perpetuating British influence for a few more years.[17]

It was felt to be necessary to persuade the Lahore Durbar, which held supreme power, to amend the treaty as the Maharajah was a minor. A lever lay to hand in that the *sirdars* could be confirmed in their *jagirs* which were fiefs held in return for money and services. In other words their present conditional ownership could be made unconditional.[18] The Maharani, acting as regent, was against giving the British further rights and only wanted a small force at Lahore while the kingdom was reorganised and consolidated for her son. Her efforts were in vain and by the Treaty of Bhairowal on 26 December 1846, the British became in effect the rulers of the country. The terms involved the paying of the expenses of the British garrison by the Lahore government, and the taking over of the direction of military and civil administration. The Maharani was thus deprived of nearly all power and given a pension of 150,000 rupees a year. She was furious with these arrangements and bitterly resentful towards those *sirdars* who, under pressure, had even begged the British to stay; she got the young Maharajah, a lad of nine, to refuse at a public ceremony to invest Tej Singh, the 'hero' of Sobraon, with the title of rajah. This enabled Hardinge, using the Durbar, to get rid of the Maharani, who was exiled to Sheikapura with her pension reduced to 48,000 rupees—the latter action breaking the terms of the treaty.[19] British protection was to last until 1854, but naturally after these *contretemps* the Sikhs doubted whether a withdrawal was really intended.

These manœuvrings in Lahore made the traditional rulers of the Punjab very uneasy. It is easy to see why, for Lord Dalhousie, Governor-General from 1847 to 1855, was to dissolve and bring under British administration many princely states which in his opinion had been misgoverned—to the mutual benefit of the British and the embryonic Indian middle class. Unfortunately for the Punjab rajahs, the bar to British control, the Sikh army, had been weakened; there were, however, in the Punjab at this time a mass of bitter, unemployed soldiers, hating the British for religious, racial and perhaps even nationalist reasons—while the large class of worried landowners saw their political and economic power and prestige slipping from them. They had miscalculated the effect of the defeat of the Khalsa army on themselves.

Among the most prominent of these rulers was the Dewan Mul Raj who had succeeded to the fief of Multan in 1844. Owing to the disturbed state of the country he had paid no tribute to the government as a succession fee. In an agreement with the British resident he promised to pay only 20 lakhs instead of 30* but to give up his lands north of the river Ravi—one third of this province—and to raise his contribution to the central government by one third for three years. This was bad enough for the Dewan but the British started to abolish the internal customs dues exacted by him, and also began hearing appeals against his legal decisions. Both these actions cut into the Dewan's financial resources, and the latter deeply affected his prestige.[20] In disgust he submitted his resignation on 18 December 1847, but was persuaded to stay on until March. The new ruler of Multan was to be paid a fixed salary while a British official ran the state. Two British political officers, Van Agnew and Anderson, were sent to Multan where the sepoys were anxious as they feared, rightly, that the garrison would be considerably reduced, and they would be unemployed. On 19 April, just after they had arrived, the two officers were attacked and badly wounded by the soldiers. Mul Raj tried not to get involved but was elected war leader, and after the desertion of the Sikh troops who had come with the two men from Lahore, they both were murdered.

A Sikh force was ordered to march on Multan, and Gough made preparations for a British column to follow. His actions were countermanded by Dalhousie, who had become Governor-General in January 1848, though it would seem by the terms of the Treaty of Bhairowal that their duty was to ensure 'preservation of the peace of the country'. After all, the Lahore government was paying for their army at Lahore. Herbert Edwardes warned that the concentration of a Sikh army on Multan would result in its desertion, a general rebellion of the country

* A lakh was worth about £10,000.

and its inevitable annexation.[21] This was what Dalhousie was quite prepared to consider.

Edwardes, who was stationed at Dera Fateh Khan, a camp on the Indus, watching the Afghan frontier, received a pencilled note from Agnew, one of the wounded men at Multan. He collected a small force of Sikh levies and marched on that fortress, but hearing what had happened to the two men and realising his Sikh soldiers were very unreliable, he recrossed the Indus until he was able to join General Cortlandt, a Eurasian mercenary in Sikh service, who had a more dependable Muslim regiment. He also began to levy Pathans and Baluchis who were ready to join either side but who were not as likely to be as disloyal as the Sikhs. By a series of brilliant manœuvres with his force of untrained levies Edwardes checked an advance by the Multan garrison to the west and consolidated a force of 6,000 men— largely Pathan or Punjabi Muslims—whose attachment to him was fairly reliable as long as he could produce excitement and victories. His officers were all Muslim, often local gentry, save Cortlandt. Edwardes got in touch with the Muslim Nawab of Bahawalpur, who had raised a force of about 12,000 Muslim troops under Fateh Muhammed Khan and crossed the Indus on the 31st May. On the 18th Edwardes defeated the Multan force with his raw levies at Kineri and concentrating his forces, marched on the city. He had been joined by Shaikh Iman-ud-din of Kashmiri fame who with some rather unreliable troops had subdued the surrounding country. A further defeat of Mul Raj was inflicted on 1 July at Tibi and the Sikhs were driven back into Multan. Edwardes had superior numbers of men and guns and his Pathan cavalry had a great effect. Heavy casualties were inflicted and Edwardes was convinced that a few siege guns, if they arrived promptly, would enable him to take the fortress.

Meanwhile three columns of regular Sikh troops under Sher Singh had advanced on Multan, but were known to be extremely unreliable. Edwardes had been unable to invest the fortress properly and he kept these troops well to the rear, but even so he could not prevent Mul Raj allowing the Sikhs free access to the city and its bazaars. It was a ludicrous situation. Edwardes' urgent plea for British regulars and siege guns, particularly the latter, were refused by Gough who considered the season too hot for operations. A column was collected however under General Whish, consisting of two brigades of infantry and one

E

of cavalry with engineers and siege train, which was despatched on 26 July from Lahore; leading elements reaching Multan on 18 August, four months after the start of the disorders.

When the siege train had come up two alternatives presented themselves to the British; either to attempt a storm involving heavy casualties and great risk, or to open parallels in the style of Vauban. A compromise was adopted. Batteries were established on 7th September, and on the 12th an attempt was made to storm with four regular battalions including the only two British. Some 250 casualties were suffered, but the enemy was driven out of his immediate entrenchments in the suburbs. While the besiegers paused to consolidate, the Sikh column under Sher Singh, which was supporting them, defected. Whish then raised the siege and withdrew from Multan some miles to the south in order to cover Sind, his communications and the pacified area in the extreme south-west Punjab. There he awaited reinforcements to come up the Indus from Bombay. On 9 October, Sher Singh marched to join his father Chattar Singh in the north where the Sikh garrisons had also risen. He was accompanied by most of the Sikh and Hindu soldiery in Multan, the Muslims remaining. Whish did not consider himself strong enough to re-attempt siege operations until the arrival of another six battalions of the Bombay army on 22 December. Meanwhile the rebellion had spread across the north.

There is some ground for thinking that Dalhousie, who probably underestimated the military power of the Sikhs, was attempting to provoke an uprising which would give him an opportunity for annexation and also to crush the Khalsa army once and for all.[22] This would account for the delay in making up the Multan column. There were no insuperable obstacles to movement, because river transport for troops and guns was available on the Indus tributaries. Certainly Edwardes thought that the moral effect of swift operations was very important and was annoyed that there was considerable delay before the orders to march south from Lahore were finally issued. Certainly, too, the longer the rebellion remained unsuppressed the more likely it was to spread, and strictly military considerations might have been overruled—despite Sir John Fortescue's approval of the Commander-in-Chief's decisions.[23]

It was in the far north-west around Peshawar, which covered the passes from Kabul, that the main regular Sikh forces were grouped.

They garrisoned a largely Muslim area and would take the first shock for the British of any invasion from Central Asia, at that time a very unlikely contingency, though an Afghan raid was always a possibility. More important perhaps was the fact that the Sikh regular army was well out of the way. Nevertheless it was inevitable that the revolt in Multan would be reflected among the regulars. Their commander was Chattar Singh father of Sher Singh. The temper of the troops was worsened by the banishment of the Maharani in May 1848, from Sheikapura to Benares on the suspicion, perhaps justified, that she had been conspiring against the British and inciting the soldiers to mutiny. There were three or four executions but no legal proof against her existed, as the Resident at Lahore admitted. Even Dost Mohammed, the Amir of Kabul, Jalalabad and Guzni, that part of Afghanistan south of the watershed of the Hindu Kush, had informed Captain Abbott, who was Chattar Singh's 'assistant', that the Sikhs were disaffected. But Abbott behaved towards Chattar Singh as if suspecting treachery and may indeed have precipitated the danger he was trying to avoid. Chattar Singh, who was trying to marry his daughter to the young Maharajah Dulip Singh, certainly returned the suspicion for he had received in August 1848, an ominous letter from Currie, the Resident at Lahore, which stated that permission for the marriage could not 'be considered as indicative of any line of policy which the government may consider it right to pursue now, or at any future time, in respect to the administration of the Punjab'.[24] Actually Chattar Singh was probably anxious not to commit himself, yet he was forced to both by his own troops and by the British. Finally at the beginning of August 1848 a force at Pakli mutinied and Abbott responded by raising the local tribesmen to surround these troops, appealing to their hatred of the Sikhs for past wars and atrocities. Chattar Singh then took command of the revolt, which in the absence of any British soldiers continued in a desultory manner for over a month, as the armed peasantry under Abbott were quite unable to deal with disciplined bodies of men. On 23 October the Peshawar garrison mutinied and the British there escaped to Afghan territory where they were seized and eventually handed over to the Sikhs. The garrison at Bannu had mutinied also, killed their Muslim and British commanders, and marched to join the rest. Meanwhile Sher Singh, marching north from near Multan and picking up large numbers of recruits on the way, had reached Ramnagar on the Chenab. There the Bannu troops were advancing to join him. Thus all the northern garrisons had risen, the local Muslim levies being unable to make headway against them, a quite different situation from that in the south. The Sikh army was concentrating round the fords of Ramnagar, preparatory to a march on Lahore. It was composed of the regulars left to Lahore in 1846, old soldiers who had been disbanded and were as a consequence embittered, and the local gentry and nobility, who were convinced now that the British planned to liquidate their institutions and confiscate their property.

Though in some respects Sikh morale and cohesion were far higher than in the first war, the fact that many regiments were levied very quickly and artillery was in short supply made them less rather than more formidable; certainly they were less potentially dangerous, even if they had fought hard when the clash came.

At long last the British had begun to concentrate; troops marched down from the hill stations; the reductions ordered in the Bengal army at the conclusion of the first war were countermanded and men were rapidly enlisted. The British army crossed the Sutlej on 9 November 1848. This was partly to prevent mercenaries from joining Sher Singh, as Hindus and even Muslims would have been perfectly willing to fight the British. Sher Singh indeed had opened negotiations with Dost Mohammed of Kabul, who though not unfriendly to the British went along with Afghan sentiment and raised a force of 5,000 cavalry under Akram Khan for service and plunder on the plains of the Punjab.

On 10 November, Gough began to advance with his main body from Lahore. He had under him a field force of twenty-one battalions, five of them British and twelve regiments of cavalry, three of them European, together with eleven batteries. He still did not know for whom he was fighting, the Lahore Durbar or the British government. He was informed on 18 November that annexation was now the policy, although a proclamation issued then to the people of the Punjab declared rather vaguely that the British were 'restoring order'.[25]

The commander-in-chief made contact with the enemy on 22 November near the small village of Ramnagar about 70 miles north-west of Lahore. In the cool season of the year that river is a narrow channel exposing dry watercourses and flats. The horse artillery moved up to very advanced positions and opened fire on bodies of Sikhs

retiring across the ford. Sikh guns then came up and opened a heavy
fire, forcing them to withdraw, but one British gun got stuck in the
mud. The 3rd Light Dragoons charged to clear a way for it as the
enemy were coming back to capture it, and got into trouble in the

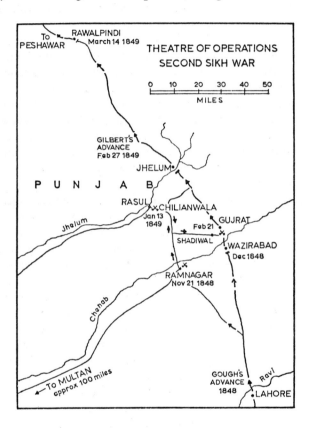

deep sand. Hereupon the 14th Light Dragoons charged and, exceeding
their orders, were badly cut up. General Cureton, commanding the
Cavalry Division, was killed, together with the Colonel of the 14th
light Dragoons. Cureton* was a remarkable officer who had risen

* He was commissioned for his gallant service in the Peninsular War being
made a lieutenant in 1816. He fought at Bhutpore in 1825-6 and made his
reputation as adjutant to a division in the First Afghan War in 1839.

from the ranks, a rare thing in those days. The action had had no very useful result as the Sikhs were withdrawing anyway. It is claimed that the cavalry inflicted heavy losses but there is no objective evidence of this, and in any case a gun had been lost. Sher Singh promptly began to fortify the opposite bank and it was evident that an attack even if successful would suffer very heavy casualties.

The only alternative was to find a way round. Considerable successes could be looked for if the enemy was driven back over the Jhelum, for there were few supplies beyond that river, even though between the Chenab and Jhelum they were plentiful. In addition the countryside became steadily more Muslim and hostile the further north-west the Sikhs retreated, local antagonism having already delayed Sher Singh in his march from Multan northward. The situation was made no better for him by the atrocities inflicted on the Muslims at Jhang by the Sikhs of the Bannu contingent, while the British were quite ready to play on these religious differences.

After stalemate for over a week a turning movement was commenced on 30 November by sending a column under General Thackwell to the right, to find an unguarded ford. Despite confusion due to the night march and the tremendous noise made by the camp followers, which it was feared had alerted the enemy, the force got across at Wazirabad. The crossing was difficult, the troops were without food and suffered great hardships, but eight battalions and five cavalry regiments got across with some horse and field artillery. Thackwell then marched down the other side of the river. He was in a very dangerous position for if the enemy had concentrated against him he might, as he had a river in his rear, have faced annihilation. Fortunately, though Gough merely cannonaded the enemy camp at Ramnagar, the Sikhs were unenterprising and did not concentrate against the turning movement. Gough tried to reinforce Thackwell by sending one brigade, Godby's, across a ford which the advance had uncovered but this force was unable to reach Thackwell until after an action had been joined at Sadulpore. Here the British found themselves (while attempting to camp and await reinforcements) under a cannonade from guns concealed in sugar cane. They deployed and the infantry lay down. After a desultory bombardment the Sikhs withdrew and the action came to an end on the evening of 3 December 1848. It was stated in despatches that the enemy had suffered severely, though this seems exceedingly unlikely. More probably the force at Sadulpore was merely covering the retreat of the Sikh main army, which fell back to a position near the villages of Mong and Rasul on the eastern bank of the Jhelum. They did not put the river between them and their pursuers, who encamped at Heylah about ten miles distant, separated by a dense belt of jungle which was gradually thinned out in the coming weeks by cutting of firewood by the camp followers of both sides. A few skirmishes occurred, while some of Chattar Singh's troops joined Sher Singh's including two excellent batteries of horse artillery trained by British officers. The lack of any decisive blow by the British resulted in some accession of strength to the enemy army, lessened, however, by the fact that it had considerable difficulty in getting enough supplies. Dalhousie, the Governor-General, was worried because he thought that Gough's communications were insecure, his commissariat by no means fully adequate and his reserves non-existent. The two armies waited for reinforcements, the British hoping for an accession of strength after the fall of Multan, the Sikhs after that of Attock when Chattar Singh's whole army and 5,000 Afghan horse would come to their aid.

Meanwhile there was action far in the south at Multan. Whish had under his command about 15,000 men in all, though many were irregulars. Many of Cortlandt's Sikhs and Hindus deserted. An engagement took place at An Suraj Khund outside Multan after Sher Singh's departure, the enemy being driven back and five guns taken. The Pathans fought well on this occasion, the cavalry frequently charging the enemy. On 22 December reinforcements arrived in the shape of the Bombay column of two regiments of British infantry and four of sepoys, together with two native cavalry regiments and supporting troops. The original position in front of the city was reoccupied on Christmas Day and on 27 December an assault involving some hard fighting cleared the enemy from the suburbs.

Batteries were established, the enemy artillery subdued and the wall so battered that the breaches were pronounced practicable by the 2nd of January 1849. The assault was commenced that afternoon—a mistake as there was not sufficient daylight left—also in the attack control was lost over the troops. One breach proved impracticable and the officer commanding the column deputed to storm it, Captain Smyth, immediately led his troops to reinforce the other attack which had already broken in. Confused fighting followed in the streets and the explosion of a magazine. Control was only reasserted in the morning after losses of about 250 men had been sustained and the garrison of 3,000 men had retired to the citadel. Mortars were established to bombard the place on the 6 January 1849, and the enemy driven from his guns. Batteries were set up on the 8th and a regular siege begun. Mul Raj now attempted to negotiate but unconditional surrender was demanded. By 22 January breaches were made in the walls and saps had been driven up them so the garrison then laid down its arms to avoid a storm. Mul Raj was imprisoned, all involved in the attacks on Van Agnew and Anderson were hanged, and the rest of the garrison disbanded. Many of the troops here had been Muslims who do not seem to have made a very determined fight of it, and in any case the keenest men whatever their religion had gone off with Sher Singh.

In the north, though the two armies sat facing one another until the middle of January, skirmishes and guerrilla operations were taking place in the Jullunder Doab—the area ceded to the British in 1846 where the peasantry were largely Sikh. Various petty chiefs took part but they were harried by a movable column controlled by John Lawrence, the commissioner. The force used to suppress the revolt consisted of several battalions of Indians. Eventually the rebels were completely dispersed on 8 January 1849. Sir John Fortescue's strictures on the diversion of force needed to suppress the outbreak seem harsh when the political need to keep a tight control on the area is realised.[26] After all, a Sikh success here would have interrupted the British supply routes from Meerut, by provoking an extension of the rising across the Sutlej among their co-religionists. Even beyond the river, where there were many dissatisfied Hindu princes with some military potential, there was danger.

On the Jhelum the stalemate was broken on the 10 January when news was received that Attock had fallen. This presaged the arrival of Chattar Singh and his Afghan allies which might put Gough in jeopardy, and he was urged to attack by Major Mackeson, his political agent. Curiously he considered himself perfectly able to deal with the Sikhs yet he had not been reinforced and could have given battle earlier. So with 66 guns and 12,000 men he marched out to the field of Chilianwala and to perhaps the hardest battle ever fought by the

British in India. The Sikhs also left their entrenchments and took up a covering position densely screened by trees and scrub. Their exact line is not clear and the conflict was so confused that the contenders themselves were muddled in their accounts of the struggle.

The Sikh army consisted of about twenty-five battalions, ten of them raised since the rebellion started, with four regiments of cavalry and 4,000 Gorcharras or irregular horse supported by 50* guns. The enemy's right, covered by a much wider belt of forest, was lightly held and echeloned back so here there was no clash at all. Gough was in fact attempting to camp where he stood, uncertain of his opponent's position, when artillery opened fire on him. He at once deployed his army and, though it was two o'clock in the afternoon, launched his attack after a preparatory bombardment. He was outnumbered but much of his enemy's infantry was in very recently raised corps. His regular cavalry ought to have been far more effective than its largely irregular opponents, while he had a marked superiority in artillery so, judging by previous battles in India, the odds could not be considered excessive. However, as at Mudki and Ferozeshah, the real European superiority, which lay in the co-ordination of cavalry, mobile artillery and infantry, was neutralised by the terrain.

The British army was drawn up in two divisions each of two brigades. On the flanks were the cavalry while the artillery was distributed along the front. Unfortunately the jungle and scrub reduced the effect of the artillery. The infantry brigades were each composed of two sepoy and one British battalions and in reserve were three Indian battalions under Brigadier Penny. On the left was Campbell's† division of two brigades under Brigadiers Hoggan and Pennycuick. Campbell personally led Hoggan's attack and drove back the Sikhs opposed to

* All but three of these were light ones, 6-7- or 9-pounders. Many of them had been buried or otherwise concealed after the first war and the political officers had not learnt about them. The British artillery, including ten heavy, and twenty-four field guns, was of superior quality.

† This was the Colin Campbell who later became Lord Clyde (1792–1863). He was the illegitimate son of a Scottish lady and a carpenter called Macilver. He was commissioned through the influence of his mother's family, and distinguished himself in the Peninsular War, being invalided home in 1813 after fighting his way to the rank of captain in five years. Lacking the money to purchase, it took him nearly thirty years to obtain a colonelcy. He was eventually lent the money, and was indirectly assisted by Fitzroy Somerset (Lord Raglan) and Lord Hardinge,

him, who were largely recently raised troops, capturing several guns, while his cavalry beat off threatening movements of the enemy's irregular horsemen on his left. Next to him on his right Brigadier Pennycuick's attack was impetuously led, masking the fire of their own guns. Pennycuick and his son were killed, while the European regiments had half their officers killed and were driven back with terrible casualties. Campbell then wheeled right and drove the Sikhs back, having brought up his guns. On the right Brigadiers Godby and Mountain, of Gilbert's division, attacked and after a savage struggle with heavy casualties forced the enemy to retire. On the extreme right, however, the cavalry brigade was badly handled by Brigadier Pope, and panicked before a charge of only 50 horsemen. The horse artillery was cut up and lost 3 guns. The panic was stopped and by nightfall the Sikhs withdrew. The British army was suffering acutely from thirst and consequently only twelve captured light pieces were removed, the rest having been taken back by parties of Sikhs during the night. It was all the British could do to bring in their wounded.

The battle had been very sanguinary, British casualties totalling 602 men killed, 1,651 wounded and 104 missing, or about 15 per cent of the total force engaged. Four guns and several colours were lost. The Sikh casualties were not recorded; they were probably higher but they had held the British to what was essentially a drawn battle. Due to lack of direction from the top, attacks were poorly co-ordinated, partly because of the smoke, dust and thick jungle. The battle was blundered into, giving the Sikhs every advantage. True, the incompetent handling of Pope's cavalry brigade and its subsequent panic leading to the loss of guns, could not have been foreseen, but Pope himself was an elderly Indian army man and physically quite unfit for command, being barely

with both of whom he had served in Spain. In 1842 he commanded the 98th regiment in China under Gough and left that country four years later as a brigadier-general. After playing a vital role in the Second Sikh War, he held various Indian frontier commands from 1850–3. In the Crimean War he rose to command the 1st Division when the Duke of Cambridge went home at the end of 1854. Three years later he returned to India as Commander-in-Chief to end his distinguished career by relieving Lucknow and pacifying the north of the country. In 1858 he was created Lord Clyde, and in 1862 was promoted field marshal. He had earned, in the words of the *Dictionary of National Biography*, 'a reputation in the military history of England absolutely unrivalled in the records of the middle of the nineteenth century'.

able to mount his horse. Even if the attack had been better managed and had not Pennycuick, for instance, by his headlong assault masked the fire of his own guns, the struggle in the centre would still have been difficult against excellent and well-posted soldiers. A common feature in the conditions of close contact of the struggle was the slaughter of the wounded, by both sides.[27] Certainly this savagery helped to give the battle of Chilianwala its legendary place in the British conquest of India.

The day after the battle the two armies withdrew to their respective camps. There followed three days of heavy rain, making it quite impossible to manœuvre the guns. The condition of both armies was wretched, unable as they were to light fires. On 17 January Chattar Singh and Akram Khan's Afghans arrived in the enemy camp and it became impractical to renew the attack. Nevertheless if Gough hesitated, some of the Sikhs did so still more after the butchery of their crack battalions: two Sikh *sirdars* deserted on the 19th while on the 20th two troopers in the 9th Lancers who had been taken prisoner in a skirmish were handed back.[28]*

Despite greater generosity towards their prisoners, the Sikh supply situation was becoming desperate, being cooped up on the Jhelum and augmented by Chattar Singh's army. The land behind them produced no great quantities of food. The fall of Multan, too, finally took place on 22 January and Whish's force started to move northward. On the 14 February as he approached, Sher Singh struck his camp and moved eastward round Gough, attempting to cross the Chenab and get to Lahore. He left behind him a position that had been very heavily fortified. His situation was difficult as to get through he had to go in an arc, while Gough was in a position to cut across the chord. A brigade on the other side of the Chenab checked the Sikh attempt to cross the river, and eventually their army was found by the British cavalry at Gujrat on 20 February. Gough caught up with them from the south-west with twenty-four thousand men and 96 guns, for Whish had joined him on the 18th. Altogether he had the equivalent of eleven regiments of cavalry and twenty-three battalions of infantry, of which three of cavalry and eight of infantry were European. The Sikh strength is more difficult to estimate: they may well have been more

---

* This uncharacteristically humane gesture was undoubtedly due to the Sikh commanders' desire to preserve their personal safety in case of defeat.

numerous, but a large proportion of their soldiers were irregulars, while they had but 59 guns.

The battleground where the armies met at Gujrat was open and grassy so that dust did not obscure the troop movements, while the battle started at 7 a.m., leaving plenty of time for a British pursuit if the action was successful. A dry nullah ran from the Sikh army to the British centre, which was drawn up on both sides of it. Both armies were in the classical formation with infantry and guns in the centre; and cavalry—and, in the case of the British—horse artillery as well, on the wings. In front of the Sikh position lay two villages fortified and held by regular infantry called Bara Kalra and Chota Kalra. As the British line advanced the Sikh guns opened fire at a distance of about half a mile, unmasking their positions. Then the British infantry lay down in dead ground, their guns pushed forward covered by skirmishers, and the cavalry and horse artillery held back the threatening movements of superior numbers of irregular horse. Gradually the artillery preparation silenced the enemy guns, dismounting some and inflicting frightful losses on the gunners. Eventually the 2nd Bengal Europeans advanced to storm Bara Kalra and, owing to inadequate artillery preparation, suffered heavily. Savage fighting took place in both villages but soon the whole Sikh front line was driven back, the irregular horsemen made off and the British cavalry rode in amongst the fugitive infantry. The entire camp and every gun was taken while the losses of the picked Khalsa troops were particularly severe. A subaltern of the 2nd Bengal Europeans recorded that many of the wounded in the camp were killed by the victors.[29] About 800 of the British had fallen, the majority being among the gunners and the 2nd Bengal Europeans who lost 148 out of 900 men. Seven battalions had borne the brunt of the action. The camp followers plundered the Sikh camp, while guards were posted on the Chenab fords with orders to let Sikh soldiers pass to their homes if they surrendered their arms. The remainder were pursued towards the North West Frontier. There, pinned down by the British, by hostile tribes and by Ghulab Singh's Kashmir army, they surrendered unconditionally on 14 March. Ghulab Singh, Maharajah of Kashmir, had vacillated while the issue was undecided. Akram Khan got across the Indus before the British came up and retreated precipitately into Afghanistan, the pursuit stopping at the Khyber. The beaten soldiers had to surrender their arms which were often their own personal weapons, but were allowed to keep their horses and were then allowed to return to their villages. They had received no pay for the campaign either, having been promised it after victory. Thus ended the Second Sikh War.

It will be noted that unlike the First Sikh War the Second was fought wholeheartedly by the Sikh people. The Sikhs started in a position much inferior to that in 1845 when they had first crossed the Sutlej. In the first place they had lost very large numbers of guns and a strong body of their picked infantrymen at Sobraon. The reductions in their regular army meant, too, that many regiments of infantry were newly raised, and had little time to become really effective. The mass of irregular horse did not really threaten the British—indeed such troops had never done so unless they could harry a column lacking cavalry support in guerrilla fashion. The estimates of numbers of the Sikh armies are much less precise in the Second War due to their more haphazard organisation. The effect of their propaganda appeals to their enemy's Indian troops was no longer effective once they had been beaten back, and the annexation of the Jullundur Doab and the stationing of a British force at Lahore meant they were cut off from their homeland, and forced to fight in Muslim territory where the peasantry were, at best, neutral. Their offensive can be said to be a last despairing throw to which they were provoked and where they were virtually certain of defeat. Dalhousie and the military certainly underestimated them and Chilianwala was regarded, judging by the clamour raised in English newspapers, as a considerable disgrace to British generalship, though not to the valour of the troops who fought and died there. Though General Gough was later created a Viscount he had been superseded after Chilianwala by Sir Charles Napier, but the latter only took command after the redeeming victory of Gujrat.

Immediately after the war ended the annexation of the Punjab was formally proclaimed. The *sirdars* and Maharajah were forced to sign a deed of abdication under threat of the confiscation of all their landed property. On 7 April 1849 Dalhousie reported to London that he had annexed the Punjab. He justified this action by charging the Durbar with vague offences, but the only one he particularised was the non-payment of the subsidy according to the treaty of Bhairowal. As the British had taken over the administration of revenue-collecting before this and considerably lowered the assessments, this pretext was weak.[30]

The results of the Sikh wars were of great importance in both the near and distant future. Immediately it brought the British frontier to the Indus and faced them with a new aspect of Indian defence. Beyond that river lay the Iranian borderlands and all the problems of frontier policing these would entail. The barren hills and mountains, with their savage and warlike inhabitants, offered little in the way of commercial opportunity. Soon beyond the Hindu Kush would appear the Russian threat,* and then it became impolitic to advance further since the State of Afghanistan could best be left in picturesque backwardness as a daunting obstacle to an invader from the north. The smashing of Sikh resistance in the Punjab—the best organised and most warlike Indian state—seemed to render the internal military situation far more secure. The ruthless way the annexation was carried out and seizures of territory in Oudh and elsewhere, though eventually of benefit to their inhabitants, alienated the old ruling class, while the progress of 'civilisation' aroused the hatred of the higher castes. This was one of the causes of the Mutiny, the great trauma of the British in India in the nineteenth century.

The conflict on the Sutlej and the Jhelum also sowed the seeds of the future Kashmir dispute. It could be argued that a more realistic policy towards the perfidious Ghulab Singh would have been quite justified in the long run, and his territory should have been annexed. Certainly, many problems in this century would have been easier to solve if this had been done. The Sikhs, despite their remarkable contribution to Britain's military power, never fully resigned themselves to being governed from Delhi, and it is a testimony to their unquenchable separatism that one hundred and twenty years after annexation their stubborn resistance constitutes no less a problem for the present Indian Government than it did for the British Raj.

---

* After the failure of the British Afghan adventure and the collapse of the Russian Khiva Expedition in 1841–2 there was much less interest in Russia in expansion towards India until the movement into Turkestan in the 1860's.

References

1 Jagmohan Mahajan. *The Annexation of the Punjab*. Allahabad and Karachi: Kitabistan, 1949; p. 22. Lord Colchester (ed.). *The Indian Administration of Lord Ellenborough in his Correspondence with the Duke of Wellington and the Queen*. London: Richard Bentley, 1874; pp. 98, 399–400.

2 Fauja Singh Bajwa. *The Military System of the Sikhs 1799–1849*. Delhi: Motilal Barnisadas, 1964; pp. 57, 234–8. The main Sikh arsenals were at Lahore, Amritsar, and Shahsadabad.

3 Capt D. H. Mackinnon. *Military Service and Adventures in the Far East*. London: Olliver, 1859; 2 vols, II, p. 153. He refers to Sikhs letting the camp followers go free after Buddowal 'having no quarrel with the natives of Hindustan'.

4 Rev J. Coley. *Journal of the Sutlej Campaign 1845–6*. London: Smith, Elder, 1856; pp. 23–4, 48. Coley was the Chaplain attached to the Governor-General. He has an entertaining evangelical style and refers to talk of the Sepoys firing high, deserting to the rear, and shooting Europeans by mistake. See also Hon. Sir John Fortescue. *History of the British Army*. London: Macmillan, 1927, vol. XII, p. 347.

5 Fauja Singh Bajwa, op. cit., p. 179. G. C. Smyth. *The Reigning Family at Lahore*. Calcutta: Thacker, 1847; pp. 87–8.

6 Lord Colchester (ed.), *The Indian Administration of Lord Ellenborough*, op. cit., p. 424.

7 R. A. Huttenback. *British Relations with Sind 1799–1843*. University of California Press, 1962; pp. 113–14. The Indus was not really navigable by steamboats of any size. It was the Directors of the East India Company in London in particular who had high hopes of this project.

8 Mahajan, op. cit., pp. 26–8.

9 Memorandum relative to a paper given by Henry Lawrence to Raja Lal Singh as sanctioned by the Governor-General in the letter of the Secretary to Government No. 166 dated 14th May 1846. Sir Frederick Currie to Henry Lawrence July 28th, 1846. L.2/Bk 169, Punjab Government Records. (P.G.R.) Cited by Mahajan, p. 30. These are extracts from a journal kept by John Nicholson and forwarded to the records after his death in 1857. For Nicholson's brief but brilliant career see Hesketh Pearson. *The Hero of Delhi*. Penguin Books, 1948.

10 Coley, op. cit., pp. 23–44.

11 Ibid., pp. 26–7.

12 Mackinnon, op. cit., p. 153.

13 Ibid., p. 169.

14 Ibid., pp. 1798–9. Mackinnon is the only diarist who was present at Aliwal. Sir Harry Smith's *Memoirs* only quote his despatches.

15 Mahajan, p. 30. Memorandum relative to a paper—op. cit. See also Herbert Edwardes. *Reminiscences of a Bengal Civilian*. London, 1866.

16 Fortescue, op. cit., vol. XII, pp. 384–5. Lt-Col R. G. Burton. *First and Second Sikh Wars*. Simla: Govt Press Office, 1911; p. 39. E. Buckle. *Memoir of the Services of the Bengal Artillery*. London: Allen, 1852; pp. 482–91.

17 H. Hardinge. *Viscount Hardinge*. (Rulers of India Series.) Oxford: Clarendon Press, 1891; p. 133. Mahajan, pp. 46–7.

18 Sir Frederick Currie (Secretary to the Indian Government) to Henry Lawrence (Resident at Lahore) September 25th 1846. L.81/Bk 169, P.G.R., quoted by Mahajan, p. 52.

19 Governor-General to Secret Committee, 19 September 1846. Parliamentary Papers relating to the Articles of Agreement conducted between the British Government and the Lahore Durbar on the 16 December 1846. London, 1847. Also cited by Mahajan, p. 59.

20 Mahajan, p. 80.

21 Edwardes to Currie (Resident at Lahore from December 1847), 4 May 1848. L.55/Bk 191 P.G.R., cited by Mahajan, p. 90.

22 J. G. A. Baird (ed.). *Private Letters of the Marquess of Dalhousie*. Edinburgh: Blackwood, 1910; pp. 25–7, 30, 33. He constantly refers to the eventual need for annexation.

23 Fortescue, op. cit., p. 424. Fortescue tends to rely on the evidence of certain 'favourites'. He dislikes Harry Smith but cannot fault him, and upholds Gough and his decisions by straining the evidence. He dislikes the local political officers whom he thinks interfered too much in military matters.

24 Currie to Edwardes, 3 August 1848, no. 1174, p. 104, 5 May 1848, P.G.R., cited by Mahajan, p. 104.

25 Proclamation by the Resident at Lahore 1849. The Directors were not anxious for further commitments but accepted Dalhousie's judgement as to their necessity.

26 Fortescue, p. 430. Fortescue's prejudice against the military powers exercised by the political agents is apparent here. See also vol. XIII, p. 525.

27 J. H. Lawrence-Archer. *Commentaries on the Punjab Campaign 1848–49*. London: Allen, 1878; p. 105.

28 Anon. *Leaves from the Journal of a Subaltern during the Campaign in the Punjab*. Edinburgh: Blackwood, 1849; pp. 118–19, 124, 155. The ferocity towards the wounded during the battle was accounted for by the British as the responsibility of the Khalsas. The Sirdars were regarded as more humane— they were also less fanatically committed enemies.

29 Ibid., p. 155.

30 John Lawrence to Elliot, 23 February 1848; and Currie to Elliot, 6 April 1848. Parliamentary Papers 1847–49, cited by Mahajan, p. 176.

The Third China War
1860

The Third China War
1860

John Selby

By 1860 China had been in conflict with the West for many years. It started in 1757 when an Imperial edict drastically changed the arrangements which allowed foreign vessels to trade at several Chinese ports and confined them to Canton. There were other irksome restrictions as well. Europeans were not allowed to live in the Chinese part of Canton; they were confined to the suburbs, and neither women nor arms could be brought to their trading factories. Two other matters, however, rankled even more. The Chinese insisted on trying foreigners for offences according to the Chinese laws, and refused to open proper diplomatic relations. This meant that British attempts to establish ambassadors at Peking always failed, and that her representatives were compelled to deal with erratic local dignitaries. Also by the 1830's, the Emperor would not receive in person political emissaries at all.

The ending of the East India Company's monopoly in 1833 produced no improvement in trading conditions. Rather the reverse; without the tactful Company's agents to smooth matters, they became worse for everyone. In 1836 the Imperial Government appointed a new High Commissioner for Canton called Lin, and he was given the task of stopping the opium trade which had long been a bone of contention between the British traders and the Imperial Government. Up to this time opium-smuggling was rife. There was a huge demand for opium in China, and the sale of the 'pernicious article' helped the East India Company who monopolised its production, the Government of India who collected revenue from its sale, and Britain's balance of payments to China. Until the appointment of Lin, Chinese officials, and even the Chinese anti-smuggling fleet, were quite agreeable to allow opium to come into China—for a personal consideration. The trade in opium, in fact, was beneficial to everyone concerned except the poor addict, the opium-smoker.

The stage was now set for the three so-called opium wars; but only the First China War of 1840 deserves such a name. This was the result of the 'siege of the factories'. Lin had the foreign merchants' warehouses and quarters surrounded; he ordered their Chinese servants to leave their masters, and followed this up by confiscating twenty thousand chests of British-owned opium; but the war was also caused by a Chinaman being killed at Kowloon by a shore party of British and American sailors. When the British refused to hand over the murderer, Lin cut off all supplies and all Chinese labour, and instructed the Portuguese Governor of Macao to expel the entire British community from his territory.

The British merchants and their families, who had been based on Macao and, for the permitted season, had traded from their factories in the suburbs of Canton, now moved to Hong Kong. The combination of the confiscation of all opium in China and Chinese waters and the expulsion of the British community from Macao and Canton were together sufficient provocation for a war. Palmerston as Foreign Secretary sent a formal ultimatum to the Imperial Government demanding the restoration of the confiscated goods or their monetary equivalent, and security for future British trade. 'In making these demands Palmerston did not dispute China's right to prohibit opium imports. The Queen of England, he explained, wished her subjects in foreign countries to obey the laws of those countries, but Her Majesty could not allow them to be treated with violence, and when wrong was done to them, she would see they obtained redress.'[1]

The main cause of the war, then, was not so much the restriction of the opium trade as the cramping conditions of trade generally and the drastic action taken against British traders and nationals.

An expeditionary force of 2,500 troops of all ranks with 100 sailors and marines was formed under General Gough, and the First China War followed. This saw a naval action to clear the channel, the silencing and occupation of Canton's forts, and the breaching of

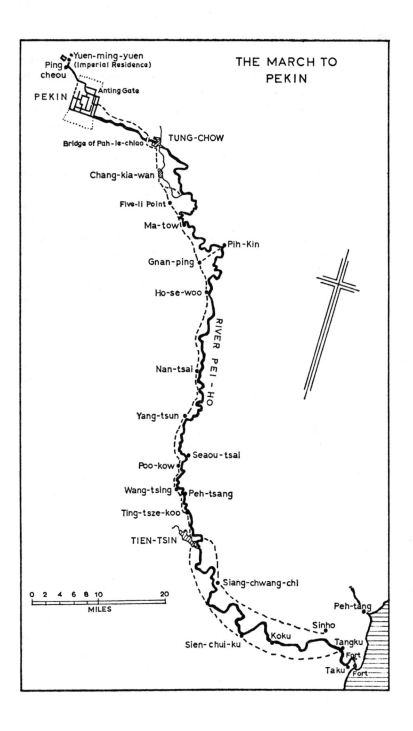

THE MARCH TO
PEKIN

Yuen-ming-yuen
(Imperial Residence)
Ping
cheou
Anting Gate
PEKIN
Bridge of Pah-le-chiao
TUNG-CHOW
Chang-kia-wan
Five-li Point
Ma-tow
Pih-Kin
Gnan-ping
Ho-se-woo
RIVER PEI-HO
Nan-tsai
Yang-tsun
Seaou-tsai
Poo-kow
Wang-tsing
Peh-tsang
Ting-tsze-koo
TIEN-TSIN
Siang-chwang-chi
Peh-tang
Sinho
Koku
Tangku
Sien-chui-ku
Taku Fort
Fort

0 2 4 6 8 10   20
MILES

Canton's walls, all interspersed with cease-fires, conventions and the like, as the beaten Chinese employed their customary, seemingly endless, delaying tactics. In August 1842, however, after the British had captured a number of cities on the Yangtse, cut the route by which the tribute of grain was sent by the Grand Canal to Peking, and threatened Nanking, the Treaty of Nanking was signed. Under this Britain obtained Hong Kong; the Chinese agreed to accept a British representative in China; and Canton, Amoy, Foochow, Ningpoo and Shanghai were opened up to foreign trade. Except for a compensation indemnity for the opium seized, not very much was said about the 'pernicious article', so smuggling still continued. Under a series of further treaties, however, several other countries, including the United States of America and France, obtained the same privileges as Britain as regards legitimate trade, and in most of the treaty ports foreign consuls acquired from the Chinese Government special areas as homes for their nationals, called concessions, in which their own laws operated. These privileges came to be known as extra-territorial rights.

In 1856 a further dispute arose between France and Britain on the one hand and China on the other. Auguste Chapdelaine, a French missionary, whose only crime was to preach Christianity in China, was tried and executed by the Chinese; and twelve Chinese seamen from the *Lorcha* Arrow* were taken off the (Hong Kong) British registered ship by mandarins and soldiers and tried by them for piracy. Although the men were returned unharmed these incidents were sufficient for the renewal of war. In the Second China War the forts outside Canton were again captured, Canton itself bombarded and its walls breached, and a naval action against junks fought. Once more the war dragged on, and the Chinese were slow to come to terms. It was not until the 26 June 1858 that the Treaty of Tientsin was signed by cowed and reluctant Imperial Commissioners with Lord Elgin and Baron Gros representing Britain and France. To reach Tientsin the British had to capture the Taku forts at the mouth of the Peiho River, and small warships cleared the river up to the town—see map. On this occasion it was easily accomplished. The modest defences at the mouth of the Peiho River, consisting of a boom of spars, chains, and hawsers, were snapped at once when a small British steamer struck them at full

* Lorcha means schooner.

speed. Other vessels followed, and although guns were fired from the forts, the heavier guns of the British ships soon silenced them, and no defence was offered when the landing parties went ashore. The terms of the Treaty of Tientsin provided for the rights of foreign diplomatic missions to live in Peking, the confirmation of extra-territorial rights, the right to travel through China, the protection of missionaries, the addition of further treaty ports, making sixteen in all, and an indemnity to cover the expenses of Britain and France for the recent expedition.

Great store was set on compelling the Imperial Court itself to handle foreign relations; and it was therefore decided to send British representatives in the following year up to Peking to obtain the ratification of the Treaty of Tientsin. What happened on the journey there was the direct cause of the Third China War. In 1859 the naval force under Admiral James Hope was repulsed at the Taku forts at the mouth of the Peiho and could not force a way through for the British and French emissaries. This rebuff could not be allowed to go unavenged. Both Britain and France decided to send considerable forces to punish the Chinese for their insulting behaviour. The Third China War was about to begin.

*   *   *   *   *   *

The Allied plan was for the French to assemble at Shanghai and the British at Hong Kong. Then the two contingents were to proceed independently to forward bases in the north, the French at Chefoo and the British at Talien-whan, which were on either side of the Gulf of Pechili, or Po Hai as it is now called. The forces would then approach together the Taku forts at the mouth of the Peiho River. To begin with the French planned to land south of the Taku forts and the British at Peh-tang (or Peitang) north of the forts. In the event both forces made an unopposed landing at Peh-tang. The Taku forts were attacked and taken from the rear, not without some difficulty, and the expedition then proceeded up the Peiho River towards Peking. On the way up the Peiho there were several incidents of importance. In the neighbourhood of Tung-chow, just short of Peking, two battles were fought, at Chang-chia-wan south of Tung-chow and at Pa-le-chiao bridge just west of the town. At this period some of the diplomatists were captured by the Chinese when they went forward to negotiate the details for the ratification of the Tientsin Treaty. Lord Elgin refused to parley until the prisoners were released and marched on Peking, approaching that city from the north-east and threatening to break in the Anting Gate. This threat led to the surrender of the city and the ratification of the Tientsin Treaty; but not all the prisoners were released, some having been murdered, others having died; and as a punishment to the regime, not, Lord Elgin said, to the Chinese people, the Emperor's summer palace nearby, which had already been sacked by the French, was burnt to the ground.

The expedition was a joint affair in two ways. It consisted of a French force and a larger British contingent, and the latter was composed of Indian and home troops; yet in spite of the handicap of being such a mixture, it must surely rank as one of the most successful small wars ever conducted by Britain.

Control of the expedition on the British side had the same duality. Sidney Herbert, the Secretary of State for War, appears to have held the main responsibility; but he gave few definite instructions to the force commander, Lieut.-General Sir Hope Grant. Writing to the latter, he says: 'It is left to the discretion of yourself and colleagues, naval and military, French and English, all acting—which is most important—in concert with the two plenipotentiaries (Elgin and Gros), upon whom the ultimate question of peace or war must rest. All I can undertake is that you shall be honestly and heartily supported at home.'[2]

As far as the military operations were concerned others besides Sidney Herbert were involved. The Duke of Cambridge, the Commander-in-Chief of the British Army, played a part in the appointment of the British officers of the force, and kept up a regular correspondence with its commander. The following undersigned memorandum, apparently forwarded to Sir Hope Grant by Sidney Herbert in 1860, illustrates the relative positions of the War Office and the Horse Guards at the time:

'The despatches sent home by Sir Hope Grant addressed to the Secretary of State for War are, it appears, sent under cover to the General Commanding in Chief. The result is great delay occurs in the receipt by Mr Sidney Herbert of Sir Hope Grant's despatches. It has always been usual for an officer commanding an army in the field to send despatches to the Secretary of State for War direct to the War Office. If Sir Hope Grant would follow this course in future, it would prevent the delay which at present results from the despatches intended for the Secretary of State for War being sent in the first instance under cover to the Horse Guards.'[3]

The Viceroy of India, from which country the bulk of the troops set out, was concerned particularly with the size of the force. This had risen to over thirteen thousand, while the French who wanted something like parity with the British could reach barely six thousand. The Home Government wanted the British force reduced to please the French, but the Viceroy does not seem very worried about it. He writes: 'The despatch which I was obliged to send you last month respecting the undue excess of our force will, I hope, give you no trouble. The truth is that, as therein shown, we exceed the prescribed ten thousand by very little.'[4]

Then the Commander-in-Chief in India, Sir Colin Campbell—created Lord Clyde in 1858 after quelling the mutiny of the sepoys of the Indian Army—took a hand in the selection of officers from the Indian establishment for this new venture, not always to everyone's satisfaction. 'I go', writes Wolseley, 'as third swell in the QM General's Department instead of second which I had hoped would be given to me, and on good grounds too for Sir H. Grant applied to have me made first, but Lord Clyde is a bigotted Scotchman with a host of greedy friends about him.'[5]

Palmerston as Prime Minister might have been expected to play an active part in this 'gun-boat war'. He does not, however, appear to have done so. Sidney Herbert is recorded as having consulted him in April 1860 about the risks of an advance on Peking, to which Lord Palmerston replied that the decision should be left to the military commanders in consultation with the diplomatists—Sidney Herbert's own formula—but that he did not believe that an occupation of Peking would lead to the overthrow of the dynasty, an opinion verified by subsequent events.

The Foreign Secretary was Lord John Russell—making a formidable partner with Palmerston. Lord Elgin seems to have been given a free hand by him, as a secret minute from the Foreign Office of 17 April 1860 shows: 'It is the opinion of H.M. Government that ... the Plenipotentiaries should be sole judges of all matters pertaining to negotiations—when they should commence, when break off, what terms be accepted, what refused. signed J. Russell.' Every incident was reported by Lord Elgin to Lord John, as the Foreign Office records show, but Lord Elgin was left to make decisions on the spot. The records also show the close co-operation between Lord Elgin and his military commander: 'As I had the good fortune to be within reach of Lieut.-General Sir Hope Grant at the time when this letter (from Lord John) reached me, I thought it proper to confer with him before answering it.'

The Allies had in Lord Elgin a notable plenipotentiary with previous diplomatic successes to his credit in Canada and China. The son of the Lord Elgin who brought back the 'Elgin' marbles from Greece, he was a mild-mannered ambassador with the face of a bewhiskered cherub, 'his snow-white hair contrasting strongly with his sun-scorched face'.[6] He worked very closely and amicably with Sir Hope Grant, taking the initiative when the Chinese showed themselves willing to parley, staying in the background, and leaving matters to the military when the Chinese became obdurate. It is doubtful whether a more skilled negotiator could have been discovered, for he possessed considerable experience in dealing with orientals, and, at the same time, was able to establish an excellent relationship with his French opposite number, Baron Gros.

Lieutenant-General Sir Hope Grant came from a well-to-do Scots family. He was educated in Switzerland, and being musical, learned to play the violoncello. Hope Grant joined the 9th Lancers, and by the time of the Third China War had seen a great deal of active service. He had fought with distinction in the First China War, the First and Second Sikh Wars, and the Indian Mutiny, before being chosen to command the expedition to march on Peking.

The nature of the new war was indeed extremely strange. In and around Nanking there had been for eight years the powerful kingdom of the Taipings. Led by a converted Chinaman called Hung Hsiu-chan, the rebel sect practised a perverted form of Christianity. At one time it was hoped that the rebellion might further the spread of Christianity in China, but the barbaric nature of the activities of its followers precluded help from the West. On the contrary, it was considered necessary to support the Manchu Emperor against the Taipings even when, in the area further north, war was being waged against the Chinese Imperial Armies; in the middle of the struggle the 44th Regiment was

diverted to assist the Imperial Governor of Shanghai against the
Taipings in the neighbourhood of that town, and to protect the
foreigners in the 'concessions' there. This confusing state of affairs
made the best method of conducting the war a very difficult one to
determine. Sufficient force to obtain what they wanted had to be gauged
to a nicety by the diplomatists, Lord Elgin and Baron Gros, in conjunction with the leaders of the military force. Britain wanted the
Imperial Government to ratify the Treaty of Tientsin so that trade
could be freed and a proper relationship set up with China; but they
did not want to use too much force to obtain these ends in case defeat
should cause the Manchus to lose control over their vast empire and
anarchy be the result. In that case there would be no one with whom
the British and French could make treaties at all!

The British were suspicious of the French and did not welcome them
as allies; they would have preferred to have mounted the expedition
on their own. 'It is a great bore (between ourselves) being tied down by
the French,' General Grant writes, 'their force is so small that by the
time it gets to China, having in all probability a five months' voyage,
it will scarcely be of much use.' Sidney Herbert asked his general to be
friendly. 'I need scarcely impress upon you the necessity of a most open,
cordial, and conciliatory bearing towards the French forces.' Grant
likes what he hears about the French admiral, 'a nice person—as long
as we have gentlemen to deal with we shall get on well'; but he is not
so sure about the general. 'I hear that Montauban is a great Turk.'
Nevertheless the two commanders got on well enough. It was arranged
that they should take alternate days for commanding in the field to
start with, but later on they went their own ways. Grant was annoyed
by General de Montauban's delay in preparing his force for the march
on Peking, 'I regret very much you have found it necessary to send them
[chiefs of staff] to Hong Kong . . . I hope you will be ready to
commence active operations at the Pei-ho as soon as possible as time
is of so much importance.'[7] The French held the British back and it
seemed they would never be ready to start—they had after all no
convenient base like India—but when it came to action they tended to
dash in first, not always with very happy results. General de Montauban
liked to disagree with Grant's plans, but usually adopted them in the
end. The French general stated that he would land south of the Taku
forts but in the end both forces landed in the place chosen by Grant.

Grant's final plan for subduing the Taku forts was also not approved of by the French general, yet he co-operated in carrying it out. In fact, Grant showed commendable skill in dealing with his allies. He was friendly and did not nag. He stated firmly what he planned to do himself and then left de Montauban to go his own way if he wanted to. The Frenchman protested—once in an official document meant for his government—but conformed to the British plan every time except at the end when the French decided to dash off and sack the Summer Palace at Peking in an independent and unexpected manner. The French fought very well indeed; but the British soldiers behaved better. 'Our Allies have behaved very badly to the inhabitants here [Peitang], pillaging and destroying everything: a large number of women have been maltreated by them so that many women have taken poison: our soldiers set them a good example and are behaving as well as any men could under the circumstances.'[8]

The French force was sent direct from France; the British from England, the Cape of Good Hope, and India, the bulk of the force from the last place. The British force had been reduced in numbers by the time the spearhead reached its final base at Talien-whan. Wolseley writes, 'We have the 2nd Queen's Regiment here, and as it had such a time at the Cape and has not ever suffered by war or disease it is a splendid specimen of old English infantry as it was before the Crimean War; we have eight English infantry regiments here [including battalions of the Royal Scots and Buffs], three native Punjab corps, two regiments of irregular cavalry,* half of the KDGs, and artillery: altogether a nice little force.'[9] There were also Royal Engineers and Madras Sappers.

The field artillery consisted of smooth-bore 9-pounders and two batteries of the newly invented Armstrong rifled breech-loading guns (see sketch between pages 100 and 101). Sir Hope Grant thought well of these new 12-pounders. 'I am very happy to give Your Royal Highness a favourable report of the Armstrong guns,' he writes to the Duke of Cambridge, 'their precision is most excellent and their range very great, when the percussion shell explodes nothing can be more effective, but I am sorry to say the damp has done injury and many I

* Fane's and Probyn's Horse; the former Sikhs, Pathans and Punjabi Mussulmen; the latter Sikhs, 'black princes' to the Chinese.

fear do not go off, the time fuzes are also not good for the same cause.' Mr Bowlby, *The Times* correspondent, liked them too, and grossly exaggerated their achievements in his reports home; but not every one was so approving; several shells exploded in the breech on loading and killed members of the gun detachment; and observers on reaching the Chinese side of the battlefields were disappointed to find fewer dead Chinamen than they expected.

It is significant that the British Army reverted to muzzle-loaders for a period after the China War. Such a complete 'about face' is so surprising that some explanation is necessary to understand it. The reason seems to have been that manufacturing methods could not produce reliability in breech-loaders. For example, a committee set up in 1865 reported: 'Breechloading guns are far inferior to muzzle-loading as regards simplicity of construction and cannot be compared to them in this respect in efficiency for active service.' A new committee in 1865 also reported that the balance of advantages was in favour of muzzle-loading field guns. It is difficult to understand that at a time when the rest of Europe was beginning to realise that breech-loading was a great step forward in the manufacture of guns, Britain was to revert to muzzle-loading, but the trials had been conducted fairly and muzzle-loaders had held their own in range, accuracy, rapidity of fire, and finally, not least important, in simplicity and cost.

Much of the honour for the success of the expedition must go to Grant's senior staff officer, Colonel Stephenson, Scots Fusilier Guards (now Scots Guards); and indeed a large number of the officers employed on the 1860 expedition achieved great distinction later on, the most notable being the commander of Grant's 1st Division, Sir Robert Napier, who became Lord Napier of Magdala,* Lieutenant-Colonel Garnet Wolseley† who became a Field Marshal and Commander-in-Chief of the British Army, and Major Probyn who gained the VC and later became a general. Probyn was considered the beau-ideal of a leader of irregular cavalry.

* See following chapter, 'The Expedition to Abyssinia, 1868'.

† Garnet Joseph Wolseley: born 1833; first commissioned into the Cameronians; Burmese War, 1852–3; Crimea, 1855; Indian Mutiny, 1857; Third China War, 1860; Red River, Canada, 1870; Natal, 1875; Cyprus, 1878; Egyptian Campaign, 1882; Gordon Relief Expedition, 1884; Commander-in-Chief, 1895–1900.

The administrative services worked well, mainly because there were so many alternatives to choose from. The Military Train was handicapped by shortage of suitable transport animals, and by being too military in its organisation. It had been used as cavalry during the Indian Mutiny, and its officers did not seem content to organise efficiently the humdrum services required from a transport corps. There were, however, other possibilities. In the earlier China wars a coolie corps of Chinamen had been organised for supply. This was set up again, and the Canton Coolie Corps was worth its weight in gold to the British and French alike; even during action they brought up supplies, and, being from the south, watched the defeat of their fellow-countrymen with satisfaction. Their only failing was bad behaviour in billets and their looting and wrecking propensities in the towns of their fellow Chinese. 'Patient, lusty, enduring, but the scourge of the inhabitants of occupied cities', was how they have been described.[10]

The campaign was opened by a landing from the sea, and proceeded along a navigable river towards Peking, so that help as regards transport of supplies could also be undertaken by the Royal Navy. The most fortunate feature of the campaign, however, was the plentiful supply of food and provisions which could be purchased locally. Unlike the terrain met with in many of Britain's colonial conflicts, North China was both fertile and healthy.

In the Crimea the medical arrangements had been deplorable; in China they were almost beyond reproach. Yet the medical side was not without its problems. For example, Hong Kong was notoriously unhealthy. In 1852, the 59th Regiment, after only twenty months, buried a hundred and eighty men there. It also had few areas of flat land suitable to provide large-scale camping grounds. Because of this the healthier and flatter peninsula of Kowloon on the mainland side of the harbour was acquired. It was leased from a most willing local Chinese governor for the payment of a yearly rent of a hundred and sixty pounds. Another example of the topsy-turvy nature of the war! Surgeon D. F. Rennie, whose brother was also serving in the same capacity, has much to say about the health of the troops during the expedition:

> 'Before leaving Talien-whan, I reported to the principal medical officer upon the health of the troops during the encampment on shore. A large amount of sickness prevailed. The symptoms

closely resembled those which prevail at Hong Kong—fever, dysentery, etc. Yet the position is remarkably healthy; there was no intemperance as intoxicating liquors could not be obtained beyond the ration, the army had been weeded of its weakly and sick at Hong Kong, the troops having at the first been selected in India as men of known robust health. The lowest amount of sickness occurred in the 99th Regiment and I observed that that regiment alone is furnished with the Indian tent, the rest of the infantry use the bell tent.'

He came to the conclusion that the bell tent with fourteen men in it was unhealthily stuffy. At Peh-tang he discovers a sanitary paradox: 'It would be difficult to indicate a more filthy and foul smelling locality than Peh-tang . . . it was expected that the troops would suffer severely from malaria disease; such, however, was not the case, their health having been much superior to what it was in the beautiful climate and pure atmosphere of Talien-whan.'[11] Allied casualties throughout the campaign were relatively slight and the close contact with the navy enabled medical services to be excellent. 'Soon after the forts were occupied . . . our own wounded had been carefully conveyed on board the hospital ships where every comfort that skill and invention could supply was prepared for them.'[12] Even during the advance towards Peking, the wounded could be evacuated by boat down the Peiho River.

The Allies had a great advantage over the enemy in weapons. Judging by the numbers captured, the Chinese had a quantity of guns suitable for firing from forts, some similar in size to the 8″ guns and howitzers, 32-pounders and 8″ mortars of the Allied siege train; but they had nothing like the Armstrong 12-pounder field guns. In the open their strongest weapons were gingalls. These were long pieces throwing balls from four ounces to a pound. They were used as field artillery as well as for firing over the walls of forts. In the field the gingall was carried on one horse and the stand on another. Other than this, they had only matchlocks, bows and arrows, self-loading crossbows, spears, pikes and swords. The Tartars and Mongolians, however, who were the main opponents of the Allies in the field, showed considerable dexterity in handling these weapons. The matchlock men were frequently seen, when retreating at full gallop, to turn round, fire off their pieces, and reload as they galloped away. The bowmen, also, discharged their arms at full gallop. In shock actions, however, the Tartar cavalry was no match for the King's Dragoon Guards or the Allied irregular cavalry. The KDGs won a tremendous reputation in this war. 'I am happy to say the First Dragoon Guards did very well and charged into a body of Tartars riding over a ditch and bank on the way and killing a great many,'[13] Grant writes. Rennie describes the Tartar cavalrymen, after a good view of them through his glass:

> 'The Tartars were dressed in the ordinary Chinese hat of black silk, with the brim turned up all round, and had two squirrels' tails projecting from the hat behind, which are the decoration only worn by military men. They had on light coloured jackets over a long under-garment of darker material, and blue trousers tucked into black Tartar boots. They were armed with spears, having red horse-hair hanging from the shaft where it joins the ironwork. They rode in short stirrups, and were mounted on stout hardy working ponies.'[14]

The Emperor's field armies were mainly manned by Tartars; in the forts, however, the personnel were Chinese. Contrary to some reports the enemy fought bravely everywhere. There was a story that the Chinese had to be tied to their guns or they would run away. This was almost certainly untrue. Rennie comments, on looking round the Taku forts after the action, 'Some [of the dead Chinese] I noticed had their port fires, in the shape of ropeyarn fastened round one wrist, which fact immediately afforded data to some imaginative individuals for setting the report in circulation that, to keep them from running away, the artillerymen had to be tethered to their guns!'[15]

On leaving Talien-whan and Chefoo the Allies sailed across the Gulf of Pechili towards the Taku forts at the mouth of the River Peiho. Before reaching the forts, however, they veered off northwards and landed at Peh-tang, eight miles from Taku.

> 'It was an interesting sight seeing the ships getting under weigh, every available steamer being employed in towing large sailing

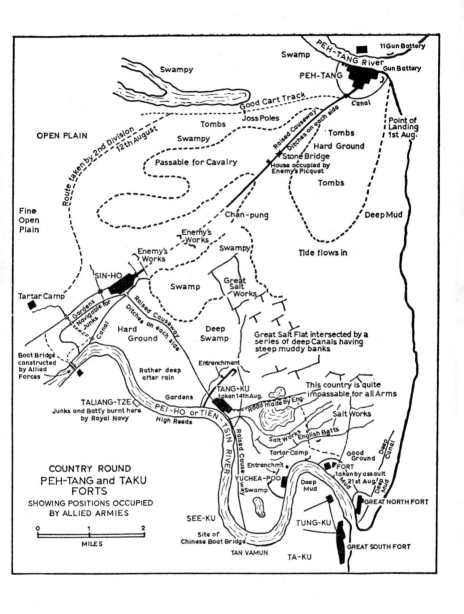

COUNTRY ROUND
PEH-TANG and TAKU
FORTS

SHOWING POSITIONS OCCUPIED
BY ALLIED ARMIES

0   1   2
MILES

transports clear of the harbour, while others, impatient to be off, relied on their own efforts. The steamers were dashing backwards and forwards, while the despatch vessels and gunboats were enforcing orders and bringing up the lazy and slow, and by noon upwards of two hundred ships and steamers were bowling along before a strong breeze.'[16] 'At noon I counted ninety vessels under full canvas bearing down on the anchorage, a fine strong and fair wind having set in. The sight was a magnificent one, not likely soon to be witnessed again. At this time a number of junks that had been cruising in the neghbourhood, though at a respectable distance, made sail in the direction of the Peiho, in all probability to report our approach . . . looking out for land I saw in the distant haze three dark masses, apparently equidistant from each other and of symmetrical shape, looming obscurely above the horizon. I looked at them through my glass and concluded they were the Taku forts.'[17]

As the weather became unsettled and Peh-tang was still ten miles off, it was decided to defer the landing till the next day, 1 August; and by then, although the day opened with heavy rain, the sea had gone down.

The landing party consisted of General Sutton's brigade of foot, with a 9-pounder and a rocket battery carried in large troop boats, each holding fifty soldiers. All were towed ashore by two small gunvessels. The boats anchored under the mud bank on the southern side of the river about a mile from the forts.

'No enemy showed himself beyond what we should have called a couple of squadrons of mounted Tartars who kept near the gate through which the road (a raised causeway) leads to Sinho and the Taku forts. There was about a mile of deep muddy flat to be waded through immediately on landing, so there was little of the pomp and circumstance of war about that operation. The first man to jump ashore and lead up the mudbank was the brigadier. He was an old campaigner well known for his swearing propensities, and famous as a game shot in South Africa. I shall never forget his appearance as he struggled through that mud, knee deep in many places. He had taken off trousers, boots and socks, and hung them over his brass scabbarded

sword which he carried over one shoulder. Picture a somewhat
fierce and ugly bandy-legged little man thus accoutred in a big
white helmet, clothed in a dirty jacket of red serge, below which
a very short slate-coloured flannel shirt extended a few inches,
cursing and swearing loudly "all round" at everybody and
everything as he led his brigade through the hateful mire. I
remember many funny scenes in my soldiering days, but I never
laughed more than I did at this amusing disembarkation of the
first brigade that landed in northern China.'[18]

As the landing proceeded, the Tartars rode off, and the Allies
moved across the mud to the causeway and bedded down for the
night, spending it, not very pleasantly on the mudflats and causeway,
without water, or anything to eat; wet through and lying on very
moist ground.

During the night Mr Parkes, the interpreter, accompanied by a staff
officer, entered the town and learned that the forts, though mined, were
deserted. Next morning the town, noisome, smelly and surrounded on
all sides by mud, surrendered. When the inhabitants had evacuated it
and hobbled off to Taku—many of the women with their tiny bound
feet having to be carried—it was divided equally between the French
and British for quarters. Not a very happy arrangement as the British
commander noted: 'I regret very much that our troops are thrown so
closely in contact with the French. We have been obliged to occupy
the town, the French taking one side and we the other. The plunder and
robbing that has been committed by them is a very bad example to
our men. The officers appear not to try to stop it.'[19] Among other things
the French soldiers, in search of food, chased pigs and dogs through the
muddy streets, and when they caught them bayoneted them. On their
behalf it must be said that, unlike the British, they did not get full rations
and had to live off the country.

The main advance on Taku, via Sinho and Tang-ku, was not started
until eleven days after the landing at Peh-tang. There were several minor
enemy defence works on the causeway and road leading to Sinho, and
against these had been sent bodies of skirmishers to test their strength.
A larger-scale reconnaissance had also been completed. Colonel
Wolseley with a party of cavalry had followed a cart track to the west

of the causeway and found quite a good route, muddy at first, but passable for cavalry and artillery, by which Sinho could be approached from the north.

General Grant and General de Montauban had come to an agreement that their forces should take precedence of march by turns, and that the British should have the first right to the privilege. The British commander, therefore, planned to lead the advance on 12th August with a drive down the causeway by Sir John Michel's 1st Division, and a right flanking attack at the same time by Sir Robert Napier's 2nd Division down Wolseley's cart track. The French, after complaining of the state of the muddy ground, agreed to help, but only with a thousand men. There followed a series of minor engagements against the entrenched camps protecting Sinho, attacking what were described as 'merely strong cavalry outposts';[20] and then the occupation of Sinho itself.

Sinho offered a most pleasing contrast to Peh-tang. It was surrounded by well-kept kitchen gardens, full of vegetables, and beautiful to eyes accustomed for the last few days to look upon nothing but mud. Although the opposition had been slight, a very large force, some said twenty thousand, of Tartar cavalry had been stationed in the area, and a plentiful supply of grain for the troops and enough hay to last six weeks were taken over. It seems that the Chinese General San-ko-lin-sin himself may have been there, for behind one of the crenellated walls blocking the road stood a very large blue awning set up on poles suitable for the use of a very high-ranking mandarin.

General San-ko-lin-sin had won renown by once defeating the Taiping rebels. He did not shape so well against the Allies. The British soldiers turned his name into 'Sam Collinson', and there was a most unlikely story among them that he was a renegade Irishman from the Royal Marines. On the approach to Sinho, Napier's 2nd Division, which had advanced along Wolseley's cart track, were assailed by a mass of San-ko-lin-sin's Tartar cavalry. It was here, as already described, that the Chinese horsemen showed their skill at shooting from the saddle. After being fired at by the British infantry and artillery, and charged by cavalry, the Tartars galloped off followed by the KDGs on horses still not fit to catch the sturdy Chinese ponies.

The British moved on, but after their departure, bands of Tartar horsemen came out again over the same area; this time they scored a small success; they managed to capture sixteen coolies and two British soldiers following a cart containing rum and supplies in the rear of the 1st Division. This was not all. The captured stragglers were brought before the Chinese commander, resulting in a well-known story of British military history; for, written up by the enthusiastic Mr Bowlby of *The Times*, and further dramatised in Doyle's poem, there emerged the famous legend of the 'Private of the Buffs'.

This is how it is described in the Buffs' regimental history:[21]

'It was at the end of the operations on this day that there came to light an incident that had occurred in the morning which, though of no military significance, led to the name of a man of the Buffs being handed down to posterity as an example of the dauntless spirit of the British soldier. It appears that on the 12th August whilst the 2nd Division was toiling along the track to Sinho, a body of Tartar cavalry, having worked round to the rear of the column, came upon a body of coolies carrying the rum of the division who, due very probably to the state of the ground, had lagged some distance behind. In charge of the party was a sergeant of the Forty-fourth Regiment who had with him No. 2051 Private John Moyse of the Buffs and a number of Indian followers (Chinese coolies). The whole party was captured by the Tartar Cavalry, and taken off to the Chinese camp. On the morning of the 13th, Moyse and his companions were brought before the Tartar mandarin, San-ko-lin-sin, who declared to them that if they would but *kow-tow*** or touch their foreheads on the ground before him no harm would befall them. Moyse refused to do this and he was then warned by an interpreter that if he did not obey he would be beheaded by one of the escort on a given signal by the mandarin, but he still stoutly declared that he would sooner die than disgrace his country, whereupon, he was instantly cut down and killed, and his body was dragged away. His companions who had complied with the demands of the mandarin and thus saved their lives, were brought back under the flag of truce on the evening of the 14th August

* The *kow-tow* was the conventional form of obeisance in China and consisted in a series of triple kneelings, bowing the head to the ground. In the earlier period refusal to make this servile gesture was one of the reasons why the Emperor would not receive our ambassadors.

to Colonel Sargent's advanced post in front of Tang-ku, and here the circumstances of Moyse's death were made known by them. Very soon after this event the action of Private Moyse was immortalised by Sir Francis Hastings Doyle in the poem, the first stanza of which is quoted below:

THE PRIVATE OF THE BUFFS

Last night among his fellow roughs
He jested, quaffed and swore:
A drunken private of the Buffs,
Who never look'd before.
Today beneath the foeman's frown,
He stands in Elgin's place,
Ambassador from Britain's crown,
And type of all her race.'

There is some doubt whether this story is quite true. Wolseley and others who heard about it considered that Moyse had died of drink; or at any rate not so dramatically as they had been led to believe.

After Sinho came Tang-ku. This was a more formidable proposition. A causeway with deep ditches on each side joined the two towns, and there were swamps on the east of the causeway and firmer ground on the river side. Tang-ku's fortifications consisted of a crenellated wall three miles long encircling it from a point on the river to the west round to the river again in its rear. General Grant commanded again—the French had made an abortive rush alone on Tang-ku immediately after the capture of Sinho, and had thus lost their turn. The attack was made on the firmer ground on the right of the causeway, with the English near the river and the French along the causeway. Sir John Michel's 1st Division led for the British. By throwing bridges across the ditches flanking the causeway towards the river, and then over several little intervening streams, the Allies found that they could approach to the very walls of Tang-ku on an extended front. While they were doing so the enemy opened fire on them from the other side of the river with some guns in two junks hauled up on the mud near the village of Taliang-tze, and from a battery on rising ground in the same vicinity. The Allied guns soon silenced this fire, and a naval officer crossed the river with a few men and spiked the guns.

On the night previous to the assault of Tang-ku, trenches were dug within seven hundred yards of the wall to give cover to the riflemen, and the protective ditch was dammed near the river to check its flow. Thirty-six guns, French and British, including two batteries of Armstrongs, supported the attack, and in addition a rocket troop was used. The heavy fire from these guns soon silenced the Chinese weapons and knocked the wall to pieces; for the commander Royal Artillery advanced his guns cleverly by alternate batteries so that 'the enemy pieces were dismantled and the parapets ruined'.[22] The flags with which the walls had at first been bedecked were fast vanishing. One brave fellow mounted on the battlements, and proudly waved a banner in the air, until a shot from one of our guns struck him and he disappeared. Meanwhile some companies of the Royal Scots and 60th Rifles crept through the orchards and sedge along the bank of the river, crossed the dam, reached the foot of the fort, and succeeded in forcing their way through the broken wall. The French on the left had also scaled the wall gallantly in their sector at about the same time and, caught in the flank as well, the Chinese abandoned the wall and fled. Inside the Chinese scampered back from the wall across to the village, with rockets whizzing through the air to accelerate the speed of their flight. From Tang-ku the fugitives made off down the causeway in the rear of the village, over a floating bridge of boats, and then to the safety of Taku. Forty-five cannon were captured from behind the wall. There were not a great many casualties on either side, though a few dozens of Chinese bodies lay about the guns. There were no Allied killed—unless General Michel's horse be included—and only about fifteen wounded.

After Sinho, Tang-ku; and after Tang-ku, Taku; and each Chinese defence work was becoming progressively more difficult to assail. The attack on Taku forts saw also the first major difference of opinion between the British and French commanders.

On the 20th August Mr Parkes and Captain Graham, with a flag of truce, were sent by Sir Hope Grant to demand a surrender; but the Chinese showed no sign of yielding, and the two envoys were compelled to return. The Taku forts were very formidable, having the usual crenellated walls, but with two broad ditches round them, and on the space between the walls and the ditches the ground was thickly studded with upright bamboo spikes—see photographs between pages

100 and 101. They had also, like the Peh-tang forts, a ramp inside leading to a cavalier, or raised platform, from which guns could be fired in all directions. The country between Tang-ku and the first northern fort was much as before, saltmarsh and swamp; but without a causeway leading across it. The British built a road north of the main swamp, bridging ditches, and carrying it forward until firmer ground near the forts was reached. The Allies also built a bridge of boats across the Peiho.

The French general now proposed that the two armies should cross the river and attack both the entrenched town of Taku and its triple southern fort. This plan had the advantage of bottling up the enemy in the fortifications and not allowing him to escape to fight another day. It appeared, however, too hazardous for Sir Hope, as the Allies would lose the right flank protection of the river, which they had in operations on the north bank. Sir Hope Grant had also made a careful survey of the positions of the forts, and had come to the conclusion—confirmed in the event—that if they captured the first small fort on the north side, now immediately in front of them, they would command by fire from it all the others, and would have them at their mercy. General de Montauban disagreed. 'L'attaque des forts qui reste sur la rive gauche [north forts] me semble complètement inutile,' he said. Sir Hope was still determined to go ahead with his plan. It looked like stalemate; but in the end de Montauban did co-operate with the British. He was satisfied with writing a memorandum to free himself from military responsibility with reference to his own government in the event of its judging the question in the same way as he did.

The attacking force on Taku consisted of two thousand five hundred British and a thousand French. Heavy guns were used as well as six batteries of field guns and a rocket battery. The Allies had a stroke of luck when an eight-inch shell falling on the powder magazine of the nearest fort blew it up with a terrific explosion. For some time the fort was so shrouded in dense clouds of vapour and smoke that it appeared to be completely destroyed; but by degrees it cleared away; the enemy recommenced firing and seemed determined not to give up the place without a desperate struggle. Heavy guns from the cavalier were still firing, but these did not keep it up for long after being struck time and time again by the shells of the massed Allied guns. The British marines brought up ontoons to try to bridge the broad ditches near the fort; but met with too much matchlock fire from the walls to do so.

The French were more successful and constructed a way across the ditch by means of scaling ladders carried by Chinese coolies. The Chinamen jumped into the water up to their necks and supported the ladders on their hands and shoulders, to enable the French soldiers to get across. The Allied force now pushed forward. Some of the British swam across the ditch, and others got across with the French. Sir Hope's aide-de-camp, Major Anson, getting across by a raised drawbridge cut the ropes keeping it up, and let the bridge fall down into position. This made a good way across. The difficulty now was to get over the high walls by scaling ladders. There was, however, a small breach made by the guns, and both the British and French, at the same time, forced their way in through it. Ensign Chaplin of the 67th Regiment (now Royal Hampshire Regiment) was one of the first of the British to get inside, and managed to plant the Queen's colour of his regiment on the cavalier, being severely wounded in doing so. For this, along with five other officers and men, he won the VC. The *London Gazette*, announcing the awards, speaks of them swimming the ditches, entering the North Taku Fort by an embrasure during the assault, and being among the first of the English established on the walls of the fort. Lieutenant Rogers, 44th Regiment (later the Essex Regiment) is given as the first.

The combined navies had brought up their gunboats near the forts at the mouth of the Peiho, and one of their shells exploded a magazine in the other northern fort. After the capture of the first northern fort white banners were seen on all the other forts, but this did not appear to mean very much at the time, for when the willing Mr Parkes was sent to summon the other northern fort to surrender, he got 'a very insulting answer'. Another joint attack was therefore staged on the bigger fort, but the French would not wait for the British, and this time it paid off; dashing ahead alone as they had done after Sinho, they entered the fort through a large embrasure without a shot being fired, and they captured it, two hours after the fall of the first fort, without resistance.

Next, flags of truce were sent across the river to Hang-Fu, the Governor-General of the province. By this time General San-lo-kin-sin and his Tartars had fled back up river towards Tientsin and Peking, and according to Mr H. B. Loch, Lord Elgin's private secretary, who accompanied the peace mission across the Peiho, Hang-Fu, although friendly, was not prepared to treat for some considerable time, not seeming willing to take responsibility, and at least pretending to search for the missing Chinese general. By the next day, however, all the forts on both sides of the river were taken over by the Allies, and the formidable obstacles, chains, stakes, spikes, and booms were removed by the navies from across the mouth of the river; obstacles which had for so long blocked the route to Peking. The first task of the expedition had now been carried out; the guns which had sunk the ships of Admiral Hope in 1859 had been captured; the obstacles which had stopped him going up the river with the plenipotentiaries had been removed. The British defeat of the year before had been revenged. 'My dearest Mother, the Third China War is over,' Wolseley wrote,[23] after the surrender of the Taku forts. But he was quite wrong; there was a great deal left still to be done.

Up to the surrender the main operations had been military. Although Hang-Fu, the Chinese Governor-General of the province of Chihli, had tried to ward off the blow threatening China by writing a series of letters to Lord Elgin asking him to appoint some time and place so that an amicable settlement might be arranged, Lord Elgin studiously avoided negotiating with the provincial official. He was aware that Hang-Fu's only purpose was to gain time until the onset of winter would halt operations. Lord Elgin, however, in consultation with Baron Gros, did write to Hang-Fu telling him the terms on which he was willing to call off naval and military operations, namely: an apology for the attack at Taku in 1859, the ratification of the Treaty of Tientsin of 1858, the payment of an indemnity to the Allies for the expenses of the war, and before their capture, the surrender of the Taku forts. To further correspondence from Hang-Fu, he made the same invariable answer.

With the Taku forts in Allied hands diplomatic action, as opposed to military, began in earnest; and it was agreed that a meeting and discussion should be arranged in Tientsin. Thus an advance was made on that city, with gunboats moving forward in the van, taking with them Lord Elgin's diplomatic assistants, Wade, Loch and Parkes. Parkes, a former consul at Canton, and a firm believer in Palmerston's 'gunboat' methods had done important work already. Always to the fore, he had arranged the purchase of Kowloon, he had found Peh-tang unmanned and discovered the nature of the mines left in its forts, and he had persuaded Hang-Fu to sign the document of surrender of the Taku forts, including nominally the whole of the province and the town of Tientsin. From now on he was to play an even greater part.

There were two roads from Taku to Tientsin, one on either side of the Peiho, the high embankments of which could occasionally be seen from the river. The countryside on leaving Taku was cultivated, and there were a few trees near the villages. The villagers were friendly, and anxious, as in 1858, to sell fowls, vegetables and eggs to the invaders at 'twenty times the proper value'.[24] Ice and grapes were particularly popular with the troops and sailors. The Chinese saved the ice from the winter, and not only drank it melted, but laid it under rugs on which to partake of cool siestas.

Admiral Hope led the Allied advance, and finding the Tientsin forts empty, took over the town. The river was crowded with junks and boats, and the people flocked in thousands to the banks showing no alarm. Lord Elgin and Sir Hope Grant were not far behind, and Baron Gros arrived in one of the French gunboats which had been sent out from France in pieces and bolted together on arrival. These were poor things with thin plates, and too small to be of much service.

Mr Parkes and Mr Wade put the terms to the three Chinese envoys, now Kweilang, who had drawn up the Treaty of Tientsin, Hang-Fu and Hang-ki, the last a member of the group of Chinese who wanted peace.

There were a series of meetings and discussions and all seemed to be going well; but when it came to signing it was discovered that the envoys from the Emperor had neither the official seal nor yet the power to agree to anything. It seems that the Chinese were at their old game of trying to delay the Allies until the winter, when, with the help of the cold weather, they thought they could drive the 'barbarians' away.

So that no time should be given the Chinese to prepare new defences, the order was at once given for a further advance on Peking. During the march from Tientsin, Lord Elgin received almost daily letters from the Chinese authorities imploring him to stop his army; but he replied that because they had tried to mislead him at Tientsin, he would not think of signing any convention until he reached Tung-chow, a city about twelve miles from Peking.

Approaching Tung-chow, but with only part of the main force on the move owing to the time needed to bring supplies up the river, Parkes and Wade again went forward to negotiate. This time Tsai, Prince of I, was the principal Chinese commissioner. The comings and goings of the British envoys now become extremely difficult to follow.

When Parkes and Wade returned after the first visit to the Chinese commissioners the preliminary arrangements appeared almost settled. The Allied armies were to advance to an area ten miles from Tung-chow and then encamp while Elgin and Gros proceeded with a large escort to Peking.

Unfortunately Parkes had to go back to Tung-chow to make a few final arrangements. He took with him, under a flag of truce, De Normann, a diplomat, Loch, Bowlby, *The Times* correspondent, Colonel Walker of the quartermaster's department, Thompson of the commissariat, and an escort of about two dozen troopers of the KDGs and Fane's Horse under Lieutenant Anderson. All of these men except Walker and Thompson and a few troopers were captured or killed, in spite of the flag of truce in the form of a white flag on a lance under which they moved.

As has been stated, Parkes' party's movements are difficult to trace. They first inspected briefly the camping area short of Chan-chia-wan. This lay on a plain between the road and the river, just short of a stream with a bank along it. On the left of the road, as they approached, was a small village near which they noticed trees had been felled—the first sign of treachery. They passed through the walled town of Chan-chia-wan safely and reaching Tung-chow were taken to their quarters in a temple.

At the meeting with the commissioners, Lord Elgin's letter accepting the conditions of a convention was read; in it he said he hoped there would be no delay in being received at Peking, and in the delivery of the letter of credence to the Emperor. On this request the Prince of I became almost offensive and refused to continue with negotiations until Parkes agreed to defer the question of the letter and also cut down the size of Lord Elgin's escort. After this it was arranged that the Chinese would set up and provision the camp for the Allies, and issue a proclamation to tell the people that peace had been established between the Emperor of China and the Allies.

On the next day Parkes, Loch, Walker and Thompson, with an escort went back to the camping ground with the intention of leading the Allied forces to it. The remainder of the party went sightseeing all innocently in Tung-chow.

When Parkes' group reached the camping ground they found it in the process of being occupied by the enemy. Obviously a trap was being prepared to catch the Allied forces when they came forward to use the area. Enemy troops were manning the bank by the stream, and masked batteries were being set up along it. On the flanks and to the front cavalry were manœuvring. The position of Parkes' party was a most critical one; it was now only too apparent that treachery was intended. After a hasty council, it was decided that, to prevent an immediate attack on the party, it was better not to show any distrust of the Chinese; Walker, Thompson, and five of the KDGs were therefore to remain moving backwards and forwards along the bank, ready on the first appearance of hostility to turn their horses' heads and gallop for their lives over the plain, across which the Allied forces would soon be advancing. While they were doing so, Parkes was to ride back to Tung-chow to find out from the Prince of I what was happening, and to warn those left behind of their danger, and Loch was to try and push through the Tartar cavalry screen and warn Hope Grant of the trap awaiting him. The first Chinese line of cavalry which Loch had to pass through was about a quarter of a mile in advance of the village with the felled trees. They made no movement to stop Loch and his Indian escort, so he pushed on at a canter through their open ranks, and came up with the Allied advance guard half a mile further on. Hope Grant was both indignant and perturbed to learn that Chinese troops and guns were occupying the very site which had been promised to the Allied force.

Loch, very gallantly, went back to help Parkes and the others escape; and Captain Brabazon persuaded Grant to let him accompany him. By the time that Loch found Parkes, seven of the original party had made their way to safety.

'We looked through our telescopes along the line of Chinese troops, and made out Colonel Walker and some men of the Dragoon Guards on their horses, but to our surprise they did not come out to meet us. . . . Suddenly we heard a heavy fire of matchlocks and gingalls, and a number of horseman were seen galloping furiously towards us. They turned out to be Colonel Walker and his party. They soon reached us, and told us their story. They had been detained by the enemy, but were civilly treated, when a French officer rode up and began a dispute with some Tartars about a mule he was riding. At last he draw a pistol and fired it, when his mule was immediately shot and himself murdered. Colonel Walker rode to his assistance, but his sword was struck out of his hand; and though it was restored to him by a Chinese officer fresh efforts were made to wrest it from him, and in his endeavours to retain it, his fingers were so badly cut that his hand was disabled. Then finding that their only hope of safety was to force their way out, he shouted to his party to ride for their lives. All charged through the enemy and made their escape—viz., Colonel Walker, Mr Thompson of the commissariat, one sowar, and four Dragoon Guards, one of whom was shot through the leg. Mr Thompson received several spear-wounds in the back; and one horse was shot through the body, but managed to convey its rider back in safety.'[25]

Meanwhile Parkes was not able to find the Prince of I, who, having laid his plot, had gone to Peking to report to the Emperor. Parkes then sought out San-ko-lin-sin, the commanding officer, and asked for a free pass for himself and the remaining members of the mission; but San-ko-lin-sin laughed in his face and accused him of having caused all the trouble that had arisen in China. This time Parkes accepted his fate. 'I fear we are prisoners,' he said to Loch.

After Loch and Brabazon had been absent for two hours, and it was evident they had been detained, Hope Grant gave the order for the attack. The French advanced on the right and got into difficulties; but to assist them the British had lent a squadron of Fane's Horse, and this gallant little force of cavalry, with half-a-dozen Spahis—mounted orderlies, and all the cavalry the French had—the whole led by Colonel Foley, the Commissioner with the French, now charged the Tartars, and, though a handful compared with them, used their sharp swords with such effect that the enemy were compelled to retreat.

On the left among the British it was much the same, with the Tartar cavalry over-running the position. Here relief was given by a charge by Probyn and a hundred of his Sikhs. Then, when reserves were brought up—the 99th Regiment, a 9-pounder battery, an Armstrong battery, and the KDGs—the enemy crumbled and their whole position was captured. Wolseley describes thus the battle of Chan-chia-wan:

'Our force then advanced, when the action became general along the whole front, the hordes of Tartar cavalry trying to surround us and intimidate us by their vast numbers, but john bull is not easily frightened so in we went at them over and over again. Through and through them until all had retired behind the river [stream] leaving all their guns in our possession amounting to over seventy in numbers. We pursued them through the town of Chan-chia-wan, and took a number of their camps which we consigned to the flames.'[26]

After the battle of Chan-chia-wan the Allies moved forward west of Tung-chow towards Peking, with the French on the right, the British infantry and artillery in the centre, and the cavalry on the left. A canal joining Tung-chow to Peking lay across the Allied front. The French were approaching the Pal-le-chiao bridge over the canal, and the British a wooden bridge on their left, when the French left was attacked by Tartar cavalry, the enemy coming between the Allies. Hope Grant immediately turned a battery on them at two hundrd yards' range, and then sent in the KDGs and Indian cavalry—it was here that the KDGs so distinguished themselves, and chased off the enemy cavalry over a ditch. But the battle was not finished. When Montauban's French troops advanced on the Pal-le-chiao stone bridge they found the élite of the Chinese Imperial Guard drawn up to resist them. After some gallant fighting, however, spurred on by their general, they secured the bridge. The battle of Pal-le-chiao was over.

The enemy had apparently disappeared; but there was one final incident before the day ended. The British camp was being pitched by the bridge when the enemy opened fire from across the canal. The Musbee Sikhs,* however, soon dealt with this. They crossed the canal, took the guns, and killed seventy of the enemy.

The next morning, the 22nd of September, a flag of truce was sent in from the highest mandarin of the empire, Prince Kung, who from now on played the main part in the negotiations. He and Hang-ki seemed genuinely to be seeking for peace, but there was still pressure in the opposite direction from a war party with the Emperor at Jehol, a town away to the north where the Royal Court had now moved.

Prince Kung announced that the Emperor was willing to call off hostilities if the Allies agreed to restore the Taku forts and leave the

* Musbee Sikhs—low-caste sikhs enlisted as pioneers who fought and did pioneer work as well.

country. Lord Elgin replied that he would not even discuss terms until all the prisoners were returned; and unless they were sent back, the Allies would move up and storm Peking. It must have been a difficult decision to make, particularly as the Chinese said the prisoners would be massacred if they did so. There was, however, a delay. As at Taku Sir Hope Grant was not prepared to attack without his siege train—the 8″ guns and howitzers, the two 32-pounders and three 8″ mortars, without which he believed it would be futile to try to break down the rampart walls of the city. These were thirty-five to forty feet high and sixty feet wide at the top, and presented a formidable obstacle even against heavy guns. Nevertheless the deliberate nature of the campaign as fought by Grant met with disapproval from the diplomatists, and even from some of the officers. 'I wish we had either of our Major Generals at the head of the army,'[27] one wrote home.

The poor prisoners—and there were French as well as British—certainly suffered from this delay. Captain Brabazon and Abbé Voss had been executed. The remainder were divided between 'the worst prison in China', Parkes' description of the headquarters of the Board of Punishments, where he and Loch were first in custody, and the cells of the Summer Palace, where Bowlby of *The Times* and De Normann died. The casualty rate among the prisoners was high. The Chinese prisons were infested by small maggots. If these got into wounds caused by the rubbing of fetters, inflammation, fever, delirium and death followed in succession. Parkes and Loch were luckier than the rest, although the Peking prison itself was very bad. Loch says of his arrival:

> 'I found myself in the presence of, and surrounded by, as savage a lot of half-naked demons as I had ever beheld; they were nearly all the lowest class of criminals, imprisoned for murder and the most serious offences (they were kindly disposed to the Englishmen all the same). On one side of the room, running the whole length, was a wooden bench extending about eight feet from the wall, sloping a little towards it; this was the sleeping place; chains hung down from several of the beams, reaching nearly to the bench, with the use of which I was soon to be made practically acquainted. . . . My hands were handcuffed, the short chain which connected them being passed through the link in the one which descended from my neck to my feet. . . .

Previous page:
The Sikh Wars.
Charge of the
Lancers at
Aliwal, 1846.

Ibid. The Battle
of Gujrat, 1849.

Ibid. Brigadier-General Cureton.

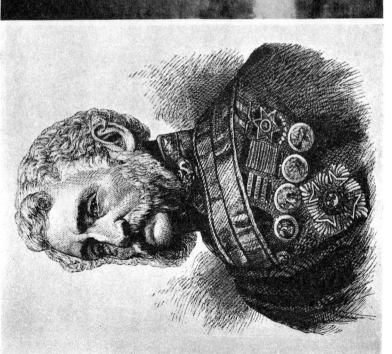

Ibid. Sir Harry Smith.

The Third China War. The Fleet at Talien-Whan in 1860.

Ibid. Rear of Taku Fort: British and French flags flying.

Ibid. Taku Fort: breach, and scaling ladders.

Inside Taku Fort after capture: note rope-yard port fires attached to dead Chinese, which led to the story that they were tied to their guns.

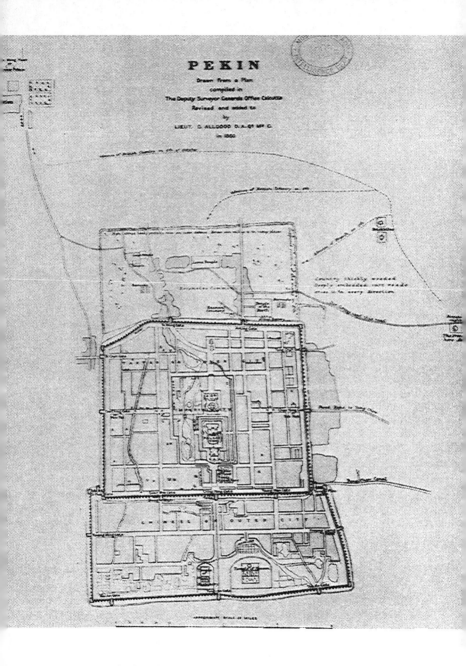

Ibid. Plan of Peking in 1860.

Opposite page: *Ibid.* Pehtang Fort: French flag flying.

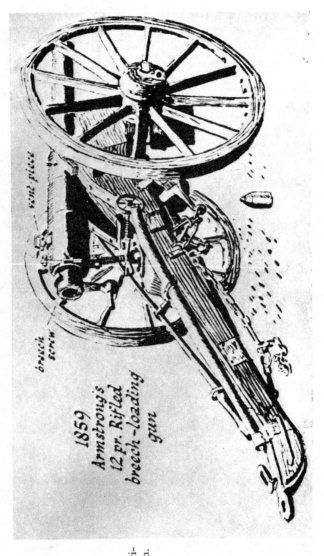

1859
Armstrong's
12 pr. Rifled
breech-loading
gun

vent-piece

breech
screw

Ibid. Armstrong's 12-pr.
rifled breech-loading gun.
First employed by the British Army in this campaign.

Opposite page: *Ibid.* The
Walls of Peking in 1860.

Sir Hope Grant.

Opposite page: *The Abyssinian War*. Sir Robert Napier and Staff. The officer in native dress (right) is believed to be Captain Speedy, the head of the expedition's Intelligence branch.

This photograph is one of the earliest taken by an official army photographer on active service.

Ibid. Part of Zula Camp. The foreground group illustrates the number of different nationalities employed in support of the army.

Ibid. The 10th
Company,
Royal Engine-
ers, in camp at
Upper Soroo.

Ibid. Kassai's Prime Minister and Abyssinian warriors. The habit of taking 'official' group photographs at top level conferences would seem to have been already well established by 1868. Note the double-barrelled muskets of Kassai's entourage.

I was then laid on the bench which I have described, with my feet towards the wall, directly under one of the chains hanging from the beam above; to this the chain round my neck was attached, and I was thus only able to lie flat on my back, and even that was painful with my elbows pinioned.'[28]

Parkes and Loch, however, were later used as a means of communication with the Allies; and were moved to comfortable quarters near the Anting Gate—even having their meals sent in from a nearby restaurant. While there, they composed several letters at the dictation of the Chinese. They were also allowed to receive fresh clothing from outside. On the letters and the clothing secret messages were sent in both directions. Hindustani was used, a language unknown to the Chinese. Finally, to placate the Allies, Hang-ki persuaded Prince Kung to release them. The two Englishmen were returned secretly in a closed cart to the Allied lines outside the city. Apparently, only just in time, for soon after they left Peking a message arrived from the war party at Jehol enclosing the Emperor's orders for their execution.

Parkes and Loch, and some of the others, returned on 8th October; the remaining survivors on the following day; but two had been killed, and eighteen had died.

While arranging for the final attack on Peking, Elgin lost touch with the French. They had moved northwards, and, coming on the Summer Palace a few miles outside Peking, had turned aside to plunder it. Montauban assured Elgin and Grant, when they rode over, that the soldiers were strictly forbidden to loot, although even while he was speaking, French soldiers could be seen helping themselves to jade, jewels, silks and furs. In the end it was agreed that the British should have a share. Their allotment was sold by auction and the money distributed among the officers and men of the force. Generals Grant, Michel and Napier declined to accept anything; but every British private got about four pounds.

Before the final move on Peking, the later famous Charles George Gordon* joined the engineers of Sir Hope Grant's force. While

* Charles George Gordon: born 1833, RMA Woolwich; served in the Royal Engineers; Crimean War, 1855–6; Peking, 1860. He fought thirty-three actions against the Taipings, crushed the rebellion and became known as Chinese Gordon. He was murdered at Khartoum in January 1885.

H

negotiations were going on Gordon also utilised the period of inactivity by going on the 8 October 1860 to see the Summer Palace. The grounds covered a large area and in addition to the main building contained more than two hundred summer houses and kiosks. Gordon describes the inside of the main house as follows:

> 'You would scarcely conceive the magnificence of this residence or the tremendous devastation the French have committed. The Throne room was lined with ebony carved in a marvellous way. There were huge mirrors of all kinds, clocks, watches, musical boxes with puppets on them, magnificent china of every description, heaps and heaps of silk of all colours, embroidery and as much splendour and civilisation as you would see at Windsor. Carved ivory screens, coral ditto, large amount of treasure, etc.; and the French have smashed everything in the most wanton way.'[29]

The main objective was now the occupation of Peking; and as all demands for its surrender were refused, the heavy guns were placed in position opposite the Anting Gate with the intention of breaking it in with gunfire unless the Chinese capitulated. Gordon, who helped with his engineers to mount the heavy guns in a protected position, indicated how the Chinese left their surrender to the last moment. He writes: 'The Chinese were given until twelve on the thirteenth to give up the gate. We made a lot of batteries and everything was ready for the assault on the wall which is battlemented and forty feet high but of very inferior masonry. At 11.30 p.m., however, the gate was opened and we took possession.'[30]

With the Emperor still at Jehol, it was left to Prince Kung to conclude the matter. On 24 October 1860, Elgin, with a large and imposing escort, marched to the Hall of Ceremonies. All he demanded was now granted; and in addition, Kowloon was ceded to Britain, and Tientsin added to the list of open ports. At last the Treaty of Tientsin, under the new name of the Treaty of Peking, was ratified; two days later a similar treaty was signed with the French.

Meanwhile, the Summer Palace, having been plundered by the French, was consigned to the flames by the British and burnt to the ground. Both Loch and Wolseley thought that the burning of the Summer Palace 'hastened the final settlement of affairs and strengthened our ambassador's position', and 'was felt acutely by the Chinese authorities as a punishment directed specially against the Emperor and themselves'. But Gordon who helped do the job of burning believed it 'a wicked shame'.

Elgin, in a letter to the Foreign Secretary from Peking on 25 October 1860, justifies his action—which caused horror throughout the world—in these terms:

> 'It was necessary, therefore, to discover some act of retribution and punishment, without attacking Peking, and in such a manner as to make the blow fall on the Emperor who was clearly responsible for the crime committed [murder of the envoys] without, however, so terrifying his brother [Prince Kung] whom he had left behind to represent him, as to drive him from the field. . . . The destruction of the Yuen-ming-yuen Palace ... seemed to me to be the only combination which fulfilled ... these conditions.'[31]

The Third China War had achieved what it set out to do. Except for the murder of the envoys, it was carried through, albeit slowly, without any real hitch. The administrative arrangements were sound, and the soldiers fought well. With remarkable skill the plenipotentiaries got the China Treaty ratified in Peking itself. It was, moreover, a lasting settlement. The friendly relations established between England and China by this treaty remained unbroken for forty years.

After the settlement it only remained for congratulations to be given and awards made. Elgin was offered, and gratefully accepted, the post of Viceroy of India, General de Montauban was raised to the French nobility as Count Palikao—after the bridge captured so gallantly by the French—and Grant received the GCB. He also received a letter from Sidney Herbert, which sums up this successful little war: 'The public here are, I think, very pleased with the way everything has been done in China—firmness, temper, skill, success ... a first-rate general, a capital staff, an excellent commissariat, and a good medical department are four things the English public are especially pleased to see, and the more so when all are got together.'[32]

References

1   E. Holt. *The Opium Wars of China*. London: Putnam, 1964; p. 65. This is a valuable recent book on the period.
2   General Sir Hope Grant, ed. H. Knollys. *Incidents in the China War of 1860*. Edinburgh: Blackwood, 1875; p. 142.
3   Hope Grant Despatches, British Museum. (See Notes on Sources.)
4   Grant, ed. Knollys, op. cit., despatch from Viscount Canning, 9 May 1860; p. 27.
5   Garnet Wolseley to Caroline W., 14 January 1860. *Wolseley Letters*, Hove Public Library.
6   D. F. Rennie. *British Arms in China*. London: Murray, 1864; p. 30. (For the correspondence between Lords Elgin and Russell see F.O. 405/5.)
7   Hope Grant Despatches.
8   Garnet Wolseley to Matilda W., 4 August 1860. Hove.
9   Ibid., to Richard W.
10   Holt, op. cit., p. 272.
11   Rennie, op. cit., pp. 84–5.
12   Robert Swinhoe. *Narrative of the North China Campaign of 1860*. London: Smith, 1861; p. 144.
13   Hope Grant Despatches, op. cit.
14   Rennie, p. 90.
15   Ibid., pp. 99–100.
16   H. B. Loch. *Personal Narrative of Lord Elgin's 2nd Embassy in China*. London: Murray, 3rd ed. 1900; p. 24.
17   Rennie, p. 69.
18   Field Marshal Viscount Wolseley. *The Story of a Soldier's Life*. London: Constable, 1903; 2 vols. II, p. 23.
19   Hope Grant Despatches.
20   Swinhoe, op. cit., p. 144.
21   *Regimental History of the Royal Hampshire Regt.* vol. I, and C. R. B. Knight. *Historical Records of the Buffs, part II, 1814–1914*. London: Medici Society, 1935.
22   H. Knollys. *Life of General Sir Hope Grant*. Edinburgh: Blackwood, 1894; vol. II, p. 100.
23   Garnet W. to Mother, 27 August 1860, Hove.
24   Loch, op cit., p. 73.
25   Knollys, op cit., p. 136.
26   Garnet W. to Caroline W., 22 September 1860, Hove.
27   George Allgood. *Letters on the China War*. London: Longmans, 1901; p. 57.
28   Loch, p. 108.
29   Gordon Letters, B.M. Add Mss. 52389 no. 27, 9 October 1860.
30   Ibid, no. 29, 9 October 1860.
31   *Confidential Print on Affairs in China 1859–61*, FO 405/5 no. 143, 25 October 1860. This Print gives the correspondence between Lord Elgin and Lord John Russell, Foreign Secretary.
32   Grant, ed. Knollys, p. 161.

The Expedition to Abyssinia
1867-8

The Expedition to Abyssinia 1867-8

D. G. Chandler

British governments have long regarded the protection of the life and property of the citizen living abroad as an important, if often irksome, responsibility. The rulers of mid-Victorian England proved no exception. By sending a military expedition of considerable size into the rugged interior of Abyssinia to rescue two relatively minor diplomatic representatives and a total of 58 other European hostages of various nationalities and ages, the administration of Lord Derby and Mr Disraeli amply demonstrated both humanitarian and patriotic leanings. In the end it proved no small undertaking. No less than 13,000 British and Indian combat troops and a total of 291 vessels of all sizes were employed in the operation, besides a veritable host of servants and workmen, and over 36,000 animals. To reach Magdala, release the prisoners and evacuate the expedition took nine months from the day the first troops set foot in Africa, and the financial cost proved enormous, although the loss of life was miraculously slight, considering the scale of the enterprise and the undoubted martial courage of the Emperor Theodore and his warriors.

This episode is of interest and considerable significance for several reasons. In the first place, it proved a convincing demonstration of the martial power and resources of the British Empire at a time when men could still remember the confusions of the Crimean War and the terrible problems caused by the Indian Mutiny, and this did a great deal to re-establish the reputation of Queen Victoria's British and native troops in the eyes of Europe and the world. Secondly, the planning and execution of the Abyssinian Expedition illustrates the interaction of politician and soldier—showing the high degree of co-operation that could emerge in spite of the rivalries and jealousies over the demarcation of responsibility which at times gravely aggravated the problems faced by the Commander-in-Chief, Sir Robert Napier. Thirdly, the military interest lies partly in the way that truly daunting administrative difficulties were tackled and overcome, and partly in the way that the organisation and equipment of the force that marched to Magdala both foreshadowed the future and at the same time reflected the past.

Napier's army consisted of extremes. On the one hand, his European troops were armed with breech-loading rifles and modern artillery (including even a rudimentary type of rocket), whilst the miracles of modern science were further demonstrated by the building of a railway, the laying of a field telegraph line and the provision of fresh water by means of condensers on the coast and the very latest types of well-boring equipment in the interior. On the other hand, the Indian components of the striking force were still equipped with smooth-bore, muzzle-loading muskets which had changed little in design since the eighteenth century, whilst the huge transport train that alone made the operation feasible included 44 elephants as well as many thousand mules, ponies and camels. Some of the troops were clad in the new-fangled khaki uniforms; others still wore the traditional red coats of Waterloo and the Crimea. The greater part of the shipping that carried and supplied the force consisted of sailing vessels, but an innovation was the provision of three specially equipped hospital ships for the care of the sick and wounded. The old and the new, the traditional and the forward-looking were thus inextricably mingled.

Then again, a fascinating human interest underlies the story. Although the day-to-day history of the expedition is prosaic enough, the rescue of innocent captives from 'durance vile' in one of the most inaccessible and daunting countries on earth is in itself a romantic concept, whilst the paradoxical character of the villain of the piece, Theodore III, who was undoubtedly a man of personality, a ruler of some talent, and a warrior of fair courage, as well as a bestial and half-demented tyrant, attracts a degree of grudging admiration as well as justifiable detestation. There is also a particular fascination in studying the conflict between a semi-civilised race of mountain dwellers, with little but the facts of geography and their own bravery to sustain them, and the relatively modern forces of the greatest imperial power of the nineteenth century, with all the latest inventions of science at their disposal. For all these varied reasons, therefore, the Abyssinian Expedition of 1868 forms a colourful and significant episode in the history of the Victorian Empire.

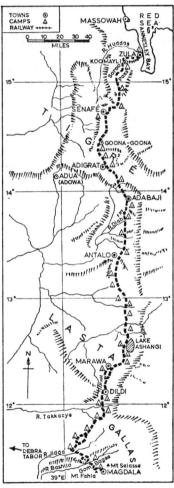

Napier's Route from Zula to Magdala

It would be quite wrong to imply that the British Government was primarily moved to undertake the expedition by imperialistic or jingoistic motives. It was one thing for Lord Palmerston to send a blockading squadron of the Royal Navy in 1850 to enforce the payment of debts due from the Greek Government to a British subject, Don Pacifico, a Gibraltarian Jew of questionable honesty. It was quite another to order a sea-borne invasion of a distant and inaccessible country some 17 years later to free a handful of nationals from the power of a local despot who might well massacre his captives the moment the relieving forces appeared. Accordingly, the decision to employ troops for this delicate mission was only reached after every other form of persuasion—even discreet bribery in the form of gifts—had failed to induce the Emperor Theodore to free his captives. Negotiations of one sort and another were to drag on for more than three and a half years before British patience at last reached breaking point. By then, of course, considerations of national prestige had come to reinforce purely humanitarian motives. The ruler of a backward and obscure country could not be allowed to heap indignities on Her Majesty's accredited representatives indefinitely if the image and dignity of the British Empire were not to suffer in the eyes of the Middle East and Asia. On the other hand there was not the least desire to extend the imperial boundaries to include the barren highlands of Abyssinia. As one of the official historians, Captain Henry Hozier, accurately described it, the expedition was inspired 'by no thirst for glory, by no lust of conquest. Unwillingly entered upon for the sake of humanity by the government of England, it was vigorously carried through in the same cause by the officer to whom its conduct was entrusted.'[1]

As has already been mentioned the British Government's quarrel with Theodore was already of several years standing when the point of complete crisis was reached in mid-1867. The original incident took place on 4 January 1864, when the Emperor ordered the close confinement of Her Britannic Majesty's Consul, Captain Cameron. To explain this impolitic action, it is necessary to describe the ruler of Abyssinia and the recent history of the British connection with the region.

In the years of his prime, the self-styled 'King of Kings' was an imposing figure. Dark-skinned, five feet eight inches tall, well-proportioned and endowed with a naturally dignified bearing, Theodore was every inch a ruler. The famous American newspaper correspondent, H. M. Stanley, saw the body of the dead ruler in Magdala, and described his facial appearance.[2] His face was broad with high cheek-bones and a prominent forehead; even in death, the eyes retained some of their fanatical and piercing qualities; a high aquiline nose with wide-set nostrils was set above a well-defined and thin-lipped mouth. His long hair was divided into three plaits.

The Emperor Theodore was a most complex personality. He was a combination of robber-chieftain, idealist and madman. Periods of great courtesy and generosity frequently gave place to fits of insensate rage. Deep religious convictions contrasted with a complete disregard for human life and suffering. In his last years his moods varied inconsistently and unpredictably from hour to hour, but at no time did his personal courage desert him.

Although he claimed direct descent from the illegitimate offspring of the Queen of Sheba and King Solomon, Liz Kassa was in fact born in 1818, the son of a minor Abyssinian nobleman living in the province of Kouara. Educated by Coptic monks, Liz Kassa eventually succeeded an uncle as provincial governor. This experience of local power awakened his ambitions and developed his obsessional dreams. He was soon in revolt against his immediate overlord, and over a period of years gradually carved and intrigued his way to a position of paramount authority over the assortment of feudal states and petty princedoms that made up the main part of mid-nineteenth-century Abyssinia. In March 1855, aged 37, he felt strong enough to have himself crowned 'Emperor Theodore III, King of Ethiopia, King of Kings and the Chosen of God' by the *Abuna* (or primate) of the Coptic Church. Still his territorial ambitions remained unsatisfied, and he soon turned to the conquest of the remaining unsubdued portions of Ethiopia and a series of wars against neighbouring Moslem tribes. By this time he had developed a considerable degree of martial skill (especially in mounting night attacks), and from this later period dates his capture of the fortress-mountain of Magdala from the Moslem Gallas peoples.

As a ruler, Theodore was inspired by two ambitious dreams. In the first place he saw himself as the pre-ordained champion of Christianity, whose destiny would be to defeat and destroy all his Moslem neighbours before leading a great crusade to liberate Jerusalem from the Turk. Secondly, as a means to this end, he realised the need to modernise his backward country and to force it to emerge from the prevalent conditions of superstition and semi-feudalism which had gripped Ethiopia for more than a thousand years. From the first, however, lasting success proved elusive. Several campaigns against neighbouring Mohammedans ended in near-disaster, and when Theodore turned to genuinely enlightened attempts to introduce social and political reforms amongst his own people he soon found himself faced by crippling obstruction. Nevertheless, despite disappointments, he persisted in his reforming endeavours, introducing a number of skilled European workmen and technicians to start the modernisation of his country. During these brighter, more hopeful years, Theodore drew much advice from an Englishman named Walter Plowden, who had been appointed the first British consul in 1842.

Unfortunately Theodore's idealism found little reciprocation amongst the Ethiopian peoples. Soon conservative obstruction was transformed into bitter civil conflict as revolt after revolt broke out against his rule. In one of these, Plowden—the trusted adviser—was murdered (1860). A second disaster was the death of the Empress, the adored Tavaritch, who had served as a restraining and moderating influence. These sudden catastrophes seem to have affected Theodore's reason, for very soon the highly unstable and utterly tyrannical sides of his paradoxical personality were becoming dominant. His second marriage to a princess of Tigré provided no solace despite the birth of a son, and soon the Emperor 'devoted himself to mistresses and intoxication'.[3] Endless wars engaged almost all his attention, and little by little his power began to decline.

It was to the court of this changed Theodore that Lord Palmerston's government decided to send out a new consul, Captain Charles Cameron, an ex-officer of the Indian Army. Cameron first met Theodore in February 1862. The gifts presented to the Emperor in Queen Victoria's name proved most acceptable, particularly a fine pair of engraved pistols. Unfortunately in this apparently auspicious beginning lay the germ of all the troubles that were to follow.

The Emperor lost little time in sending a letter of thanks to the Queen, and announced in it his intention of sending an Abyssinian delegation to visit London. He requested a guarantee of safe conduct through hostile neighbouring territories for his representatives. 'I wish to have an answer by Consul Cameron', the letter concluded, 'and that he may conduct my embassy to England. See how Islam oppresses the Christian.'[4]

Unfortunately an oversight on the part of the Foreign Office caused this missive to be overlooked, and not even a formal acknowledgement was returned. As month after month passed with no reply from the Queen, Theodore's resentment and suspicions rapidly mounted. His fevered imagination began to imagine a deliberate slight—and even a conspiracy was not ruled out. The irate monarch began to regard Cameron in a less favourable light—but that stolid and rather unimaginative character was no match for Theodore's shifting moods and took slight notice of the cooling in their relationship. Obeying the instructions of Whitehall, in 1863 Cameron journeyed to Kassala in the Sudan to investigate both the slave-trade situation and also the cotton-growing potential of the region (in the hope of alleviating Lancashire's cotton shortage caused by the American Civil War)—but Theodore chose to interpret this innocent mission as proof of a growing Anglo-Moslem intrigue. The final straw was in November 1863, when an assistant for the consul reached Abyssinia—but without the long-awaited royal reply. His rage now knew no bounds, and in the new year of 1864 he ordered the detention of Cameron and his staff. The monarch's suspicions now bordered on paranoia; every European in Abyssinia appeared to represent danger, and in the weeks that followed Cameron's arrest a considerable number of innocent missionaries and their families were rounded up and imprisoned. Only the European workmen survived the purge—for their services in casting artillery and other weapons were irreplaceable, and without them what little was left of Theodore's power would inevitably collapse.

It took some little time for news of these developments to reach London through Aden, and even when the situation was appreciated the Foreign Office refused to regard the matter as more than a temporary misunderstanding. In due course, however, it was decided to send a formal reply to Theodore's original long-neglected letter, and include in it a polite request for the release of the captives. The delivery of this document was entrusted to an Iraqi named Hormuzd Rassam—a member of the British Political Officer's staff at Aden—and in due course a Lieutenant Prideaux and a Dr Blanc were added to his party.

Rassam proved no hustler, and it was not until January 1866 that his letter (dated 26 May 1864) was in Theodore's hands! The Emperor, beset as always by local rebellions, expressed his satisfaction with the content of the reply—and the accompanying gifts—but it was not until April that he agreed to free the captives and allow them to proceed towards the coast. Nevertheless it seemed to Rassam that his mission had been successful, and that the methods of diplomacy had triumphed.

Any such self-congratulatory considerations proved tragically over-optimistic. Theodore's tortuous mind suddenly veered again, and on his orders the missionaries and consular officials were intercepted, whilst Rassam and his party were also seized during a farewell audience. Their conditions of captivity varied considerably. Some of the missionaries had already been cruelly tortured—and Cameron had spent two complete years in chains before Rassam's arrival—but in other ways their circumstances were not too difficult. They were permitted to send and receive letters, their servants remained to wait upon them, and there was no shortage of food or money. On the other hand the knowledge that their future was dependent on the unpredictable whims of a half-demented tyrant imposed a grave mental strain upon one and all. Each day might hold torture and death—or alternatively the arrival of some gift from the inconsistent Emperor, who treated his captives with alternate benevolence and severity, most particularly Rassam.

In the meantime one of the missionaries—Mr Flad—was on his way to England with a new message for the Queen. In this Theodore thanked her for the latest consignment of gracious gifts, and did not fail to indicate that further donations would be very welcome—most particularly a number of skilled workmen, various types of machinery and an expert manufacturer of ammunition. Mr Flad reached London on 10 July 1866, and shortly thereafter a slightly apprehensive White-hall came to realise that Theodore's cunning had been underestimated. Although it was now clear that the ruler of Abyssinia was impudently blackmailing the British Empire, the new Tory Ministry of Lord Derby and Mr Disraeli was in no position to take immediate retaliatory action. Crises nearer home were absorbing all their attention: the financial equilibrium of the City had been shaken by the recent Austro-Prussian War; there was also much political agitation occasioned by the proposed Reform Bill; and a severe outbreak of cattle-plague was threatening the agrarian economy. For these reasons the government continued to play down the Abyssinian affair, and the Secretary of State for Foreign Affairs, Lord Stanley, decided to comply with Theodore's demands and return yet another pacific reply. A party of volunteer workmen was recruited and sent off to Aden en route for Abyssinia. It was still hoped that the Emperor would see reason and thus avert the need for direct action.

Flad returned to Abyssinia in December, by which time Theodore had transferred most of his captives to Magdala, which, under the prevalent conditions of declining power, the Emperor was coming to regard as both his capital and refuge. The envoy found his fellow-captives in reasonable health—and their captor in an amiable mood. The Emperor again expressed his pleasure at the content of Lord Stanley's letter—but gave no sign of any intention of freeing his prisoners immediately. He merely indicated to the Political Agent at Aden that the workmen and other gifts should be sent into Abyssinia without delay.

This insolent reply at last elicited a sterner reaction from London. The Foreign Office first ordered the holding of the workmen at Aden (they were subsequently shipped back to England), and then despatched a formal note, dated 16 April 1867. Still Theodore remained intractable, and Colonel Merewether, the Political Officer at Aden, was soon reporting to Whitehall that all communication with the Abyssinian court had broken down.

As its hands were now freer of home crises, the Government cautiously began to entertain the idea of direct intervention. There was still, however, a notable reluctance to take binding decisions. In 1867 very little was known about Abyssinia; apart from a handful of intrepid explorers, missionaries and traders, the interior of the mountainous country had hardly been visited. Since 1800, when the British Government's attention had first been drawn to the strategic significance of the Upper Nile and adjacent regions during Sir Ralph Abercromby's invasion of French-occupied Egypt, there had been few attempts to remedy this ignorance, and in consequence all kinds of strange tales and rumours were soon circulating. Nobody was sure whether the country could support an expeditionary force—nor what geographical and climatic difficulties the troops would be called upon to face. Then there were doubts in some quarters as to whether the Army was capable of achieving success. Certainly Abyssinia was very inaccessible. The Suez

Canal was not yet open, so it would not be feasible to send troops from Great Britain direct. Aden's port and water facilities were inadequate for the support of a major force. Therefore it was clear that any rescue operation would have to be mounted from India, with a specially constructed base area somewhere on the east coast of Africa. As Abyssinia was completely hemmed in by Moslem powers, this would involve complicated negotiations with Egypt and perhaps Turkey, and the statesmen had no wish to find Turkish or Egyptian forces attempting to take part in the expedition—or eventually taking over Abyssinia from its Christian rulers. All in all, it was a complex problem—but underlying every objection to direct action were considerations of cost and fears of humiliating failure.

Nevertheless, it was soon clear that the problem would have to be tackled. The public conscience of Great Britain was slowly stirring; awkward questions were being asked and the Government was soon aware of a tide of mounting indignation. Accordingly, in June 1867 the Cabinet began to seek information concerning military ways and means. It soon became evident that any expedition would best be mounted from the Presidency of Bombay. Not only was 'the merchant queen of the eastern seas' (Hozier) the largest naval station in British India, with plentiful resources of both supplies and shipping, but the Presidency's army was in cantonments conveniently close by. Its British units had recent experience of frontier fighting conditions; the native components were considered loyal and capable, whilst in the person of the local Commander-in-Chief, Sir Robert Napier, the Bombay Government possessed an experienced and distinguished soldier. And so, on 10 July, the Secretary of State for India telegraphed to the Governor of Bombay the question how soon—*if* an expedition were determined upon—a force could be ready to start fully equipped and provisioned. This cautious and carefully-hedged enquiry constitutes the true genesis of the Abyssinian Campaign.

Mr Seymour Fitzgerald, the Governor, at once passed the enquiry over to Sir Robert Napier. For two weeks the General studied every available book and record pertaining to Abyssinia with the assistance of his quartermaster-general, Colonel Phayre, and drew up a carefully considered appreciation which was transmitted to London on the 23 July (and subsequently expanded on 8 August).

The gist of Sir Robert's recommendations was as follows. In his opinion any expedition would have to be landed in the vicinity of Massowah on Egyptian territory, and a large base established. The distance from Massowah to Magdala was computed to be 400 miles. An intermediate base would have to be established about 200 miles inland near Antalo. The General advised that no less than 12,000 combat troops would be required, 5,000 to form the spearhead of the advance and the remainder to safeguard the bases and the lines of communication. To support these forces a large number of servants would also have to be transported to Abyssinia, and although he hoped that local resources would provide a considerable amount of forage, meat and corn, he was insistent that a sufficiency of stores and baggage-animals should be provided to ensure adequate supply facilities. Napier estimated that at least three months would be required for the basic preparations to be completed—especially in connection with the provision of adequate shipping and beasts of burden, which, he repeatedly stressed, would both inevitably be extremely costly. He mentioned the need for mountain artillery, for tents, blankets and groundsheets to protect the men's health on the Abyssinian plateau, for adequate supplies of specie with which to make local purchases and secure the co-operation of the local inhabitants. In conclusion Napier advised the issue of immediate orders authorising the collection of shipping and animals, and the despatch of a reconnoitring party to the Massowah area.

This appreciation caused not a few raised eyebrows in Whitehall. The suggested scale of the expedition was larger than most had anticipated—and many continued to advocate that a small force of a couple of thousand men should suffice for a 'flying column', which would execute a lightning dash to Magdala and back to the coast. Clearly the expense involved in an expedition on the scale envisaged by Sir Robert Napier would be immense. Could it be justified? Was so comprehensive an expedition really necessary? From the start Sir Robert strenuously resisted all suggestions of a reduction in size, and at the same time repeatedly stressed that the expenses of the campaign would be daunting. 'It is to be hoped that the captives may be released by the diplomatists at any cost of money', he wrote to the Duke of Cambridge on 25 July, 'for the expedition would be very expensive and troublesome, and if not a hostile shot is fired the casualties from climate and accident will amount to ten times the number of the captives. Still, if these poor people are murdered, or detained, I suppose we must do something.

I

I believe some proposals for a much smaller force have been made. It is quite possible that, all being smooth, a very small force might do what is wanted, but it is exactly when a force is small that things do not go smoothly.'[5]

After digesting this information, on 13 August the British Cabinet finally made up its mind to order intervention—although it was not until 9 September that the final ultimatum to Theodore was issued. Even then, many officials optimistically hoped that a show of force would bring Theodore to terms. On the suggestion of the Government it was also determined to offer Napier the command of the expeditionary force, with Sir Charles Staveley as second-in-command.

At the time of accepting this appointment, the General was 56 years of age. He was tall, well-built and dignified. 'His face was remarkable for the kindliness of the blue eyes, the genuine gentleness of the countenance lit up by them and the smile that continually played around his lips,' recorded H. M. Stanley. 'To all Sir Robert was extremely bland, affable and kind; sometimes there lurked in his tone something akin to sarcastic *politesse*, and at such times he was more plausibly phrased than ever.'[6] This courteous exterior concealed a fine brain and a wealth of military experience accumulated over 39 years of service. He was a soldier of great determination with an unflinching sense of purpose, who earned the respect of his superiors as well as the loyalty of his subordinates.

Born in Ceylon in 1810, the son of a gunner officer, Robert Cornelis Napier was from the first destined for service in the Indian Army. After several years at Addiscombe (the military school of the East India Company), he gained a place at Chatham and emerged as a sapper subaltern in mid-1828. The next seventeen years which he spent in Bengal brought him no active service, but in 1845 he took part in the Sutlej campaign and was promoted Brigade Major in recognition of his valorous conduct in fighting against the Sikhs. After several more campaigns he was eventually appointed Chief Engineer to the Punjabi Government, but his personal life was clouded by the death of his first wife in 1849. So far his career had followed a fairly normal course, but the grim period of the Indian Mutiny really made his reputation. Accompanying the first relief column to Lucknow, he subsequently became deeply involved in the renewed siege—and performed his duty so well that he was appointed Brigadier-General after the final relief, and a little later awarded the K.C.B. His next chance of distinction came during the China War of 1860.*

After returning to India at the conclusion of the campaign, Sir Robert entered into a phase of his career which greatly expanded his administrative experience. As First Military Member and subsequently President of the Indian Council, he became deeply involved in politics. During this period (which lasted from 1861–5) he married happily for the second time. Then, in July 1865, he was appointed Commander-in-Chief of the Bombay Army with the rank of Lieutenant-General.

Thus Sir Robert Napier was a soldier of no mean operational or administrative experience when he was chosen to lead the expedition to Abyssinia, although it was the first time an Engineer had been selected for such an appointment. His variegated career had taught him three main lessons which he now strove to apply to his new task. First, the paramount importance of a properly organised and equipped commissariat, especially when operating in largely unknown terrain. Second, the advisability of retaining as free a hand as possible over the conduct of the expedition as a whole—especially in connection with the political side. And thirdly, the need to resist all pressures to mount ill-advised, hasty operations; in his expressed opinion a policy of 'slow but steady' was most likely to succeed in the present instance.

Some of the problems facing the expedition were both novel and formidable, and not at first sight capable of rapid solution. The basic operational problems were four in number. Although it was not anticipated that much opposition would be encountered before Magdala was reached, the complete lack of good roads—and the extremely precipitous nature of much of the terrain to be crossed—would inevitably impede the 400-mile advance from the coast; transport and supply difficulties would consequently be immense, especially as the scale of obtainable local resources remained very uncertain. Then there were problems of climate and health to be considered. With morbid fascination concerning the perils to be faced by others, the British public wrote endless letters to the Press warning of malaria epidemics on the coast, the prevalence of tropical conditions and chronic water shortages all the way to Magdala. As Captain Hozier noted, 'animals were to perish by flies, men by worms'.[7] Insurance companies pushed

* See the previous chapter.

up their rates, but despite the general atmosphere of impending doom spread by ignorant pessimists there proved to be no dearth of volunteers to accompany the expedition. Thirdly there would be the difficulty of catching Theodore. If he chose to abandon Magdala without a struggle and wage a war of evasion and movement, the British forces would be facing an almost insoluble problem. And lastly there was the need to consider the fate of the prisoners: any ill-considered move might result in their immediate execution. On the other hand a measure of assistance might be forthcoming from some of the dissident tribes if they were properly handled.

Political and administrative difficulties bedevilled the organisers from the outset. On the very day that the expedition was confirmed, Napier was writing to the Governor that the presence of an all-powerful Political Officer alongside the commander would not be acceptable. 'I respectfully submit', he wrote, 'that the political responsibility should be included with the military command.'[8] A protracted and acrimonious dispute followed. He was informed that this request was not 'in accordance with the previous custom in India', but the General had not the least intention of playing second fiddle to a Political Officer appointed by the Viceroy. He found his case supported by the Duke of Cambridge at home, and in the end the soldiers won their way. Political trammels were to be kept to a minimum. Napier for his part agreed that he would consider the suggestions of Colonel Merewether, Political Officer designate, but made it clear that he would not consider these as directives. The final decisions would rest with him alone.

Relations with the Viceroy's Government were not improved by this victory. Thereafter the central Indian Government certainly did its best to interfere with the choice of officers and units for the campaign. 'I quite understand that the Home Government has left everything in your hands', wrote the Viceroy rather acidly on 25 August, 'and therefore everything which has been said must be treated as mere suggestions on our part. We all think, however . . .'[9]—such was the tone of many a supposedly 'helpful' communication. But Napier was an old enough hand to know how to withstand such pressures. Inter-Army jealousies were also aroused when Napier declared his intention of employing principally troops from the Bombay Presidency. The armies of Bengal and Madras wanted fair representation, and the Commander-in-Chief (India)—Sir William Mansfield—agreed with their argument and persuaded the Viceroy to intervene on their behalf. 'I am *very* sorry that you could not take a division of native troops from us', wrote the Viceroy at the end of September. 'I still think it is the right course to pursue.'[10] Soon there were differences of opinion over every possible issue. Napier's plans were criticised and his competence queried; his request for a special Cooly Corps of labourers was strenuously opposed; his requirement for 20,000 baggage animals was declared impossible; his ideas relating to the organisation of the commissariat were rejected; the reliability of his Bombay native regiments was questioned. The Viceroy also chose to challenge Sir Charles Staveley's suitability for second-in-command—although he had originally put forward his nomination. 'I make no apology to you for interfering in this way', ran a pompous viceregal letter of 25 September; 'The safety of the Army and the honour of England are involved in this matter.'[11]

Napier, however, refused to surrender one tittle of his prerogatives, and the Home Government backed him over almost every issue. 'I feel every confidence in my plans,' he wrote on 3 October. 'There is nothing rash in them—I make no hasty moves. If I do not succeed there can be no disaster, and some better man will come up and complete on my foundations. . . . The Army is in the highest spirit and I have no fear of my Bombay Regiments. Mansfield never knew them.' He was equally adamant about Staveley's suitability. 'I knew him in China as a Brigadier and have seen him for nearly two years here.'[12]

Such difficulties and obstruction notwithstanding, stage by stage preparations went steadily forward. The Home Government certainly spared no pains. The Foreign Office secured Egyptian permission for the establishment of a temporary base on their territory, and sent its representatives scouring Spain and the Middle East for baggage animals. On the advice of the explorer, Dr Beke, negotiations were concluded with Vienna for the special minting of half a million Maria Theresa dollars of 1780—the only currency univerally accepted throughout Abyssinia.

The Admiralty undertook the lighting and buoying of the approaches to Massowah, provided three hospital ships and vessels specially converted for shipping animals, and agreed to supply three fresh-water condensers. The War and Ordnance departments similarly did everything in their power. Two batteries of 7-pounder mountain guns (adapted for carriage by mules) with a thousand rounds apiece, a battery of 12-pounder, breech-loading, rifled Armstrong guns of the latest pattern, and four 'rocket machines' (supplied with 340 6-pounder 'Hale's War Rockets'), were allocated to the expedition. Similarly, 4,000 new Snider-Enfield breech-loading rifles were sent out for the European troops, and the latest types of tube-wells and chain-pumps provided. Although almost all the troops were to be found from the Indian establishment, a number of specialist officers and the newly-formed 10th Company, Royal Engineers, were sent out from Great Britain. Two novelties were the inclusion of a team of nine photographers and an electric telegraph unit, supplied with sufficient equipment for laying up to 450 miles of line. At one time it was also proposed to ship out a complete railway—locomotives, lines and rolling-stock—but the task of providing this bulky equipment was eventually transferred to Bombay.

The services of interpreters and experienced travellers (including Captain Speedy from New Zealand and Major Duncan) were procured, and to ensure the accurate recording of the expedition, the British Museum found a geographer, an archaeologist and a zoologist, while the Press was represented by Dr Austin of *The Times*, Whiteside of the *Morning Post*, Lieutenant Shepherd of *The Times of India*, not to forget G. A. Henty of the *Standard* and the American special correspondent of the *New York Times*, H. M. Stanley. In every way the Victorian talent for thoroughness was amply displayed. 'Truly the rulers of England did well,' noted Hozier. 'The experiences of the Russian War were not forgotten.'[13] And although he saw fit to add that 'Europe in general looked upon the undertaking with the smile of quiet scorn' this did not prevent the attachment of a considerable number of foreign military observers, including Prussians, Italians, Austrians (both army and navy), French, Dutch and Spaniards—some 13 in all.

In India, meantime, the work of preparation also proceeded, if fraught with rather more difficulties. After several months of negotiation and remonstration, on 11 November the detailed composition of the force was announced. There were to be four British and ten native infantry battalions, a squadron of British cavalry and four regiments of native horse, five batteries of artillery, a rocket brigade (eventually manned by the Naval Division), and a total of eight companies of Sappers and miners—comprising one British and seven native units.*

* See Appendix, p. 157 for the organisation of the expedition at the climax of the campaign and a list of the main units employed.

In round terms this constituted a fighting force of 4,000 European and 9,000 native troops. Of these, virtually all the Europeans and two-thirds of the Indians were drawn from Bombay; the Presidency of Bengal provided one infantry battalion, two lancer regiments, a battery of British gunners and a regiment of pioneers; scarcely 400 men were taken from the Madras Army—all of them sappers. Over 7,000 public and private followers accompanied these units to perform menial tasks.

The organisation of the supply and maintenance of this fighting force posed an entirely different set of problems, and here Sir Robert found himself at even greater variance with the local governments. General Napier pressed strongly for the formation of a unified Land Transport Corps (which would be directly responsible to his Quarter-master-General)—of a type similar to the one raised to accompany the Persian Expedition in 1856. He also requested the services of a Cooly Corps to provide a labour force. These requirements faced a storm of opposition. The official view was that all such matters should come under the authority of the Commissariat Department—an organisa-tion responsible to its own senior officer, the Commissary-General. In the end Napier was forced to concede this individual's authority in India, and it was not until the opening of the campaign had been con-siderably delayed owing to the proven deficiences of the old organisa-tion that the General got his way completely. On the other hand his proposals for adding a considerable number of light carts to the establishment and re-ordering the chain of command of the various transport units were grudgingly accepted (15 October). As a result several hundred Maltese and bullock carts were provided and 18 inspectors of varying grade (mostly volunteer NCOs) and 20 'Head *Muccadums*' or native overseers were appointed for every 2,000 mules. All in all, however, the Commissary remained a huge and unwieldy organisation prior to the implementation of Sir Robert Napier's further reforms in early 1868, controlling no less than 14,500 followers, 3,000 horses, 16,000 mules and ponies, 8,000 camels, 4,000 pack and 1,000 draught bullocks, and 44 elephants. The separate Land Transport and Bengal Cooly Corps increased the number of natives by a further 2,000.*

* In all, 62,220 men and 36,094 animals were eventually transported to Zula. These numbers included 13,088 troops (4,038 European and 9,050 Indian), see Holland and Hozier, vol. I, pp. 235-6.

The provision of adequate shipping for so large a force and its vast quantities of stores of every kind taxed the authorities sorely. In the end, the naval officers charged with the task engaged 205 sailing vessels and 75 steamers, and purchased a total of 11 small craft. The hire of this amount of shipping alone cost £449,000 per month, and it took no little time to assemble.

While all these arrangements were being pressed ahead in England and India, a reconnaissance party was on its way to Massowah to commence surveys. Commanded by a Committee consisting of Colonel Merewether and five senior officers, this party—perhaps 400 soldiers and servants in all—left Bombay in two ships on 16 September, and eventually anchored off Massowah on 1 October. Several days were spent in studying the port and its environs before it was decided that it would not provide an adequate disembarkation point for the expedition. The survey then moved on 30 miles south to Annesley Bay, and in due course a practicable site was discovered near the village of Zula on its western side. A certain amount of fresh water was found near the village whilst its close proximity to the Abyssinian mountains some 13 miles away was a further point in its favour. The local Moslems seemed friendly enough, and the bay would provide the shipping with fair shelter. On the other hand the inshore water was very shallow, which meant that piers at least 700 yards in length would have to be constructed to enable the steamers to discharge their cargoes of men and material without complete reliance on lighters. Furthermore the surrounding countryside appeared most uninviting: the prevalent steamy heat promised the presence of disease, whilst there was a great shortage of fodder for animals. Nevertheless, it constituted the best site available—and the survey party reported in these terms to Bombay. Their advice was immediately adopted and the first convoy of shipping set sail from Bombay. Several officers and parties of cavalry then explored inland, seeking for the best place to penetrate the mountains and gain access to the Abyssinian highlands. Some time was spent investigating the Huddas Pass, but Colonel Phayre, the Quartermaster-General, eventually decided that the Koomayli Pass would provide the better route.

Then, on 21 October, the Advance Guard of the expeditionary force anchored in Annesley Bay. The first shiploads carried mainly sappers and their materials, and very soon work had begun on the proposed piers, tramway and camp sites. Over the days and weeks that followed, more men, horses, mules and material made their appearance, and the Zula base gradually began to take shape. Despite the difficulty of finding sufficient stone, one 900-yard jetty was in operation by December, and in due course a water condenser was established at its end. A start was then made on a second pile-driven pier, whilst a water-shoot was constructed from a small artificial island (on which a second condenser was eventually situated) to the shore. A number of store sheds were soon built, camp lines laid down and tents erected. A tram-way leading to the pierhead proved of the greatest assistance in landing

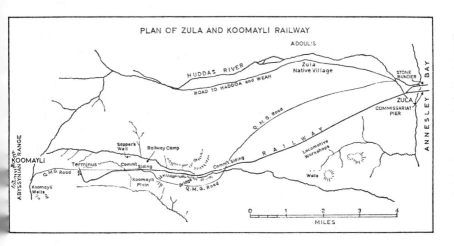

stores and materials. Meanwhile some of the engineers were hard at work further inland. 'A tramway having been proposed to be laid in the lowland country between Zula and the base of the mountains at Koomayli, a distance of about 12 miles, Lt. Willans, R.E., Assistant Field Engineer, commenced surveying the line in November and the works were commenced in December when the ships with the plant from Bombay began to arrive.'[14]

As a consequence of all this endeavour, by mid-December 2,000 British and 5,500 native troops were accommodated ashore, with 5,000 mules and ponies, almost 2,000 camels, 962 bullocks and 956 carts besides a host of followers and labourers. In the process of building up the quantity of supplies required, five thousand tons of provisions had so far been landed, including six million pounds of forage for the animals.

In spite of this considerable achievement, however, everything did not always go smoothly at Zula. The local Egyptian governor showed no inclination towards providing practical assistance and it was soon found that the local fresh water resources were incapable of providing the minimum ration of $1\frac{1}{2}$ gallons per man each day and also to water all the animals, and serious trouble developed amongst the native labourers. Prior to the arrival of the condenser equipment (operational on 1 January) the prospect would have been grim, had it not been for the efforts of Captain Edye, R.N., who managed to ship 120 tons of water ashore every day from the steamships in the bay. As it was many animals died of thirst and plague, and the roads around the Zula base were soon littered with stinking carcasses. Not surprisingly morale soon began to sink under these unpleasant conditions.

Affairs at the base took a turn for the better after the arrival of Sir Charles Staveley to take over command on 6 December. The Egyptian Government was induced to appoint a more helpful local governor, the dead animals were buried, comprehensive health regulations enforced and the water supply more closely controlled. On the other hand the hybrid collection of workmen drawn from every part of the Middle East and India continued to present disciplinary problems, while the unloading facilities were proving incapable of handling the large number of ships arriving almost daily in Annesley Bay.

On 2nd January 1868 H.M.S. *Octavia* arrived off Zula carrying Sir Robert Napier and his staff. Once ashore he immediately conducted a thorough inspection of the work in hand. He was pleased to learn that the reconnaissance party was pushing ahead into the interior of the Abyssinian mountains, sending agents before them to contact chieftains hostile to Theodore, and approved the news that the advance guard had reached Senafé, some 40 miles from the coast at a height of 8,000 feet where they were busily organising a forward camp. He was less enchanted with what he found at Zula. To date some 7,500 troops had been landed with three months' worth of European rations and double the quantity of Indian stores. Certain important items, however, had failed to materialise, and the General was soon telegraphing the Secretary of State for India requesting the provision of (among other items) 15,000 pairs of ammunition boots (mainly for the Indian troops), as many pairs of woollen socks and 15,000 blankets (which he estimated would be very necessary amidst the cooler regions of the Abyssinian highlands), 500,000 lbs of biscuit, 100,000 lbs of salt meat, and 30,000 gallons of rum. To simplify the over-crowding problem at Zula, Napier further instructed the authorities to retain for the time being the remaining parts of the expedition (some 6,500 men) at Bombay and Aden.

Three weeks of hectic administrative preparations ensued. On account of an outbreak of disease among the horses, the Commander-in-Chief soon moved most of the cavalry to new camps near Koomayli, where water had been discovered, and further ordered the transfer of men and stores to the foot of the mountains to be hastened. The inadequacies of the transport arrangements were now fully revealed. By mid-January the railway only extended four miles beyond Zula. and the commissariat and Land Transport trains were on the point of breaking down. Napier was particularly disappointed at the slow rate at which stores were being passed forward up the difficult Koomayli and Soroo passes to the forward base at Senafé—but at least these difficulties enabled him to implement the series of reforms he had suggested the previous autumn. Determined to improve the quality of the mule-drivers, Sir Charles Stavely began to plan the replacement of the troublesome Turks, Arabs, Persians and Egyptians by more reliable Indian labour, imposed a more rigid system of supervision, and increased the allocation of draught-mules and light carts. These measures were soon giving results. Work on the railway-line was proceeding despite grave difficulties, while the telegraph detachments of the Engineers were hard at work laying a wire to link Zula and Senafé. Meanwhile up at the front the survey parties had pushed ahead beyond Goona-Goona towards Adigrat, choosing camping sites, assessing local food and fodder resources and looking for water, while at Senafé piles of stores were now rapidly accumulating.

By mid-January Sir Robert Napier had made an assessment of the problems facing the expedition and had also worked out a compre-hensive plan. Obviously the sooner the main body set out for Magdala the better. The coastal plains were very disease-ridden, and it was absolutely essential that the whole expedition should be completed before the onset of the heavy summer rains. Furthermore a report dated 18 December had arrived from the interior revealing that the

Emperor Theodore was already slowly wending his way with some 8,000 warriors, six large guns and 14 wagons of munitions from Debra Tabor to Magdala, laboriously making a road for his artillery. If it were at all possible, Napier would prefer to forestall Theodore at Magdala and rescue the prisoners before trying conclusions with the Emperor's main army—but as 400 miles lay between Zula and his objective, this would be difficult to achieve if a properly-managed form of advance was to be adopted.

Napier was by now completely convinced that an elaborate full-scale operation was necessary. No 'rapid dash' of the sort so dear to the hearts of the arm-chair strategists of Whitehall could guarantee a successful outcome. In the first place, the attitudes of the princes through whose provinces Napier would be forced to pass on his southward journey were still unclear. Two of these were of greater importance than the rest. Kassai, Prince of Tigré, who controlled the first 150 miles of country, was known to be a bitter enemy of Theodore, but by the end of January he was still concealing his hand and seemed to be even more pre-occupied in feuding with his immediate neighbour, Wagshum Gobaje, Prince of Lasta. This was a considerable complication, for Napier depended in no small degree on their friendly co-operation to ease his logistical problems and assure the troops of a free passage. How could Kassai be wooed without giving offence to Wagshum Gobaje, and vice versa? Another prospective ally would be Prince Menelek of Shoa, but there was no accurate knowledge of his present whereabouts. Beset by so many political uncertainties, it certainly behoved Napier to make his dispositions with care, and to protect his lines of communication—which would inevitably be very lengthy—from the possibility of any treacherous attack. This would inevitably take both time and men.

If political difficulties would beset Sir Robert Napier from the out-set, he had long recognised that problems of movement and supply would constitute his gravest burden. Even if the various tribes re-mained friendly, the sheer ruggedness of the Abyssinian tableland would greatly hinder the advance of his guns and supply convoys. Inevitably the latter would be very extensive—for it was already becoming evident from reports sent back by the advanced brigade that scant supplies would be forthcoming from the countryside. A little meat, barley, fodder and firewood might be procurable—at a price—

but never enough to support the whole striking force. Water was also likely to be critically scarce for much of the journey. At the height of the dry season the streams were low, and one river which the survey party had optimistically described as capable of supplying 'abundant water' turned out to be a trickle 18 inches wide and half an inch deep! Every type of military store—and even water—would therefore have to be carried or dragged over long distances.

Once these problems had somehow been overcome, the expedition would still be faced with a series of the trickiest difficulties. It was by now clearly wishful thinking to suppose that Theodore would tamely submit without a struggle, and Napier had to devise means of assuring the successful outcome of any engagement against hardy mountaineers fighting deep in their own country. This meant that all the guns would have to be taken to Magdala no matter what natural obstacles lay in their path. Then the safety of the hostages had to be taken into account. How far could Napier press his measures without fatally compromising their safety in the hands of a mad tyrant? And even if everything went well, what was to be done with Theodore after his capture? Certainly Sir Robert Napier was not going to find his command any bed of roses.

In simple outline, the Commander-in-Chief's plan for overcoming all these associated complications was to march a column of 5,000 combat troops to Magdala, taking with them everything they might require, by the most direct available route. While this spearhead (later named the 1st Division, commanded by Sir Charles Staveley, KCB) travelled southward through Senafé, Adigrat, Antalo (the half-way point where another forward base would have to be established) to Lake Ashangi and thence to the river Bashillo and Magdala itself, the remainder of the troops (the 2nd Division) were to be employed in detachments to safeguard the ever-lengthening lines of communication and protect the ceaseless stream of convoys travelling to and from the front.

On 25 January the Commander-in-Chief decided that the time had come for the main movement to commence. The troops held back at Aden and Bombay were forthwith summoned, and measures announced for the safeguarding of the base at Zula. As the new troops arrived, they would release rear units for service further forward. That same day the long red, green and khaki clad columns with their seven-mile 'tail' of mule-trains, gun-teams, elephants and servants, began to snake their slow way over the coastal plain and up the steep and uneven paths through mountainous defiles towards the Abyssinian plateau.

Four days later found Napier in person at Senafé, whilst the advanced brigade entered Adigrat some 35 miles ahead. On the way up the Commander-in-Chief had halted near the head of the Koomayli Pass to await the arrival of the first convoy of 75 bullock-carts up the steep gradients. Leaving Senafé, he next rode on towards Adigrat, which he reached on 6 February. Here a fortnight's lull ensued. Although the cooler, healthier atmosphere of the high ground was a welcome relief from the steamy heat of the coastal plain—and the men were glad of their groundsheets and blankets at night—the going was proving so bad for the supply convoys that a period had to be set aside to let them catch up. Napier was still dissatisfied with the performance of the commissariat trains, so he decided to send to the rear large numbers of unreliable drivers and then proceeded to divide the entire transport organisation into two formations: a highland division (which would operate from Adigrat southwards) and a lowland division responsible for moving stores from Zula to Senafé and Adigrat. The mules were sub-divided into groups of 2,000 and troops of 150, with European overseers drawn from the ranks of the battalions under the direct supervision of the Quartermaster-General and his staff.

By the time the thirsty and foot-sore columns had reached Adigrat it had become clear to every participant that the campaign was going to call for prolonged exertions. 'It is so simple for people at home to say "Why don't you advance?" ' wrote Lieutenant William Scott, one of Napier's aides-de-camp, 'while here we are . . . barely able to do more than keep ourselves in food.'[15] The Horse Guards still needed convincing of this, however, for on 18 February the Duke of Cambridge wrote to Napier that 'what is desired here is that a flying column or a succession of flying columns should be pushed forward and operate to the front, so as to make a dash if possible and finish the business before the rains set in'.[16] Whitehall's anxiety was partly due to the mounting expense of the expedition and partly to the threatened intervention of an Egyptian army. The Government had no desire to share the honours of the expedition with the underlings of Turkey, and had certainly not the least intention of allowing Abyssinia to be overrun by the Moslems. But Napier quite rightly refused to be hustled into premature action. Before leaving Adigrat he wrote: 'I am risking much by advancing beyond what I consider prudent before supplies have been passed on, but I do so in the hope of drawing something from the country . . . but beyond Antalo I cannot advance until supplies come up and they are backward even at Zula.'[17]

One factor that made these pauses necessary was the generally disappointing progress being made by the railway across the coastal plains. It had been hoped that this rear link would prove capable of moving almost all the requisite supplies to the foot of the mountains at Koomayli, a distance of almost 13 miles. Even by 19 February, however, only six miles of track had been laid. From the start, the railbuilders were beset with harassing difficulties. Most of these were directly due to the Bombay authorities, 'five different descriptions of rail having been provided for the work on four different principles of fixing'.[18] Much vital equipment had been packed in the wrong vessels, and there was a great shortage of experienced plate-layers. Several of the engines and much of the rolling-stock proved defective. Then again the blazing sun and the meagre water ration of $1\frac{1}{2}$ gallons per man made it impossible to extract more than $6\frac{1}{2}$ hours of labour a day from the native gangers, and to cap it all, once the expeditionary force began to move south, 'so many trains were in requisition for other purposes (particularly commissariat) that it was almost impossible to keep the plate-laying parties at the end of the line supplied with material'.[19] In the end the Engineers completed some 14 miles of 5 ft 6 in gauge track (including a loop at the Koomayli terminus) and the railway certainly contributed to the movement of supplies although rather less effectively than had been originally anticipated. Apparently 13,000 tons of stores and 24,000 troops and followers were carried between March and June.

The advanced brigade reached Antalo—200 miles from the coast—on 14 February, and four days later the main body set out from Adigrat to join them. The going proved worse than ever, and it was extremely difficult for even the reorganised highland transport division to bring up the 170 mule-loads a day needed to keep the force supplied. This induced Napier to order a large reduction in the amount of personal equipment being carried. Before leaving Zula, headquarters had restricted each officer to one servant and a single baggage mule, while three officers or 12 NCOs and men were expected to share a single bell-tent. Many had evaded this instruction, so from 20 February it was decreed that all officers should be restricted to 75 lbs of kit and every other rank to 25 lbs. At the same time, practically all the native servants were sent back to Zula. A month later, near Lake Ashangi, even direr reductions were to be enforced. Thenceforward 12 officers or 20 other ranks were expected to share a single tent—very necessary as heavy storms of rain occurred almost every night—all private baggage was discarded, and all but the Indian mule-drivers were sent to the rear. Soon afterwards, a British soldier was put at the head of every animal to assist its journey over the ravine-cut terrain, where many mules were lost down the precipices. Thus the expedition progressively reduced its equipment as the problems of forward supply grew acuter, and eventually even the coveted daily rum issue had to be suspended.

Despite these deprivations the health, morale and discipline of the British and the Indian units remained satisfactory for the greater part of the long march. There are no recorded instances of soldiers marauding—there wasn't very much to loot—and, in the carefully measured words of Captain Hozier, 'no swarthy damsel was subjected to any rude gallantry on the part of the redcoats'.[20] As for the officers, they somehow found time and energy to visit Coptic churches to stare at ancient manuscripts, and many enjoyed shooting wildlife when opportunity offered. It was indulgence in this gentlemanly pastime that caused the expedition's first European fatality, when Colonel Dunn of the 33rd had the misfortune to shoot himself on his way to Senafé.

The hybrid collection of muleteers, however, presented a very different picture. 'The muleteers are a good instance of what Babel must have been like,' noted Lieutenant Scott. They argued, grumbled and fought amongst themselves, losing no opportunity that offered to loot the stores with which they were entrusted. Worst of all, they neglected their mules, and it was not until some sharp disciplinary examples had been made, and (latterly) that the worst of the riff-raff had been replaced by Indian drivers, that matters improved significantly.

Each day brought its own crop of difficulties. Reveille was sounded half an hour before dawn, and the next night's camp was rarely reached before dusk, but it was exceptional for a day's march to cover more than ten miles. The route of the expedition led it inexorably over mountain chains and down into deep chasms worn in past ages by fierce torrents, which were now often little more than trickles of water. The rough trails blazed by the advance guard and the pioneers often proved extremely perilous. The elephants baulked at loose scree, the mules tended to become sick at high altitudes. 'The march into Adigrat was the stiffest of all for the artillery; they were out nearly all day at one bad place; the horses had to be taken out, and the guns and carriages lowered by ropes.'[21] Almost every day's march brought similar problems.

The staff found it increasingly difficult to ensure an adequacy of supplies. Sometimes a few bushels of grain were purchased from a local chieftain, but on most occasions there was little to be found. Inevitably the locals pushed up their prices to the maximum, and the fact that they would accept nothing but the Maria Theresa dollars often meant that they drove some very hard bargains. At one stage Major Pritchard's Army Signals Corps ran out of suitable poles for their precious telegraph line (which eventually extended to Antalo) but the difficulty was overcome by offering a dollar for every few poles the natives could bring in. Many Abyssinians virtually demolished their rude hovels in taking advantage of this opportunity. However, no formal opposition was offered to the columns during the advance—for the Abyssinians were considerably over-awed by the sight of the tame Indian elephants, and clearly greater profits could be made from a semblance of co-operation.

Almost every day political agents and spies were now returning with news from Magdala or from the encampments of the intervening chieftains. It was not until late in February, however, that the long-awaited meeting with Prince Kassai took place. After several delays, a rendezvous was arranged on the banks of the river Diab (25 February). The Prince appeared with an imposing escort of 4,000 warriors— the first native soldiery the expedition had yet encountered—and the British troops were favourably impressed with their fierce bearing and reasonably modern firearms. For two days the discussions and associated feastings went on. Napier spared no pains to impress his visitor. The guns fired, cavalry wheeled, infantry manœuvred; gifts were exchanged and toasts drunk; even a group photograph was taken. Lieutenant Scott was not above a little sleight of hand when it came to the matter of gifts. 'Sir Robert also presented him [Kassai] with the horse he had ridden on to meet him. I grudged very much having to hand him over ... he was the best of the lot. So I slipped out, had the

K

saddle and bridle whipped off and put on another horse, and got *him* ready for presentation.'[22] The exchange went unnoticed, and when the two leaders parted on the 27th, Prince Kassai had promised Napier every possible assistance. Sir Robert for his part was particularly pleased at gaining Kassai's good will without giving any undertakings to assist Tigré against Wagshum Gobaje. Nevertheless, stringent security arrangements remained in force.

Headquarters reached Antalo on 2 March, and another ten-day pause ensued while the Commander-in-Chief reduced the bulk of the force's baggage, waited for his hospitals to be brought up, and extemporised a secondary line of communications back to the coast. The same period saw the final organisation of the expedition into its two divisions, the 1st, commanded by Staveley, was designated the striking force, comprising some 5,000 men divided into two brigades and an advance guard, and all the guns. The 2nd, under Major-General Malcolm, CB, was made up of the Antalo, Adigrat and Senafé garrisons, the Zula command, and all other communications detachments.*

The columns of the strike force set out from Antalo at daily intervals, the first starting off on 12 March. Eight days later Lake Ashangi was reached, and further drastic reductions in the 'tail' announced. In addition to the restrictions mentioned earlier, ambulance allocations were reduced to three 'doolies' (a form of mule-born litter) for every hundred men, and rations were also slightly cut to enable each brigade to carry 15 days' supplies with them. No attempt was made to drive a waggon-trail beyond Lake Ashangi; only men, mules, horses and elephants were to proceed, the last-named carrying the heavy Armstrong guns in dismantled sections on their backs. Magdala now lay about 100 miles ahead.

The speed of the advance quickened when Napier learnt that Theodore had won the race to Magdala, and had even managed to manhandle his pride and joy, a huge 70-ton mortar named 'Theodorus', into the vicinity of the fortress. The time for the long postponed 'dash' had clearly come—but the going proved more difficult than ever. Under the continuous strain of long marches and short water rations, discipline occasionally wavered. During the hard march from Marawa to Dildi, for example, the men of the 33rd openly swore at their

* See Appendix p. 158.

officers, some even 'falling out from the baggage guard, throwing themselves down and refusing to move',[23] calling out for water. Napier immediately dealt with this act of indiscipline by ordering the King's Own to take over the head of the column, relegating the recalcitrant 33rd to the rearguard. This lesson had the desired effect, and the march went on.

Contact was made with Wagshum Gobaje, Prince of Lasta, on the 30th, when another short halt was authorised to allow the brigade columns to close up with the advance guard. This prince proved as accommodating as Kassai, although a tricky moment was experienced on 2 April when a picquet fired on part of Gobaje's entourage after mistaking it for an enemy band, killing one and wounding another. The incident was smoothed over with a compensatory payment to the bereaved, and the advance proceeded unhindered. The tension was now mounting. News was still filtering through from Magdala describing Theodore's preparations to meet the invasion, and at the end of the first week of April Napier thought fit to send a formal demand for surrender to the Emperor. It elicited no reply, but Napier was somewhat reassured to learn that the Moslem Gallas had sealed off the fortress from the south. After crossing the river Jidda, the 1st Division converged on the river Bashillo, the last obstacle between Napier and his quarry. During this stage of the advance it was joined by the 45th Foot, which had made a phenomenal march of 300 miles in only 24 days. The leading brigade reached the watercourse on the 8th and the expedition again halted to complete its final arrangements. Magdala now lay on 12 miles ahead.

Theodore, meanwhile, was busy whipping up confidence and enthusiasm amongst his 10,000 warriors. He promised rich booty for one and all if they performed well, and threatened dire retribution on any waverers. None doubted his word concerning the latter part of his declaration. For, after watching the approach of the distant columns from the summit of Mount Fahla throughout the 9th, Theodore returned into Magdala and spent the night butchering several hundred of his hapless Abyssinian prisoners, hurling many chained in pairs down a precipice. His rage subsiding, the demented Emperor had resort to prayer for forgiveness, and interviewed a not unnaturally apprehensive Rassam about what the future might hold. The night passed without further incident, however, and early on the 10th the warrior-monarch left Magdala, and marched out to occupy the Height of Fahla where seven cannon, including 'Theodorus', had already been sited. The climax of the campaign had been reached.

On several counts the prospect facing Napier's expedition was hardly alluring. The almost total absence of water between the Bashillo and Magdala meant that every drop would have to be carried forward from the river—and any slight hold-up in the supply of this vital commodity might well have a disproportionate effect on any fighting the future might hold. Secondly there was the fate of the prisoners to be considered. Would Theodore choose to go down fighting after massacring them—or would he try to escape, carrying his hostages with him? To try and avert this latter possibility Napier decided to attack without further delay, but was not inclined to underestimate the fighting capabilities of his opponent. While he had every confidence in the ability of his men to defeat the Emperor's feudal hordes in the open—their huge mortar, field artillery and reasonably-modern firearms notwithstanding—it might well prove a very different matter to bring them to account amidst the precipices, ravines and rocky slopes which constituted the greater part of the Magdala position. The reports brought back by his probing patrols seemed to indicate that Magdala was a natural fortress which might turn out to be virtually impregnable—or at least take a heavy toll of casualties—if properly defended. Report placed Theodore's strength at over 10,000 warriors.

The fortress of Magdala itself forms part of an inaccessible mountain range which roughly describes a half circle from west to east some five miles in diameter. Three heights dominate the range. Closest to the current British position towered the flat-topped mountain of Fahla, overlooking both the Arogee plain and the King's Road, which constituted to all intents and purposes the sole practicable approach to Magdala. This road clung to the northern slopes of Fahla before passing over a saddle on to the equally precipitous southern slopes of neighbouring Mount Selasse, which constitutes the cente of the range. This mountain rises to a height of 9,100 feet above sea-level, and comprises the second highest point in the region. Beyond Selasse lies the plateau of Islamgee, and at the easternmost point of the range stands the mountain fortress of Magdala, looming some 300 feet above Islamgee, and resembling an inaccessible eagle's eyrie. A precipitous wall of rock protected the northern, western and southern aspects of this natural stronghold; 'the eastern side', noted Stanley, 'rose in three terraces of about 600 feet in height, one above another. Its whole summit was covered with houses, straw-thatched of a conical shape'.[24]

Napier was under no illusions about the line of attack he would have to follow. Despite the presence of the friendly Gallas tribes hemming in Magdala from the east and south, the General was aware that Fahla and Selasse constituted the keys to the Magdala position, and that he would consequently have to attack from the west, tackling each obstacle in turn. The utter inhospitality and impassability of the surrounding terrain ruled out any other course.

Accordingly, on 9 April, force headquarters issued the following orders: '1st Brigade, 1st Division, with the exception of the cavalry, under command of Brigadier-General Schneider, will take possession of the Gombagee (Affijo) spur, and encamp there tomorrow.'[25] Four companies of sappers would build a rough road along the spur ahead of the leading infantry battalions, while the rest of the brigade moved up to the foot of the pass to await the opening of the trail. Colonel Phayre, meantime, was to push ahead with an escort to reconnoitre the Arogee plain and Fahla. The remainder of 1st Division was to close up to the Bashillo.

Shortly after dawn on Good Friday, Colonel Phayre set off towards the head of the pass, taking an escort of sappers with him. Soon left far behind, the infantry of the leading brigade laboured their way over the uneven countryside. The going proved exceptionally difficult, even for Abyssinia, and within a few hours several men had collapsed from heatstroke. The Engineers ahead of the column soon became dubious about the possibility of their task, but news from the Deputy Quartermaster-General that the head of the pass on to the Arogee plateau had been found undefended and was now secure, caused everyone to redouble their efforts. Reporting by mounted messenger, Phayre suggested that Napier might now send forward the baggage and guns up the King's Road with no more delay. The Commander-in-Chief accepted this advice without demur and very soon the mule-trains were moving up the rough road towards the supposedly secure head of the pass.

Napier and his staff set spurs to their horses and rode off ahead of the infantry on to Affijo, which overlooked the point where the King's

Road breasted the slope and entered the Arogee plateau. An unpleasant surprise awaited them. Despite Phayre's earlier assurances, they were unable to detect any sign of troops holding the vulnerable defile. 'When I came up and found my order about the road not executed', wrote Napier to his wife, 'I got very uneasy, and pushed on just in time to see the mountain guns and rockets emerge from the pass close under the enemy's position [Fahla].'[26] The baggage of the army, and, even more important, its precious guns, were consequently very exposed to enemy attack. So much for the reliability of Colonel Phayre's report that the head of the defile was safely held!

Fortunately Sir Robert Napier was a man of instant decision. Hoping to forestall Theodore, he instantly ordered the 23rd Punjab Pioneers (leading the 1st Brigade) to move left so as to secure the head of the pass and join the mountain guns. This move proved not a minute too soon, for as the leading mules of Colonel Penn's batteries emerged from the pass a salvo thundered out from the seven cannon on the summit of Fahla, and at the same instant a mass of native warriors could be seen swarming down its slopes. The time was four o'clock in the afternoon; the action of Arogee had opened.

Watching from the crest of Fahla, the Emperor Theodore had noted the mule-trains approaching up the King's Road, but had failed to spot the position of Napier's infantry column. In the firm belief that the English general had committed a bad blunder, Theodore immediately ordered his favourite chieftain, Fitaurari Gabi, to take 500 chiefs and 6,000 men and with them swoop down to loot the apparently unprotected convoy. Such an easy success, he hoped, would serve to put a fine edge on his men's mettle. The Emperor himself remained on Fahla to direct the covering fire, compelling his unwilling German artisans to reload and train the pieces. In spite of the range being all of 3,000 yards, Theodore's very first salvo fell uncomfortably close to Napier's staff and the deploying Punjabis. The accuracy of the enemy's fire at such extreme range came as something of a shock to our Lieutenant Scott. 'Being my first time under fire, I must say, hearing the hissing of the shot above . . . I felt much inclined to duck my head down to the saddle. I, however,' he proudly adds, 'resisted the impulse.'[27] Fortunately little damage was done by this or subsequent discharges, for the technical problems associated with firing plunging shot on to the British troops at extreme range proved too much for the Abyssinian master-gunners, and they insisted on using considerably too much powder in their charges, thus causing their projectiles to overshoot. Moreover, the Emperor's vaunted secret weapon, the 70-ton mortar, 'Theodorus', disconcertingly and noisily burst its barrel the very first time it was discharged.

Meanwhile, under the cover of this fire, the whooping hordes of Abyssinian warriors, led by scarlet-clad chiefs on horseback, were drawing closer to their objective, but owing to the considerable distance they had to cover the 1st Brigade was afforded sufficient time to complete its counter-measures. On Sir Robert's order, the Naval

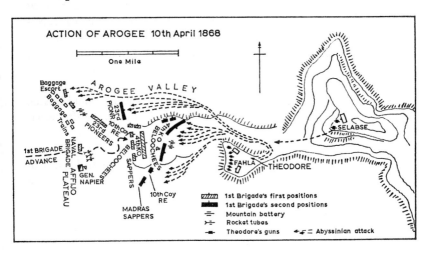

Brigade came hastening up the road to site its rocket-tubes on a spur of the Affijo overlooking Arogee. Very soon, Lt.-Commander Fellowes had opened fire upon the oncoming masses, but despite the havoc caused by his hissing and bounding rockets, which exploded in all directions, the human tide continued to surge nearer. At the same time, however, Sir Charles Staveley was able to lead the King's Own, part of the Beloochees, 10th Company R.E. and the Bombay sappers on to the western edge of the Arogee plain. 'Fourth to the Front!'[28] shouted Brigadier Schneider, and the troops deployed into two lines to await the onset of the enemy. In the excitement of the moment the men quite forgot their parched throats and swept forward with a rousing—if hoarse—cheer.

The King's Own fanned out into skirmishing order, and opened fire on Theodore's warriors at a range of 150 yards with telling effect. 'How they just about did catch it!' enthused Lieutenant Scott. 'You never saw such a sight.'[29] Faced by the sustained fire of breech-loading rifles, the *élan* of the Abyssinians soon started to ebb away—but it was nevertheless some little time before they sullenly began to fall back towards Fahla, whereupon the centre and right of Napier's force advanced to a second position. Many warriors took cover on Fahla's lower slopes behind bushes and boulders and opened a sniping fire against the British right, causing several casualties. Then a force of warriors tried to work their way round the brigade's right flank, but this move was countered by bringing up the Madras Sappers and a detachment of the Bombay Cavalry with part of the Naval Brigade and two guns. Within half an hour, the attacks against Staveley's right and centre had been driven back, and Lt.-Commander Fellowes was able to switch his rocket-fire against Theodore's guns on the summit of Fahla. In spite of the range, the sailors made good practice. One hissing rocket narrowly missed the Emperor, who exclaimed: 'What a terrible weapon! Who can fight against it?'[30] before covering himself with his shield.

Meanwhile another sizeable part of the Abyssinian horde had swept forward against Sir Charles Staveley's left flank, thus threatening the brigade's baggage trains which had halted short of the crest along the sides of the King's Road. Colonel Milward at once opened fire with the steel guns of 'A' Battery, R.A., but was soon forced to summon up a detachment of the King's Own into line alongside the 23rd Punjabi Pioneers to safeguard his 7-pounders. Once this measure was successfully completed, the Punjabis advanced to counter-attack. A tough bayonet-fight ensued, for the Indians were still armed with muzzle-loading firearms which were slow to reload—whilst a fair proportion of Theodore's men, on the other hand, were equipped with superior double-barrelled percussion muskets. On this occasion cold steel served the Indians well, and soon the Abyssinians were in full flight on their sector.

Simultaneously another party of the enemy came into close contact with the baggage guard on the extreme left of the British line. Although he was greatly outnumbered, Lieutenant Sweeny, the officer in command, kept his head admirably. Massing the baggage in a relatively safe place, he drew up the three companies of the baggage guard into line, and poured several withering volleys into his opponents. They, too, broke and fled.

Now the tide of battle on the left swung decisively in the British favour. Attacked frontally by the baggage guard, taken in flank by the 23rd Pioneers assisted by a further two companies of the King's Own detached from the centre, the Abyssinians suffered heavy casualties from bullet, shell and bayonet. At least 100 were killed in a narrow ravine—and many more corpses were lying thick upon the ground. By this time it was seven in the evening, and the action of Arogee was practically over. All the combatants were soaked to the skin, for torrential rain fell during part of the action. After the last shot of the day had been fired no less than 700 Abyssinians lay dead in the field—including Fitaurari Gabi—whilst 1,200 more lay wounded. For their part the British had sustained 20 wounded (of whom two subsequently died). Once again the superiority of well-trained and well-armed troops over less sophisticated masses had been amply demonstrated. The new Snider-Enfield rifles, steel guns and rocket tubes had proved their worth as weapons, and all the undoubted courage of the Abyssinians had availed them nothing. Theodore's gamble had not come off.

As dusk descended, Sir Robert Napier ordered his jubilant troops to halt. The men built their bivouacs near the baggage trains, but as the tents had not come up—and since the supply convoy was similarly delayed on the road—most of them spent a cold and hungry night. Early on the morning of the 11th, however, the convoys reached the encampment, closely followed by the 2nd Brigade which took over the forward positions. Meantime the doctors and orderlies were doing their best for the wounded of all nations, and numerous parties were detailed to bury as many of the slain as possible.

Theodore had spent the night with his shaken army on the in-hospitable slopes of Mount Selasse. Although he soon discovered that early pessimistic estimates of the previous day's losses were hugely exaggerated, he sorely felt the loss of his favourite chieftain, and accordingly, shortly after midnight, the Emperor decided to have further recourse to negotiation. A message was sent to Rassam in Magdala, imploring his aid. As a result of lengthy consultations, Dejatch Alami and two of the prisoners—Mr Flad and Lt Prideaux—were sent down to the expedition's camp early on the 11th to sound

Sir Robert's intentions. The Commander-in-Chief, however, refused to even hint at a reconciliation, but forthrightly told the envoys that the prisoners must be handed over with no further delay, and that Theodore should immediately surrender himself unconditionally into Queen Victoria's hands—in return for a guarantee of fair treatment. To enable Theodore to make up his mind, Sir Robert announced his willingness to observe a 24-hour armistice. Before the delegation was dismissed it was treated to a demonstration shoot by the Armstrong guns. They were suitably impressed. 'There is no escape for us', lamented Dejatch Alami, 'we must surrender or be killed.'[31]

During the absence of his envoys, however, Theodore's attitude had hardened. Daylight had revealed the true extent of his losses, and his warriors' morale seemed better than expected. Consequently he received Napier's message with scorn, and even returned his letter unopened. The Emperor gave vent to one of his hysterical outbursts, calling down the wrath of God on his persecutors.

This insulting rebuff left Sir Robert in a considerable quandary. He could certainly not ignore Theodore's recriminations—but if he were to order a new attack what would prevent Theodore from murdering his hostages without further ado? To gain a little time, the General ordered the delegation to return again to Theodore with a stern message, insisting that the rejected letter contained Napier's final offer. Meanwhile, dramatic events had been taking place in Theodore's camp. After his rage had calmed down, the Emperor summoned a full council of chiefs, and debated his future moves. Some spoke of killing the prisoners forthwith, but the majority favoured their release—and to everybody's surprise Theodore tamely consented. Then suddenly a new spasm of maniacal fury convulsed the Emperor, and seizing a pistol he attempted to shoot himself through the mouth—but the weapon misfired. This Theodore chose to represent as a revelation of God's will—but he confirmed his intention of releasing the Europeans.

Soon a jubilant Rassam was leading Consul Cameron and several more members of the European party down the hillside, escorted by the German engineers. Meeting the returning delegation, on its way back to Magdala, they decided to go to Napier together. The troops cheered as the party reached the lines. All was not quite over, however, for several European families still remained in Magdala through illness or other circumstances, and they were clearly still vulnerable. Anxiety on their behalf was somewhat relieved with the arrival on the 12th of a more moderate letter from the Emperor. In it he asked forgiveness for his earlier brusqueness, and announced that he was sending down a gift of 1,000 cattle and 500 sheep for the Commander-in-Chief.

Sir Robert took counsel with his advisers and the leaders of the ex-hostages, and concluded that any acceptance of this present would be tantamount, in Abyssinian eyes, to 'burying the hatchet'. The outposts were accordingly ordered to drive the beasts back. However, to humour Theodore a little the General told the German artisans to return to their master with the body of Fitaurari Gabi for burial in Magdala. A renewed summons to surrender accompanied this gesture. As had been hoped, Theodore was touched by this action, and took no steps to hinder the evacuation of the remaining families; he also permitted his artisans to go down to the British camp. Thus, by early afternoon of 12 April, the last of the hostages were safe. A wave of relief swept through the expeditionary force. 'I send the prisoners to the rear tomorrow,' wrote Napier to his wife. 'It is not easy to express my gratitude to God for the complete success as regards the prisoners.'[32] One object of the campaign had been safely accomplished. It only remained to punish the upstart ruler.

All this while Theodore was persuading himself that his pacific gestures would induce Napier to relent. As a further conciliatory move, the Emperor ordered the evacuation of his guns from Fahla. 'Surely it is peace, now that they have taken my power from me—surely it is peace!'[33] he exclaimed to his entourage. Slowly, however, he came to realise his error as the British outposts turned back his herds. In great despondency, Theodore returned into his fortress. Early on the 13th, he made a bid to escape with 2,000 men from the northern side of Magdala but changed his mind when he realised that all effective exits were blocked by taunting and blood-thirsty Gallas tribesmen. Back in the town, Theodore gave formal permission for any of his followers who so wished to make their way to Napier's camp and surrender. Soon a veritable multitude of warriors, their families, cattle and possessions were taking advantage of their release from allegiance to Theodore. Several hundred, however, freely chose to remain with him to the end. Their master had now determined to sell his life dearly, and was making plans for a last-ditch stand within his redoubtable natural fortress.

By the early hours of the 13th, Napier had decided that Magdala would have to be stormed without further delay. Not only had Theodore refused to surrender, but the original 24-hour armistice had already lasted more than two days. The longer the attack was postponed the greater the danger that Theodore might find some means of slipping away and eluding capture.

As a preliminary move the complete division was paraded on the Arogee plateau preparatory to advancing up the King's Road towards Fahla and Selasse and thence on to the plateau of Islamgee—the last approach leading to Magdala. To cover the advance, the Armstrong battery was to be sited on the saddle between the peaks of Fahla and Selasse, where it could open fire against the western side of the fortress. The actual attack was to be carried out by the 2nd Brigade, supported by the 1st. The division would have to detach considerable bodies of troops to occupy Fahla and Selasse as the main columns marched up the King's Road, and a small party of cavalry was at once despatched to parley with the large numbers of Abyssinian warriors who were desirous of laying down their arms. As the bulk of the expedition's cavalry was still back at the river Bashillo on account of the water shortage at the front, Napier next found it necessary to extemporise a second mounted force from his escort and orderlies, under his aide-de-camp. Scott's orders were 'to lose no time in circling round Fahla to the rear of the enemy's position to take prisoner, or to cut up, any people trying to escape'.[34] He would be relieved as soon as the regular cavalry appeared on the scene.

About 9 a.m. on Easter Monday the advance began. First went 10th Company R.E., followed by the 33rd Foot and the batteries of mountain artillery. As far as the saddle connecting Fahla and Selasse, the whole of the 2nd Brigade marched along the rough surface of the King's Road, but then three companies were detached to the right to occupy Fahla and two more of the 33rd Foot, later supported by part of the 1st Brigade, scaled Selasse. By midday a flood of disarmed Abyssinian warriors and their families were streaming down from both peaks on their way to the rear—some eye-witnesses placing their number as high as 25,000. Three mountain guns were somehow man-handled on to the summit of Selasse, the rest of the artillery continuing up the road below.

So far everything was going remarkably well. It was fortunate that no opposition was encountered for 'all the officers admitted that a few Europeans stationed behind the projecting masses of rock to contest the approach would have materially changed the aspect of affairs',[35] so precipitous and difficult was the going. However, with both mountains secured soon after midday, Napier felt justified in calling up the Armstrong guns on elephant-back to site them on the saddle, and soon the 12-pounders were in action, firing across the inner side of the concave range of mountains into Magdala at a range of 2,700 yards.

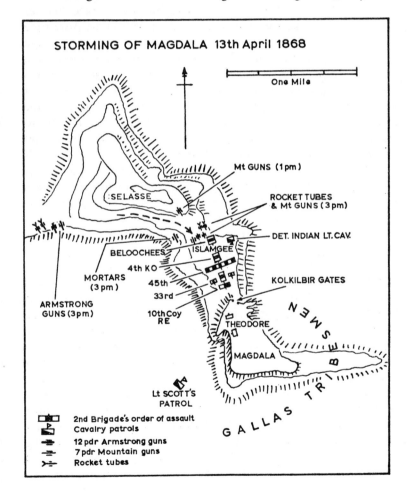

STORMING OF MAGDALA 13th April 1868

One Mile

Mt GUNS (1 pm)

ROCKET TUBES
& Mt GUNS (3 pm)

SELASSE

DET. INDIAN LT. CAV.

BELOOCHEES   ISLAMGEE

4th KO

MORTARS   KOLKILBIR GATES
(3 pm)   45th

33rd

ARMSTRONG
GUNS (3 pm)   10th Coy
RE   THEODORE

MAGDALA

Lt SCOTT'S
PATROL

GALLAS TRIBESMEN

2nd Brigade's order of assault
Cavalry patrols
12 pdr Armstrong guns
7 pdr Mountain guns
Rocket tubes

In the meantime, a squadron of Indian cavalry pressed forward on to Islamgee where they interrupted Theodore and a band of his warriors attempting to manhandle their guns into Magdala from the park near the native market. The Emperor rode forward waving his sword, challenging all comers to single combat, but the troops ignored the taunts and posturings of the single unidentified horseman, and pressed ahead to prevent the movement of the guns into the fortress. This they were able to do with the help of the advanced company of the 33rd. Frustrated on both counts, Theodore abandoned his guns and moved back into Magdala, where he shut himself in with his remaining 300 loyal followers.

Gradually the plain of Islamgee filled with British and Indian troops as the brigades and guns arrived. They soon discovered the putrefying bodies of Theodore's victims of the 9th at the foot of a precipice. 'The sight of wholesale slaughter caused a deep feeling of hatred to Theodore among the British soldiery,'[36] noted Captain Hozier. 'A more horrible sight it is impossible to imagine; it is the sort of thing to dream about for nights after,'[37] recorded Lieutenant Scott.

Sir Robert Napier had now completed his reconnaissance of the natural and man-made defences guarding the northern approaches to Theodore's lair. They appeared imposing. Beyond a sharp dip at the southern end of Islamgee towered a steep cliff-face 300 feet high, scaled only by a single narrow, twisting path. Two gates four foot wide, and associated obstacles, guarded this slender avenue of approach. The lower Kokilbir Gate stood 230 feet above Arogee, consisting of a small barbican flanked by long walls of stone and wooden stockades, twelve feet high and topped with thorn bushes. Seventy feet higher stood the upper gate with similar defences, giving final access on to the Magdala plateau. 'Although these defences were rudely constructed, and could not have stood even against field artillery,' noted a sapper officer who inspected the works in detail after the storming, 'they were admirably adapted for resisting the attack of an enemy armed only with muskets and spears, for which purpose, no doubt, they were originally constructed.'[38] At the time Theodore had further strengthened these defences by piling blocks of stone against the inside of the closed lower gates, rendering them virtually impenetrable. It was decidedly fortunate that Theodore had only a few hundred followers and a handful of light guns at his disposal; otherwise success would have been dearly bought.

Faced by such an obstacle, Napier's plan of assault could hardly be subtle. Only a frontal attack up the path and through the gates was practicable. To provide close covering fire, the rockets of the Naval Brigade and all 12 cannon of the Mountain Artillery were brought forward and sited on the lower slopes of Selasse some 1,300 yards from the scarp, and shortly after 1 p.m. these pieces opened up against the gates, adding the weight of their fire to that of the Armstrong guns which had also been moved a little closer up the King's Road on the Commander-in-Chief's orders. Supported by this bombardment (which appears to have done remarkably little damage to the enemy), the assaulting column formed up. First to advance would be two companies of the 33rd, deployed in skirmishing order; on reaching the foot of the cliff their task would be to fan out on either side of the path and engage the defenders above their heads. Through this screen would pass 10th Company, Royal Engineers, followed by 'K' Company, Madras Sappers and Miners, equipped with scaling ladders, charges of powder for blowing the gates, picks and crowbars. Behind these troops would come six companies of the 33rd commanded by Major Cooper, with a further two in support. A couple of companies of Bombay Sappers were to bring up the rear of the column, but behind them the 45th Foot, drawn up in line, would constitute the first reserve. The other troops of the 1st Brigade were restricted to a mainly passive role—but they could console themselves with the knowledge that they had the action of Arogee already to their credit.

Shortly after 3 p.m. the expedition's guns thundered out in a renewed and sustained bombardment, but elicited no reply from the silent ramparts of Magdala, where the defenders were lying low. An hour later Sir Robert Napier ordered the storming column to advance to the assault. Final instructions were issued. 'Before starting', records Ensign Wynter, carrying the Regimental Colour of the 33rd that day, 'Sir Charles Staveley, our General of Division, rode up to Melliss (carrying the Queen's Colour) and myself, and told us to wave our colours as soon as we got in.'[39] The troops marched off, and soon the leading units had reached the foot of the cliff-path. They at once began to climb, covered the while by the fire of the two companies deployed on either side of the line of advance. The defenders replied with musketry, but caused surprisingly few casualties. The lower gate was reached—but then a disconcerting pause ensued. It was discovered that the sappers had forgotten to bring their powder-charges and scaling ladders—or else dropped them on the way up. They set to work with a will on the gates with their crowbars, but these were so massively reinforced with stone that little impression could be made. Next, rather than allow the entire impetus of the assault to die away, three companies of the 33rd, accompanied (against the specific orders of his senior, Ensign Melliss) by young Wynter and his Regimental Colour, turned off the track to the right and began to seek a way round the troublesome obstacle.

Now took place the celebrated incident that earned the 33rd Foot its first two Victoria Crosses. A tall private soldier named Bergin managed to hack away with his bayonet some of the protruding thorn-bushes from a section of the twelve-foot-high palisades and then asked a neighbouring drummer, Magner, to give him a leg up. It proved easier, however, for Bergin to heave the drummer toward the top of the wall until his fingers could just hook over the edge. A stalwart shove from the butt of Bergin's rifle quickly deposited the drummer fair and square on top of the wall. Ignoring heavy enemy fire, Magner was just able to lean over and haul his companion up beside him, whereafter he continued to assist more comrades up in the same way while Bergin fired away single-handed at every Abyssinian he could see—killing several. A way was thus opened through the lower line of Magdala's defences.

Soon Ensign Wynter reached the breach. 'It was a tough pull up, but I was hardly ever on my feet as the men took me and the colours in their arms and passed us on to the front . . . I shall never forget the exhilaration of that moment, the men firing and shouting like madmen.'[40] As more and more men appeared over the gap in the wall the defenders turned and fled for the upper defences. Losing no time, Bergin's party rushed forward in hot pursuit and managed to prevent their adversaries from closing the gates. Another party helped the main body penetrate the obstinate lower gate, and soon the 33rd was inside Magdala. An exuberant Wynter signalled this success, as ordered, by waving his Colour.

To all intents and purposes the capture of Magdala was now an accomplished fact. A few stalwarts continued to offer resistance, but the majority proved only too willing to throw down their arms when word reached them that Theodore, their leader, was dead. His body was found a short distance within the inner gate. At the moment when it became clear that all was lost, the Emperor had turned to his gun-bearer, Welder Gabre, and said: 'Flee. I release you from your allegiance; as for me, I shall never fall into the hands of an enemy.'[41] Then, drawing rather ironically one of the pistols originally presented by Queen Victoria, he shot himself through the mouth and fell dead instantly. The tyrant was no more. Britain's honour had been vindicated.

The two colours of the 33rd were lashed to the top of the highest roof in the fortress, and Napier was undisputed master of Magdala. The cost of the assault had only been two officers and 13 other ranks wounded. The Commander-in-Chief could congratulate himself on achieving both the main purposes of his expedition. The captives were safe; their persecutor lay slain. Theodore's death was in many ways a God-send for Napier, as it relieved him of awkward decisions regarding the tyrant's fate. It only remained for him to evacuate the Magdala area, destroy the fortress, and then march his men back to the coast for re-embarkation.

The last days of the expedition at Magdala did not prove uneventful. First there were 265 native prisoners to liberate—including in their number no less than 36 Abyssinian princes and senior chieftains, some of whom had been incarcerated for as many as 30 years. A board of enquiry looked into Theodore's death, and the Emperor's body was buried. Then it was necessary to protect the inhabitants of Magdala and the disarmed warriors of Theodore's ex-army from the vengeful and loot-lusting Gallas tribesmen, and in the course of this several incidents took place. Severe regulations had to be issued to stop the troops of the expedition from doing a little scavenging on their own account. Every item of booty that had not actually been captured in combat 'at point of sword or bayonet' was rigorously collected by the Prize-Master for future auction—to the disgruntled annoyance of the soldiers. Living conditions around and in Magdala remained tough, for the shortage of water within the fortress was almost as dire as in the surrounding countryside, and so everybody was pleased when on 15 April Sir Robert Napier ordered preparations for the return march to Zula.

Two days later the Engineers destroyed the 15 smooth-bore cannon (three of them being 56-pounders), 13 howitzers and nine mortars captured in the Islamgee market or within Magdala. Charges were then placed beneath the fortifications of Magdala, and fire was set to every building on the plateau as the rearguard evacuated the area. As the long column of troops, accompanied by tens of thousands of Theodore's ex-subjects who had to be escorted beyond the grasp of their hated Gallas foes, wended its way down the King's Road for the last time, they left behind them a massive column of smoke ascending into the sky— symbolic testimony of the folly of twisting the British lion's tail.

The march to the coast proved as difficult as the advance. The wet season was now approaching, and frequent storms were encountered. All excitement was now over, and morale steadily sank as the seemingly endless columns toiled northwards. Passing through Lasta and Tigré the tired and grumbling troops were frequently called upon to drive off bands of marauding tribesmen, whose expectations of massive loot from Theodore's eclipse had proved illusory, and who now turned all their attentions against the expedition and its horde of followers. Antalo was reached on 9 May, and after packing up or destroying all the accumulated stores and equipment in the camp there, Sir Robert divided the force into five brigade columns, which continued the march to the sea at daily intervals. The rearguard quitted the half-way staging post on the 15th. That same day Theodore's queen, who had been ailing for some time, died and was buried. The Commander-in-Chief then appointed himself guardian of her son.

Nine days later the rearguard reached Senafé, and prepared to evacuate the base there and follow the preceding columns down from the Abyssinian Highlands on to the steaming coastal plains. Here Napier held a last series of meetings with his erstwhile ally, Prince Kassai of Tigré, who came to the conference clearly expecting great rewards. He received half a dozen mortars and as many howitzers, with 200 rounds for each piece, together with 850 muskets, 350,000 rounds of small arms' ammunition and 28 barrels of gunpowder, besides numerous other articles. In presenting these not inconsiderable munitions of war, Sir Robert somewhat hopefully stressed that they were solely for use 'in the defence of his country'. The Prince was also promised delivery of several mountain guns at some future date. All in all, these 'gifts' left Kassai the strongest war-lord in Abyssinia, but inevitably heralded another series of desperate civil wars as their owner battled for the paramount leadership against his fellow-rulers.

It is revealing that Napier's mandate included no clear directions for reorganising the chaotic political condition of the country he had just traversed. By the time he reached the edge of the plateau the mass of Theodore's ex-subjects had dwindled away to practically nothing, and the liberated chiefs had left for their own territories after being advised to give some form of allegiance to Kassai—but in other respects nothing was done to assure a settled future for the country. Napier's political masters had no desire to incur the least responsibility for the region; the expedition had achieved its specific purposes, and that was enough. The hostages were free, the national honour had been vindicated, and nothing else troubled the Victorian conscience.

After a rather dangerous passage down the flooded Soroo Pass, where a number of servants and baggage animals were swept away, the last troops of the expedition descended on to the plain and by 2 June all the troops were in the Zula encampments. The only thought in men's minds at this juncture was to get away as soon as possible, and a period of hectic endeavour ensued as everything that could be moved or dismantled was packed aboard ship. Even the defective locomotives, rolling-stock and rusting rails of the Soroo railway were re-embarked, and by the time the last men were aboard there were few traces left of the vast encampment. About 13,000 animals were sold or given back to the local natives. Napier himself set sail for England on 10 June, leaving what little remained in charge of the Egyptian governor. Those of his men destined for England returned via the Suez-Alexandria, railway and thence by sea. The native regiments sailed for India. In all 42,700 men and 15,000 animals were re-embarked at Zula. The very last troops left African soil on 18 June. The vessels of the Royal Navy sailed next day.

For a while Victorian England basked in the success of its soldiers. 'We landed at Portsmouth about the 20th June,' recalled Ensign Wynter of the 33rd. 'All the ships in harbour and at Spithead were dressed and manned, and bands were placed on Southsea and other piers and played "Home Sweet Home" and "See the Conquering Hero Come". A tremendous crowd were in the streets who chaffed our ragged clothes, and one big woman took my Captain, a very little man, in her arms and kissed him, much to his fury. It was funny to see his struggles.'[42]

The mood of relief and rejoicing did not, however, linger long in high places. Very soon awkward questions were being raised in both

Houses of Parliament concerning the cost of the expedition which had almost doubled the original estimate.* A Select Committee was appointed to examine the Abyssinian War in the greatest detail from the financial angle. The Indian Government proved particularly critical of Napier's showing in this respect—but he had warned them from the very outset that the expense would be enormous. Much of it was linked with inefficient departments and short-term financial policies resorted to at the time, heedless of his protests. To cite a few examples, the refusal to reform the transport and commissariat services led to great waste and avoidable charges; much outworn and outdated equipment had been unloaded on to the expedition (*viz.* the railway materials); an unimaginative policy of hiring all available shipping— which proved the greatest single item of expense—heedless of its suitability, was certainly not of Napier's choosing. In these and a thousand other ways an unwillingness by the Indian authorities to accept primary expense had proved a devastatingly false economy. Inefficiency in packing the vessels had led to waste and confusion. At one point no less than 4,000 mules had been 'lost' at Bombay, and their failure to reach Abyssinia forced the staff to purchase local animals at inflated prices to make good the deficiency. Yet pinch-penny attitudes in high places had provided only three barges to assist the unloading, and the officer who later purchased a further half-dozen was held personally responsible for the cost of five of them.

On the whole, however, the Home Government backed Napier to the hilt. Rising in the House to propose a vote of thanks to the army, Disraeli proclaimed (somewhat inaccurately) that 'the standard of St George has been hoisted upon the Mountains of Rasselas',[43] and on another occasion, with reference to the financial furore, he publicly stated that 'Money is not to be considered in such matters: success alone is to be thought of', and that high expense was 'likely to be the case in all wars for which I may be responsible'.[44]

* The original estimate of the cost of the expedition—to the end of 1867— suggested a sum of £2,000,000, with a forecast of expenditure at a rate of some £600,000 a month if operations continued into 1868. Parliament thereupon authorised a vote of £2,000,000 from the Consolidated Fund, and raised Income Tax by 1d. in the pound (to a total of 5d.) in November 1867. When all items of expenditure had been met, however, it was found that the expedition had cost all of £8,600,000. See *Report of the Select Committee on the Abyssinian War*, 1869, Appendix 29.

On balance it can fairly be said that Sir Robert indubitably earned the promotion and peerage conferred upon him. Although Theodore had made a serious error in not opposing the expeditionary force at an earlier date and was certainly outclassed in terms of weapons, training and equipment, Napier had carried through no easy task. To take a force of 14,000 men and numerous supporters to a virtually unknown land, march 400 miles through unmapped, roadless, arid and mountainous country and then defeat a demented monarch in his inaccessible fortress, and at the same time effect the release of the hostages, the original *casus belli*—called for no little military skill and application. Every mule-load, every source of water, had to be carefully calculated; the whims of touchy local chieftains had to be allowed for and their willing support elicited; the discipline and well-being of his men amongst very difficult circumstances had to be carefully maintained. What might have happened had a less capable and thorough soldier been in command is shown by the terrible fate of the Italian Expedition in 1896, which was severely mauled at the battle of Adowa by the same ferocious warriors that Napier had faced and defeated (one wonders whether the guns provided by a grateful Britain had a part to play in the outcome!). In the light of this comparison, the Commander-in-Chief's achievement is truly revealed. Whereas the Italians lost no less than 6,000 killed and 1,700 wounded in this single action, the total deaths amongst the British troops throughout the whole nine-month expedition of 1867–8 amounted to exactly 35 (about 1·3% of the British contingent), and only a further 333 were seriously wounded or afflicted by illness. Total British admissions to hospital for all reasons amounted to 1,332 over a period of nine months' active operations. The losses incurred amongst the Indian troops and the mass of followers were somewhat higher, but not dramatically so. Whatever might be said concerning the high financial expense of the operation, no one could have expected a lower rate of mortality. And yet, all goals had been achieved. 'Though a little war, it was a great campaign,' wrote H. M. Stanley in a just summary. 'The fame of it resounded with loud reverberations over wide Asia and established her [England's] prestige on a firmer base than ever.'[45] The honour of England had been vindicated, and the martial qualities of the post-Crimean and post-Mutiny Army had been tested and not found wanting.

However, the deeper lessons of policy and statecraft were soon being pointed out in the columns of the more influential newspapers and periodicals. 'June is not yet out', ran the editorial of the *Illustrated London News*, 'and the military expedition to Abyssinia, so reluctantly determined upon, so carefully organised, so wonderfully successful, has come to a close.' After a laudatory summary of Sir Robert Napier's achievement and a survey of the difficulties overcome, the editor hailed the campaign as 'the most astonishing feat of modern days. It was a triumph of which science may well be proud; and it shows how large a part science will hereafter bear in military administration.' The real pith of the article came in the final paragraphs. After enthusing on the discomfiture of Britain's military critics, and the object-lesson in moderation that the rulers and soldiers of the British Empire had provided for the hostile powers who dared to accuse Victorian England of unscrupulous imperial aggrandisement and insatiable colonial appetite, the editor put his finger on the real issue at stake. 'But we must learn a lesson for ourselves, as well as impress one upon others. We have been taught by costly experience how necessary it is to keep ourselves clear from political contact with nations that are not yet sufficiently advanced in civilisation to conform to the canons of international good faith and decorous demeanour. We have been too much in the habit of leaving the contingency of peace or war in the hands of subordinates, naturally over-zealous in magnifying their office and their personal importance at our risk. There was no conceivable need for our setting down a Consul on the African side of the Red Sea. To an experimental appointment of this kind we are indebted for an expedition which will cost us something upward of £5,000,000. Government will, we trust, be chary in future in opening consular stations at out-of-the-way places, and will firmly resist being dragged into political relations with barbarous chieftains. We can ill-afford a perpetual succession of "little wars". We have no right to expect that they will all end as fortunately as, thanks to Sir Robert Napier and his gallant army, the war in Abyssinia has ended.'[46]

As the next 30 years were to show, this plea for a policy of non-involvement was to prove a very pious hope. The future was to hold a whole succession of 'little wars', many of them in Africa.

As a postscript to Napier's Abyssinian campaign, it is interesting to note the scale and effect of a similar rescue operation which took place on the African continent 94 years later. To rescue more than a thousand Europeans from the hands of the Congolese rebels at Stanley-ville and Paulis in 1964 required a force of 600 Belgian paratroops and 14 American transport aircraft, operating from the British airfields of Ascension Island. The entire operation took only four days (25–29 November). A comparison of the scale and length of this expedition with the facts of Napier's campaign certainly reveals dramatic changes over the course of a century—and yet the basic humanitarian motivation of the two operations was identical. It is also interesting to note the international repercussions of these two highly successful incidents. In 1868 certain powers—most notably Turkey—chose to misrepresent the British intention as a concealed attempt to extend the bounds of the Empire. In 1964, amongst the many international protests caused by the rescue operation in the Congo, was a denunciatory statement issued by the Ethiopian Minister of Information, who claimed that the incident must be 'considered as a shameful and disgraceful action . . . a veritable manifestation of neo-colonialism on the African scene'.[47] Memories clearly die hard in Abyssinia.

References

1 Capt H. M. Hozier. *The British Expedition to Abyssinia.* London: Macmillan, 1869; p. 11.
2 H. M. Stanley. *Coomassie and Magdala.* London: Sampson Low, 1874; p. 451.
3 Major T. J. Holland and Capt H. M. Hozier. *Record of the Expedition to Abyssina, compiled by order of the Secretary of State for War.* London: H.M.S.O., 1870; vol. I, p. 9.
4 Ibid., vol. I, p. 11.
5 Lt-Col H. D. Napier. *Field Marshal Lord Napier of Magdala,* London: Edward Arnold, 1927; p. 203.
6 H. M. Stanley, op. cit., p. 352.
7 Hozier, op. cit., p. 62.
8 Napier, op. cit., p. 204.
9 Ibid., p. 206. (Viceroy's letter of 25th August 1867.)
10 Ibid., p. 207. (Viceroy's letter of 31st (sic) September.)
11 Ibid., p. 209.
12 Ibid., p. 211.
13 Hozier, op. cit., pp. 61–2. For a full list of stores provided from England, see Holland and Hozier, op. cit., vol. I, chapter IV.
14 *Professional Papers of the Corps of Royal Engineers,* Woolwich, 1870. Vol. XVII (New Series), Paper XI, p. 142.

15 Lt W. W. Scott, *Letters from Abyssinia during the Campaign of 1868.* Privately printed, London, 1868; p. 1.

16 Field Marshal Lord Napier of Magdala, *Letters of Field Marshal Lord Napier of Magdala concerning Abyssinia etc.* (ed. by Lt-Col H. D. Napier). London, 1936; p. 15.

17 Napier, op. cit. (see 5, above), pp. 223–4.

18 *Professional Papers*, op. cit., vol. XVII (New Series), Paper XI, p. 144.

19 Ibid., vol. XVIII (New Series), Paper XII, p. 165.

20 Holland and Hozier, op. cit., vol. I, p. 391.

21 Scott, op. cit., p. 39.

22 Ibid., p. 51.

23 Ibid., p. 84.

24 Stanley, op. cit., p. 444.

25 Holland and Hozier, op. cit., vol. II, pp. 34–5.

26 Napier, op. cit., p. 232.

27 Scott, op. cit., p. 110.

28 Col L. I. Cowper. *The King's Own—the Story of a Royal Regiment.* Oxford, 1939, vol. II, p. 158.

29 Scott, op. cit., p. 110.

30 Holland and Hozier, op. cit., vol. II, p. 37.

31 Hozier, op. cit., p. 204.

32 Napier, op. cit., p. 233.

33 Holland and Hozier, op. cit., vol. II, p. 48.

34 Scott, op. cit., p. 120.

35 Stanley, op. cit., p. 440.

36 Hozier, op. cit., p. 231.

37 Scott, op. cit., p. 130.

38 *Professional Papers* etc., op. cit., vol. XVII (New Series), Paper XII, p. 151.

39 *Memoirs of Ensign Wynter, 33rd Regiment*, p. 15—an unpublished source kindly made available by Brigadier B. W. Webb-Carter, D.S.O., O.B.E. Considerable parts of this account are quoted in his article for the *Journal of the Society for Army Historical Research*, vol XXXVIII, 1960; pp. 144–9.

40 Ibid., *S.A.H.R. Journal*, vol. XXXVIII, p. 149.

41 Holland and Hozier, op. cit., vol. II, p. 59.

42 Wynter, op. cit., Ms., p. 17.

43 E. T. Raymond. *Disraeli—the Alien Patriot.* London: Hodder and Stoughton, n.d.; p. 263.

44 H. Pearson. *Dizzy.* London: Methuen, 1951; p. 177.

45 Stanley, op. cit., p. 253.

46 The *Illustrated London News*, 27th June 1868, p. 622.

47 *Keesing's Contemporary Archives*, 1964, No. 20562.

Appendix

ORGANISATION OF
THE EXPEDITIONARY FORCE

w.e.f. early March 1868
(Simplified from tables in Holland and Hozier, Vol. I, pp. 428–30)

A. *Headquarters Staff*

Commander-in-Chief: Lieutenant-General Sir Robert Napier, K.C.B., G.C.S.I.

Deputy Adjutant-General: Colonel the Hon. F. A. Thesiger.

Deputy Quartermaster-General: Colonel R. Phayre (serving with Pioneer Force, First Division).

Assistant Quartermaster-General: Captain T. J. Holland (in temporary charge of Q.M.G. Department).

Military Secretary: Lieutenant-Colonel M. A. Dillen.

Assistant Military Secretary: Lieutenant H. M. Hozier.

Political Officer: Brigadier-General W. L. Merewether, C.B.

Intelligence Department: Major Grant, C.B.

Amharic Interpreter: Captain Speedy.

Aides-de-Camp: Lieutenant R. Napier; Lieutenant W. Scott; Lord C. Hamilton.

Headquarters Escort
10th Company, Royal Engineers.
25 sabres, 3rd Bombay Light Cavalry.

B. FIRST DIVISION. All troops from Antalo to the front.
Divisional Commander: Major-General Sir Charles Staveley, K.C.B.

Pioneer Force
Commander: Brigadier-General Field.
Troops: 40 sabres, 3rd Light Cavalry;
        40 sabres, 3rd Regiment Sind Horse.
        3rd and 4th Companies, Bombay Sappers and Miners.
        Two companies, 23rd Regiment, Punjab Pioneers.

First Brigade

Commander: Brigadier-General Schneider.

Troops: H.Q. Wing, 3rd Dragoon Guards (en route).

3rd Regiment Light Cavalry.

3rd Regiment Sind Horse.

'G' Battery, 14th Brigade, Royal Artillery (four Armstrong mountain guns).

'A' Battery, 21st Brigade, Royal Artillery (six 7-pounder mountain guns).

4th King's Own Royal Regiment.

H.Q. and eight companies of the 33rd Regiment (the Duke of Wellington's).

H.Q. and two companies of the 27th Regiment Native Infantry (Beloochees).

H.Q. Company ('wing') of the 10th Regiment Native Infantry.

Second Brigade

Commander: Brigadier-General Wilby.

Troops: H.Q. Wing, 12th Bengal Cavalry.

'B' Battery, 21st Brigade, Royal Artillery (six 7-pounder mountain guns).

Detachment, 5th Battery, 25th Brigade, Royal Artillery (two 8-in. mortars).

Rocket Battery, Naval Brigade (four rocket-tubes).

'K' Company, Madras Sappers and Miners.

H.Q. and seven companies, 23rd Regiment, Punjab Pioneers.

Detachment ('wing'), 27th Regiment Native Infantry (Beloochees).

(45th Regiment, the Sherwood Foresters, joined the Brigade on 8th April).

C. SECOND DIVISION. All troops at and from Zula to Antalo.
Divisional Commander: Major-General G. Malcolm, C.B.

Antalo Garrison

Commander: Brigadier-General Collings.

Troops: Wing, 12th Bengal Cavalry.
5th Battery, 25th Brigade, Royal Artillery (in fact detained at Zula).
'H' Company, Madras Sappers and Miners.
45th Regiment (The Sherwood Foresters)—joined First Division on 8th April.
3rd Regiment Native Infantry.
Detachment, 10th Regiment Native Infantry.

Adigrat Garrison
Commander: Major Fairbrother.
Troops: Squadron, 10th Bengal Cavalry.
'G' Battery, 14th Brigade, Royal Artillery (two guns).
2nd Company, Bombay Sappers and Miners.
Wing, 25th Regiment Native Infantry.

Senafé Garrison
Commander: Brigadier-General Stewart.
Troops: Squadron, 10th Bengal Cavalry.
1st Battery, Native Artillery.
Three companies, 21st Punjab Native Infantry.
Wing, 10th Regiment, Native Infantry.
Depots of all Regiments in the advance.
26th Cameronians (en route).

Zula Brigade. Composed of all troops at Zula and stationed in the passes.
Commander: Brigadier-General Russell.
Troops: Squadron, 10th Bengal Cavalry.
'G' Company, Madras Sappers.
1st Company, Bombay Sappers and Miners.
2nd Regiment, Native Infantry (Grenadiers).
18th Regiment, Native Infantry.
H.Q. and five companies, 21st Punjab Pioneers.
5th and 8th Bombay Native Infantry (on arrival).

The Ashanti Campaign
1873-4

The Ashanti Campaign
1873-4

John Keegan

'The white man brings his cannon to the bush but the bush is stronger than the cannon.'

KWAKU DUA,
King of Ashanti, 1838–67.

The shore of the Gulf of Guinea, from Cape Palmas to the delta of the Niger, was still divided by Victorian cartographers into the Ivory, Gold and Slave Coasts, so called from the exports which had characterised the first decades of trade between the European merchant venturers of the fifteenth century and the littoral tribes. But ivory and gold had early come to occupy a minor importance in the coasts' commerce: by the middle of the seventeenth century the West African trade was largely in slaves, by the end of the eighteenth almost wholly so, when some eighty thousand souls were embarked each year for the plantations of North and South America and the West Indies. Some were bought and transported by individual entrepreneurs, running perhaps a single ship a year on the triangular route from Europe to Africa and the Americas. Such men did not linger on the fever coast, cruising its length only long enough to complete a cargo. A more permanent European presence was provided by the tiny garrisons of the coastal forts built by the European trading states or their chartered monopoly companies. Nine had maintained fortified factories on the Gulf of Guinea, since the Portuguese set up their first at Elmina in 1482. The majority was concentrated along the shores of the modern State of Ghana, some forty in all belonging, in the main, to the English, Dutch and Danish companies; the rest to the French, the Brandenburger and the Portuguese.

But though the export in slaves was wholly in the hands of Europeans, they intervened in the business in Africa only at the point of outlet, buying the slaves wholesale at the gates of their castles from African brokers. These, chiefs or notables of the coastal tribes, were themselves middlemen whose profits came as much from the re-sale of trade goods—-textiles, metals, hardware, liquor and firearms—as from the traffic in flesh. The source of wholesale supply lay in and beyond the deep forests, regions which the coastal people did not visit and which were quite unknown to Europeans until the beginning of the nineteenth century. It was there that the working of the slave trade exerted its most important effect upon West African society.

Slavery was an established feature of West African society long before the Europeans came. 'Human beings could be born to slavery; they could be enslaved in punishment for a civil or criminal offence; they could sell or pledge their kin or even themselves in payment of or as surety for a debt; they could be enslaved as the result of capture in inter-tribal wars. [But] the domestic slave was not, as the slave was only apt to be on the American plantations, a mere beast of labour working in a gang of similar beasts. He was for the most part a member of the owner's household, an individual with recognised social rights.'[1] The institution, then, was almost a benevolent one; but with an important proviso: 'the status of slave could never be lost and, when necessity arose, or . . . human sacrifice became the vogue, an otherwise kind and considerate master would turn instinctively to the man who had no friend in the world, in order to satisfy the need for money or a victim';[2] there was, then, no moral or legal restraint to inhibit the West African slave-owner when the Europeans first indicated that slaves were an acceptable, even preferred, item of exchange for the goods their ships brought, as they began to do with the establishment of a plantation economy in the Americas during the sixteenth century.

But the number of souls readily enslaved was limited. As the market expanded, and individual kidnappings or enslavement for petty debt failed to meet the demand, tribes turned increasingly to raiding and to war to supply it, activities in which ready access to firearms gave the

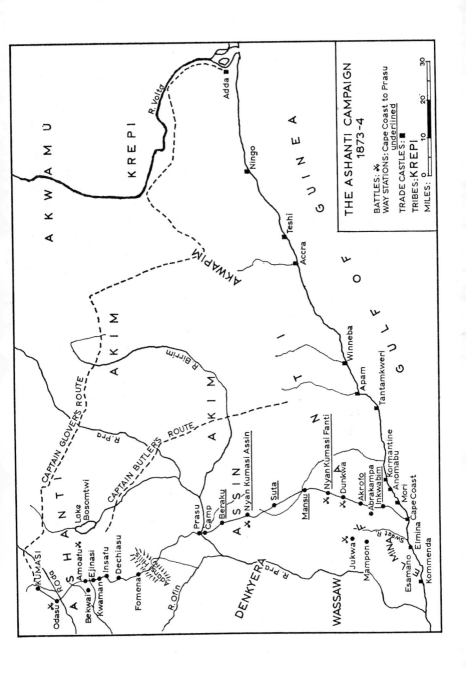

THE ASHANTI CAMPAIGN
1873-4

BATTLES: ✗
WAY STATIONS: Cape Coast to Prasu
<u>underlined</u>
TRADE CASTLES: ■
TRIBES: **KREPI**
MILES: 0 10 20 30

forest peoples advantages over their inland victims and in which large nations enjoyed security and opportunities denied to smaller. The history of West Africa during the three centuries of the Atlantic slave trade was destined then to be one of almost uninterrupted warfare and of the rise to power of strong martial states, of which the most notable and enduring were Oyo and Benin (in what is now Nigeria), Dahomey and Ashanti.

All owed their origin to a southerly movement of related Akan peoples, beginning a thousand years ago, from the Savannah belt below the Sahara into and through the deep forests between it and the narrow coastal plain. But those who achieved the sea did so only in small numbers. The forest barrier itself provided a favourable environment for settlement so that there were already by the fourteenth century populous and important states established within it. The circumstances which elevated Ashanti to power among them are unclear, for its history, like that of its neighbours, has come down through oral traditions alone, traditions moreover long guarded as tribal secrets and further obscured by the duty the Ashanti enforced upon tribes newly subjugated to accept the paramount power's history as their own. But it would seem that, at the beginning of the seventeenth century, the chiefs of Kumasi, at that time a minor forest kingdom, assumed the leadership of other small Ashanti states in order to resist the advance of the powerful Doma people. The struggle was protracted but eventually successful.

Tradition is quite specific about the turn events next took. Osei Tutu, Chief of Kumasi, 1679–1731, and his chief priest, Okomfo Anokye, determined that this loose military confederacy must be transformed into a more lasting union. It is impossible now to assess the weight of economic and strategic motive behind this decision. But the power of the Doma to the west had been checked, not overthrown, while to the east lay the mighty Kingdom of Denkyera to which the Ashanti, like most neighbouring Akan peoples, was tributary. Clearly there existed a strong material incentive to formalise the association between the Ashanti states; but no reference to it nor any account of the necessary diplomatic negotiations finds a place in the story of the making of the union, which has come down only in the form of a myth. It is a myth, however, which is central to the Ashanti's picture of their past. The myth-making was deliberate for the peculiar genius of Osei

Tutu, or more probably of Okomfo Anokye, lay in recognising that only by the enlistment of spiritual and magical powers could loyalty to a central government be implanted among the states of the confederacy. The first step seems to have been the creation of a commonly recognised throne or stool, located at Kumasi. The second was the bringing down, at a great meeting of chiefs and peoples there one Friday, of a Golden Stool which alighted on Osei Tutu's knees and was declared to embody henceforth the spirit of the Ashanti nation, whose power would prevail as long as the stool itself was kept from harm. Upon it the assembled chiefs swore fealty. Though one may find it difficult to accept unreservedly the circumstances of the Golden Stool's arrival, there can be no question that Osei Tutu and Anokye had provided a remarkably enduring and powerful focus for Ashanti national feeling, a feeling which was to carry them far along the road to power in West Africa during the next two hundred years.

The first step was clearly the overthrow of Denkyera which in 1699 obligingly but unwisely anticipated events, attacked and was defeated. Much of its territory was annexed while its westernmost clients took the opportunity to cast off their allegiance. Ashanti was thus established as the chief forest power of the Gold Coast and for the next fifty years was, despite temporary setbacks, to carry its conquests far beyond its original frontiers. At Osei Tutu's accession these had enclosed a territory some thirty by forty miles. At mid-century, the Ashanti empire extended 150 miles to east and west and some ninety north and south. Without lay a ring of states, Banda, Gyana and Bono beyond the rain forest to the north, Akim, Assin and the range of Denkyera to the south, over which Ashanti claimed authority and from which it drew tribute.

But, though the Ashanti were well-nigh invincible in war they seemed unable to consolidate their conquests and to transform them into a peaceful community. For this there were two reasons. Firstly, the Ashanti system, which gave a conquered chief a place on the national council and left him internal autonomy in return for guarantees of military service, worked well only with states closely akin to the original members of the union. The outer vassals, however, had well-established histories and identities of their own, and though Ashanti was in many respects a highly developed state with a well-regulated constitution and legal code, it seemed unable to create the sort of strong imperial administration which alone could have kept them subject.

It was forced therefore to live *toujours en vedette* and to hold what it had by threat of force. But more important were economic pressures. European goods, in particular firearms, were an expensive commodity in the interior and Ashanti, like the other forest powers, soon found that only by slave-raiding could it assure large regular purchases of these necessaries. Hence the incessant marauding which took their armies at times as far as the upper Volta. Moreover, the Ashanti were not content to act as mere wholesalers. Direct access to the sea, which Benin and Dahomey had already achieved, would clearly improve the terms of trade, both in the export of slaves and the distribution of European imports. Their gaze turned more frequently and unkindly towards the Fanti middlemen of the coast.

The Fanti states, many in number but all small and unwarlike, had responded to the threat of Ashanti expansion, first sensed through southward pressure from the buffer states, by entering towards the end of the century into a loose confederation. Its principal object was mutual defence, but an important subsidiary was the settlement of terms of trade, for monopoly offered obvious advantages in the Gold Coast where all movement of goods began or ended in Fanti territory. There were also advantages to be wrung from presenting a united front to the British and Dutch whose forts were interspersed and whose companies were usually at odds. Neither enjoyed extraterritorial rights (the 'Notes' by which they held their forts were much prized as spoils: Ashanti had captured that for Dutch Elmina in the Denkyera war) and by playing upon their antagonisms the Fanti extracted regular profits in bribes and subsidies.

The Fanti, however, overestimated the security which association conferred, for when first directly confronted by Ashanti power in 1806 they decided to resist and were swiftly and thoroughly defeated. More importantly for European interests, the British had taken their side. The case concerned an issue of suzerainty: an Assin chief had fled from Ashanti justice, been granted sanctuary by the Fanti and then offered refuge, with his followers, by the British. Torrane the Governor, was, however, quite unable to resist the Ashanti force which arrived to recover them and handed the fugitive chief, Otibu, over to torture and his people to slavery. He was also compelled to recognise Ashanti title to his forts and their rights of conquest over the Fanti. They, however, and the buffer states would not acquiesce; their attitude provoked two further Ashanti descents in 1811 and 1814 and these were decisive. By 1816 there was no power between the forest and the sea to oppose the Asantehene's will. The buffer states were overawed, the Fanti broken; the Dutch, who had lost two of their forts to his attack, were quite humiliated, and as for the English, 'from the hour Torrane delivered up Otibu,' the Asantehene Osei Bonsu later said, 'I took [them] for my friends, because I saw their object was trade only and they did not care for the people'.[3]

In this he was of course mistaken. The Ashanti's achievement of access to the sea had coincided with the parliamentary victory of the abolitionists; its concrete advantages were thus jeopardised as soon as gained. Moreover the abolitionists had, besides the influence to insure naval enforcement, the firm conviction that preventive action was not enough, a conviction reinforced by a net rise in the export of slaves, from 80,000 to 125,000 annually, between 1810 and 1830. It was inevitable, they argued, that while there was a trans-Atlantic market, there would be smugglers to serve it and, unless offered viable commercial alternatives, African slave-raiders and brokers to supply it. They came to define their objects, then, as 'the overturning of the Slave Trade by civilisation, Christianity and the cultivation of the soil' and 'the deliverance of Africa by calling forth her own resources'. A beginning had already been made by the establishment of the colony for freed men at Sierra Leone which, after initial setbacks, had become the bridgehead for that range of activities, commercial, agricultural, educational and missionary, which the abolitionists expected to transform the quality of African life.

They had however underestimated the extent to which slaving was interwoven with the fabric of West Africa's economy. 'Calling forth her own resources' meant in practice not much more than encouraging the trade in palm oil, whose production was confined to the coastal states; it neither could nor did tempt away the peoples of the interior from their ingrained habit of slave-raiding. As the African Company protested in 1809, it was too much to expect that 'natives of the vast continent of Africa . . . [should] contribute to and even acquiesce in the destruction of a trade not inconsistent with their prejudices, their laws or their notions of morality and religion and by which alone they have been hitherto accustomed to acquire wealth and purchase all the foreign luxuries and conveniences of life'.[4] Official action at sea and the private endeavours ashore of missionaries and legitimate traders were to prove an insufficiently effective combination in bringing West Africa out of slavery. But since Britain from the first committed herself to the trade's extinction, the unforeseen and unwished consequences of the abolitionists' victory was the certainty of direct and deepening involvement in the native affairs of the coast and its hinterland.

But in the immediate aftermath of abolition, it seemed by no means certain that Britain would any longer maintain her presence there. Freetown in Sierra Leone was essential as a base for the preventive squadron, but the trade forts cost more in subsidies than they returned in revenue. Since the African Company which staffed them 'had been formed largely to promote the slave trade, its survival after 1807 was anomalous'[5] and no government of the time was anxious to take on the administration of unprofitable colonies. Had the country been at peace, Parliament might well have abandoned the coast to the navy but when, in 1816, it at last found time for a decision, opinion had moved against withdrawal. The imperfections of naval blockade had emerged and the continued activities of the slavers, often under the very walls of the forts, had become a scandal. The abolitionists used these as arguments in securing the transfer in March 1822 of the Gold Coast forts to the Governor of Sierra Leone Colony.

This departure proved, however, a false start to the colonial era, for direct British control lasted only six years. It was beset by difficulties from the start. Some of these stemmed from genuine misunderstandings between the British and the Ashanti over coastal suzerainty and title to the forts, matters exacerbated, if anything, by treaties in 1817 and 1820. But the real trouble lay deeper. Though both wanted order on the coast, neither wanted the bother of ruling the Fanti. To complicate affairs, while the Ashanti regarded the Fanti as their vassals (though the Fanti themselves did not), they held the British, because of their *de facto* jurisdiction, responsible for Fanti good behaviour. And that in its strictest sense, for the Asantehene, whose power was essentially feudal in character, was prone to take offence at the smallest slights. The Fanti knew this. Sir Charles McCarthy, the new Governor, did not. It is possible that he did not care for he was dedicated to the abolitionist cause and when, within weeks of his appointment, the Asantehene declared himself insulted over some trifling affront by a Fanti policeman, he put the coast into a state of defence. Not content, however, with re-inforcing the white garrison, he suspended arms shipments to the interior, organised a Fanti militia and put out feelers to the buffer states. Thoroughly provoked, the Asantehene mobilised his whole army and on 22 January 1824, caught the Governor, who had quixotically ordered an advance, near the border village of Bonsaso. Sir Charles, whose force numbered under five hundred, had 'God Save the King' played, apparently in the belief that it might move disaffected contingents in the Ashanti host to change sides, but without avail. The Ashanti came on in hordes in their traditional crescent formation and he and almost all his men were overwhelmed. He fell wounded and, fearing torture, took his own life. The Ashanti, however, had been much impressed by his intrepidity; they removed his head and bore it back with them to Kumasi where, its features long recognisable, it was customarily carried in procession at the more important state ceremonies.

This indignity was fairly swiftly avenged. Because the Ashanti's purpose had been to discomfit the subordinate Fanti they did not, during their two years' campaign on the coast, move against the forts whose Governor, Hope Smith, was thus left free to organise countermeasures. On 7 August 1826, with 11,000 men, he brought them to battle at Dodowa, near Accra. The fighting was confused and very bitter, since he had enlisted strong contingents from Akim, Denkyera and other traditional enemies of the Ashanti, but the battlefield was in open country, which did not suit Ashanti tactics, and his army was equipped with Congreve rockets, whose discharge at the moment of crisis put the panic-stricken Ashanti to flight.

It took longer to bring them to terms, for the Fanti insisted on a campaign of revenge against the Elmina people, their former coastal allies. But in 1831, when all fighting had at last simmered down, a new Governor, George Maclean, succeeded in negotiating satisfactory terms with Kumasi. These provided for the giving of two princely hostages (who were taken to England for education and were later to be present at Queen Victoria's coronation), the deposit of securities, the abjuration of rights over the Fanti and the forts, the fostering of free trade and the reference of disputes between the signatories, who included all the Dodowa combatants, to Cape Coast. This treaty 'settled the relations between the British and the coastal peoples on the one hand, and the Ashanti on the other for the next forty years. In half that time, it is true, peace was greatly endangered but the treaty of 1831 was regarded as containing the normal footing on which the affairs of the Gold Coast should stand.'⁶

The British Government, however, was less than constant in its own Gold Coast policies during that period. Maclean, for example, though negotiating in the name of the Crown, was not its servant, for the Government had chosen the battle of Dodowa as a suitable occasion to relinquish direct control. It had wished to disengage completely but, in the face of mercantile protests, had eventually granted a committee of London merchants a small annual subsidy to administer the forts, provided its jurisdiction was confined to their immediate limits. Maclean however was a remarkable man; the Fanti sought his adjudication in disputes so frequently that his thirteen years' governorship effected a marked increase in British influence. Encouraged by the efficiency and cheapness of his administration, and prodded by the second wave of abolitionists, the Government resumed control in 1842; but when it tried to formalise the relationships he had fostered, by persuading the Fanti and buffer states to enter into 'Bonds' guaranteeing the rule of law it was less successful; his achievement had been personal. Moreover the informal 'Protectorate' thus established was as strong or weak as the Government chose to make it.

During the forties and fifties, under abolitionist pressure, British involvement was strong: in 1850, the Government bought out the Danes from their forts, extended protection to their client states and made Cape Coast independent of Sierra Leone; in 1852 it encouraged the Fanti chiefs to found a legislative council; and in 1853, challenged by one of Ashanti's recurrent claims to suzerainty in the buffer states, it made a resolute show of force and outfaced them. But in the sixties, British policy weakened. In the most important affair of the decade, a further instalment of the suzerainty question, we first acquiesced in an Ashanti occupation of the Protectorate, sent reinforcements when they retreated with the rains, then refused permission for an advance into Ashanti but sent more West Indian troops, and finally sanctioned an invasion by an even stronger force but when disease began to reduce their numbers at an alarming rate, withdrew them. The Asantehene fortunately felt honour satisfied and, though reserving his claim, did not re-invade. The Government however had lost all taste for a firm West African policy. Admiral Hay, whose brother had died in the camp at Prasu, nearly carried a vote of censure through the House of Commons, and the subsequent Select Committee recommended that though it was 'not possible to withdraw . . . wholly or immediately . . . all further extension of territory or assumption of government would be inexpedient . . . and that the object . . . should be . . . more and more to transfer [to Africans] the administration . . . with a view to our ultimate withdrawal'.[7]

Within nine years Britain was to have launched a major military expedition against Ashanti, defeated its armies and occupied Kumasi. What lay behind this total reversal of policy?

The explanation is not to be found in any sudden increase in the coast's commercial importance: indeed the annual value of Gold Coast trade remained stable at about £500,000 while the cost of administering the settlements tripled to £170,000; nor in any surge of public enthusiasm to take up the white man's burden; nor in an internal revolution at the Colonial Office. It lay in the Government's response to a series of crises on the Gold Coast itself, crises precipitated by persistence in traditional policies. In 1867, Britain and Holland agreed, in the hope of operating an effective tariff and so offsetting budgetary losses, to consolidate their interests into two blocs, the Dutch to the west, the British to the east of Elmina. The Africans of the British towns listed for exchange objected, however, to losing her protection. The Kommenda people in particular were so outraged that they took up arms against their new masters and were joined first by other Fanti contingents, then by those of Wassaw and Denkyera, whose informal dependence on British support had also been written away by the same measure and who knew they could expect mere appeasement of the Ashanti by the Dutch in times of trouble. Inevitably this 'New Fanti Confederation' soon turned its attention against Elmina which responded vigorously, no doubt expecting that Kumasi would come shortly to its rescue.

Ashanti, however, was temporarily unable to intervene since its court was in uproar over an incident preceding the 'enstoolment' of the new Asantehene, Kofi Karikari; by an unfortunate mistake, the nephew of an important general had been included in the quota of royal attendants selected for ritual sacrifice. It was not until late in 1868 that the even tenor of court life was sufficiently restored for consideration to be given to Elmina. But the decisions then taken were of far greater moment than anyone on the coast could have expected. They were for nothing less than a comprehensive attempt to reverse the tide of events which had set against Ashanti since the implementation of abolition sixty years before.

It is difficult to establish what effect abolition had had upon Ashanti society. The most obvious was an increase in the practice of human sacrifice since the cash value of captives had so declined. It would be tempting further to argue that the denial of Atlantic outlets had depressed Ashanti purchasing power to intolerable levels; but too little is known of the mechanics of inland trade in Victorian Africa. What evidence there is suggests that Ashanti had found some compensation in the internal slave traffic and in the transit trade. Its principal trouble, and that it was a troubled kingdom is undoubted, seems to have stemmed ultimately from a failure to adapt its ethos to changed times. For it had carried forward all the arrogance and aggressiveness of a slave-raiding state into an age when slave-raiding no longer provided any real basis for power in the land. Indeed like many societies stranded by change, it had tended to exaggerate its traditional characteristics. Above all, it resented the erosion of its authority over peoples which had once trembled at rumours of its anger. Under Kwaku Dua, a wise and long-lived Asantehene, these traits had been moderated. But his youthful successor had fallen into the hands of a faction who saw in the withdrawal of British protection from Wassaw and Denkyera the opportunity to re-assert over them those feudal rights whose loss so rankled. The plan they devised called not simply for an expedition to Elmina but for two other thrusts, one on to the lower Volta and the eastern Protectorate, and one in greater strength down the Kumasi–Cape Coast axis (though whether this was to be directed against the forts themselves is unclear).

The triple thrust would take time to prepare, however, and the main effort was postponed. But the Elmina and Volta expeditions, the former a small one under a general named Akyeapom, the latter much larger under Adu Bofo, set off at the end of 1868. Both were delayed for much of 1869, Akyeapom over rights of passage through neighbouring states (Wassaw and Denkyera had naturally closed the direct route), Adu Bofo by the determined resistance of the Krepi with whose enemies, the Akwamu, Ashanti had made alliance. Akyeapom did not therefore reach Elmina until late in 1869 and brought little more than moral support to its people. Adu Bofo was so unsuccessful that he was forced to give hostages as surety for good behaviour. Both expeditions, however, returned some important results. At Anum, in the Krepi country, Adu Bofo captured two German missionaries who provided Kumasi with valuable bargaining counters. And, with Akyeapom in Elmina, Ashanti reinforcements expected, and trade at a standstill, Holland decided to leave the Gold Coast for good.

She had already shown signs of wishing to quit but the decisive influence on her African policy stemmed from the instalment in 1868 of a colonial secretary with strong views on retrenchment. It was De Waal's belief, reinforced by the opening of the Suez route in 1869, that Holland should concentrate colonial expenditure in the East Indies. His eagerness to be rid of Elmina and the other stations was tempered only by his anxiety to extract British agreement to an extension of Dutch sovereignty in Sumatra. But by the end of 1871 he seemed to have persuaded both capitals to accept cession. Dutch traditionalists were mollified by the prospect of Asiatic compensations, British non-extensionists by the representation of cession as an economy, since divided administration was believed principally to underlie the expensive feuding.

It seemed too that Kumasi was prepared to swallow cession, for although the Asantehene had at its first rumour in 1870 objected in the strongest terms, claiming that Elmina had 'from time immemorial paid annual tribute to my ancestors by right of arms' and that 'the Dutch delivered [it] to Osei Tutu as his own',[8] he did not press the claim and the Dutch were able to persuade Lord Kimberley, the Colonial Secretary, that the Elmina Note was 'a mere record of an agreement to pay an annual free gift for the encouragement of trade'.[9] Later next year the Asantehene sent ambassadors who conceded that he had exaggerated, and in August despatched a written 'Certificate of Apologie' whose genuineness the ambassadors confirmed. The Elmina people maintained their objection, thus delaying ratification until early in 1872, but were eventually persuaded that resistance was fruitless and in March agreed to the banishment of Akyeapom whose continued stay occasioned London's last objection. On 6 April, a new Governor of the West African Settlements, John Pope Hennesy, arrived to implement the transfer.

Hennessy, 'who has strong claims to be regarded as the worst colonial governor of the nineteenth century',[10] spent exactly a year on the coast. Almost every act of his governorship was a miscalculation, but none more so than his negotiations for the release of the missionaries. Believing appeasement the best form, he first arranged for the Elmina stipend to be not merely continued but doubled, then for the arms embargo to be lifted, finally, when the Asantehene demanded double his offer of ransom, for the hostages whom Adu Bofo had given in 1869 to be sent home. Since it now seems clear that each Ashanti démarche, from the original despatch of ambassadors to their verification of the 'Certificate of Apologie', was a calculated move to gain time for re-armament, he played into their hands. The 1869 campaign had been essentially opportunistic in origin. The cession of Elmina which the Ashanti chose to regard as an integral part of the kingdom, imposed by contrast the necessity for a war *à outrance*. On 9 December 1872, their munitions replenished, the Asantehene's armies left Kumasi for the front.

The plan again was for three thrusts. Adu Bofo, marching this time on the western flank, was to lead five thousand warriors against Wassaw and Denkyera, while a small diversionary force raided eastwards against Akim. The main body, of at least twelve thousand (estimates of its eventual strength are as high as forty thousand) under Amankwa Tia, was to march straight down the main Kumasi–Cape Coast road. It reached the Pra on 22 December and, after a delay attributed to a well-timed stroke of human sacrifice by a chief on the opposite bank, crossed and assembled around Atasi where it sacked several villages and skirmished successfully with an Assin force, losing three men whose heads were sent down to the coast as evidence of the invasion.

The news at first caused little stir there. The Governor refused to believe it. Pope Hennessy, who was about to leave, denied that it was an invasion. His successor, Robert Keate, feeling that even if it were the Ashanti would not attack the forts, declined to send reinforcements from Freetown and warned the Fanti, in the spirit of the 1865 report (p. 173), that they must depend upon their own exertions. For this they might have been better prepared had his predecessors not so intemperately squashed the New Fanti Confederation's attempts, in 1871, to make itself an effective body. As it was, the Ashanti were opposed piecemeal and were able to defeat each contingent in turn. On 9 February 1873, the Assin were beaten at Assin Nyankumasi and forced back on to Fanti Nyankumasi, only thirty miles from Cape Coast. Reinforced there by many Fanti, some Denkyera and a token troop of Hausa police under a British officer, they were again beaten and fell back four miles to Dunkwa. Much reinforced, they were able, on 8 and 14 April, to hold their positions, despite the arrival of Adu Bofo to Amankwa Tia's assistance, but they could not then bring themselves to carry the battle to the enemy and opted for a further retreat to the coast, during which most of the army dispersed. Fortunately the Ashanti, disheartened by casualties and their already considerable losses from disease, had themselves been preparing to withdraw and did not at once follow.

It was now obvious even to the most complacent that the allies would need more than exhortation to stiffen them. It seemed moreover by no means certain that the Ashanti would spare the forts. Accordingly, at the news of Dunkwa, a meeting was convened between Lord Kimberley, Edward Cardwell, Secretary of State for War, and G. J. Goschen, First Lord of the Admiralty, to consider their protection, and it was agreed as not inconsistent with the Government's policy of non-extension to order four companies of the West Indian Regiment from Barbados and to send a hundred marines to Elmina.

That the cession of Elmina underlay the invasion was a conclusion that had at last begun to glimmer through the confusion of news from the coast. On 20 March 1873, the Asantehene had told the Administrator as much by letter, though he also laid claim to Denkyera, Akim and Assin, which he had specifically foresworn in 1831. And a week earlier the King of Elmina, in refusing to swear an oath of allegiance, had made it plain that he had long expected Ashanti relief. Thus, while Kimberley had had to confess ignorance of the invasion's cause in the House of Lords on 7 March, by early May Knatchbull-Hugessen, his Parliamentary Under-Secretary, was able to tell the House of Commons that 'the invasion was the result of the cession of Elmina . . . and that [the Asantehene] was determined to retake it'.[11]

It seemed however as May drew into June that the crisis might evaporate. Confidence in the rightness of non-extension revived. Kimberley wrote: 'If we wish to weaken ourselves we cannot adopt a better course than . . . conquering Ashantee and establishing a West African Empire. It is to be hoped that no Government will be mad enough to embark on so extravagant a policy.'[12] There was no news at all during June, which boded well and the Ashanti question, which

Kimberley had begun to think must be raised in Cabinet, disappeared from Government business.

The calm was spurious: two mail ships had been lost. On 10 June, the worst news yet reached London. On 5 June, the Ashanti, who had left Dunkwa and drifted westwards towards the rallying-ground of the Denkyeras, had fallen upon them and their Fanti followers and destroyed them at Jukwa. A flood of refugees, soon swollen by women and children, had poured down to Cape Coast where some twenty thousand huddled around the fort, a number quite beyond the power of the garrison to feed or safeguard. The victory had brought the Ashanti to within a day's march of Elmina and on 13 June, to forestall a *coup de main* by their supporters, the marine detachment had been landed in the town and fought a sharp, though successful, action.

Kimberley was thoroughly alarmed. On 15 July he arranged for another two hundred marines to be sent and for four companies of an infantry battalion to be held ready. *The Times* meanwhile called for the despatch of Gordon, echoed on the 24th by the *Daily News*, on the grounds that he was 'the best leader of irregulars that the world contains'.[13] But Kimberley was moving away from the belief that affairs might be settled by a local force. On 26 July he advised Cape Coast they might tell the Fanti that 'while HMG expected them to do their best to defend themselves, they will on their part give them cordial and active support to end this disastrous war' and wrote to Cardwell about organising such support: 'We cannot leave [the Ashanti] quietly in occupation of the Protectorate. Public opinion would not allow us to do so, if we ourselves desired it. . . . Are we to contemplate an attack on Coomassie and could we assemble a force sufficient enough for the purpose?' These were questions the two preferred to keep meanwhile to themselves. The only initiative which the Cabinet was asked to approve before it dispersed on 2 August was the financing of a native diversion on the Volta, under the remarkable Captain Glover, R.N.

Nevertheless there is little doubt that Kimberley and Cardwell had by now privately agreed to jettison the policy of non-extension and, for the first time, to commit European troops. The appointment on 13 August of Sir Garnet Wolseley as Administrator and Commander-in-Chief on the Gold Coast merely set the cap on consultations of some long standing between the three. Cardwell had arranged for his protégé to prepare expeditionary plans perhaps as early as May, minuting them when complete, 'Sir Garnet Wolseley ... is now ready to capture Kumasi'.[14] And Kimberley himself seems to have decided well before August that less extreme measures would no longer serve. When his first choice as Administrator, a witness at the 1865 Committee, proposed a simple clearing of the Protectorate, he rejected it and transferred his favour to Wolseley and his far more ambitious project. They sensed however that neither the Cabinet nor the country was yet ready to accept open preparations for a white expedition into the deep forests. Kimberley therefore gave Gladstone no warning of Wolseley's appointment nor did he allow the latter's instructions to commit the Government to the use of white troops.

Wolseley's instructions however left him wide discretion to recommend all necessary means, and in fact he had decided from the first for a white expedition and for directing it into the heart of Ashanti. Though he offered to begin by taking 'a number of specially selected officers for the purpose of raising an efficient native force, if that were possible ... to drive back the Ashantee ... and secure our possessions', he added that 'all the information ... gathered ... made me think it would be impossible to accomplish what was wanted without ... white troops' and he therefore warned Cardwell that while he would do his best 'to avoid the terrible necessity of having to employ our soldiers in such a climate', it was 'essential to have two first-rate battalions told off ... for a campaign beyond the Prah' should he send for them.[15] The exceptional calibre of his staff suggests, too, that he had more in mind than a pacification of the coast with native levies. Of his chosen twenty-seven—and he had the pick of the Army—almost everyone was later to distinguish himself in command, in combat or with the pen.* But the appointment of Wolseley himself was the

* The 'Wolseley Ring' on the Ashanti expedition included: Major G. Colley (afterwards Major-General Sir George Colley), Lieutenant-Colonel E. Wood, VC (afterwards Field-Marshal Sir Evelyn Wood), Captain R. Buller (afterwards General the Right Hon. Sir Redvers Buller), Lieutenant-Colonel McNeill, VC (afterwards General Sir John McNeill), Major G. Greaves (afterwards General Sir George Greaves), Major B. C. Russell (afterwards General Sir Baker Russell), Major T. D. Baker (afterwards General Sir Thomas Baker), Lieutenant F. Maurice (afterwards Major-General Sir Frederick Maurice), Captain W. Butler (afterwards Lieutenant-General Sir William Butler) and Captain H. Brackenbury (afterwards General Sir Henry Brackenbury). See Alan Lloyd. *The Drums of Kumasi*, Panther edition, 1965; p. 75.

strongest guarantee that the campaign would be pressed *à outrance*. At forty the youngest general in the army, he had already won a reputation as a ferocious warrior, a surpassingly able staff officer, a successful field commander and, most recently, an author and military polemicist. He had embraced wholeheartedly the cause of military modernisation, enjoyed the patronage of Cardwell, the protagonist of reform, and the hearty dislike of its opponents. His character, his achievements and his known views were argument enough that he would settle for nothing short of a clear-cut military decision. His instructions allowed him the latitude to attempt it.

He had first, however, to go through the motions of trying to settle things with local forces. On 27 September 1873, fifteen days after leaving Liverpool, Wolseley and his staff (henceforth to be known affectionately or derisively to the Victorian Army as 'the Ring') arrived at Freetown. There, and at Bathurst and Cape Palmas, he complied punctiliously with his instructions to raise men. The results were unspectacular: fewer than six hundred responded and these, filled out with Cape Coast militia and Hausa police, were sufficient to form two irregular regiments, known as Russell's and Wood's after their Colonels. The only disciplined force to hand was the 2nd West India Regiment which was broken up into small garrisons and could find only the smallest mobile detachment. On 4 October Wolseley, now at Cape Coast, held a palaver at Government House to persuade the Fanti and their allies to make up his manpower deficiencies. They were ready with promises but not with men. Wolseley himself found this understandable: 'Seeing that we left them entirely to themselves at the beginning . . . it is scarcely to be expected that . . . the whole of a much dispersed and dispirited people will suddenly come to believe in our serious intention vigorously to aid them. To get the people to act with that rapidity which . . . is essential we must act energetically ourselves.'[16]

To this end he at once assembled the most powerful striking force he could find and, putting it about that he was off to help Glover on the Volta, embarked it during the night of 13 October for a descent on the Ashanti encampments round Elmina. He had already summoned the headmen of that district to meet him in the castle where he would have warned them to cease providing the invaders with food, of which they were their principal suppliers. The chief of Esaman had answered, 'Come and get me: White man dare not go into the bush.'[17] Less than

half Wolseley's force was white but these two hundred swiftly dis-
abused the chief, striking directly into the coastal scrub, driving off
those who attempted ambush, putting a number of villages to fire and
retiring safely to their ships before nightfall.

The effect of this little fight was wholly salutary both in denying
food to the Ashanti and in heartening the allies. It raised Wolseley's
spirits too. But it had served other purposes: to demonstrate the
difficulty of controlling 'even the best native troops in his bush-
fighting', to lend weight to his conviction that 'the very best officers
and the most highly disciplined troops are alone capable of bringing
this war to a successful and speedy issue', as he argued in his report, and
to justify his request, already written on the eve of the action, for the
despatch of the European battalions.[18]

He had also on the 13th opened the correspondence with the
Asantehene as his instructions required. 'Your Majesty,' he had written,
'The Queen ... has heard, with profound concern, of your recent
doings. ... But ... as she is strong she is patient. ... She wishes only
well to the great Ashanti people [and] has sent me therefore to arrange
with you a lasting peace. As, however, it is not our custom to discuss
terms of peace with one who persists in an attitude of aggression, I have
to require as preliminaries to negotiation (1. Withdrawal by 12
November; 2. release of captives; 3. guarantee of compensation).
If you will ... consent ... I will be ready to treat you in a friendly
spirit. ... But if ... not ... I hereby warn you to expect the full
punishment your deeds have merited. ... Rest well assured that power
will not be wanting to that end ... Her Majesty's dominion reaches
far and wide over the earth. Against you ... she has hitherto never
found it necessary to employ more than an insignificant fraction of the
special forces which guard this petty corner of the vast realms which
own her as sovereign. ... How then, when [she] puts forth her might
against you, can you hope to resist her? ... I am,' the proconsul ended,
'your Majesty's well-wisher.'[19] No copy of this letter reached Kumasi.
One went astray. The other two were intercepted by Amankwa Tia,
still encamped at Mampon, and it was he who answered on 20 October.
'For what purpose I came here is that: Assin, Dunkwa, Akyem,
Wassaw. These four nations belong to [the Asantehene] and they
refused to serve and escaped away unto you. ... But the King did not
send me to Cape Coast, and then, you deliver [them] ... and I shall

N

bring to the King there is no any quarrel with you. I send my love to you.'[20] He then paraded the army before the messengers, who reported that it took two days to march past.

Yet despite their overwhelming superiority, the Ashanti were on the point of breaking camp. They had suffered heavily from disease and had already requested the Asantehene's permission, which was a prerequisite, to withdraw. He had refused, charging that 'You wished for war and you have it',[21] but they could now plead the defeat at Esaman and some ominous rumours of infiltration (in fact, the movement of a survey party) across their rear to excuse a disengagement. Amankwa Tia therefore sent off the sick on 16 October and prepared to follow with the main body. Its route home lay along minor tracks which would put it on the main road twenty miles north of Cape Coast. News of the decampment soon reached the British who at once undertook the reinforcement of their small posts along the road at Dunkwa, Abrakampa, Akrofo, and Mansu. On 23 October, a reconnaissance found an abandoned staging-camp on the route near Mampon where 'a rough drawing of a hand, traced in blood'[22] had been left to guide stragglers, and four days later a patrol under Colonel Festing from Dunkwa fell upon a large force near Iscabio. Wolseley, who had got firm word of the retreat from the fugitive slave-wife of an Ashanti chief on 25 October, hurried up from Cape Coast hoping to co-ordinate with Festing a dual attack against the Ashanti's flanks, but neither of their forces, still largely African in composition, dared to attack and the Ashanti got away. The manœuvre had however frustrated Amankwa Tia's strategy. He had divided his army into two, with the idea of attracting the British garrisons above Dunkwa on to his right wing which was then to disengage, rejoin the uncommitted left and march straight up the unblocked road to Prasu. But Wolseley had fastened upon his left and the garrisons had stood fast. He had therefore to fight his way on to the road, moving first against a sizeable force under Russell at Abrakampa. This, of about a thousand West Indians, sailors and men of Russell's Regiment, was well entrenched and withstood his assaults throughout 5–6 November. Wolseley, who had been alerted on the second day, reached the scene before nightfall; but his Africans were even more stubborn than before in their refusal to attack. Amankwa Tia, however, drew off and, despairing of clearing the road, ordered a parallel path to be hacked through the bush to a point above the northernmost British roadblock. Not until 26 November did the British again make touch with his army and it had by then regained the road and secured a two days' start. Its rearguard severely mangled the pursuit and by 29 November it had got clear away. The retreat was an achievement of which, Wolseley's private secretary wrote, 'the army of a civilised nation need not have been ashamed'.[23]

The Ashanti had just managed to preserve their constitutional proprieties for at the last moment and only on the war party's promise to reimburse the treasury for the cost of the campaign, the Asantehene had issued the necessary order of recall. Since he thus fulfilled the most important of Wolseley's conditions and since the army had lost half its strength, he and most of the council hoped that the British would call off the campaign. But Wolseley had the bit between his teeth. And the accounts in his published despatches of his allies' humiliating behaviour had won wide support for a more active prosecution of the war from the British public whose sensibilities were clearly outraged by disclosures of Ashanti barbarities; feelings which were shared by the Queen and which the Cabinet could not ignore. Its resolve had wavered during October, when Kimberley advised Wolseley that he would be satisfied with an honourable peace, but on receipt on 17 November of his request for the regular battalions (of which he now wanted three), the Cabinet at once consented and they sailed from Southampton two days later.

Much of the reluctance to commit this force, which had been standing by in barracks since early September, stemmed from the coast's reputation as 'the white man's grave, that dreaded bourne whence few travellers return',[24] and a great part of Wolseley's reports had been devoted to dispelling these apprehensions. He had maintained from the first that, were the campaign confined to the dry months, December to March, and were the troops got immediately off the coast and kept on the move, which was possible if a good road and way-stations were constructed before they arrived, a march on Kumasi would 'not involve great risk'.[25] Kimberley's instructions covering the use of the white battalions confined him closely to those terms. Besides reminding him that the aim was to conclude a peace satisfactory both to the British and to the Ashanti, whose legitimate desire for free trade deserved respect, and warning him that if the campaign were prosecuted too vigorously he might find no one with whom to treat at Kumasi, he made it clear that the Cabinet expected him to re-embark a largely undepleted force by March at the latest.

Arrangements for its reception had been set in hand within a week of his arrival. By 27 October the road had been cleared as far as Mansu, thirty-five miles inland, the sites for the seven way-stations at ten-mile intervals between Cape Coast and Prasu chosen and some fitted up. Each was to have hutted accommodation for four hundred soldiers, a hospital, water-purifier, and ablution and store sheds; two were to have bakeries and four, abattoirs. The forward base at Prasu, seventy miles from the coast and sixty from Kumasi, was an even more elaborate establishment, to house two thousand Europeans, with a hospital for a hundred patients, a magazine, battery, canteen, post office, headquarters and a two-hundred-foot bridge across the Pra, the largest of 237 constructed along the route.

These were provided rather to keep the soldiers dry than to ease their progress since dampness was believed the principal cause of disease; for the same reason all the huts had sleeping platforms. Teams of porters with travelling hammocks were to be stationed at each way-station to evacuate those who were nevertheless taken sick to the coast, where one regular and two auxiliary hospital ships lay off to receive them. There was a fourth for convalescents at St Vincent, and an arrangement for the Cape Town liners to embark patients for transfer to England or Gibraltar. These services were sufficient to deal with 450 sick a month and could at a pinch cope with 1,425, though such an incidence of sickness would have put an end to the expedition.

North of Mansu however the work of preparation became increasingly difficult. By 18 November, Major Robert Home, the responsible engineer, was only six miles further on and Wolseley's timetable, which depended on the road's completion by early December, was in jeopardy. Home's greatest difficulty lay in getting and keeping men, for whom he had to compete with both the tactical and transport staffs, while all were driven to despair by the inroads of desertion. For the Fanti had now apparently come to regard this war as a European affair, and though there was a superfluity of labour on the coast, the normal market processes were failing to attract it. Wolseley was constrained at this time to characterise his allies as 'too cowardly to fight their own battles and too lazy, even when well paid, to help those who are risking their lives in their cause'.[26]

This was not wholly fair, as he might privately have admitted, for during the first weeks the transport organisation was thoroughly mismanaged. The administrative services of the Army had undergone a paper transformation five years before but the established principle of civilian control had been perpetuated; it worked scarcely better in West Africa than in the Crimea. The commissaries were competent enough at landing stores in bulk at the base but the business of sending them forward to the troops, which demands a ready understanding of operational necessities, an easy intercourse with regimental officers and a capacity for handling men, was beyond them. But this fault, as Wolseley recognised, was not theirs; it was the belief on which the system was based, that separating administrative from operational responsibilities left a commander free to get on with winning battles, that was false. When, therefore, in December the Professor of Military Administration at the Staff College, Colonel Colley, arrived on the coast, Wolseley appointed him to his staff as commander of transport. He effected an immediate improvement in the system. Hitherto there had been no proper recording of payment, loads or journeys and the gangs had been thrown together without regard to the tribal origins of the porters or the gang chiefs who distributed pay. Colley reorganised the gangs on a tribal basis and put them under command of military officers. He also instituted the distinction between regimental and line-of-communication transport, dividing the latter into four groups and the road to Prasu into four stages. Each group was to work only along its own stage, the receipt for each gang's deliveries providing the sole authority for payment on its return to base. Regimental porters, conversely, were to remain permanently with their unit, their officers coming under its commander.

Admirably progressive though this system was, it did not wholly succeed in preventing desertion and it could not of itself procure men. By dint of disarming the levies, recruiting the splendidly energetic market women of Cape Coast and making peace with the suppliant chiefs of Elmina conditional upon the provision of porters, the transport corp's strength was got up from about 1,300 to 6,000 between 8 November and 22 December, sufficient to complete the road and establish the Prasu base. But most of these had been found while the civilian Control Department was still in charge and 'handing carriers over to [it]', wrote Wolseley, 'is like pouring water into a sieve; they run away after making a single journey'. Colley calculated on taking over that he needed at least 8,500 porters, 2,500 for daily subsistence, 2,500 for provisioning Prasu and 3,500 for regimental transport. The base at Prasu was to hold 1,100,000 rounds of Snider ammunition (expenditure was known from earlier skirmishes to be abnormally high in the bush) and thirty days' rations for 6,500 men—400 tons of food alone. Wolseley had been forced on 9 December to wave off the first transport of Europeans because these stores were not yet on site. When they returned the base was ready but the regimental porters suddenly lost all stomach for the march on Kumasi and made off in droves. At this Wolseley quite lost his patience. He warned the chiefs that without carriers he could not invade Ashanti and that, if he did not, the Ashanti would return; in earnest of his warning, he re-embarked the Royal Welch Fusiliers and the Royal Artillery detachment. The chiefs were at once profuse with offers to punish the deserters. Colley himself set off to drive the villages round Dunkwa; and at Agoonal, whose porters had deserted en masse and mistreated the messengers sent to recall them, he burnt the houses to the ground. This razzia did its work. Within a few days, the transport service was back to strength, stores were going forward and, by 19 January 1874, the European battalions were in camp at Prasu. Wolseley's timetable was less than a week behind.

The force at his disposal amounted, after the re-embarkments, to four thousand combatants: 1st Black Watch, 2nd Rifle Brigade, 2nd West India Regiment, 250 sailors, Russell's and Wood's Regiments and Captain A. J. Rait's Hausa Artillery. After regimental representations, a detachment of a hundred Royal Welch Fusiliers was included in the party; the rest of the battalion, as his original plan had provided, remained in reserve. The 1st West India Regiment, fresh from Jamaica, was left in support at Cape Coast. The British had shed their scarlet or rifle green, and the West Indians their zouave costume for sensible reach-me-down suits of grey homespun, and both were to carry the barest essentials on the person; the impedimenta held essential to life in the bush—veils, respirators, spare cholera-belts, groundsheets and tent halves—were borne by porters, one to three soldiers. All ranks had been taught the rudiments of health discipline and each man was to be dosed with quinine before the day's march.

Wolseley had also taken the unusual step of circulating to the troops his tactical instructions, a document remarkable for concealing its originality beneath much conventional exhortation. 'Fighting in the bush', he wrote, 'is very much like fighting in twilight; no one can see further than a few files to his right or left.' But because of the Ashantis' preference for envelopment, the troops would have to fight in open files and, despite the sub-division of companies into four sections and the distribution of officers and NCOs as widely as possible, would therefore have to exercise much of the fire-discipline and intercommunication themselves. They were not, however, to worry about their flanks (he intended to form a loose square at the approach of combat) nor to retire. Above all, they were to trust in their moral and material superiority and to conserve ammunition. 'Soldiers and sailors, remember that the black man holds you in superstitious awe: be cool; fire low, fire slow and charge home.'[27]

His tactics then were to be of the simplest. The strategic direction of the campaign was, in theory, far more demanding, for it entailed the co-ordination of four independent columns: his own, Captain Butler's, Captain Dalrymple's and Captain Glover's. The first were two of his own special service officers detached to recruit and lead contingents from the more martial of the allies. The third, a former Administrator of Lagos whose expansionist beliefs had incurred Pope Hennessy's displeasure, owed his appointment to Kimberley whom he had persuaded at the end of July, when there was still some hope of avoiding the commitment of regulars, to finance his raising an expedition against eastern Ashanti. He had subsequently been subordinated to Wolseley who allotted him, with the other two, a diversionary role. Dalrymple was to raise his standard among the Wassaws and cross into Western Ashanti by the Ofim, Butler to take a route east of and parallel to Wolseley's with an army of Akims, Glover to ascend the Volta from Accra and march across country into eastern Ashanti; all were to concentrate against Kumasi in early February.

But these enterprises were to fall far short of success and for the same reason: lack of volunteers. Butler found no more than 1,400 Akim willing to march and lost them all when an allied force attacked them in error. Dalrymple rallied only fifty of the thousand Wassaws expected and could not get them across the Ofim by any means. Glover began more promisingly, for in the Hausa police recruited from the Muslim people of the Upper Niger, for whom he had formed one of those enthusiasms for warlike minorities to which the extrovert Victorian was so prone, he had the nucleus of an organised force. They had been concentrated at Accra where he believed there to be a sizeable Hausa community; round them he hoped to assemble important contingents of Accras, Akwapims, and Krepis. The 'Hausas' of Accra proved to be, however, not the true 'Sikhs of Africa'[28] but captives of theirs bought into domestic slavery by the coastal people, who resisted his efforts to recruit them while refusing to enlist themselves. Thus although he had promised Wolseley to reach the Pra on 15 January with at least 15,000 and perhaps 30,000 men, he eventually crossed with no more than 750, the original disciplined nucleus; and although he was to reach Kumasi with 4,000 it was only after the city had fallen and when the eastern allies felt it safe to join him. News of his flanking approach did however draw off a major Ashanti division, the Juaben, at a critical moment. This was the sole achievement of the three subsidiary columns.

All, then, was to depend upon Wolseley. But before marching off, he made one more effort to bring Kofi Karikari to terms. On 1 November he had sent off another copy of the letter which had fallen in Amankwa Tia's hands, mounting the bearer, an Ashanti captive, on one of the otherwise useless traction engines shipped by the Control Department. 'The experience . . . had little or no visible effect on him, and he seems to have regarded the whole proceeding as a ponderous prelude to his own execution.'[29] He completed the journey between the first hill and Kumasi on foot. The Asantehene's answer, brought into Prasu on 2 January, showed that neither this nor other manifestations of the force preparing against him had yet shaken his composure: it denied any quarrel with the British but complained about attacks on Amankwa Tia's rearguards and reasserted his claim over the Assins and Denkyeras. Since bearers of bad news to Kumasi were believed to suffer a traditional fate, Wolseley decided that Kofi must be ignorant of the true situation which he therefore described in detail in his reply, arranging meanwhile for the envoys to witness a demonstration of the Gatling gun. They seem to have been more shaken by the unmistakeable signs of his intention to invade: the bridge across the Pra and the parties of scouts encountered on the homeward journey. Even more ominous was the sight of the fallen Kuma tree, from which the city took its name, outside the palace on their return to it; it had crashed on 2 January, the date which headed the letter they bore. Many of the council which convened to consider it, and particularly the veterans of 1873, argued against further resistance. But the indemnity required— 50,000 ounces of gold—and the demand that soldiers escort any embassy to Kumasi, were too heavy to be borne. The vote eventually was for war but it was agreed to temporise with Wolseley while the outlying divisions rallied. The arsenals, fortunately for them, were full since British merchants had run large quantities of guns and powder into the French ports adjoining the Gold Coast throughout the previous year.

Wolseley however was in no mood for prevarication and was softened neither by the appearance of the first of the missionaries, Kühne, at Prasu on 12 January, nor by that of the other, together with his wife and child and a French hostage, with fresh representations, eleven days later. He had by then begun the invasion and, far from heeding the Asantehene's new proposals which were distinctly conciliatory, hardened his own demands and pressed the column forward. On 24 January he wrote from Fomena: 'I intend to go to Coomassie. It is for your Majesty to decide whether I go there as your friend or your enemy.' If as a friend, all the Fanti prisoners were at once to be sent down, half the indemnity and, as hostages, the queen mother, the heir apparent and the heirs of the four most important vassals. This last, to the matrilineal dynasty of Kumasi, was an impossible demand. How impossible Wolseley was perhaps unaware; but even if not it seems unlikely that he would have been deterred. From the first Kumasi had beckoned and he was now within thirty miles of the city.

He did however agree to advance more slowly for the next few days, though admittedly the need to accumulate supplies and the knowledge, gleaned from the Ashanti envoys' attendants, that the enemy was hanging back, made this convenient to himself. Between 24 and 28 January he halted at Fomena; ten days' supplies were accumulated, the road run forward six miles to Dechiasu and the surrounding villages patrolled. All the signs pointed to the proximity of large enemy forces and on 26 January a strong force under Colonel McLeod skirmished with a party of 200 Ashanti at Atobiasi. Two further appeals from Kumasi to halt came down to him at Dechiasu on 29 January but negotiations had reached an impasse: the Asantehene argued that since all his chiefs had left 'to guard the roads' he needed time to consult them; Wolseley, who was unaware of the Asantehene's dependence on conciliar agreement, riposted 'you have taken advantage [of the pause at Fomena] to collect your armed men'.[30] There was a larger skirmish later the same day and on 30 January, sensing the approach of a general action, Wolseley issued his orders for the deployment.

His command, now reinforced by 200 Fusiliers to replace the sick, numbered 1,509 whites and 708 blacks. It was to advance in hollow square, the Black Watch forming the front with Rait's two 7-pounders in the centre and two rocket projectors at each wing, sailors at the head of each side column, with Russell's Regiment following on the left and Wood's on the right, and the Rifle Brigade closing the square in rear. Headquarters, the medical service, the ammunition limbers and the tactical reserve of Fusiliers were to march within the square, the Royal Engineers and their labourers ahead, hacking paths parallel to and 300 yards from the main road to open a way for the square's sides. The heavy baggage and the sick would be left at Insafu and Akankwasi, just forward of Dechiasu, but under guard for there were rumours of Ashanti infiltrations across the line-of-communication.

Wolseley's intelligence was that 'the enemy had concentrated . . . about Amoafu . . . Becquah, a mile to the west . . . was . . . full of men and it appeared . . . that the enemy would fight at Amoafu and again in front of Coomassie'.[31] This was remarkably accurate. Once convinced of Wolseley's intention to go to Kumasi and compelled by his impossible demands to oppose him, the Ashanti had settled for a spider and fly strategy. Wolseley had been lured as deep as possible into their territory and was now to be enveloped by drives against his front and across his rear. The main army, numbering 'many thousands'[32] under Asamoa Nkwanta, was lying in wait for him just south of Amoafu. The Juaben division, however, had been detained at the last minute by the news of Glover's approach on their territory, but given the Ashanti's numerical superiority, an encirclement of the battlefield itself was well within their powers.

Asamoa Nkwanta had prepared the trap well. The road to Amoafu, after leaving the village of Ejinasi, followed the course of a sluggish stream through a steep and heavily wooded defile until, five hundred yards on, it crossed the stream's swampy bed and climbed the scarp of a ridge ahead. The Ashanti, who were deployed along the rim of the horseshoe in traditional fashion, left and right wings thrown forward of the main body, scouts ahead, chiefs with their umbrellas and sacred stools to the rear, thus dominated the square's advance; and their positions, among 'great cotton trees, with high undergrowth ... interlaced everywhere with creepers' were quite invisible.[33]

The trap was sprung by Lord Gifford's Assin scouts as they pushed down the road on the morning of 31 January. Brigadier-General Alison, in tactical command, at once sent forward two companies of the Black Watch, then, as the fire swelled and was taken up on the left, a third to join them and two more to take the western ridge and hack a parallel path along its crest. He himself followed with the remaining three and Rait's guns. Beyond Ejinasi he got a clearer view of the lie of the land and grasping at once the Ashanti's plan, hurried on to reinforce the centre. The bush was so thick that the Ashanti muskets could for once take effect and wounded Highlanders were coming down in dozens from the firing line. As Alison reached it he was rejoined by the two left-hand companies which had found the bush too thick to allow a sympathetic advance and he pushed them into the main fight, reporting at 9.30 a.m. that he had 'only one company in reserve', that 'the enemy is holding his ground stoutly' and that 'some relief to my men would be advantageous'.[34]

This was on its way, for the two flank columns were marching to the sound of the guns. McLeod's, on reaching Ejinasi, took the route lately abandoned by the Highlanders on the left, reached the crest at heavy cost to its cutting party, and there opened a clearing to deploy. A charge by the Hausas of Russell's Regiment, covered by rocket salvoes, then drove the Ashanti out of the bush and captured their encampment. Shortly afterwards, the sailors of Wood's column, having passed through Ejinasi, began to cut a path diagonal to the road and towards the Ashanti encampment on the right-hand ridge, but musketry from the crest was so galling that they had to halt and clear fields of fire.

Wolseley meanwhile had reached Ejinasi with the tactical reserve and the Rifle Brigade. The village echoed with the sound of musketry from three fronts, none more than 800 yards distant, but it raged most fiercely ahead and he sent the Fusiliers straight on down the road. He then had left only the eight Rifle companies to meet calls for help or to reinforce success. Minor Ashanti attacks forced him to commit two of these to assist Wood's Regiment in the defence of the village, another to McLeod and a fourth to Wood's sailors, in each case to fill gaps in their skirmishing lines, so that when at 10.30 a.m. he got Alison's appeal for four companies he could safely release only one. Alison's difficulties were however almost immediately eased by the arrival of Rait's guns which had had to be manhandled through the swamp. 'Fourteen or fifteen rounds fired in quick succession caused such a slaughter as shook the Ashantis and enabled the position to be carried with a rush. It was found to have covered a large camp.'[35] The Ashanti fell back upon a secondary ridge and re-formed, but Rait's 7-pounders again did their work and by noon the road was open to Amoafu which the Highlanders entered a few minutes later.

The two other columns, however, were still held up and parties of Ashanti were filtering through the open corners of the square and attacking the two Fusilier and Rifle companies strung out inside it along the road south of the swamp. At points they were crossing freely, for Brackenbury noticed that a chief's body had been removed between two of his trips along it. Wolseley's scheme of deployment had undoubtedly saved the expedition from disaster but the conformation of the ground had inevitably disrupted the square and the advance of the Highlanders, though very short, had finally broken its slender cohesion. At 1.30 p.m. therefore Wolseley ordered Wood's Regiment out of Ejinasi, and on to the right-hand heights which it cleared in great style, going on to meet the sailors in their clearing. McLeod's men (though peppered by Snider bullets from the companies on the road) had meanwhile cut a path down from the left-hand ridge, which was now clear of Ashanti, and rejoined the road south of the swamp.

By 1.45 p.m. all firing had ceased and Wolseley began the work of getting the baggage up to Amoafu—which Alison reported large enough to hold the whole force—and the wounded down to Insafu, some miles distant from each other. But at about 3 p.m. sounds of fighting were heard from Kwaman, the intervening village, which was held only by a few West Indians. A company of Rifles was sent down to their relief and had driven off the Ashanti by 4 p.m. But an hour later, as the head of the main baggage column, some five miles in length, approached, they came out of the bush again, both around the village and along the road, panicking the carriers and maintaining a harassing fire until well after dark. Their numbers however seemed small, and though many loads were lost and Colonel Colley swept away in the rush to the rear, he was able to stop the rout at Insafu and gather in the jetsam during the night. Next morning the road between Insafu and Amoafu was lined by nine companies of riflemen and Highlanders and the supplies got up. The wounded had by luck escaped ambush and reached Insafu safely.

Their number, considering the prodigious expenditure of powder and shot, was small: 21 officers, 144 British soldiers and 29 African. One officer, two Highlanders and an African had been killed. The expedition had the inefficiency of the Ashanti muskets, which would not wound beyond fifty yards, to thank for its escape. Its artillery and Sniders had killed in return at least 150 Ashanti, whose bodies were found near the road, and probably many more lay undiscovered in the depths of the bush. Three great chiefs, Amankwa Tia on the right, Appia, in the centre, and Kwabena Dwumo, King of Mampon, on the left, and several lesser had fallen.

But the Ashanti, though shaken, were not yet broken. They were still in strength at Bekwai, which had to be cleared on 1 February, and to the south near Fomena, now an important staging post, which they attacked the same day. The West Indian garrison drove them off but the carriers, of whom there were 10,000 on the road, were panic-stricken and refused to advance beyond the place. Wolseley calculated however that stocks in the regimental transports would sustain a dash to Kumasi, now only fifteen miles distant from his encampment north of Amoafu. He had received a last desperate appeal from Kofi for him to understand that 'my old mother and young brother are both my counsellors and helpers in every way' but had replied, 'I cannot halt until the hostages are in my possession'.[36]

At daybreak on 3 February, the expedition, stripped to the bone and deployed for speed in column, set out from Ejinasi. Its advance was contested by Ashanti pickets at every turn of the road and at halfway point, on the Oda river, it came up against the main body. The river was too wide for any but the scouts to ford, and the sappers bridged throughout a night of torrential rain. At first light, the main column pressed across and almost at once came under heavy fire. But the road ahead ran along the crest of a ridge which was easily cleared in rushes by the Rifle Brigade, working in concert with a 7-pounder. By nine o'clock the van had reached Odasu and, by half-past twelve, the rear-guard and the carriers had been passed through a double cordon into the village. Already before these had closed up, Wolseley had ordered on the Black Watch who, with flank companies extended in the bush and the pipers leading down the road, drove through ambush after ambush to within four miles of the capital. Their colonel then ordered a halt but sent down word that he would be in Kumasi by nightfall, news which raised so loud a cheer around Odasu that the Ashanti, who had kept the village under fire all afternoon, at once gave up the fight and slipped off through the bush. The column stepped down the main road.

The Black Watch met no further physical resistance though on the outskirts they came upon a group about to perform human sacrifice as a final stay to their advance. The victim was spared and at 5.30 p.m. they entered the capital. At a little past six Wolseley arrived and was received in the palace square with a general salute.

Kumasi was found by light of morning an almost empty city. The throngs of armed men who had watched and even approached to shake the hands of their conquerors the evening before had quite disappeared. The palace was deserted, for though the Asantehene had been present at Odasu he had not taken part in the retreat to Kumasi but found refuge in the bush; as Kimberley had warned, Wolseley was 'in possession of Coomassie without any government or ruler to treat with'.[37] And it was clear that he could not long remain there; the shortage of supplies and the approach of the rains prompted an early departure. During 5 February, while the soldiers and correspondents toured the long streets of the city, and savoured the horrors of Death Grove (said to hold the remains of 120,000 victims), the royal treasures, which were of course not found to include the Golden Stool, were collected for auction, the palace mined and the residential quarters prepared for burning. At 6 a.m. on 6 February, the expedition paraded; at seven, it marched off and at eight the fuses were lit; 'by nine o'clock, when the Black Watch took their last look at the place, all that remained of Kumasi was a heap of smouldering ruins'.[38]

Once across the Oda, which had risen two feet over the bridge, the downward march was swift and uneventful. Each regiment embarked as it reached Cape Coast, the Fusiliers on 22 February, the Rifle Brigade on the 23rd, the sick on the 26th and the Black Watch on the 27th. Russell's Regiment and Rait's Artillery were disbanded at Cape Coast and Wood's at Elmina. The 2nd West India Regiment returned to the Caribbean. The 1st remained as the West Africa garrison. The force was largely intact. Counting the trifling losses at Odasu (two killed, sixty-six wounded), total casualties amounted to eighteen killed or died of wounds, and 185 wounded, most of them only lightly. Fifty-five Europeans had died of disease.

It had been, then, a model campaign and most of the credit for it rightly went to the Major-General. For if the battle-winning factor had been the fire power of the Sniders and the 7-pounders, the battles themselves had been almost incidental to the outcome of the campaign. The real difficulties, which Wolseley had foreseen and provided for with almost startling prescience, had laid in supply, movement and the care of health. It was for these administrative triumphs, for making 'arrangements every one of which resulted in complete success',[39] for vindicating the efficiency of the newly re-formed army, that the honours were laden upon him: the G.C.M.G. and the K.C.B., the parliamentary vote of thanks and grant of £25,000, the City's address and sword of honour and the universities' honorary degrees. For he had 'within inexorable limits of time' taken 'a handful of forces' into a climate 'fraught with danger to the health of Europeans', 'a dark valley of the Shadow of Death' against 'a warlike, crafty and ferocious . . . nation'[40] and brought them home safe and victorious; and all for £800,000.*[41] Wolseley's subsequent career described a path of unbroken ascent— except for his failure to save Gordon—culminating in his appointment as Commander-in-Chief, 1895-1900. The individual fortunes of the survivors of the Ring were equally assured: nine became generals and one a field marshal.

But though the campaign had proved that Britain's soldiers would be 'found equal to any demands made upon them by the exigencies of the future',[42] it had done curiously little to settle the future of the Gold Coast. Messengers from the Asantehene, it is true, had caught up with Wolseley at Fomena on 13 February and agreed with him a draft treaty which secured his principal demands: an indemnity of 50,000 ounces of gold, renunciation of suzerainty over Denkyera, Assin, Akim, Elmina and (by its own request) the Ashanti state of Adansi, abjuration of rents for the forts, free passage on the roads and the suppression of human sacrifice. But almost all these terms might

* £767,093. 1. Admiralty: £280,000; 2. Colonial Office: £150,000; 3. War Office: £257,093 (warlike stores, £30,000; provisions, £100,000; clothing, £38,750; medical, £4,000; labour, £40,000; field allowances, £9,000; daily pay, £31,267; miscellaneous, £4,076); 4. Obsolete stores and transferable or deferred charges: £80,000.

have been calculated to undermine the stability of the Ashanti state, with which, the Government had always recognised, that of the whole coast was bound up. The indemnity was far too large (only 4,000 ounces were ever paid). Sacrifice, however deplorable, was an essential ingredient of the religious character of Ashanti monarchy. And suzerainty was the basis of its political system. 'That the critical hour had arrived', one of the captive missionaries wrote, '[the Ashanti chiefs] all acknowledged, when the news came of the surrender of Elmina' in 1872. But Elmina had never been more than an outstation. Adansi was a founding member of the union. It had fought hard against Wolseley and its secession, a mere stroke of opportunism, should never have been countenanced by a power which professed a desire 'for the establishment between [Ashanti] and the Queen's subjects and allies of those commercial and friendly relations which are so essential to the well-being of all'.[43] Its action was shortly imitated by most of the other important Ashanti states, Mampon, Bekwai, Kokufu, Juaben and Agona and by the outlying provinces of Kwaku, Gyaman, Sefwi and Banda. In September 1874, Kofi Karikari was therefore 'destooled' by his counsellors and twenty-five years of unbroken trouble, both within Ashanti and between it, the coastal peoples and their protecting power, ensued. The government at Cape Coast, raised to the status of a colony in 1874, relapsed into its time-worn policy of disengagement, leaving the new Asantehene and his successors to restore by arms or threat of arms their power over their errant vassals, intervening, and then usually ineffectually, only when appeals were made against the Asantehene's rule. It was a policy designed to foster discord and depress trade and it was only the steady penetration of French power to east and west of the Gold Coast which at last woke Britain to an awareness of its dangers. The eventual extension of the protectorate to Ashanti and its formal annexation involved, between 1890 and 1901, the despatch of two military expeditions and the prosecution of operations far more lengthy and expensive than Wolseley's 'most horrible war'.[44]

References

1 J. D. Fage. *An Introduction to the History of West Africa*. C.U.P., 1961; p. 78.
2 R. S. Rattray. *Ashanti Law and Constitution*. Oxford, 1929; p. 42.
3 W. E. F. Ward. *A History of Ghana*. London: Allen and Unwin, 1958; p. 155.
4 O. K. Dike. *Trade and Politics in the Niger Delta*. Oxford, 1956; p. 12.
5 David Kimble. *A Political History of Ghana*. Oxford, 1963; p. 2, fn.
6 Ward, op. cit., p. 188.
7 *Parliamentary Papers*, 1865, V (412), p. iii.
8 Douglas Coombs. *The Gold Coast, Britain and the Netherlands, 1850–1874*. Oxford, 1963; p. 81.
9 Coombs, op. cit., p. 84.
10 John D. Hargreaves. *Prelude to the Partition of West Africa*. London: Macmillan, 1963; p. 168. These claims have been vigorously attacked by his grandson, James Pope Hennessy, in a biography, *Verandah*. London: Allen and Unwin, 1964.
11 W. D. McIntyre. 'British Policy in West Africa: The Ashanti Campaign of 1873–1874', in the *Historical Journal*, vol. VI (1962).
12 McIntyre, loc. cit.
13 McIntyre, loc. cit.
14 Sir Robert Biddulph. *Lord Cardwell at the War Office*. London: Murray, 1904; p. 221.
15 Field-Marshal Viscount Wolseley. *The Story of a Soldier's Life*. London: Constable, 1903; vol. II, p. 262.
16 W. W. Claridge. *A History of the Gold Coast and Ashanti*. London: Murray, 1915; vol. II, p. 52.
17 Joseph H. Lehmann. *All Sir Garnet*. London: Cape, 1964; p. 173.
18 Henry Brackenbury. *The Ashanti War*. Edinburgh: Blackwood, 1874; vol. I, p. 184.
19 Ibid., pp. 201–3.
20 Ibid., p. 204.
21 F. A. Ramseyer and J. Kühne. *Four Years in Ashantee*. London, 1878; p. 239.
22 Brackenbury, op. cit., I, p. 227.
23 Ibid., p. 303.
24 Capt E. Rogers, in 'The Ashantee War' in *United Service Magazine*, 1873, II, p. 497.
25 Brackenbury, I, p. 198. Wolseley to Cardwell, 13.10.73.
26 Claridge, op cit., II, pp. 92–3.
27 Brackenbury, I, pp. 361–7.
28 Capt Sir John Glover, 'The Volta Expedition, During the Late Ashantee campaign' in *R.U.S.I. Journal*, 1875, p. 330.
29 Claridge, II, p. 81.
30 Brackenbury, II, pp. 150–1.
31 Ibid., p. 157.

32   Ibid., p. 182. There are no more precise estimates.
33   Sir William Cope. *The History of the Rifle Brigade*. London: Chatto, 1877; p. 488.
34   Brackenbury, II, pp. 164–5.
35   Ibid., p. 169.
36   Ibid., pp. 203–4.
37   Ibid., I, p. 349. Kimberley to Wolseley, 24.11.73.
38   Claridge, op. cit., II, p. 144.
39   Biddulph, op. cit., p. 244.
40   *Illustrated London News*, 4 April 1874, pp. 310–11.
41   W.O. 33/26 Confidential Print 1874 (W.O. 0563).
42   *Illustrated London News*, 4 April 1874, p. 311.
43   Brackenbury, I, pp. 201–2.
44   Wolseley, II, p. 370.

The South African War
1880-1

The South African War
1880-1

Brian Bond

'For forty years', declared Mr Gladstone shortly after the cessation of hostilities in 1881, 'I have always regarded the South African question as the one great unsolved and perhaps insoluble problem of our colonial system.' This was a very frank admission after a war which, though short in duration and comparatively inexpensive in loss of life, had cost the Liberal Government dearly in terms of political prestige, and had also cruelly exposed the limitations of British military power when confronted with a civilised but unorthodox opponent.

In the context of Victorian imperialism the interest of this minor campaign—the period of hostilities lasted only from 16 December 1880 to 22 March 1881—lies in two aspects: in the Government's handling of the situation from the moment of taking office in April 1880 up to the hasty conclusion of the war; and in the dramatic sequence of military events, culminating in the disaster on the Majuba mountain and the death of General Colley.

'The South African crisis which led to the First Boer War occurred because the British Government claimed to be the paramount authority and trustee of South Africa and the trek Boers rejected the claim.'[1] For over half a century British imperial policy had aimed to secure the Cape route to our eastern empire without becoming involved in the interior.[2] This strictly limited objective, however, was persistently thwarted by the Boer trekkers who carried colonisation ever further into the interior. Still, so long as these poor farmers could be kept politically ineffective the Colonial Office was prepared to allow them a certain amount of self-government. This policy of indirect imperialism was exemplified by the Bloemfontein Convention of 1852 and the Sand River Convention of 1854, which recognised the independence of the Orange Free State and the Transvaal respectively. But the severe limitations of Boer independence were soon made clear: the two republics were forbidden to unite; further expansion inland was denied to them; and, most seriously of all, they were cut off from the coast. Faced with the prospect of endless native wars as the Boers strove to extend their holdings, the imperial authorities turned, in the 1860's, to the solution that promised so well in Canada: confederation. This policy was in perfect accord with mid-Victorian schemes designed to reduce expenditure and devolve authority without sacrificing imperial supremacy. The problem was to cajole the Boer republics into a federation with the Cape and Natal colonies. The sooner this could be achieved the more predominant would Cape Colony be in relation to the Orange Free State and the Transvaal. Gladstone's ministry of 1868–74 attempted, quite unsuccessfully, to bring about a confederation. The republics were embittered by British annexation of Basutoland and Griqualand West; while the Cape Dutch were unwilling to bear the defence burden of British imperialism.

By the mid-1870's the discovery of diamond fields at Kimberley had greatly exacerbated the problem for the new Conservative ministry (1874–80). 'The diggings at Kimberley brought a surge of development to the stagnant South African economy. . . . The investment of the Eighteen seventies gave a filip to colonisation inland. The inflow of immigrants and speculation in rising land values gave fresh impetus to the colonists' expropriation of the tribal lands. . . . The frontiers were ringed with explosive land disputes and potential native wars.'[3] The Colonial Secretary, the Earl of Carnarvon, felt the urgency of preventing this 'balkanisation' of southern Africa with its accompanying dangers to the vital British route to the Far East. Again confederation was attempted, at the London Conference of August 1876, but neither the Cape nor the Orange Free State leaders would cooperate.

Meanwhile the British civil and military administrators in Natal and Cape Colony were becoming sceptical as to the Transvaal Boers' ability to govern themselves. In the first place—and this was ironic in view of their subsequent achievements—the Boers seemed incompetent to defend themselves against increasingly menacing native tribes, among whom the Zulus were the most formidable. This view seemed confirmed by the ignominious failure in 1876 of a strong Boer Commando to capture a mountain stronghold held by Basuto clans

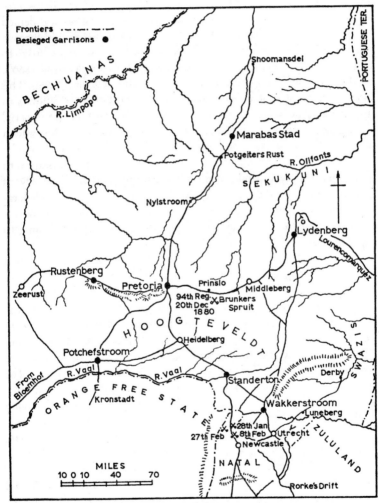

Laing's Nek and the Transvaal

under Chief Sekukuni. The second weakness was the Boers' complete inability to run their finances. In the words of a British official report: 'The Government had become paralysed beyond hope of recovery. The finances, which had never flourished, had wholly gone to ruin under the strain of war expenditure and a foreign loan. The public servants were unpaid. The treasury was empty ... the people would no longer pay taxes and the banks refused further advances. ...'[4]

Prompted by the fear that anarchy in the Transvaal would undermine the security of Britain's position throughout South Africa, Disraeli's Government accepted the advice of its experienced agent on the spot, Sir Theophilus Shepstone, and annexed the Transvaal in June 1877. The Colonial Secretary, Lord Carnarvon, acted under the impression that a large proportion of the Boers—there were only about 8,000 adult males in a total 'Dutch' population of 23,000—would welcome the protection and greater efficiency of British rule, as a stepping stone to confederation. That this was a serious mistake was made increasingly apparent in the remaining months of Conservative government. Two delegations led by Paul Kruger visited London to plead for the restoration of independence, and a series of petitions and mass meetings demonstrated that opposition was bitter and almost unanimous.

The British Government refused to reconsider the annexation. In the autumn of 1879 Sir Garnet Wolseley, the most able soldier and political 'trouble-shooter' of the day, became High Commissioner of the Transvaal, and issued a proclamation confirming the will and determination of the Queen's Government that the territory should continue for ever an integral part of her dominions in South Africa. Wolseley sought and received explicit confirmation of this policy on the last day of the old Parliament, 9 March 1880, and in announcing it employed picturesque language which served to harden the dissident Boers' resentment. As Kruger recalled, Wolseley declared that 'so long as the sun shines, the Transvaal will be British territory; and the Vaal River shall flow back to its sources before the Transvaal is again independent'.[5]

The speedy abandonment of annexation in face of armed rebellion should not obscure the fact that there was a strong case for maintaining British rule. There were, as Carnarvon's successor at the Colonial Office, Sir Michael Hicks-Beach, perceived, 'The interests of the large native population who now ... are quiet and contented; [and] of the European settlers who have acquired property in the province in the full belief that the annexation will be maintained . . . .' But it was Wolseley who foresaw the future history of the Transvaal most clearly and prophetically. 'The Transvaal', he wrote in October 1879, 'is rich in minerals; gold has already been found in quantities, and there can be little doubt that larger and still more valuable gold fields will sooner or later be discovered. Any such discovery would soon bring a large British population here. The time must eventually arrive when the Boers will be in a small minority, as the country is very sparsely peopled, and would it not therefore be a very near-sighted policy to recede now from the position we have taken up here, simply because for some years to come, the retention of 2,000 or 3,000 troops may be necessary to reconsolidate our power?'[6] Here, in essentials, was outlined the clash of interests—economic, imperial and Boer nationalist—which were to trouble British policy in South Africa for the rest of the century. Neither party in Britain seems to have given adequate consideration to Wolseley's memorandum before the outbreak of war in 1880.

Had a consistent policy of either determined military occupation or of generous concessions towards self-government been followed, it is unlikely that war would have occurred. Inconsistency was not, however, simply due to the change of government in 1880. Certainly in the pre-election campaign both Gladstone and the temporary Liberal leader, Lord Hartington, said enough to convince the Boer leaders that annexation would promptly be repealed should they take office. On coming into power, however, Gladstone's Government found official reports all to the effect that Boer opposition in the Transvaal was dying down. In these circumstances how could ministers justify abandonment of annexation that might again plunge the Transvaal into chaos? On the positive side, the powerful and controversial High Commissioner at the Cape, Sir Bartle Frere* still held out

---

* Sir Bartle Frere (1815–84) entered Bombay civil service and made his reputation as a brilliant administrator as Commissioner of Sind (1850–9) and Governor of Bombay (1862–7). In 1877 he became High Commissioner and Governor of the Cape with the task of creating a South African Federation. In 1879 his decision to wage war against the Zulu Cetewayo was much criticised. He did not again hold public office after his recall in 1880.

good prospects for a confederation in which the Transvaal would form an integral part.

The indecisiveness of British policy towards the Transvaal in 1880–1 is to a large extent explained by dissension within the Government. In the Transvaal, as in Ireland, the Liberals had to decide whether to meet a nationalist movement with coercion or concession. W. E. Forster, Secretary of State for Ireland, stood for the humanitarian imperialists who stressed the need of the African natives for British protection against the rapacious Boer colonists. The Whig peers, notably Kimberley and Hartington, were more conventional imperialists, determined to uphold British prestige and supremacy. On the other hand the Prime Minister, Chamberlain, Bright and Dilke all sympathised with the Transvaal's demand for independence and inclined to concession. Indeed all that united the two groups was a desire to keep imperial expenditure in southern Africa to a minimum.[7]

The new Cabinet decided to overlook the awkward pre-election speeches and for the time being adopted the policy of their predecessors. On 12 May the new Colonial Secretary, Lord Kimberley, informed Frere that the sovereignty of the Queen over the Transvaal could not be relinquished; and a month later the Prime Minister rejected yet another plea by Kruger on the grounds that 'obligations had now been contracted, especially towards the natives, that could not be set aside'. Under British sovereignty, however, ministers desired that 'the white inhabitants should enjoy the fullest liberty to manage their local affairs'.

Disillusionment spread quickly among the Transvaal Boers, and it was their opposition exerted on the Cape Colony Dutch which speedily put paid to plans for a confederation. In the face of mounting Parliamentary criticism, including that of pro-Boer Radicals like Leonard Courtney, the Government modified its policy to the extent of ordering the recall of Sir Bartle Frere on 1 August 1880. This, however, was a barren gesture, for no political concessions followed. Solemn and deliberate as Gladstone's promise sounded, commented his biographer John Morley, 'no step whatever was effectively taken towards conferring this full liberty or any liberty at all'.

In the months following Frere's recall the ambivalence of Liberal policy towards the Transvaal became steadily more galling to the Boers. It was not merely that constitutional reforms were delayed. To justify their continuation of a policy they had so often denounced when in opposition 'the Government had at least to show that they ruled the Transvaal by the wish of the people, and that it was not a costly possession held by force alone. They had in fact to make it pay. Military expenditure must be reduced, taxes collected.' Thus while latent hostility was fanned into flames, the forces which might have controlled it were simultaneously reduced. Major-General Colley, who had succeeded his friend and mentor, Wolseley, in the civil and military command of Natal in June 1880, reported to the War Office in September, 'I have now, I hope, definitely arranged for the withdrawal of another regiment from the Transvaal, reducing the garrison there to two infantry regiments and one battery.' He added that this measure had received only grudging assent from the military commander in the Transvaal, Colonel William Bellairs, who anxiously anticipated further mass meetings and disturbances.[8]

There can be no question that the Government remained oblivious of the threat from the Boers right up to the moment when the Transvaal rose in open rebellion. The problem is to decide where culpability lay.

Colley cannot be entirely freed from blame, but on closer inspection he too, like Lord Kimberley, seems to have been the victim of circumstances and faulty information. His responsibilities as Governor of Natal and High Commissioner for South East Africa were anomalous and unwieldy in that, while he exercised direct control over Natal and Zululand, he was only indirectly concerned with the Transvaal, since that province remained the immediate charge of its Administrator, Sir Owen Lanyon. On arrival in Natal, Colley found so many pressing issues to deal with, such as conferring a constitution on that state and investigating tribal problems in the recently conquered Zululand, that he genuinely had little opportunity to visit the Transvaal and judge for himself.

Sir Owen Lanyon*, Administrator in the Transvaal since March 1879, must be held chiefly responsible for underestimating both the seriousness of the Boers' disaffection and their military capability. Indeed his judgement was astonishingly wide of the mark. Through

* Colonel Sir William Owen Lanyon, K.C.M.G., formerly and subsequently commander of the 2nd West India Regiment and A.D.C. to Wolseley in Ashanti in 1873. Administrator of Griqualand West 1875-9. See following chapter p. 264.

October and November he minimised the significance of growing signs of unrest, and even when, on 4 December, he realised that an armed rising might be imminent, dismissed it with the comment: 'They cannot do much, for their commissariat will be limited, as the greater part will have to come on horseback on account of the short notice.' A week later he wrote again to Colley: 'I don't think we shall have to do much more than show that we are ready, and sit quiet and allow matters to settle themselves. . . . They [the Boers] are incapable of any united action, and they are mortal cowards, so anything they may do will be but a spark in the pan.' He repeated this opinion on 18 December, after the Boers had proclaimed a Republic, and described the rebellion as 'an impulse that . . . could not have been premeditated'.[9]

One manifestation of this prevalent attitude of almost contemptuous over-confidence was the casual despatch to London by mail steamer of information or advice which in retrospect was to appear of critical importance and was to be frequently cited by critics of the Government. Of the many instances provided in the published documents the following, by the temporary Administrator of Cape Colony, Sir George Strahan, was perhaps the worst. On 6 December 1880, President Brand of the Orange Free State, whose indefatigable efforts to secure peace were to win the admiration of all parties in the months to come, telegraphed to Strahan: 'I read with very deep concern the account of the very serious aspect of affairs in the Transvaal. The gravity of the situation will, I hope, be accepted as an excuse . . . for asking whether your Excellency will not devise some means by which a collision, which seems imminent, may be averted, a collision which will have the most disastrous results and seriously imperil the prestige of the white man with the native tribes.' This well-founded warning was received by Lord Kimberley on 30 December—nearly a fortnight after the outbreak of war.[10]

Thus Lord Kimberley and other ministers had some grounds for their post-war self-justification: that they had been misled until it was too late to take action by the false optimism of the civil and military authorities on the spot. An examination of the voluminous despatches in the pre-war months, however, shows that sufficient information did filter through to the Colonial Office to have worried a minister who was not predisposed to believe that things were improving in the Transvaal. The salient fact is that the Government had been in office

eight months without making a single concession towards self-government. It is perhaps an indication of the Cabinet's inattention to the
problem, in the midst of their Irish troubles, that the private papers of
John Bright (Chancellor of the Duchy of Lancaster)—usually a champion of 'oppressed Nationalities'—contain not a single reference to the
Transvaal before 15 February 1881.[11]

When the insurgent Boers proclaimed a Republic on 16 December
1880 the British military position in the Transvaal was extremely
vulnerable. The recent reductions had left only 1,759 troops in the
Transvaal and 1,772 in Natal. Colley's withdrawal of the 58th regiment
to Natal in October was a step in the right direction, as was also the
belated decision to concentrate some of the smaller outlying garrisons
in Pretoria. Unfortunately the Boers took action and forestalled this
move so that there remained seven isolated forts to be held—and
relieved. As a recent student of the campaign has commented, 'It is
difficult to see how any other arrangement could have suited the
Boer leaders better.'[12] The latter could calculate how many men were
needed to coop up each garrison while the remainder—some 3,000 of
the best soldiers—could be despatched to the Natal frontier to await
the relief column in a natural defensive position.

Disadvantage in numbers and disposition was not offset, as might
have been expected, by high morale on the part of the redcoats. The
aimlessness of existence in those remote stations, a steady diet of bully
beef, and long periods under canvas on the monotonous veldt had
badly affected the troops' discipline and morale. The Orange Free State
provided a convenient sanctuary for deserters and their number grew
alarmingly in 1880. This disturbing situation had been reported to both
the War and Colonial Offices, and indeed it was partly in order to
combat desertion that Colley had reduced and begun to concentrate
the garrisons.

One other weakness must be stressed at this point since it was to
cripple British action from first to last. The Transvaal garrisons were
entirely lacking in regular cavalry, and indeed had scarcely any
mounted troops at all. Against a mounted enemy bred to the saddle,
skilled in horsemanship and operating in the immense open spaces of
the veldt the consequences were unavoidable. The garrisons had no
choice but to surrender the initiative, dig in, and await relief by an
almost equally immobile column from Natal.

Although there had been shooting at Potchefstroom on 16 December, where a ludicrously small detachment from Pretoria had been sent to restore order, the first real action came on 20 December, when the Boers demonstrated the moral tonic which results from beginning with a dramatic victory. Lieut-Colonel Anstruther of the 94th Regiment (or Connaught Rangers) with 9 officers and 254 other ranks was marching from Lydenburg to Pretoria when he was ambushed 37 miles from his objective at Bronkhorstspruit. He had been informed of the Boer rising and warned against being surprised, but even so the Boers' tactics were of doubtful fairness since it was by no means certain that a state of war existed. The straggling column of waggons was halted by a few Boers in an exposed spot, the Colonel was handed a proclamation ordering him to turn back; he was given only two minutes to reply, and when he refused fire was opened at once. The Boer leader, Joubert, had concealed about a thousand men in excellent firing positions, clearly expecting a refusal. The action lasted less than half an hour and amounted to a massacre—all the officers were killed or wounded in the first burst of accurate fire.

No general lessons could fairly be drawn from such a one-sided action, though in retrospect it was apparent that certain military weaknesses which were to hamper the British throughout the campaign were foreshadowed at Bronkhorstspruit. Even allowing for the fatal lack of a mounted escort the precautions taken against surprise were inadequate; there was an excess of impedimenta; and British shooting was innocuous.[13]

At this point we may anticipate the course of the campaign on the frontier of Natal by recounting the fate of the garrisons in the Transvaal, isolated as they were after 20 December by superior though fluctuating numbers of Boers. None of the garrisons was relieved before the armistice and none surrendered, despite alarming rumours that reached Natal. The Boers pursued a policy of loose or 'open blockade', in some cases placing their laagers as far as eight miles out. Each siege constituted a minor epic with numerous sorties and skirmishes, though only at Pretoria where both sides had about 1,200 men was there anything approaching regular action. Nevertheless on the credit side the garrisons performed a valuable role in occupying far more than their own number of the enemy. The Boers showed perhaps an excessive respect for British artillery and rifle fire and refrained from trying to storm the 'forts' some of which, such as Potchefstroom, were very cramped, ramshackle and hurriedly improvised affairs.[14] As in the greater conflict of 1899, however, British strategy was restricted by the urgent need to relieve the garrisons, especially in view of Boer atrocities alleged to have been perpetrated at Bronkhorstspruit and elsewhere.

The Transvaal rebellion was thus kindled by disillusionment with Gladstone's Government and sparked off by the rigorous efforts to collect taxes. The important issue of how many Boers were initially prepared to resort to the apparently futile gesture of war with Britain remains obscure. Though the great majority were hostile to British rule, Sir Owen Lanyon was probably correct in believing that at first only a small minority, led by Kruger and Joubert, were willing to fight. These men were driven beyond endurance by a sense of grievance; inspired by the justice of their cause; and hopeful of gaining the sympathy of liberal opinion in Britain, and more than sympathy from fellow-Dutchmen in the Orange Free State and Cape Colony.

Hardly distinguishable from political justice in the Boer mind was religious zeal. Kruger wrote characteristically in an official letter concerning the action at Bronkhorstspruit: 'we are bowed down in the dust before God Almighty who has been so near to them [the Boers] and who, against the hundred [British] soldiers killed, has caused only two of our own men to perish. . . .' Even their greater and more worthy victories the Boer leaders ascribed, not to their own skill, but to the intervention of the Almighty. Their almost frenetic reaction to Colley's occupation of the summit of Majuba mountain was partly due to the fact that the British had violated the sanctity of the Sabbath.

If the Boers took up arms with the initial advantages of much higher mobility and morale, the long-term odds against them were overwhelming. There were only about 7,000 men fit for service and there was no organisation other than the loose 'Commando' system to ensure that even these would remain on duty. They had no artillery, and began with only about 15 rounds of rifle ammunition per man. Even the rifle which most of them carried—the Westley Richards—was inferior in range and loading rate to the British soldier's Martini-Henry.[15] It would seem that once British reinforcements had reached Natal and moved up to the Transvaal border—say three months at most—the Boers must inevitably be defeated. A bold offensive strategy seemed their only hope: to destroy the British troops on the spot and thereby strike politically at the hesitant home government and, equally important, to induce the Orange Free State to come in on their side. In fact, as in 1899, after opening moves of startling boldness the Boers' strategy and tactics alike were cautious and defensive. They isolated the garrisons and with their main force quickly occupied the only viable entrance to the Transvaal from Natal at Laing's Nek. Thereafter they launched only tentative probing raids into Natal and returned the initiative to the enemy. Joubert, the Commander-in-Chief, impressed the British generals as the most moderate and statesmanlike of the Boer leaders, but he was if anything too respectful of British military power and lacked the essential spirit of boldness.

A combination of material and numerical weakness allied to timid strategy ought thus to have ensured the Boers' defeat. Instead a remarkable series of military miscalculations and diplomatic manœuvres by their enemy led them to military victory and political triumph.

For reasons already given the British Government was caught unprepared for the outbreak of rebellion in the Transvaal. The treacherous attack at Bronkhorstspruit—and other stories of Boers abusing the white flag—aroused the feeling, particularly among the Whig members of the Government, that the rebels must be taught a lesson and the humiliation wiped out before there could be any thought of a settlement. This instinctive, but far from unanimous, reaction was to cause the Government endless embarrassment in the months to come.

The Transvaal and Irish crises broke simultaneously upon Gladstone's already badly disunited Government, and brought the friction between the Whig and Radical wings to a climax. It was not merely that the discordant groups tended to view both problems in the same light, the Whigs favouring coercion in Ireland and the Transvaal and the Radicals concessions and conciliation. The two crises interacted: the Radicals utilised the support of the Irish Nationalists in the House of Commons 'to dish' the Whigs' policy in the Transvaal. Thus also Chamberlain and Dilke fought for the Transvaal's independence 'not only on principle, but as a weapon against the Whigs on the Irish question, and as a means of forcing Kimberley's resignation'.[16]

At first the Whigs carried the Cabinet. Three diplomatic actions in particular embodied the Government's decision to take determined military action. On 30 December Lord Kimberley rejected a suggestion by certain members of the Cape Legislature that the Government

The Abyssinian War:
Group of British soldiers outside hut. Note the newly introduced 'khaki' uniforms.

The Abyssinian War.
The Battle of
Arogee.

Opposite page: *Ibid.*
The storming of
Magdala from a
sketch drawn at the
time. Note the sup-
porting fire from the
rockets manned by
the Naval Brigade.

The Ashanti War.
Artillery Park at
Prah-su.

Ibid. Gifford's
Scouts.

Field Marshal Viscount Wolseley—a photograph taken when he was
Commander-in-Chief of the British Army, 1895–1900.

Opposite page: *The Ashanti War*. Headquarters at the Battle of Amoafu.

The First South African War. Major-General Sir George Colley.

Opposite page: *Ibid.* Majuba, a contemporary photograph.

Above: *The First South African War.* A Boer Commando.

Left: *Ibid.* General Piet Joubert. A later photograph of the Boer Commander of 1881.

Opposite page: *Ibid.* O'Neill's Farm, with Majuba in the background: the house served as a temporary hospital after the battle, and the Anglo-Boer Convention was signed there after the war.

Major-General Hector Macdonald, a photograph taken at the time of the Second South African War. 'Fighting Mac' was one of the few Victorian generals who rose from the ranks.

Opposite page: *The Egyptian War*. Fort Pharos after the British Naval bombardment. Note the ancient cannon and mortars.

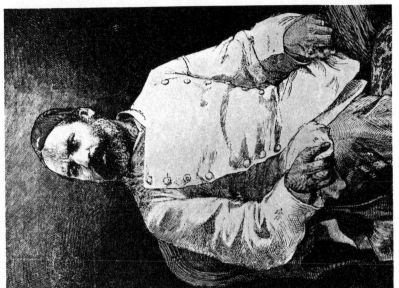

Right: *The Egyptian War.* Colonel Arabi in exile in Ceylon.

Left: *Ibid.* Sir Drury Lowe, who commanded the spectacular cavalry dash to Cairo which speedily ended the war after the Battle of Tel-el-Kebir.

Opposite page: *Ibid.* Battery W at Tel-el-Kebir. This photograph taken soon after the battle gives some idea of the desert terrain which provided the greatest obstacle to Wolseley's advance.

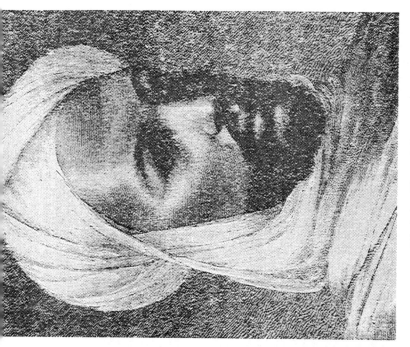

The Sudan. The Mahdi.

The Sudan. Sir Horatio Herbert Kitchener as Commander-in-Chief of the Egyptian Army in 1896.

should send a special commissioner to enquire and report on the true state of Boer feeling in the Transvaal. The extent of the rebels' support from their own people was to remain a matter of debate throughout and after the war. On the same day the instructions given to Sir Hercules Robinson, Frere's replacement as High Commissioner for Cape Colony, contained the sentence 'It is useless to discuss arrangements [with the Boers] which can only be practicable when the authority of the Crown has been vindicated.' Finally, in the Speech from the Throne a week later, the Queen proclaimed that the rebellion 'has of necessity, set aside for the time any plans for securing to European settlers full control over their own local affairs. . . .'[17]

Meanwhile General Colley, also deeply distressed by the Boer rebellion and anxious above all to check 'this extraordinary fever spreading beyond the Transvaal', began hastily to gather together a scratch force to march to the relief of the beleagured garrisons.

George Pomeroy-Colley at the age of forty-six was already set in the mould of the great Victorian servants of Empire. In appearance he was slight and well-proportioned; his hair was dark brown; and in the last three years of his life he wore a beard. His brow was 'strong and massive', 'the nose large and straight, the nostrils wide and curving backwards very finely at the edge. The whole face was . . . beautifully modelled, a strong countenance developed to the utmost and informed with thought. . . .' Colley possessed an admirable personality of deep integrity and charm, and, moreover, was widely regarded as the most promising young general of the modern British Army, recently re-formed by Edward Cardwell. The scion of an ancient and prosperous Irish family, Colley passed out top of his class at Sandhurst at the early age of sixteen. But it was at the Staff College, after service in South Africa and China, that his intellectual brilliance was demonstrated. Finding the compulsory courses and the schoolroom attitudes boring and irksome he decided to work on his own and to take the examinations after one year instead of the normal two. After barely nine months he passed out first with 4,274 marks, the largest total ever yet obtained and more than 500 in excess of the nearest rival. To his ability in examinations was added a love of travel, skill in sketching and painting, and a passion for reading very uncommon in a soldier of that time. Through his contribution to the Cardwell reforms Colley secured the interest of Sir Garnet Wolseley and in 1873 he joined the charmed circle

P

of the 'Wolseley Ring' when summoned to Ashanti to take charge of communications. He seized the opportunity to demonstrate that as well as being a scholar he was also a first-rate military administrator. In 1880 he was recognised as the most brilliant member of the 'Ring' and it was from Wolseley himself that he inherited the Natal Command. By this time, his wife noted, he had thrown off 'some earlier traces of gentle tentativeness', and now possessed 'the quiet assurance of a man of great affairs. . . .'[18] But until January 1881 he had never had a chance to exercise independent command in the field.

On 1 January 1881 Colley informed the War Office that he aimed to reach Standerton, well inside the Transvaal, by 25 January, by which time his inexperienced troops would already have marched nearly 400 miles. Then, depending on the strength of Boer opposition, he would either press on to Pretoria or wait about a month for reinforcements to come up. Rumours had reached him that the Boers intended to attack the column as it crossed the saddle of Laing's Nek just inside Natal. Far from daunted by this the General commented: 'very good-natured of them if they will thus give me the opportunity of meeting them close to my base. . . .'[19]

But it was in no over-sanguine or vainglorious mood that Colley began his advance, leaving Maritzburg for the front on 10 January. He was well aware of the inadequacy of his force both in quantity and quality. His twelve infantry companies were taken from four different battalions and comprised mostly young and inexperienced soldiers; he had only six guns and, above all, was chronically short of cavalry, having only 120 mounted troops, many of them infantrymen barely able to keep their seats. From this motley column—'as queer a mixture as was ever brought together,' thought Colley—not many more than a thousand men could be put into battle. And the Boers were reported to have 2,000 men at Laing's Nek alone.

Also, as a highly intelligent man who had devoted much of his career to the enlightened government of South Africa, Colley did not see the political issue in simple terms of right and wrong. He feared the spread of Anglo-Afrikaner racial hatred throughout all the South African provinces and had already made noble efforts to discount rumours of a long-nursed Boer plot to drive the British into the sea, and to play down reports of Boer atrocities. Shortly before the war began he had been considering the restoration to the Transvaal of 'as free a constitution as might be consistent with continued connection with the English Crown'.

In view of the tortuous transformation in Cabinet policy during the war it is interesting to read Colley's ideas for the post-war settlement before his first contact with the enemy. 'It seems early yet to be talking of the resettlement of the Transvaal', he wrote to Lord Kimberley early in January, 'but the breaking-up of the Boer force is only a matter of time . . .' To punish the rebels he proposed a heavy war tax of £10 per farm with exemptions for those who had remained loyal or had suffered as pro-British. Treatment must depend on how the Boers accepted defeat. 'They may remain sullen and carry on a guerrilla war or, what I am hopeful of, may accept their defeat and curse the leaders who have misled them . . .' Should this happen Colley favoured the introduction of a limited form of representation believing that 'a certain amount of the discontent is due to a feeling of being muzzled and of having no opportunity of ventilating their grievances or sharing in the government'.[20] At this stage, however, the Government forbade Colley to offer any terms except 'promising protection to the inhabitants of the districts occupied', and as it happened a British victory was never forthcoming to enable the strength of moderate and conciliatory opinion among the Boers to be assessed.

Unknown to Colley, as his improvised column painfully marched towards Laing's Nek, determined diplomatic efforts were already in progress to end hostilities without further bloodshed. These negotiations, though abortive, reflect the greatest credit on President Brand of the Orange Free State but less on Lord Kimberley and the divided Cabinet.

To a message from Brand dated 10 January hoping every effort would be made to stop further bloodshed, Lord Kimberley replied 'providing only the Boers will desist from their armed opposition to the Queen's authority, H.M.'s Government do not despair of making a satisfactory arrangement'. This completely unsatisfactory attitude was maintained in answer to a succession of increasingly anxious telegrams from Brand. He suggested on 11 January that the Government should 'send someone without a moment's loss, say Chief Justice de Villiers of Cape Town, to the Transvaal burghers with a view of stopping further collision, and with a clear and definite proposal for the settlement. . . .' Kimberley replied that armed opposition must cease before this move could be considered. Brand reiterated on 16 January that 'the only way in which further bloodshed and great calamities to South Africa can be prevented' was that the Government 'make a clear and distinct proposal to the Transvaal people without delay'. The Colonial Office twice repeated that armed opposition must cease first and added vaguely that in such an event the Government 'would endeavour to frame such a scheme as in their belief would satisfy all enlightened friends of the Transvaal community'. President Brand's almost frantic reply, urging that these terms be clarified and transmitted to the Transvaal before Colley went into action, reached London on 28 January in company with a telegram announcing that a battle was being fought at Laing's Nek. This ended the first abortive efforts to bring about a settlement.[21]

Lord Kimberley's non-committal replies to President Brand were consistent with the Government's declarations, mentioned earlier, that 'the Queen's authority must be vindicated' before there could be any question of a political settlement. There was also the important consideration that the Boer leaders had as yet made no use of Brand's declared willingness to mediate. Another explanation of British policy is consistent with the documentary evidence though it cannot be proved. It is that the Government's overriding concern was to prevent the situation worsening through the adherence of volunteers from the Orange Free State (or possibly the State itself) and also Cape Colony to the Transvaal cause. Should this happen Colley's tenuous line of communications to Newcastle, and indeed to Natal itself, would be endangered from the flank. Thus vaguely encouraging messages could be exchanged with Brand until Colley had won the anticipated victory near Laing's Nek, and after that the bargaining position should immediately improve. Indeed the rebellion itself might be deflated by this first pin-prick.

What may be concluded with certainty is that General Colley received no instructions to fetter his military initiative before he went into action at Laing's Nek.

Under the shadow of humiliating reverses critics were to ask why Colley had advanced so precipitately. In January the South African summer was at its worst. The roads were quagmires, the rivers were in flood, progress by men on horseback or on foot was slow and on wheels almost impossible. In a month large-scale reinforcements, including regular cavalry, could be expected. Against these disadvantages, however, Colley's mind was decided by the urgent need to offset the stunning effect of Bronkhorstspruit and to relieve the beleagured garrisons. Potchefstroom in particular could not be expected to hold out beyond mid-February; and if it fell the Boers would be materially strengthened and morally encouraged. The war would be protracted. At this stage it was an understandable error to underestimate the Boers' resolution and ability to resist regular troops.

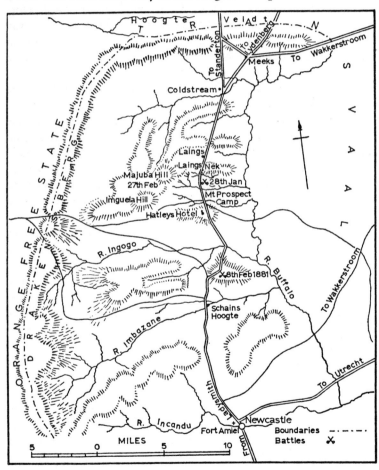

Colley's Operations at Laing's Nek

On 28 January almost the whole British force—just under one thousand men—set out from their camp on Mount Prospect, three miles from Laing's Nek, to challenge nearly twice their number of Boers who were concealed in the natural bastion formed by the converging ridges at the Nek where the main route from Natal crossed a saddle of the Drakensberg Range into the Transvaal.

There was no alternative to a frontal approach, but Colley's plan for the infantry of the 58th Regiment to attack the Boer left flank under cover of a simultaneous charge by his mounted men a little to their right, promised well to seize a thinly defended spur from which the Boer defences could be turned. Meanwhile the Naval Brigade and the artillery were to shell the remainder of the Boer lines in order to cover the attack and keep the weak spot isolated.

Unfortunately the mounted attack went in prematurely and against a more rugged slope than Colley intended. The first line charged gallantly but was halted by devastating rifle fire at short range, and before its impetus was recovered the second line turned and fled. This happened before the infantry had even begun their ascent of the neighbouring slope, but it was too late for the attack to be called off. The 58th were led up the steep hill much too fast and so reached the crest breathless and in confusion, there to be exposed to demoralising fire not only from their front but also from the unprotected flank. The officers all became casualties and only the accurate covering fire of the artillery prevented the retreat from becoming a rout. As it was the regiment suffered 160 casualties out of 480. The Boer losses were given as 14 killed and 27 wounded; the total British loss being 83 killed and 111 wounded. The attack was thus a complete and costly failure. It was also, incidentally, the last occasion when British regiments carried their colours into action.

In a letter written to Sir Garnet Wolseley two days after this disappointing beginning Colley characteristically admitted he had underrated his opponents' skill and courage. Already the Boers had given a foretaste of their marksmanship; they had shown themselves adept at concealment, and had not, as anticipated, been demoralised by the British guns. To the Secretary of State for War Colley wrote that he felt justified in making the attack and had very nearly succeeded. 'Had Major Brownlow's force consisted of trained cavalry, I have hardly a doubt but that the position would have been ours, and without much loss. But one cannot blame mounted infantry and untrained horses for not doing all that trained cavalry might have done.' But, Colley concluded, 'The men are in excellent spirits, eager to attack again.'[22]

To impress the Boers with his determination to take the Nek at a second attempt Colley resisted the temptation to retire to Newcastle, and remained at Mount Prospect to await reinforcements. On 4 February Colley detailed his plans in a long letter to Sir Evelyn Wood* who, though senior to Colley in the Army List, had agreed to come out from Chatham and serve as his second-in-command. Colley hoped to be ready to advance by 20 February by when the 15th Hussars, the 2nd Battalion 60th, and the veteran 92nd Regiment—fresh from the Afghan campaign—would have joined him. His column would then consist of about 2,200 infantry, 450 cavalry and 8 guns and Gatlings. 'If we clear the Nek satisfactorily', wrote Colley, 'I shall probably leave you one regiment at Wakkerstroom, and push on with a lighter column to Pretoria, leaving you in command of all the forces below the Vaal river ... You will understand', he concluded, 'that I want to take the Nek myself!'

Three days later, however, the Boers precipitated another action by sending a patrol round Colley's flank to cut his communications with Newcastle, twenty miles away. Rather than allow a few Boers to interrupt his postal service, and also threaten the reinforcements as they struggled forward unsuspectingly, Colley decided on immediate action.

Early on 8 February the Commander in person led a force of about 300 men—(5 companies of the 60th and 38 mounted men) with four guns—from Mount Prospect to escort the mail half way to Newcastle. At midday, some eight miles from camp and after fording the Ingogo river, the party was confronted by a strong force of mounted Boers, who at once began extending their wings, Zulu fashion, to surround the British. From noon to dusk (at about 6 p.m.) the British bravely clung to the crest of a small plateau in face of superior numbers and

* Sir Evelyn Wood (1838–1919), Field Marshal. Entered the Navy in 1852 as a midshipman and served in Naval Brigade in the Crimean War. Purchased his majority in 1871 just before the purchase system was abolished. Like Colley he joined the 'Wolseley Ring' in the Ashanti War 1873–4. In 1878–9 he commanded a column in the Zulu War and was present at the final battle of Ulundi. In the late 1880's and 1890's he was perhaps the best trainer of troops in the British Army.

more accurate shooting. The Boers were firing uphill at 300 yards range and under and, making excellent use of cover, presented few targets. By contrast the defenders enjoyed scanty cover and the Riflemen in their white helmets and dark jackets made good aiming marks. Nevertheless the inexperienced troops put up a fine stand, husbanding their ammunition and holding their ground. Their persistent fire saved them from being rushed—the Boers refusing an order to do so—and by dusk both sides were more or less fought out. Despite a terrific thunderstorm, which turned the Ingogo into a swirling torrent, the survivors escaped under cover of darkness, and by a heroic effort saved the guns. British casualties, including those left on the field, totalled 150; the Boers lost not many more than 20.

The military significance of these two minor actions can easily be exaggerated. At Laing's Nek the Boers had merely retained an immensely powerful position against a weaker attacker; and at the Ingogo, though taken by surprise, the inexperienced British infantry had defended tenaciously and accomplished a successful withdrawal. Nevertheless there can be no doubt that the Boers had gained enormously in self-confidence: unbelievably the farmers had proved themselves far better riders and marksmen than their professional opponents. After only a fortnight in action no less than a third of the British force were casualties.

Colley's resolution did not waver but his private correspondence reveals how keenly he felt the loss of his soldiers and staff. He was in fact the sole survivor of the original five officers in his mess. 'I have to look cheerful,' he wrote to his sister on 16 February, 'and I dare say am thought callous . . . but sometimes it is hard not to break down. However, reinforcements are now arriving, and I hope it will not be long before I have force enough to terminate this hateful war.' He grew daily more anxious that even Brand's efforts would fail to prevent the Orange Free State from giving military support to the Transvaal.[23]

It is now necessary to outline the stages by which the British Government's policy was transformed between the action at Laing's Nek and the culminating disaster at Majuba on 27 February. Up until the former action, as we have seen, Lord Kimberley's communications with the High Commissioner at the Cape, with Brand and with Colley all gave the impression that the Government would not consider peace terms until the Boers ceased from armed opposition. In particular

Colley was not permitted to assure the Boer leaders that if they submitted they would not be treated as rebels.

A slightly more promising note is heard in Lord Kimberley's message to Colley on 8 February, directing him to inform the Boers that the Government would be ready to give all reasonable guarantees as to the treatment of Boers after submission, if they would cease from armed opposition, and a scheme would be framed 'for permanent friendly settlement'. Unfortunately Lord Kimberley repeatedly refused Brand's requests over the next three weeks for details of this scheme which he wished to transmit to the Boers.[24]

The military events from Bronkhorstspruit to the Ingogo inevitably intensified the Government's internal disagreements and placed the Cabinet in a most awkward situation. In the words of Sir William Butler, 'A single victory on our side would have made compromise easy, but every defeat barred the diplomatic roadway as completely as in a military sense it blocked the movement into the Transvaal.'

The impasse was resolved by the first overture from the Boers. This was a letter from Kruger to Colley, dated 12 February, and reached the Colonial Office by telegraph two days later. The essence of it was that 'the Boers had been driven to arms in self-defence and their views had been continually misrepresented. If annexation was cancelled they were willing to co-operate with the British Government for the good of South Africa. They did not fear enquiry by a Royal Commission . . . If British troops were ordered to withdraw from the Transvaal they would give them free passage and withdraw from their own positions. But if annexation was upheld they would fight to the end'. Neither in this note of 'fierce defiance' nor at any other time did the Boer leaders mention submission; in fact they utterly rejected the suggestion and agreed to negotiate only on the understanding that annexation would be ended.[25]

This diplomatic overture forced the Cabinet to decide whether to commence negotiations from an inferior military position on terms that would clearly favour the Boers, or continue to refuse specific terms until a crushing victory obliged the Boers to take a less arrogant and more realistic view of the situation.

The Radical group had already demonstrated their determination to reverse the Government's policy on 21 January when Dilke, Bright, Chamberlain and Courtney—all members of the Government—

ostentatiously walked out of a House of Commons debate on the Transvaal. On the other hand the Chancellor (Lord Selborne), the Duke of Argyll, Earl Granville and Earl Spencer 'all more or less demurred to so large a concession to the Boers at this moment'. 'They put strongly that after having said we would re-establish the Queen's authority we should be in a very awkward position if after our reverses we send such an answer as is proposed to the Boers. . . .'[26]

Gladstone's decisive personal influence was thrown on the side of the 'peace party' and agreement was obtained to accept the Boer note as a basis for discussion in a Cabinet meeting on 15 February. Colley was directed to inform the Boers that on their desisting from armed opposition the Government would be ready to send commissioners to develop a scheme of settlement; and that meanwhile, if this proposal were accepted, the General was authorised to agree to the suspension of hostilities.

These diplomatic exchanges were clearly only tentative, and it seemed certain to Colley that if the Government insisted on a real 'submission' the Boers would fight on. In the light of the Boer victories and their self-righteous proclamations it was inconceivable to the soldiers that the Government would depart from its stated intention to restore order before considering a settlement. In the immediate future there was the reverse of Laing's Nek to wipe out and the desperate garrisons to be relieved. On a wider view an unavenged humiliation of British arms might be expected to have long-lasting repercussions throughout South Africa.

The ambiguity of the instructions sent to Colley by the War and Colonial Offices provides the key to much of the later recrimination. 'As respects the interval before reply from Boers is received,' wrote Mr Childers on 16 February, 'we do not bind your discretion; but we are anxious for your making arrangements to avoid effusion of blood.' Colley was even more puzzled how to interpret the phrase 'the Boers ceasing from armed opposition', and telegraphed Lord Kimberley on 19 February, 'Latter part of your telegram of 16th . . . not understood; there can be no hostilities if no resistance is made, but am I to leave Laing's Nek in Natal territory in Boer occupation, and our garrisons isolated and short of provisions, or occupy former and relieve latter?' Colley felt that an armistice on these lines would not only tend to increase the Boers' military advantage, but would also imply tacit recognition of their political demands.

Lord Kimberly replied: 'It will be essential that garrisons should be free to provision themselves and peaceful intercourse with them allowed, but we do not mean that you should march to the relief of the garrisons or occupy Laing's Nek if arrangement proceeds. Fix reasonable time within which answer must be sent by Boers.' On 21 February Colley despatched a letter to Laing's Nek, where he believed Kruger to be, stating that on the Boers ceasing from armed opposition the Queen would appoint a commission. Should the proposal be accepted within forty-eight hours he would agree to a suspension of hostilities. He waited in vain for a reply until the evening of 26 February and then began a movement which ended the following day in a military disaster and his own death.

Did the diplomatic situation outlined above justify Colley's decision to take military action on 26 February? His letter was acknowledged by General Smidt at Laing's Nek on 24 February, but he reported that Kruger had gone to Heidelberg and consequently his reply could hardly be expected in less than four days. On the 26th, however, Colley heard that Kruger had strayed even further afield to Rustenberg—'where the natives were restless'—and so his reply would be even longer delayed.

Meanwhile there was no question of either side believing that hostilities had been suspended. The Boers continued to strengthen their earthworks around the Nek; guns were fired from Mount Prospect; and shots were exchanged by vedettes. The movement contemplated by Colley did not contravene his instructions and, even if the negotiations should succeed, was he to be debarred in the long interval from taking up any position on Natal territory which might strengthen his own line and weaken the Boers'? Above all there was the consideration that every day the Boers' reply was delayed brought nearer the capitulation of the British garrisons. When forty-eight hours had elapsed from Smidt's acknowledgement Colley felt free to move, and on the information available to him, this decision seems entirely justified.[27] Had his daring plan succeeded it is unlikely that the subsequent accusations by British Liberals of his 'rashness' and 'aggression' would have been heard.[28]

Kruger's absence at the crucial time has surprisingly escaped adverse comment. He personally had asked for a negotiated peace on 12 February and he knew, from Brand's ceaseless diplomatic activity, that the British Government had begun to abandon its original uncompromising stand.

The reply to his overture must have been expected daily after about 15 February yet Kruger chose to travel beyond reach of the telegraph and did not delegate authority to accept a proffered armistice. It may be that he hoped that the Government's resolution would weaken still further. At least it may be said that he displayed no sense of urgency; indeed his reply eventually reached the British camp only on 7 March.

Despite subsequent rumours that Colley had acted in a mood of gloomy defeatism, the General's last private letters show that he remained confident of military success if only the Government allowed him time. In his last letter to Wolseley, begun on 21 February, he writes, 'The Home Government seem so anxious to terminate the contest that I am daily expecting to find ourselves negotiating with the "Triumvirate" (Kruger, Joubert and Pretorius) as the acknowledged rulers of a victorious people—in which case my failure at Laing's Nek will have inflicted a deep and permanent injury on the British name and power in South Africa which it it not pleasant to contemplate. . . .'[29]

Returning from Newcastle to Mount Prospect on 23 February, Colley at once noticed a significant change in the terrain; the Boers appeared to be busily entrenching on both sides of the Nek and also on the lower slopes of Majuba. Looking towards the Nek from the British camp Majuba towered to the left front, a great table-topped mountain dominating the landscape. From a broad base it rose in steep and sometimes precipitous folds to 6,500 feet above sea-level and 2,500 feet above Mount Prospect. Majuba formed a gigantic bastion flanking the Boer lines yet the Boers, rather carelessly for all their knowledge of the ground, regarded it as so inaccessible to the British that they were content to send a picquet to the top only during daylight hours and withdrew it each night. Here, Colley reasoned, lay the key to Laing's Nek. A night march to occupy the summit would completely undermine the Boer position and would compel them either to abandon the Nek or fight in a very inferior position. Most probably the route to the Transvaal would be opened without further bloodshed.[30]

In the four days between the conception and execution of this daring plan only two staff officers—Lieutenant-Colonel (later Major-General Sir Herbert) Stewart and Major (later Major-General Sir Thomas) Fraser, R.E.—were fully admitted to Colley's counsels. Two measures were taken to mislead the Boers as to British intentions. A reconnaissance in force beyond the Buffalo river to the east of Laing's Nek enabled Colley to study the reverse slopes of Majuba, and also served to suggest that the next attack would be made from that direction. Secondly, in order to suggest that no attack was immediately contemplated and so reduce the danger that the Boers would occupy the summit of Majuba permanently, a battalion of the 60th Rifles was ordered back to Newcastle.

Only seven infantry companies and a naval detachment—554 men— were detailed for the march and three of these companies were to be detached on the way to form a line of communications and supply. Thus only about 350 men would make the final ascent. Colley's intentions can be established from his marching orders and from Stewart's later report: each man carried three days' full rations, which could be eked out to six days; a greatcoat and waterproof sheet; and 70 rounds of ammunition. Each company would carry six picks and four shovels. The initial force was thus expected to hold the summit for up to six days, but supplies would be available from the first day and reinforcements soon afterwards. There is no reason to dispute Lady Colley's conclusion that the enterprise was not only daring but also reasonable: 'the military motives strong, the main scheme carefully worked out and offering a fair chance of success'.

'The night march of troops bound up on some perilous enterprise', wrote Sir William Butler, 'is of all operations possible in war, by far the most impressive.' Setting out at 10 p.m. on the bright though moonless night of 26 February, excitement gripped the troops as at last they realised their objective. As the party stumbled up the saddle between the Imquela and Majuba mountains dogs were barking at O'Neill's farm between the two camps, and it seemed impossible that they would escape detection by Boer outposts. A precious hour was wasted when the rear companies were lost, but by 1.30 a.m. the three companies had been detached with orders to entrench and the foot of Majuba had been reached. It was the final thousand feet which proved the real difficulty. The heavily-laden men were often compelled to crawl on hands and knees, helping themselves forward up the almost sheer slope by clinging to tufts of grass. Major Fraser with two Kaffir guides reached the summit about 3.40 a.m.—and found it deserted. Within an hour and before the first signs of dawn the whole party was up. General Colley personally sorted them into their companies and distributed them, half around the rim and half in reserve in the centre.

The configuration of the summit was to play a crucial part in the disaster. Majuba's volcanic origins were obvious from the shallow depression, 10 to 40 feet deep, which occupied almost the whole mountain top. The circumference of the rocky rim measured about 900 yards. On the south and west sides the rim was almost conterminous with the edge of the summit but on the northern side—facing the Boer camp—there was a rolling grassy slope of some 100 yards between the rim and the true brow of the mountain. This meant that the defended perimeter had to be extended to nearly 1,500 yards, and even then the shape of the slopes made large areas of the ascent 'dead ground' for the defenders.

With the first rays of light a magnificent panorama of mountain

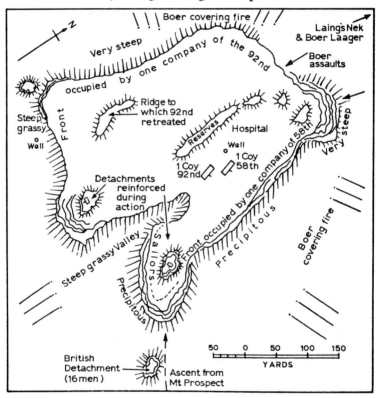

The Summit of Majuba on 27 February 1881

ranges was revealed to the soldiers, while nearer at hand—almost within a stone's throw it seemed—though in reality two to three thousand yards away—twinkled the lights of the Boer waggons. 'The valley', wrote one onlooker, 'was a mass of light. It was a thrilling sight from our point of vantage. There was our enemy at our mercy, and unaware of our proximity.' Here sounds the note of over-confidence which led to disaster. Colley's orders to remain concealed were forgotten as the view bred an overwhelming feeling of security. At 5 a.m. a newspaper correspondent saw 'at least 20 Highlanders on the ridge exposed to the full view of the Boers . . . pointing to the camp below and shaking their fists in exultation'. Soon afterwards random shots were fired and any hope of concealment was ended. The laager began to seethe like a disturbed ant-heap. Colley certainly appreciated the need for concealment and must bear some of the blame for the unsoldierly way in which his position was so quickly exposed.

It might be expected that the principal reason for delaying detection would be to enable the British to entrench on the summit. One of the main criticisms of Colley's generalship is that this was not done. Colonel Stewart, the chief staff officer, explained afterwards that the General thought the men too exhausted by their climb, and had in fact reconnoitred three positions where redoubts would be constructed the next day. This answer is clearly unsatisfactory. The high spirits of the 92nd soon after arrival on the summit belies the notion of exhaustion as do several testimonies written soon after the action; two wells were dug early in the morning; and several officers—including Lieutenant (later General Sir Ian) Hamilton—vainly requested permission to entrench. The most likely explanation, and one that is borne out by the events of the morning, is that Colley shared the popular view that the summit was impregnable. 'We could stay here for ever,' he is said to have remarked to Stewart soon after daybreak.[31]

This feeling of security, indeed of triumph, was underlined by Boer reactions to the first shots. A few groups made for the lower slopes and opened a desultory fire but the general impression seemed one of consternation. The oxen were quickly driven in and the waggons inspanned. Even the firing slackened off towards mid-morning. The *coup de main* seemed to have worked—the Boers were preparing to abandon Laing's Nek!

The messages signalled from the summit to Mount Prospect reflected this delusive sense of security. At 9.30 a.m. after messages on matters of supply and reinforcements from Newcastle, Stewart signalled: 'All very comfortable. Boers wasting ammunition. One man wounded in foot.' This set the tone for succeeding despatches until the last message was noted at 12.10 p.m. 'Boers still firing heavily on hill, but have broken up their laager and begun to move away ... I regret to say Commander Romilly is dangerously wounded; other ... casualties three men slightly wounded.'

Meanwhile at Laing's Nek Commandant Smidt quickly discovered the small size of the force holding the summit and, so eager and confident were the young Boers, volunteers were called for to storm the heights. Initially, according to a young Boer participant, Stephanus Roos, there were only about 50 volunteers and two officers—Commandant Joachim Ferreira and himself. The two parties—eventually totalling not more than 180 men, but all marksmen—began to climb at about 11 a.m., by which time patrols had reported that no British attack was impending elsewhere. In addition to the storming party about a thousand Boers opened a steady fire on the north and west sides of the mountain. It was this highly effective demonstration of covering fire which Colonel Stewart described as a waste of ammunition, and which alone made the final assault possible.

At about 1 p.m. General Colley was sufficiently unalarmed to take a short nap. By 2.30 it was clear even at Mount Prospect that the Boers were in command of the summit. What had happened in the interval?

Under intensified covering fire—the most effective coming from a ridge only 400 yards from the northern crest—the widely spaced and badly protected troops on the perimeter could scarcely raise their heads to follow Boer movements let alone move about to reduce the area of 'dead ground'—in some parts as much as 400 yards immediately below the crest. These conditions enabled the Boer commandos to climb within a few yards of the defenders at two widely separated points. Suddenly the Boers rose and poured a deadly volley into a small detachment of Highlanders holding the koppie on the north-western side. The survivors fell back on to the plateau and within minutes the Boers had gained a foothold on the summit. The reserves, in some confusion, rushed to hold this line and a counter-attack was attempted. Almost simultaneously however the Boers appeared on the northern side and took the Highlanders in the rear. The sailors on this side ran back towards the central ridge and, as one said later, 'the attack advanced firing so rapidly we could only see their rifles through the smoke as they crept up'. The absence of any sound defensive position *inside* the rim was now decisive. General Colley tried to rally the survivors on the central ridge but the view only extended to 40 yards and the Boers were able to work their way unseen round the flanks. Small groups of British troops which had been isolated by the sudden Boer assault were now picked off man by man. For example Lieutenant (later Major-General Sir Hector) Macdonald held the koppie on the west side with 20 men until only himself and one private remained alive. Meanwhile as the Boers—by now reinforced—closed around the central ridge an unidentified officer gave the order to retreat and thereafter a rout ensued as the survivors, many of them wounded, tried to scramble down the almost sheer slopes on the Mount Prospect side. Colley was killed—shot in the head at close range—just as the last attempt at defence was abandoned, and his death put a seal on the Boer triumph.

British casualties were as follows: killed 93, wounded 133 and prisoners 58. By comparison Boer losses were ludicrously small, one authority putting them as low as one killed and five wounded.

Who was to blame for the disaster? With commendable speed the military authorities in Natal gathered an impressive body of evidence from survivors and released prisoners.[32] Many testimonies were necessarily vague on such matters as time, positions, and the source of orders, but they did serve to discredit certain extravagant newspaper explanations such as those of the *Natal Mercury* which stated that the British had exhausted their ammunition and were outnumbered thirty to one. A certain acrimony entered the investigation when Colonel Stewart, who had been taken prisoner, presented his report on 4 April. He attributed the loss of the summit 'to the advance of the Boers being unseen, and hence unreported, the consequent retirement, and the fact that the efforts of the officers were fruitless to check the demoralisation ensuing thereon'. In short the troops were blamed for not observing and reporting the Boer advance, and for panicking as soon as the Boers appeared on the crest. Sir Evelyn Wood, Colley's successor, noted that Stewart's account was at variance with other officers' reports already received and he had good reasons for associating Stewart's name with an outspoken attack on the quality of the troops

Q

at Majuba which appeared in the *Natal Mercury*. Further questions elicited the fact that at least three officers had observed and reported the Boer ascent. In particular Lieutenant Hamilton, whose personal gallantry throughout the action was beyond dispute, showed at length that he had reported on *four* occasions the number of Boers he judged to be climbing the hill, three times to Colley in person and once (because the General was sleeping) to Major Hay. Colley had certainly spent a busy morning constantly visiting the perimeter, but it is hard to escape the conclusion that he—and his staff—had paid insufficient attention to this vital information because he imagined the summit to be impregnable, and the Boers in any case preparing to withdraw. The reserve, which was virtually wasted in the centre of the plateau, might have made all the difference on the Highlanders' extended front where the breakthrough came.

The second charge—that the Highlanders had panicked at the first appearance of the Boers near the crest—is difficult to judge because the officers on the spot were naturally concerned to uphold the honour of their men. When allowance is made on this score, however, certain facts suggest that the retreat from the crest, though a fatal mistake, was not dishonourable. First, Commandant Joubert confirmed a British staff officer's estimate that between 40 and 50 casualties occurred on the brow before the first retreat took place. Secondly, a British officer in the burying party said of the Highlanders' dead, 'All were shot above the chest; in some men's heads I counted five or six bullet wounds'. These testimonies bear out Sir Ian Hamilton's later comment: 'To us it was not a surprise—we were overpowered.'[33]

Complete agreement as to what happened on the summit is probably beyond reach and in any case does not conceal the general reason for the disaster; namely the gross underestimation of the Boers' tactical aptitude and courage. From the moment the British betrayed their position the Boer response showed a mastery of the principles of fire and movement which suggested how much the professional soldiers had to learn about the basic facts of modern war. British officers and men alike showed little appreciation of concealment, while the negligible Boer casualties provides sufficient comment on their marksmanship.[34] In the generous and just appraisal of Sir William Butler: 'If in this war the fighting General of the Boers [Smidt] had done nothing except the attack . . . on Majuba, the manner in which he carried out the movement would suffice to stamp him as one of the ablest leaders of mounted infantry that have appeared in modern war.'

The news of this remarkable defeat was bound to come as a shock to the British public. The death of the young and popular Colley seemed to magnify the disaster and made it difficult to regard the action dispassionately as a mere tactical reverse suffered by an isolated detachment. The popular press adopted a frankly sentimental attitude towards 'the lost leader'; the Queen lamented 'Poor Colley's death' in her letters; and her cousin, the Duke of Cambridge, described Majuba as 'a rout so complete and disastrous that it is almost unparalleled in the long annals of our Army'. Major Thomas Fraser, a brilliant Engineer who had been close to Colley on Majuba, wrote home: 'well, we have had a bad defeat, but had we all been killed, if only Colley had escaped, the country would have been less bereft. There were many brave men there, but he was the Homeric hero ...' Both Wolseley and Wood felt his death as a personal tragedy, the latter writing to his wife: 'Colley is gone: the best instructed soldier I ever met ... For him success [i.e. at Laing's Nek] was impossible, no smaller mind would have attempted to achieve it with the totally inadequate means at hand. He did not know what it was to fear and rated others by his own undaunted heart.'[35]

This unexpected defeat and the emotional public reaction to it only sharpened the Government's dilemma: whether to follow popular (and Royal) opinion and continue the war until a victory was gained; or continue to press for the policy already adopted by the Cabinet of a speedily negotiated peace irrespective of the military situation.

The reaction of the War Office was to champion the former alternative. On the very day that news of Majuba was received (28 February) it was decided to concentrate the dispersed military power of the Empire in order to defeat the Boers. The 85th Regiment was ordered to sail from India, part of the 102nd from Ceylon, and the 99th from Bermuda. As if this was not sufficient proof of determination, Major-General Sir Frederick Roberts—whose reputation fell little short of Wolseley's—was that day appointed to succeed Colley and ordered to sail at once for South Africa. Nor was this the sum of War Office assistance. On 1 March Mr Childers informed Wood that three additional regiments were being sent and implied that there was no limit to what Wood and Roberts could expect in the way of re-inforcements.[36] These gestures left no room for doubt that the Government meant to wage war more vigorously until a victory had been secured. It was a policy which coincided perfectly with Wood's own view of the situation.

The Whig triumph was short-lived. Dilke recorded the Radicals' tactics in his diary and his entry for Wednesday 2 March deserves to be quoted at length. On that day, after a long interview between Chamberlain and Dilke, the former

> 'had an hour and a half with Bright, and got him to write a strong letter to Gladstone about the Transvaal, which we put forward as the ground for a proposed resignation, although of course the strength of the coercion measures [i.e. in Ireland], the weakness of the land measures and the predominance of the Whigs in the Cabinet were the reasons which weighed chiefly with Chamberlain and myself, in the Transvaal matter, however, we should not be two but four, for Bright and Courtney must go out with us, and Lefevre might do so. On the other hand, we had reason to think that if the Whigs yielded to us on the Transvaal, Kimberley would go.'[37]

The Prime Minister's views were opposed to the policy adopted by Childers and Kimberley, even before he received the Radicals' ultimatum. After all, he argued, a proposal had been made to the Boers and their reply was still awaited. Could Colley's defeat justify the withdrawal of a proposal agreed upon by the Cabinet? 'Suppose for argument's sake,' wrote Gladstone to Lord Kimberley on 2 March, 'that at the moment when Colley made the unhappy attack . . . there shall turn out to have been decided on, and possibly on its way, a satisfactory or friendly reply from the Boer government . . .? . . . if it proved to be the case we could not, because we had failed on Sunday last, insist on shedding more blood.'[38]

On 3 March the Prime Minister sent for Bright and told him that he was 'in entire harmony' with the Radical view. As a consequence 'Kimberley at once gave in and telegraphed what he was told' and, rather ironically, the Radicals remained 'as far from resignation as ever'.[39]

Gladstone's decision not to seek military revenge and to let the peace proposals stand was, from one point of view, a courageous one which was certain to receive Conservative, Royal and Army opposition. It also opened dangerous possibilities of a wide gulf between Cabinet policy and War Office instructions to the General in the field.

Fortunately the weather intervened to impose a temporary check on Wood's determination to advance and drive the Boers from the Nek. Rain fell heavily for ten successive days, transforming the unbridged rivers into unfordable torrents—the Incandu at Newcastle rose 7 feet in one day—and the Natal roads (really tracks) into impassable ribbons of mud. On 6 March Wood's party—on horseback—took five hours to cover the twenty miles between Newcastle and Mount Prospect. With his reinforcements held up and Potchefstroom near starvation, Wood had sound military reasons for an armistice, and this was achieved on 6 March in a meeting with Joubert arranged by President Brand. The armistice was to last until midnight on 18 March. The Boers undertook to pass eight days' supplies to the invested garrisons, and inform them of the terms of the truce.[40] The Cabinet approved the ceasefire.

At the same time Wood made it clear that he intended to renew the advance at the earliest suitable moment. 'Considering the disaster we have sustained', he telegraphed Lord Kimberley, 'I think the happiest result will be, that after accelerating successful action ... the Boers should disperse without any guarantee, and then many now undoubtedly coerced will readily settle down.' 'Do not imagine I wish to fight,' he added on 8 March, 'but now you have so many troops coming I recommend decisive though lenient action; and I can, humanly speaking, promise victory.'[41]

These proposals were extremely unwelcome to the Prime Minister and the Radical element of the Government, and Wood was at once forbidden to make any military movement. Then, on 7 March Kruger's reply to Colley's letter of 21 February was at last received. So far from 'submission' the Boers welcomed the news that *the British Government* was inclined to cease hostilities—which was of course the case—but they did express hopes that a meeting of representatives from both sides would speedily lead to a satisfactory result.

This diplomatic crisis of the South African war came at a time when the Cabinet's energies were being devoted almost exclusively to the Irish Land Bill. Gladstone's private papers reveal how desperately eager he was to grasp at any solution in the Transvaal which in his opinion could be squared with the earlier Government pronouncements about vindicating the Queen's authority. Wood was therefore instructed to prolong the armistice and to inform the Boers that if they desisted from armed opposition a Royal Commission consisting of Sir Hercules Robinson, Sir Henry de Villiers and himself would consider the giving back of self-government to the Transvaal, subject to British suzerainty, with a Resident at the capital, and provisions for guarding native interests.

There followed anxious days of haggling between Wood and the Boer leaders when it looked as though the war might go on—an outcome which Wood continued to favour. Eventually, however, the Boers agreed to withdraw from the Nek and disperse to their homes. The British agreed not to occupy the Nek and not to follow up the retreating enemy. The garrisons were to remain in the Transvaal until the Royal Commission had finished its work. The Boer leaders were recognised as legitimate negotiators but, on the other hand, no Boer members were admitted to the Royal Commission.

Gladstone gratefully accepted these provisional arrangements on 22 March, his moral judgement strengthened by Brand's practical warning that if hostilities were renewed Afrikaner sympathy in the Orange Free State and Cape Colony would probably result in active support of the Transvaal. Thus the war ended with the Boers unbeaten in battle and Majuba unavenged. The British Liberals and the Irish and Boer nationalists had triumphed over the Whigs and the humanitarian imperialists.[42]

The many weak points in the Government's policy towards the Transvaal, and their handling of the campaign and the peace negotiations, were exposed in two full Parliamentary debates.[43] Earl Cairns, the former Conservative Lord Chancellor, outlined the 'six stages of the Surrenderer's Progress' from passionate determination to vindicate the Crown's authority down to negotiation on the prior assurance that the basic Boer demands would be met. Sir Michael Hicks-Beach, a former Conservative Colonial Secretary, touched a very raw spot when he said, 'You have given to men with arms in their hands what you denied to their peaceful prayers.' Government supporters argued at great length and with much hair-splitting over words like 'submission' that in fact a consistent policy had been pursued throughout the period of hostilities. There was one criticism which undermined this defence and it was never satisfactorily answered. If the scale and persistence of the rebellion had convinced the Cabinet, even before

Laing's Nek, that the Boer grievances were just and annexation must be cancelled, why was Colley not given explicit orders much earlier to avoid bloodshed? In fact both Mr Childers and Lord Kimberley had confirmed his freedom of action as late as 11 February (i.e. after the actions at Laing's Nek and the Ingogo river) and, as has been shown, the War Office continued to send reinforcements and promise more almost up to the conclusion of hostilities.[44] Sir Stafford Northcote also found the target when he pointed out that for some weeks the Government had thrown the responsibility of making peace overtures on President Brand, and had conducted negotiations with a divided mind.

The Government was admittedly defending a policy that had failed. The Prime Minister carried the fight to the opposition by enquiring what they would have done after gaining a military victory, given that a large majority of Boers were fanatically opposed to British rule. 'In the end,' said Gladstone, 'we should have been making war upon a very large portion—nay, on the whole Dutch population of South Africa, which numbers two to one of the English.' In these circumstances was it conceivable that Britain should have tried to hold the Transvaal under permanent military occupation?

The censure debate in the House of Commons (which the Government won by 314 votes to 205) was unfortunately held a few days before the Royal Commission finished its work, but even so there was a strong feeling on the opposition benches that the Government's management of the peace negotiations did not augur well for the future tranquillity of the Transvaal. 'They have secured,' said Hicks-Beach, 'not only that peace shall not be lasting, but that it shall be the precursor of infinitely worse trouble than any from which their weak yielding has for the moment delivered them.'

It is too easy to accept this inductment as an accurate prophecy. The negotiations, concluded in August 1881 by the Pretoria Convention, certainly failed to work smoothly. However, it is not easy to judge to what extent Liberal policy in 1880-1 was responsible for subsequent troubles since, as Wolseley had foreseen, the discovery of enormous gold deposits in the Transvaal dramatically altered the economic, political and military standing of that State. What can be charged against Gladstone's Government is that after having the worst of the war the British left the impression of having imposed an unsatisfactory peace under the shadow of a large army waiting to cross the frontier.

The Boers resented being excluded from the Royal Commission and also the ambiguous assertion of British 'suzerainty'. After further delegations to London the term was dropped and a full South African Republic was restored by the London Convention of 1884. The Transvaal was not after all partitioned as Lord Kimberley had intended, with the hopes of making it easier for the British to protect the natives, and this problem—together with that of the uitlanders—remained a major source of friction between Britons and Boers down to 1899.

In effect, then, the war of 1880–1 did secure to the Transvaal the independence lost in 1877, but it failed to lead to any notable improvement in the relations of the British and the Boers in South Africa. Apparent victory in the war gave Kruger and his followers—the exclusive and particularist burghers of the Transvaal—increased faith in their superiority over the despised uitlanders. On the British side Conservative and Liberal Imperialist statesmen were confirmed in their view that Boer independence represented a real threat to the empire, and one that sooner or later must be removed.[45]

Majuba—like Isandhlwana—has become a highly emotive name synonymous with disastrous defeat at the hands of an inferior foe and representing a whole mismanaged campaign. That it was a signal military disaster with very important political repercussions is undeniable. What has been less often appreciated is the complexity and confusion of the political context in which Colley made his fateful decision to occupy the mountain top, and Wood his unpopular decision to seek an armistice. This account has also underlined the advantages and disadvantages of close telegraphic contact between Government and field commander, and the hazards attendant upon Victorian generals who personally led small detachments into action.

The Liberal Government emerges with little credit for its conduct of Transvaal affairs in 1880–1. The Ministers responsible undoubtedly desired a settlement that would be in the best interests of South Africa w hile preserving Britain's strategic security; but the apparent *volte-face* on taking office, and failure to implement promises in the succeeding months, served only to provoke a rebellion for which they were militarily unprepared.

Cabinet control of policy during the war was if anything even less decisive. After apparently making a firm decision to suppress the rebellion, the Government, surrendering largely to internal pressures, retreated diplomatically to a position where they made peace hastily after three military reverses. Gladstone's decision to avoid further bloodshed in a war where justice was not demonstrably on the British side may be considered admirable from the viewpoint of domestic politics, but he certainly added to Colley's difficulties, and it is doubtful if his magnanimity was properly appreciated in South Africa. In the light of subsequent events in the Transvaal it is tempting to say that Sir Evelyn Wood should have been permitted to defeat the Boers before making peace. But it must remain an open question as to what would have happened had the Army been allowed to invade the Transvaal. The protracted guerrilla warfare of 1900-2 should make us wary of assuming that there would have been a short and satisfactory solution.

Not the least interesting aspect of the campaign was the shortcomings it revealed in the British Army. The Boer success demonstrated what patriotism, mobility and instinctive grasp of tactics allied to superb marksmanship could accomplish against regular troops with no training in individual initiative, inadequate instruction in the use of their weapons off the parade ground, and no idea of making the best use of the terrain. Colley, had he survived, was the sort of man to have benefited from his shattering experiences. As it was, Sir Evelyn Wood fully appreciated the crucial weakness in mounted men, and urged an unresponsive Duke of Cambridge that every battalion ought to train a proportion of its men as mounted infantry in peacetime.[46] Lieutenant Ian Hamilton, as he then was, set himself to improve the abysmal standard of marksmanship and made a lasting impact, first in India in the 1880's, and later in the 1890's as Commandant of the Musketry School at Hythe. Thus it would be an exaggeration to say that the British Army failed entirely to profit from the experience of the First South African War. Against these individual efforts, however, must be recorded the melancholy fact that precisely the same lessons were to be spelled out by the Boers, and on a far more impressive scale, in 1899-1902 in the Second South African War.

References

1   R. Robinson and J. Gallagher. *Africa and the Victorians*. London: Macmillan, 1961; p. 53.
2   Ibid., p. 59. Despite the opening of the Suez Canal in 1869 the Cape route

remained of great commercial and strategic importance. In 1878, for example, £91 million of British trade passed to or round the Cape compared with £65 million passing through the Suez Canal.

3   Ibid., p. 58.

4   Report by Sir Garnet Wolseley on the situation in the Transvaal in January 1877. Cabinet Papers 37/1, no. 18.

5   *The Memoirs of Paul Kruger, told by himself.* London: Fisher Unwin, 1902; 2 vols., I, p. 159. See also John Morley. *The Life of W. E. Gladstone.* London: Macmillan, 1911; 3 vols., III, pp. 20–1, and Cabinet Papers 37/1, no. 5.

6   Cabinet Papers 37/1, no. 5, and Morley, op. cit., p. 21.

7   Robinson and Gallagher, op. cit., pp. 66–7.

8   Sir W. F. Butler. *The Life of Sir George Pomeroy-Colley.* London: Murray, 1899; p. 251. Spencer Childers. *The Life and Correspondence of the Rt. Hon. H. C. E. Childers, 1827–1896.* London: Murray, 1901; 2 vols., II, pp. 6–7. Childers, the Secretary of State for War, 1880–2, was an old friend of Frere's and had been at Cheam School with Colley.

9   In fairness to Lanyon it must be noted that his contempt for the Boers was fully shared by Wolseley, see J. Lehmann. *All Sir Garnet.* London: Cape, 1964; pp. 261–81. See also Butler, pp. 252–60, 268–71, and Blue Book on South African Affairs 1881, C2740 and C2783.

10 C2783, pp. 18, 40. C2740, pp. 109, 115, 122. C2866, p. 15.

11 G. M. Trevelyan. *The Life of John Bright.* London: Constable, 1913; pp. 430–1.

12 Major G. Tylden. 'The British Army and the Transvaal 1875–85' in *Journal of the Society for Army Historical Research (J.S.A.H.R.)*, vol. xxx, 1952, pp. 159–71. The besieged garrisons were: Lydenburg, Rustenberg, Wakkerstroom, Standerton, Potchefstroom and Pretoria.

13 *Life of Childers*, op. cit., pp. 29–30. Butler, p. 277. For Bronkhorstspruit see *The Ranger 1914–20*, pp. 162–77; H. Jourdain and E. Fraser. *The Connaught Rangers.* London: R.U.S.I., 1926, vol. 2, and 'The Connaught Rangers' Papers', Royal United Service Institution MSS, no. 390.

14 Tylden, op. cit. Among the many interesting accounts of the sieges are: Lady B. Bellairs. *The Transvaal War.* Edinburgh: Blackwood, 1885; W. E. Montague. *Besieged in the Transvaal: the defence of Standerton.* London: Blackwood, 1881, and R. W. C. Winslowe. *The Siege of Potchefstroom.* London: Marshall, 1896.

15 Tylden. Kruger. *Memoirs*, p. 173.

16 Robinson and Gallagher, p. 69.

17 Morley, pp. 26–7. Gladstone Additional MSS. col. 44225 ff 261–6. C2754 para. 9: for Lord Kimberley's subsequent self-justification see Cabinet Papers 37/5, no. 10.

18 Shortly before sailing from England to relieve Wolseley, Colley wrote that he felt heavily handicapped in succeeding the great man in his first attempt at independent work, and added 'I can only hope that I may do my master credit, and I need not say that . . . I shall always consider myself at your disposal and only too proud again to follow you in any capacity from drummer boy upward.' Wolseley Papers at Hove Public Library. Lady

Colley left a fascinating analysis of her late husband's personality in an un-published manuscript now in the possession of her great-nephew Major Bruce Hamilton.

19   *Life of Childers*, pp. 13-15. Colley contemplated sending a second column from Capetown via Kimberley but abandoned the project on 6 January, when he realised that the reinforcements from India would not arrive in time. See War Office Papers 1881, 0878, no. 118.

20   Gladstone Add. MSS., vol. 44226 ff. 15-20, 30-1. C2837, p. 7.

21   Butler, pp. 322-5. C2837, nos. 35, 45, 46, 51. C2783, nos. 20, 21, 27, 32, 33, 40, 47, 52. C2866, nos. 13, 14.

22   Butler, pp. 286-90. *Life of Childers*, p. 16. Lady Colley noted that Lord Wolseley and General Sir Frederick Maurice always held that the attack was militarily justified, see 'Sir George Colley in South Africa', in *The Nineteenth Century*, March 1904, p. 408; also her letter in *The Times*, 9 January 1900.

23   Butler, pp. 311-12. C2866, no. 86.

24   C2837, nos. 45, 46, 51. Colley received his first information of the Govern-ment's negotiations from President Brand on 3 February. Lady Colley, op. cit., p. 409.

25   Colley's summary of Kruger's letter is given in C2837, no. 29. See also Gladstone Papers 44226, f. 40.

26   Dilke Papers B.M. Add. MSS. 43935, f. 19. S. Gwynne and G. M. Tuckwell. *Life of the Rt. Hon. Sir Charles W. Dilke*. London: Murray, 1917; 2 vols., I, p. 367. Gladstone Papers 44226, ff. 26-7.

27   *Life of Childers*, p. 24. Butler, pp. 357-9. Sir Evelyn Wood. *From Midshipman to Field Marshal*. London: Methuen, 1906; 2 vols., II, p. 113.

28   See for example Morley, p. 30; Lord Kimberley in *Hansard* 3rd series, vol. 260, 283; Mr Rathbone, ibid., vol. 263, 1790; Gladstone, ibid., 1755. Morley's biassed account is convincingly refuted by Lady Colley in *The Nineteenth Century*, March 1904, pp. 402-20.

29   Wolseley Papers at Hove, Colley file, letter 3.

30   The main sources used in the account of the action are: Butler, op. cit., Sir Ian Hamilton. *Listening for the Drums*. London: Faber, 1944. Major G. Tylden (translator). 'Majuba—a contemporary Boer account' in *J.S.A.H.R.*, vol. XVII, 1938, pp. 9-12. Major T. Fraser in *Royal Engineers Journal*, vol. xi, 1881, pp. 114-17, 125-6. A vivid but not entirely reliable account is given by C. E. Vulliamy in *Outlanders: a study of Imperial Expansion in South Africa 1877-1902*. London: Cape, 1938; pp. 56-85.

31   In a letter dated 30 July 1901, Col A. D. MacGregor testified that in the capacity of A.D.C. on Majuba he was asked by Major Hay and others to get permission to entrench but the General always replied, 'Not yet, that it did not require anything very substantial, as it was only against rifle fire.' See C. G. Gardyne. *The Life of A Regiment: the history of the Gordon High-landers 1816-98*. Edinburgh: Douglas, 1903; vol. 2, p. 204.

32   Correspondence relative to Military Affairs in South Africa. War Office Paper 0878 of 1881.

33   Gardyne, op. cit., p. 209.

34 It was this experience which caused Sir Ian Hamilton to become a life-long enthusiast for musketry training and it largely inspired his first publication *The Fighting of the Future*. London: Kegan Paul, 1885.

35 G. E. Buckle (ed.). *The Letters of Queen Victoria, 1879–85*. London: Murray, 1928; vol. III, pp. 198–206. *R.E. Journal* xi, pp. 114–17. Sir W. F. Butler. *Autobiography*. London: Constable, 1911; p. 217. Wood, op. cit., p. 112. Col W. Verner. *The Military Life of H.R.H. George Duke of Cambridge*. London: Murray, 1905; II, p. 223.

36 C2837, nos. 68, 69, 76. *Life of Childers*, pp. 25–7. One embarrassing consequence of the Government's *volte-face* was that Roberts had to be recalled without setting foot in South Africa.

37 Dilke Papers 43935, ff. 50–1.

38 Gladstone Papers 44226, f. 37. Lady Colley rightly stresses that the Boers never did send 'a friendly reply'. As Lord Cairns remarked: 'Opposition, my Lords, triumphed—it was *we* who ceased.' Quoted in Lady Colley, op. cit., p. 419.

39 Dilke Papers, ibid.

40 Cronje, the Boer Commander at Potchefstroom, failed to do this and obtained the surrender of the garrison's guns and ammunition by false pretences. This treachery provided a source of friction and mistrust throughout the months of post-war negotiations.

41 Wood's reluctant submission to the Government's order was bitterly unpopular with the Army and, Wood believed, permanently handicapped his prospects of high command. See his *Winnowed Memories*. London: Cassell, 1918; pp. 292–3, 336–7.

42 Robinson and Gallagher, p. 71. The Queen found it impossible to approve of the Government's change of policy and considered the repeal of annexation as 'damaging to the prestige of this Empire'. Buckle, op. cit. The Duke of Cambridge favoured another battle to restore the morale of the troops. Gladstone Papers 44129, ff. 185–6. Wood believed that 'a [British] victory would have been a gain to all' and was 'not sanguine' of enduring peace. *Life of Childers*, p. 27.

43 In the House of Lords on 31 March 1881—*Hansard*, vol. 260, 249–319; and in the House of Commons on 25 July 1881, ibid., 263, 1756–1876.

44 *Life of Childers*, pp. 18–19. Lady Colley, op. cit., p. 418. It might have been argued that reinforcements were sent out for purely defensive purposes but for the fact that the Government was well aware that Colley, and later Wood, were determined to attack the Nek and advance into the Transvaal at the earliest opportunity.

45 Robinson and Gallagher, pp. 72–3.

46 Considerable progress was made in the training of mounted infantry from the late 1880's. See Brian Bond. 'Doctrine and training in the British Cavalry, 1870–1914' in Michael Howard (ed.) *The Theory and Practice of War*. London: Cassell, 1965.

The Egyptian Campaign of
1882

The Egyptian Campaign of 1882

M. J. Williams

The Egyptian Campaign of 1882 was a striking success for Sir Garnet Wolseley; it earned him a peerage and in the short run proved to be of considerable political value for Mr Gladstone, the reluctant authoriser of the campaign. It was short, with less than two months elapsing between the decision to send a British expeditionary force to Egypt in July 1882 and the 'crowning mercy' of Tel-el-Kebir in September. The casualties were negligible and the British forces suffered no appreciable check from start to finish. Compared with the preceding Zulu, Afghan and Boer campaigns, with their disappointing setbacks at Isandhlwana, Maiwand and Majuba, and the succeeding Sudan campaign which failed to relieve Gordon, the Egyptian campaign went so smoothly that public opinion was overjoyed, and Wolseley himself always looked upon the campaign as the best-managed expedition in British military history.[1]

The campaign itself was launched because a violent nationalist reaction against the growth of European control over the Egyptian Government and administration threatened important British financial and strategic interests, so that most reluctantly Gladstone was forced to agree to send a British expedition to protect these interests. It was traditionally a principle of British foreign policy to prevent France establishing a sphere of influence in Egypt that would threaten the security of the over-land route to India and British trading interests in the Middle East. Furthermore, Egypt was still nominally part of the

Turkish Empire, although virtually independent in fact, and British policy aimed at preserving the Ottoman Empire as a shield against Russia. Until 1882, however, British statesmen had steadfastly refused to consider an occupation of Egypt by British forces. Not only would this have been to risk war with France, but the possible expense and administrative complications were unattractive. As Gladstone said in 1877: 'We cannot enjoy the luxury of taking Egyptian soil by pinches . . . our first site in Egypt, be it by larceny or be it by emption, will be the almost certain egg of a North African Empire. . . .'[2] In any case, Britain's

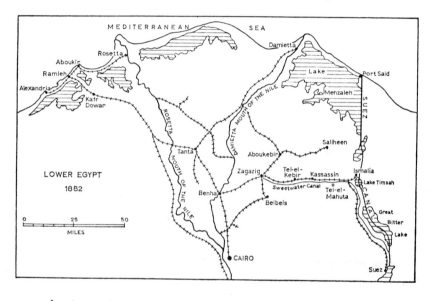

predominance in sea-power guarded against French rivalry, so that to keep France out it was not necessary to land in Egypt.

Neverthless, the construction of the Suez Canal—in use from 1869—gave an increased strategic value to Egypt itself, since it offered a shorter route to India and British Far Eastern possessions than the route around the Cape; and Gladstone's immediate predecessor, Disraeli, had, in 1875, secured a measure of financial control over the Canal by his purchase of the Khedive of Egypt's shares. Then the ambitious programme of westernisation pursued by the Khedive Ismail, nominally the viceroy of the Sultan of Turkey but in fact the ruler of Egypt, combined with a corrupt and inefficient administration, led to bank-ruptcy in 1876. Although Disraeli repudiated territorial ambitions, he felt unable to let France alone take over the reform of Egyptian finances. In order to prevent an exclusive sphere of influence being established by France against Great Britain, Disraeli co-operated with France in setting up a Dual Control of Egyptian finances in the interest of the European bondholders who were creditors of the Khedive. Disraeli's main motive was to maintain parity of influence with France, and this policy, which was also Gladstone's, had far-reaching and unintended consequences. Because of it, Britain was forced to acquiesce in a tighten-ing of the Dual Control in 1878 that greatly weakened the power of the Khedive Ismail. A liberal constitution was extorted from him and a responsible Ministry including British and French representatives was set up. Aware of the increasing growth of internal opposition to European interference, Ismail vainly attempted to defy Britain and France and overthrow the Dual Control. As a result, he was deposed and his more amenable son, Tewfik, substituted in his place, despite British misgivings. British and French Controller-Generals with wide powers of inspection were imposed on the new Khedive. In July 1880, European financial control was tightened to the point whereby two-thirds of the Egyptian Government's revenues was earmarked for repayment of Egyptian debts, while taxation, fiscal legislation, administrative expenditure, were all subject to the scrutiny and approval of the European Debt Commission representing the European powers whose leading members were, of course, Britain and France. Egypt, as Lord Milner later said, was 'tied hand and foot, unable to move, almost unable to breathe without the consent of Europe'[3].

The power of the Khedive had been gravely weakened and his prestige fatally injured. The great landowners did not welcome the proposals to enforce a more equitable mode of tax collection. The Moslem religious leaders and the officers of the Egyptian Army were angered by the spectacle of the Khedive as the tool of the European powers, and here a further motive was the Army's dislike of the proposed economies at its expense. A serious agitation against European influence and against the Khedive Tewfik was gathering strength from 1879.

The leadership of this agitation was primarily in the hands of a number of officers drawn from the Arabic-speaking peasantry or

R

fellahin, and outstanding amongst these was Ahmed Arabi Bey, who was born in 1840, the son of a small village sheikh, near Zagazig and, after studying at the Moslem Azhar University in Cairo, was conscripted into the Army at the age of fourteen. There, thanks to the patronage of the Viceroy, Said Pasha, a supporter of the fellahin against the Turkish ruling caste, Arabi enjoyed extraordinarily rapid promotion, becoming a lieutenant-colonel at twenty and A.D.C. to Said Pasha. The accession of the Khedive Ismail in 1860, however, was accompanied by a reaction against the lower-class fellah officers. Arabi fell into disfavour and, together with other officers of fellah stock and the Moslem religious leaders, he welcomed the overthrow of Ismail in 1879. The new Khedive Tewfik at first favoured him and appointed him a colonel of one of the regiments of his Guard. Then, however, the obvious growth of European control, in combination with threatened dismissal of officers and disbandment of regiments, turned Arabi into a nationalist leader. An eloquent and persuasive speaker, with considerable force of character, Arabi was a strong personality and undoubtedly guided by a sincere belief that he and his like-minded friends in the Army would regenerate Egypt. He was supported, as events proved, by most of the Army and most of the politically conscious elements—many landowners, the Moslem 'Ulemas', and the intelligentsia—and had much support even within the Khedivial family itself. Arabi was among the first of a long line of Middle Eastern and African nationalist leaders.[4]

By the autumn of 1881, Arabi and the fellah colonels had become the most important political force within Egypt, and a military demonstration had forced Tewfik to dismiss his Ministry and substitute one more acceptable to the nationalists. By the end of 1881, Arabi himself had been taken into the Ministry.

Meanwhile the British Government had been reluctantly forced to take cognizance of the Egyptian situation. Gladstone himself was preoccupied by the Irish question. His attempts to conciliate Ireland by concessions were to him the most important tasks and the Egyptian problem ranked, and continued to rank, much below the Irish problem in importance. At first both Gladstone and Lord Granville, the Foreign Secretary, were prepared to sympathise with the Egyptian nationalists' demands for reform but both accepted that the paramount necessity was to remain on good terms with France and to maintain parity of influence with her in Egypt. Thus Britain before long was drawn in France's wake and France was determined to crush Arabi and the nationalists, partly to prevent the bad example being followed in French North Africa, and partly to prevent the possibility of a strong Egyptian Government emerging which might hinder the realisation of the dream of Egypt as a French sphere of influence. Gladstone and Granville hoped however, almost to the end, that if intervention proved necessary, the Turks would restore order on behalf of the Concert of Europe. But while this hope proved fruitless, the association with France's policy led only to an increase in nationalist strength. In February 1882 Arabi was made Minister of War in a nationalist ministry. By April 1882, Sir Edward Malet, the Consul-General in Egypt, reported that: 'The country will soon be governed by none but officers.'[5] Hopes that a Turkish Commissioner would restore order were followed by the idea, held both by Malet and Granville, that a naval demonstration at Alexandria by the combined Franco-British Mediterranean fleets would 'make the acceptance of the points demanded certain'—that is, the dismissal of Arabi and the nationalist ministry.

However, although the prospect of Anglo-French aid nerved the Khedive Tewfik to dismiss Arabi, such was the latter's strength that inevitably, on 30 May, the Khedive was forced to reinstate him as War Minister. Gladstone's repeated attempts to get France to agree to come to terms with the nationalists or to agree, on the other hand, to get the Concert of Europe to sanction Turkish intervention, were in vain. Then, on 11 and 12 June, anti-European riots in Alexandria led to the death of over 50 Europeans and made it clear that the naval demonstration had failed completely.

Yet the June riots were of great importance. Gladstone was disillusioned with Arabi and the nationalists. More important still, the Radical faction in the Cabinet, led by Joseph Chamberlain, the President of the Board of Trade, combined with the Whig faction led by the Secretary for India, the Marquis of Hartington, to put mounting pressure on Gladstone to intervene. Chamberlain and the Radicals now believed that the nationalist movement was only a screen for Arabi's desire to become a military dictator, and that he should be overthrown in the interests of Egypt itself. Hartington believed that the nationalists threatened to repudiate Egypt's public debt and the security of the Canal. For financial and imperial reasons they must be crushed—

whether or not France assisted us or the Concert of Europe approved of intervention.

The combined pressure of Chamberlain and Hartington was impossible for Gladstone to resist. He could not risk the collapse of his Cabinet at a moment when the important Irish Rent Arrears Bill was in the balance. On 15 June the Cabinet discussed the propriety of preparing to send a British expeditionary force via the Mediterranean to Egypt, and the Secretary for War, Hugh Childers, informed the Commander-in-Chief, the Duke of Cambridge, and the Adjutant-General, Sir Garnet Wolseley, that confidential enquiries were to be made as to the necessary steps if an expedition were decided upon.[6]

Then on 21 June, although Gladstone and Granville still refused to hear of unilateral intervention, they were forced to consent to the sending of two battalions of infantry from Malta to Cyprus so that, if need be, they could protect the Suez Canal; and the Cabinet agreed to authorise a military expedition, other than Turkish, to Egypt. Then the British and French controllers were excluded from sitting in council with the nationalist ministers, and the British Admiral at Alexandria, Sir Beauchamp Seymour, reported the erection of shore batteries and fortifications, menacing to his fleet. On 10 July, having obtained Cabinet permission to demand the cessation of the work, Seymour exceeded his instructions, issued an ultimatum that the works must be surrendered within twenty-four hours, and upon refusal opened a bombardment. Gladstone had been powerless effectively to countermand this since Hartington approved it as the forerunner of an expedition and Granville, his main ally, was now deserting him.[7]

The only good consequence of the bombardment was that the Khedive seized upon the opportunity afforded by the hurried withdrawal of Egyptian forces from Alexandria on 12 July to take refuge with Seymour's fleet. Otherwise the bombardment increased the nationalist fervour. A Military Committee selected from the Council of Notables in Cairo appointed Arabi Pasha as Commander-in-Chief, and, outside of Alexandria, now occupied by Seymour's sailors and marines, the Khedive's sovereignty had ceased to exist. There was now no avoiding an expedition. Already, on 10 July, Childers had informed the Queen that preparations were so far advanced that within four to five weeks an expeditionary force of two divisions of infantry, a cavalry brigade and supporting artillery could be landed in Egypt.[8] Gladstone and Granville, it is true, now hoped that intervention might be limited to the seizure of Ismailia and the Suez Canal, which would be retained by the two battalions from Cyprus under Major-General Sir Archibald Alison, supported by the Fleet. But, on 13 July, the Duke of Cambridge addressed a vigorous protest to Childers against this proposal. After consulting Wolseley, he was 'most decidedly of the opinion' that unless this operation was backed up by at least 15,000–20,000 troops, it 'would be not only most hazardous but really quite unjustifiable by all the rules of war'. Cambridge pointed out that even if the Government only proposed to protect the Canal, a landing in Egypt was an act of direct hostility to Egypt and 'we must be prepared to meet it as such'.[9]

The plan of limited intervention was overruled by Hartington and Chamberlain, now determined to crush Arabi completely, and on 20 July a reluctant consent to this was extorted from Gladstone, whose remaining hopes of the Turks, or of French co-operation with the blessing of Europe, were then completely dispelled very quickly. On 23 July France refused to go beyond protection of the Canal. Then, on 29 July, the French Chamber of Deputies overthrew the Government of Freycinet and, obsessed by fear of Germany, completely repudiated intervention. Likewise the other European powers preferred to stand aside and Turkey successfully evaded offending Pan-Islamic sentiment by non-intervention.[10]

However, Gladstone, having agreed to intervention, had now persuaded himself that it was a righteous act and was then able to persuade the bulk of his Liberal supporters likewise. In the debates in the Commons between 22 and 28 July, Gladstone depicted intervention as a short-term project, a means to save Egypt from anarchy and, by restoring the rule of law, a possible means of arousing a 'noble thirst' amongst Egyptians for true civilised life. With 'infinitesimal exception', as Gladstone informed the Queen, on 28 July the House of Commons passed a vote of credit of £2,300,000. The matter was now in the hands of the armed forces.[11]

Only the previous year Childers, the Secretary for War, had carried a step further the reorganisation of the Army begun by Cardwell, by abolishing the old numbers and substituting territorial titles for the infantry regiments. But Childers had been unable to remedy the shortcomings of the Cardwell system, the most important of which was the perhaps inevitable failure to balance the much higher annual turnover of men under the short-service system by a big expansion of recruiting. The home battalions had become mere training units for those abroad and although, in 1881, Childers had decided to increase the term of service with the colours to seven years, at the same time he decreed that no troops below the age of twenty could serve overseas. Consequently a high proportion of the home battalions were either raw recruits or men who could not be sent on active service. A further difficulty was the fact that the repeated imperial campaigns since 1870 meant that the linked battalion system did not work in practice. In 1882 there were 81 battalions of infantry abroad and only 60 at home. At the end of 1881 the War Office hoped to keep 12 of the home battalions at full active service establishment of 950 and to send no more than four of them overseas on relief each year. Also, eight battalions were to be kept at an establishment of 850, the lowest considered suitable for foreign and colonial service. But it was realised that this plan presupposed no considerable demand upon home resources. In the event, the demands of the Egyptian campaign could only be met by calling out the First Class Army Reserve—men who had passed into the Reserve in 1881— quite contrary to Cardwell's original intention, which was that the Reserve was only to be called out in times of national emergency, such as an invasion. However, this problem of how to keep the home battalions up to strength and efficient was never solved in the pre-Haldane era.[12]

The possibility of armed intervention in Egypt had been 'for many months' under consideration at the War Office. At the beginning of 1882 Major Tulloch of the Intelligence Department had reconnoitred the Ismailia–Cairo line of advance. Wolseley himself had ordered the preparation of a number of papers, especially from Captain Hare of the Intelligence Department, on various aspects of the problem. On 21 June, as already mentioned, the service departments were ordered to make preliminary plans for an expedition. On 24 June a distinguished Cambridge Arabic scholar, Professor Edward Palmer, was recruited by military and naval intelligence for a mission to safeguard the Suez Canal by winning over the Bedouin tribes east of it—and, despite the tragic end of the mission, with the murder of Palmer and his companions, Captain Gill, R.E., and Lieutenant Charrington, R.N., by untrustworthy Bedouin, this mission had considerable success.[13]

Then, on 28 June, the first definite step was taken in the preparation of the expedition itself, when the Adjutant-General called upon the Commissary-General to make a return showing the number of horses, mules, carts, etc, on the transport establishments at home and in the Mediterranean bases, and showing also the amount of transport that would be required for the first line of a corps of about 24,000 men.

Childers ordered preliminary organisation to begin on 29 June, and the following day a Mobilisation Committee of the heads of departments at the War Office met, under the presidency of Wolseley, who outlined a plan of campaign, which was essentially the plan eventually followed. Two divisions of infantry and a brigade of cavalry should be sent to Ismailia, complete with regimental transport, as it would be unwise to count upon procuring much transport in Egypt before the defeat of the Egyptian Army. Then the force would advance from Ismailia upon Cairo, having first obtained possession of the Maritime Canal in order to insure the safe passage of the expedition. The railway line from Ismailia to Cairo and the Sweetwater Canal would be secured to within striking distance of the main Egyptian position already being prepared, as Intelligence reported, for the defence of the eastern side of the Nile Delta at Tel-el-Kebir. Then would follow a pause to amass supplies sufficient for the concentration of the army to deliver a final blow, to destroy the enemy in a general action.

To make the force independent of Egyptian rolling-stock, 5 locomotives with tenders and brake-vans, 100 open goods wagons, 5 break-down wagons with adequate tools for repairs and at least 10 miles of steel rails, with sleepers, nuts, bolts, etc., should be taken along. The Royal Engineers should supply the personnel to work this rolling-stock and a sufficient number of engine-fitters should be provided as well. With this provision of rolling-stock, transport could be cut down considerably. After the expected action at Tel-el-Kebir it could be assumed that any further Egyptian resistance would be insignificant.

This plan, embodied in a memorandum of 3 July which was communicated to Childers,[14] had chosen the Ismailia–Sweetwater Canal line of advance on Cairo to take advantage of the shorter route—75 miles—and of the 'hard desert' on the eastern side of the Nile Delta. The Delta itself was, of course, irrigated by a vast network of artificial canals. There were no roads for wheeled vehicles, and transport was either by boat, railway or pack-animal. Further, the months August–

October are the period of the 'high Nile', with the whole Delta flooded, thanks to the irrigation works. Thus the alternative Alexandria–Cairo route was not only longer in itself—120 miles—but could prove to be extremely difficult to follow, whereas the Ismailia–Cairo area consisted almost entirely of 'hard desert' of firm, smooth gravel and in general good marching-ground for infantry and cavalry, and, although sandy patches created difficulties for artillery and wheeled transport, conditions were still much more favourable for them here than in the Delta. Only on this side of Cairo, also, would the approach permit a rapid cavalry pursuit into the capital, whose speedy capture should end the whole campaign.

It is clear that Wolseley saw the campaign as a problem in logistics rather than in tactics or strategy. The tone of complete confidence of success was maintained, almost unwaveringly, to the end of the campaign.

On the same day that Wolseley drew up his memorandum, preparations were made to purchase extra mules in America, and for the Army Service Corps and Royal Artillery to provide as many carts, horses, etc., as possible for the expedition. The next day warning orders were sent out to the units selected for the expedition to be prepared to move at the shortest notice. It was also decided what baggage was to be left at Ismailia and what was to go forward by rail or with the troops. The advanced guard should be lightly equipped, with the men carrying one day's rations, while two days' supplies, and if possible fuel, were to move with the regiments in carts and five days' rations, including fuel, would follow by train. Ammunition reserves would follow on mules and carts and a special train. By 10 July, arrangements had been made to provide tents, and a supply of wood from Cyprus, and to establish hospitals at Malta and Cyprus. Also, it had been decided to arrange with the Indian Government for an Indian contingent to be despatched to Suez, then to join the main expedition.

The War Office had decided that the units to form the Expeditionary Force should be drawn mainly from the forces which had been chosen to take part in the autumn manœuvres, which on 7 July were definitely abandoned. The small advance force agreed upon when the plan was first considered in June, of two infantry battalions under General Alison, reached Cyprus on 14 July. On his own initiative Alison moved to Port Said, ready to seize the Canal and then, on learning of the events in Alexandria, sailed to Alexandria where he arrived on 17 July.[15] Meanwhile the limited intervention scheme of Gladstone's had collapsed, and on 9 July at Granville's request, Childers had decided to increase the forces at Malta and Cyprus to 15,000 men. Finally, on 20 July the Cabinet approved the Cairo expedition of two divisions, 15,000–16,000 men, of troops from Great Britain, to be known as the 1st Army Corps. To bring this up to strength, the First Class Army Reserve of 11,600 in all were called out by Order in Council. The remainder of the Regular Reserve totalled some 18,000 who would be available if need be, while the training of the Militia Reserve was extended to the full fifty-six days permissible, so that it would be under training until mid-September.[16]

There was no doubt as to who should command the expedition. No British general officer could compare in renown with Lieutenant-General Sir Garnet Wolseley, G.C.B., G.C.M.G., the Adjutant-General, whose competence was now a household word—'Our only soldier,' as Beaconsfield had written. His successes in Canada and Africa had not been marred by reverses. He was widely recognised as the most intellectual of Britain's generals, and had a wide circle of literary friends. He had been the assistant of Cardwell, who regarded him as his chief military adviser, and therefore had valuable supporters in the Liberal Party, although he himself was far from being an admirer of Gladstone's present administration. He had, however, aroused the resentment of the reactionary Commander-in-Chief, the Duke of Cambridge, who regarded him as a 'desperate reformer', and objected to what he considered, with much justice, to be Wolseley's passion for self-advertisement by indiscreet articles in the papers and indiscreet public speeches critical of the administration of the Army. Added to these objections was the Duke's fear that the rise of Wolseley represented a threat to his own power, which he had tried to forestall by strongly opposing the promotion of Wolseley to Adjutant-General at the end of 1881. Furthermore, the animosity of the Duke had been communicated to his cousin, Queen Victoria, who had refused Gladstone's request to give Wolseley a peerage in 1881.[17]

Wolseley was well aware of the 'formidable Royal party which is against me'. He had scornfully commented that Cambridge 'knows as much of modern warfare—or indeed of any warfare—as my top-boot does'. However, he made now a strong effort to win over the Court, while on his side the Duke was forced to admit to Queen Victoria, on 20 July, that Wolseley, who had been that day selected as the expedition's commander by the Cabinet, was 'very decidedly as able a man for the field as we have got'. Wolseley received the local rank of General.[18]

The Duke did not welcome the choice of Lieutenant-General Sir John Adye, who was fourteen years Wolseley's senior, as Chief of Staff and second-in-command, although Adye made no difficulty about serving under Wolseley. Nor did the Duke approve of the selection of so many of the 'Ashanti Ring' to serve with the expedition. In charge of Intelligence was Colonel Redvers Buller; Colonel Sir Baker Russell commanded the 1st Cavalry Brigade; Major-General Sir Evelyn Wood, V.C., commanded an infantry brigade. One Assistant Adjutant and Quartermaster-General was Lt-Colonel W. F. Butler, one of Wolseley's closest personal friends. Another friend, Major J. F. Maurice, the future Official Historian of the campaign, and one of the leading military theorists of the day, was appointed Deputy Assistant Adjutant and Quartermaster-General. Lt-Colonel Herbert Stewart was on the staff of the Cavalry Division; Lt-Colonel McCalmont was acting Brigade Major of the 1st Cavalry Brigade.[19]

As far as the Divisional and Brigade commanders were concerned, Wolseley had been ready to accept nearly all the generals chosen to command in the autumn manoeuvres. He was on good terms with Major-General D. C. Drury Lowe, the commander of the Cavalry Division. However, relations soon became strained between Wolseley and the two infantry divisional commanders, Lieutenant-General G. H. S. Willis of the 1st Division and Lieutenant-General Sir Edward Hamley of the 2nd Division. The former Wolseley came to look upon as an 'alarmist' and the latter, although a famous military writer, was donnish, autocratic and of a violent and vindictive temper, and in the course of the campaign became obsessed with the conviction that he had been deliberately slighted by Wolseley, who in turn developed a keen dislike of Hamley. Further, the number of generals was unusually large in proportion to the total strength—eighteen of brigadier-general rank and upwards, and this inevitably made for friction.[20]

Much to his annoyance, Wolseley was obliged to accept Major George Fitzgeorge, the Duke of Cambridge's son, as his Private Secretary. The Prince of Wales himself was anxious to go out with the expedition and Wolseley, although inwardly offended by what he considered had been the Prince's past ill-treatment of himself—his 'insulting "out of door relief" '—did not refuse. However, on 27 July, Gladstone declined to agree, and anyway the Queen could hardly have consented. Nevertheless, the Prince of Wales did not relinquish his plan and while at Bad Homburg in September, vainly attempted to secure the assistance of Wolseley through Lady Wolseley, then on holiday there. Unwisely, however, the Prince presumed to criticise Wolseley's strategy and appointments, both verbally to Lady Wolseley and by letter to the General himself. He thus infuriated Wolseley, who wrote acidly to his wife: 'Let him stick to tailoring, that is his province' —and more in similar strain.[21]

On the surface, however, Wolseley made a considerable effort to ingratiate himself with the Court and supported the application of the Duke of Connaught, the Queen's favourite son, to serve. After the Queen had very reluctantly consented, the Duke of Connaught was given a brigade and Wolseley was before long to complain privately that Connaught had no stamina.[22] Worse by far, however, was the Duke of Teck, a cousin of the Queen, accepted by Wolseley as an officer on 'Special Employment'. It turned out that he was full of complaints about his quarters and his hardships. Wolseley termed him 'quite an impossible human being, just like a spoiled child' and said that his 'only occupation' was 'packing and unpacking his kit'.[23] Eventually it proved necessary to detail him to look after the foreign military attachés to keep him out of the way.

However, these troublesome characteristics of the two Dukes had not made themselves apparent when on 28 July the Queen received all the generals of the Expeditionary Force at Osborne. Here Wolseley made a bid for royal favour by criticising the lack of preparedness of the administration and by speaking highly of the Duke of Connaught. Unfortunately, as events proved, Wolseley made no strongly favourable impression on the Queen, and on the way back to London he contracted a chill which turned to erysipelas and seriously indisposed him for some days. His medical advisers vetoed the intended overland route to Brindisi and then ship to Alexandria, and insisted that he proceed to Egypt by the long sea route. However, this in no way impeded the final stage of mobilisation, which proceeded smoothly thanks to the extensive preparations made in good time by both Admiralty and War Office.

The Director of Transports at the Admiralty, Admiral Sir William Mends, had begun to prepare transports on 12 July, and a total of 69 troop transports was hired at 20s. 8d. per ton from the merchant shipping lines for the transport of the main force and its equipment from England, and five more were hired to transport mules from Natal to Egypt, the main work being done between 21 and 31 July. Further, there were nine 'troopers', the Admiralty's own transports, of which five were used to assist the transport of the Indian contingent which began to prepare on 22 July. The Indian Government itself also hired a number of transports, at a considerably higher cost per ton.

While this was in progress, the troops of the main expedition were concentrated at the embarkation ports. The total was 16,416 troops including staffs,with 5,487 horses. There were three cavalry regiments and a composite Household Cavalry Regiment (2,397 men and 2,047 horses); ten infantry battalions (8,169 men); eight complete batteries of artillery (1,881 men, 1,406 horses and 54 guns); and finally Royal Engineers, Commissariat and Transport troops; Ordnance troops, military police, medical units, railway staff and telegraphists (3,851 men and 1,423 horses in all). The cavalry sailed from the London and Southampton docks; nearly all the artillery detachments from Portsmouth and Southampton. The Royal Engineers and Corps troops sailed mainly from London, but the embarkation ports of the infantry were more widely dispersed. Four battalions sailed from Kingstown and Queenstown, the rest from Portsmouth, Southampton or London.

Eight transports were needed for the cavalry; ten each for the artillery and infantry; eight for the Royal Engineers and Ordnance; twenty for the Commissariat and Transport; one each for medical units and miscellaneous Corps troops; and eleven were needed for the all-important rolling-stock upon which the supply and transport system was to depend. Sailing began on 27 July but the main movement began on 30 July, and from then until 12 August the main body of troop transports cleared daily from the ports, calling at Malta for orders and then proceeding to Alexandria. The main concentration at Alexandria was complete by 22 August, but some late-sailers arrived only on 5 September.[24]

Meanwhile the Mediterranean stations of Gibraltar and Malta were almost stripped of their garrisons which were sent on to Alexandria. Including the two infantry battalions already with Alison, nine infantry battalions (7,592 men) went from the Mediterranean stations to Alexandria and became part of Wolseley's forces. Furthermore, the Indian contingent of two British infantry battalions, three Bengal and Bombay infantry battalions and three regiments of Bengal cavalry, with Madras sappers and miners (6,930 troops in all), under the command of Colonel Sir H. T. Macpherson, V.C. (who received the local rank of Major-General on 4 August), sailed from Bombay in seven transports on 9 August to rendezvous with Wolseley's force and to form part of it. Including the drafts and depot troops (some 4,000) sent out to Wolseley, a total of nearly 35,000 troops was assembled in the Egyptian theatre during the campaign.[25]

Numbers proved no problem in fact, and as early as 18 August, when Childers informed him that the Cabinet were considering forming a 3rd Division, Wolseley was able to inform the Secretary for War that he did not anticipate needing another division after the already prepared drafts and depot troops had been sent out, although he believed the formation of a 3rd Division was a wise precaution. This was a considerable relief to Childers. While some 6,000 troops were available and the transport could be got ready in reasonable time, it would have forced Childers to embody Militia battalions for garrison duty in view of the 'heavy Irish demand', and this would have needed Parliamentary permission—and Parliament was in recess until October. Even to spare two battalions from England, he informed Wolseley on 25 August, 'would be a little questionable'. Had it been necessary 'at a pinch' Wolseley could have drawn a half-battalion from Malta and Gibraltar and the Government of India would have had to be called upon.[26]

Wolseley was given a completely free hand in planning his campaign and Childers repeatedly assured him of his 'absolute confidence' and that he did not 'much care to know your intentions unless by knowing them we can help you here'. The Queen likewise emphasised that Wolseley must be left unhampered and thus, although Wolseley reported to the War Office by telegraph daily throughout the campaign, there was no interference from home.[27]

Although Wolseley was very unwell for several days after his return from Osborne, he was quite clear about what had to be done. His first care was to prevent any premature move to Ismailia which might warn Arabi and also induce him to cut the Sweetwater Canal which supplied fresh water not only to Ismailia but also to Port Said and Suez. In case Arabi should attempt to destroy the Canal, warning orders had been sent on 24 July to Admiral Seymour and General Alison at Alexandria to prepare to seize Port Said, Ismailia and the Nefiché rail junction with the small force of troops and marines. Then Alison was ordered, on 31 July, to maintain a constant state of alarm amongst the Egypians who had fallen back from Alexandria to Kafr-ed-Dauar, where they were concentrating a force. Therefore Alison almost daily reconnoitred the enemy position, and on 5 August made a personal reconnaissance in force, with the assistance of an armoured train manned by seamen and carrying a 40-pounder gun. These reconnaissances certainly deceived the newspaper correspondents and may have had a good effect in drawing the enemy's attention. It was necessary, however, for Wolseley to veto a scheme, on learning of it by telegraph, prompted by fear of an attack on the Canal, to seize Ismailia at once, as it would have been a most fatal mistake to show the British hand too soon. Wolseley greatly feared that Arabi might not only cut the Sweetwater Canal but might block the Suez Canal itself, and, writing to Childers from his sick-room on 29 July, said he did not see how the Ismailia plan could work if this happened. A premature occupation of Ismailia by a small force might provoke the consequences he feared.

Wolseley therefore ordered Adye, who reached Egypt on 10 August and took over the command, that he was not to go to Ismailia except in an emergency, to defend the Canal, but to prepare for the movement while continuing to divert the Egyptians' attention to Alexandria.[28]

Meanwhile Wolseley himself, still far from well, on 2 August boarded at the Albert Docks the *Calabria* transport which held most of the Household Cavalry and, refusing to wait at Cowes to say good-bye to the Prince of Wales, sailed the same day. Before leaving he had prophesied that he would fight a decisive battle at Tel-el-Kebir about 16 September, and cheerfully promised his young daughter, Frances, a pony 'even if Arabi's nose escapes my pruning-knife'.[29] By the time that Malta was reached, on 12 August, Wolseley was fully fit and his only fear was due to an unfounded rumour that Turkey was to intervene after all, perhaps causing Arabi to give in. On the night of 15 August he reached Alexandria, where the Guards Brigade under the Duke of Connaught had already disembarked and strengthened Alison's defensive positions around the town. It was also known from the telegraphed reports of vessels passing Malta that by 19 August nearly all the infantry of the 1st Division would have reached Alexandria. The Household Cavalry had arrived as well as some of the artillery, while the rest of the cavalry and artillery still at sea could be directed to follow to Ismailia.

On arrival at Alexandria, Wolseley received a congratulatory telegram from the Queen which he did not appreciate, being unable to 'forget the Queen's most ungracious conduct to us both hitherto'. He was also annoyed the following morning, 16 August, to learn that Sir Edward Malet, the British Consul-General, had been made Minister Plenipotentiary, with precedence over himself and Seymour. 'I think the Government should have given the position to me, but I am not yet able to dictate upon such points and so must submit: by and by I shall have my day—at least I hope so.' Despite this disappointment the day was a rewarding one. Wolseley lunched on the *Helikon* despatch boat with Admiral Seymour, with whom he established very cordial relations, and finalised his plan 'for opening the ball'. It was arranged that the force should leave Alexandria on Saturday 19 August, ostensibly to land at Aboukir and attack Arabi's position nearby, but really to go down the Canal to seize Ismailia. It was also decided to inform Admiral Hewett, commanding at Suez, which had been seized on 2 August and where a battalion of the Indian contingent was already established, so that the whole of the Suez Canal could be secured simultaneously on the morning of 20 August. Then, after seeing the Khedive, Wolseley went off to survey the Egyptian positions at Kafr-ed-Dauar and 'did the Commander-in-Chief' with a Napoleonic air, finally returning to dine with the admiral.[30]

Strict secrecy was maintained about the plan of campaign. The Press was given to understand that Aboukir was the objective and so were all Wolseley's military subordinates except Adye. Hamley and his two brigadiers, Wood and Alison, were set to work drawing up plans for a frontal attack on the lines of Kafr-ed-Dauar combined with the 'flank attack' at Aboukir Bay, which Wolseley then gravely endorsed. These ruses did not deceive Childers but did incur the censure of the Duke of Cambridge on the grounds that it was unethical to mislead the Press.[31]

However, there was a number of serious problems that had to be overcome. Firstly there was the hostility of the great French engineer, Ferdinand de Lesseps, who was strongly opposed to any idea of British seizure of the Canal. He had already persuaded Arabi that this would not happen—which may account for the Egyptian failure to block it—as it would be regarded as a neutral zone. Wolseley feared that de Lesseps would sabotage the Canal and this fear mounted when an unfounded rumour arrived on 18 August that a French ship had been grounded—purposely?—near Lake Timsah.[32]

Also there was the problem of moving transports through the Canal itself to Ismailia. With large transports the danger of grounding was very real; many of the ships' officers of the transports had no previous experience of the Canal, and the special steering gear fitted on the regular canal ships was lacking. Moreover, de Lesseps had in his employ all the special canal pilots. It was planned to overcome these difficulties by setting a naval officer in charge of every transport and the whole working of the passage to Ismailia was placed in the hands of Captain Fisher, R.N., using the little Thornycroft torpedo boats, with their shallow draft, as his means of rapid communication. Then, as large ships going in opposite directions could not pass in the Canal, arrangements had to be made to confine northbound ships to the 'gares' or stations as the expedition moved south. Finally, at Ismailia itself there was only one small pier for disembarking so that ships had at first to anchor at least half a mile from the shore. And, after disembarkation, a narrow road then led to a single small bridge over the Canal over which at first everything had to cross. Although landing stages to supplement the inadequate pier and adequate bridging stores had been prepared beforehand in England and brought out by the Royal Engineers, the advance ships would have to be occupied by the troops needed to seize the railway and Sweetwater Canal, with their necessary guns, ammunition and supplies. Inevitably, even if the seizure of Ismailia went off faultlessly, the build-up of the main force there through the bottleneck of the Canal with the inadequate landing facilities would take time.[33]

But all obstacles were overcome. On the morning of 17 August Admiral Hoskins arrived off Port Said and the following day briefed the captains of the men-of-war that were to carry out the seizure of the Canal from Port Said to Ismailia on the morning of 20 August, while Admiral Hewett, on his side, was ordered to seize Shaluf on the 20th and Serapeum as soon as possible. With the exception of the capture of Serapeum, which was not taken until 21 August, soon after 3 a.m.

of the appointed day the operations were simultaneously and successfully carried out.

Parties from H.M.S. *Ready* under Commander Edwards occupied all barges and dredgers along the line to Ismailia and required all ships in the Canal between Ismailia and Port Said to move into and stay in the stations. Three vessels evaded this control but luckily caused no delay. Kantara telegraph station was seized without resistance.

At Port Said, Captain Fairfax of H.M.S. *Monarch* was equally successful. Here Lt-Colonel Tulloch of the Intelligence Department landed from an open boat with six marines and surprised and seized the sentries. Then companies of Marines from the *Monarch* and H.M.S. *Iris* seized the garrison in its barracks while still asleep. At Ismailia parties of Marines and seamen from H.M.S. *Orion*, H.M.S. *Northumberland* and H.M.S. *Coquette* and the *Nyanza* troop-ship seized the lock and the town in an hour at the cost of one officer wounded.

The ships then shelled an enemy detachment in the railway station and this was abandoned by the foe. The Egyptian telegraphists had informed Cairo of the fall of the town, yet telegrams continued to arrive from Cairo for the traffic manager. A reply was sent to Cairo to the effect that 5,000 English troops had landed and that any attempt to relieve the place was too late. The War Minister in Cairo politely acknowledged receipt and said he had informed all concerned! This bluff was intended to avert the danger of a counter attack, which in the event did not materialise, from the Egyptian detachments at Nefiché.

Like success attended Admiral Hewett. A company of the Seaforth Highlanders seized the important lock at Shaluf where a fresh-water canal emptied into the Suez Canal. Here there was rather more vigorous resistance but it was soon dispersed. Small-arms fire, naval Gatling guns and the guns of H.M.S. *Seagull* and H.M.S. *Mosquito* easily scattered the Egyptians and the only fatal losses were two soldiers drowned trying to swim the fresh water canal. So the way was clear for the passage of the main force to Ismailia and the rendezvous with the Indian contingent, whose main body arrived at Suez on 20 August. The whole operation had been carried out with great skill and just in time, for the Egyptian Military Committee had not been satisfied with de Lesseps' reassurances and, but for the reluctance of Arabi Pasha himself, would have attempted to block the Canal between

S

Ismailia and Part Said. Indeed, a Council of War at Kafr-ed-Dauar on 20 August decided, too late, on the 'temporary' destruction of the Canal.[34]

As it was, Wolseley feared that vigorous action by the Egyptian detachment at Nefiché, estimated at 2,000 strong, might endanger the small force at Ismailia. In fact, however, the great bulk of the Egyptian regular forces, 8,000–9,000 strong, was still at Kafr-ed-Dauar. It is true that Wolseley's Intelligence estimated the Egyptian forces at 60,000 with 6,000 Bedouin allies (an estimate soon to be inflated to 100,000), distributed as follows: 15,000 each at Kafr-ed-Dauar and Aboukir; 7,000 at Damietta; 12,000 at Tel-el-Kebir and on the eastern side of the Delta; 11,000 at Cairo with 3,000 Bedouin at Kafr-ed-Dauar and 3,000 at Tel-el-Kebir. However, Wolseley himself admitted in writing to Childers on 19 August, and referring to his Intelligence staff, that 'those employed to collect information are such wild people when any estimate of the enemy's strength is called for, that it is difficult for me to give you any statement that would be worth your having. . . . My own humble opinion is that he [Arabi] had 20–25,000 real soldiers, say 5–10,000 Bedouin and say 10,000 levies. I believe my estimate is a most liberal one.'[35] Wolseley anticipated that the landing at Ismailia would draw Arabi off from Alexandria to Tel-el-Kebir, as expected all along, and enable him to bring up the bulk of his troops from thence, leaving the town quite securely in the hands of a couple of battalions plus depot troops.

Now, just before he took the main force up to Ismailia, Wolseley was unworried about any possible enemy concentration against him so long as Ismailia was secured, and he informed Childers that whether Arabi 'has a mob of 30,000 or 100,000 is really of very little consequence to us. With our two divisions and the Indian contingent the whole of Egypt assembled at Tel-el-Kebir would be made short work of: please believe this if any croakers try to frighten the Government.'[36]

Thus the British Commander was supremely confident of success if Ismailia and the Canal were secured. While the naval task-forces were preparing to seize the Canal, the rest of the plan of deception was carried out. The Guards Brigade and all the available infantry and cavalry were re-embarked on 18 August and arrangements were made to transport to Ismailia four locomotives and eighty carriages. Then in the evening all the fleet except the despatch boats of Wolseley and

Seymour anchored outside the outer harbour of Alexandria, 8 iron-clads and 17 troop transports in all. At noon of the following day, the Commanders' despatch boats joined the fleet which then weighed anchor. Sweeping eastward, the fleet anchored about 4 p.m. in Aboukir Bay, where they remained until nightfall. Then small craft simulated an attack on the Aboukir forts while the rest of the fleet steamed off towards Port Said. Wolseley, who derived great amusement from the 'fond conviction' of Hamley and his brigadiers, Wood and Alison, that their plans of attack on Kafr-ed-Dauar were to be implemented, had left sealed orders with Hamley to be opened at daybreak on Sunday, 20 August, disclosing that 'the whole thing is a humbug'. Wolseley realised that leaving the 2nd Division commanders behind and keeping them in the dark might provoke resentment. Nevertheless, it would have been pointless to have taken a stronger force with him then because of the Canal bottleneck. Extra transports would only have been accumulated at Port Said until the port facilities of Ismailia had been much improved. Then there was the defence of Alexandria to be assured until Arabi had been drawn off from Kafr-ed-Dauar. Malet, the Minister Plenipotentiary, was somewhat sensitive on this point, though there was little serious danger of an Egyptian attack. Finally, Willis's division was rather more completely assembled than Hamley's, with more of its infantry present at Alexandria before the move, so that the 1st Division was the logical choice to form the core of the striking force. From the purely personal viewpoint, how-ever, the matter turned out badly. Hamley did not forgive being made to look a fool and Wolseley's ultimate decision to leave the brigade of Wood, the junior Major-General, at Alexandria not only infuriated Hamley, it also alienated Wood, who was, in the view of Redvers Buller, 'eaten up with personal vanity' and had had unworthy aspira-tions to take Wolseley's place.[37]

Having reached Port Said soon after sunrise on 20 August, the fleet found that the three ships which had disobeyed the naval control parties had not cleared out, but to avoid delay, Major-General Gerald Graham, R.E., with a wing of the West Kent Regiment, was transferred first into a torpedo-boat then, after the steamers had been by-passed, into a gun-boat, and landed at Ismailia at 10 p.m. Then, with the three ships moving north out of the way, the expedition entered the Canal with transports carrying lighters and working parties in the van. Slow progress was made on the forty-mile journey on the 20th as groundings were frequent. At 9 a.m. on 21 August, Wolseley himself reached Ismailia and sent forward Graham with his West Kent detachment and a battalion of Marines in the hope of catching the detachment at Nefiché. Progress in the Canal continued to be slow. Not before dusk on 21 August had the bulk of the infantry of the force reached Ismailia. However, Serapeum was captured by the Seaforth Highlanders and here the important lock from the Sweetwater Canal (as had been the case at Shaluf) was found to be open and was promptly closed. The enemy were easily driven off and their parties were in full retreat northwards across the desert.

By 22 August, the whole line of the railway and freshwater canal between Suez and Ismailia was in British hands, though not without damage at certain points. Disembarkation at Ismailia went forward as quickly as possible and by the evening of 23 August about 9,000 men, nearly all the troops, were on shore, including the remaining units of the 1st Division which had still been en route to Alexandria from England on 19 August and who had been directed up to Ismailia. But the disembarkation of supplies and equipment for the troops was far from complete. There was great congestion in the port itself, as had been expected. Under the direction of Colonel Sir W. O. Lanyon (2/W India Regt.), the Base Commander, and his deputy, Captain J. H. Sandwich, R.M.L.I., the engineers, assisted by large fatigue parties, greatly extended the landing stage, erected two additional landing piers and laid new roads. Even so, and despite a plentiful supply of lighters, horse boats and flats, it was necessary to swim many mules and the supply cattle ashore. It was already clear that the supply situation was going to be the one big problem that could delay a speedy build-up of the force.[38] Repair work on the railway began at once and the engines brought up from Alexandria were sent on to Suez to await the re-opening of the line.

Meanwhile the level of the fresh water in the Sweetwater Canal was falling and it was learned that the enemy had constructed a dam at Magfar stopping the flow of the Canal. Beyond Magfar the land rose steadily towards Tel-el-Mahuta and it was considered that while the Canal could still be dammed above Magfar, it would be far less easy to break down the banks where they were so much higher. Thus, to safeguard the water supply, it was necessary to press on to Magfar, six miles ahead. Moreover it was already clear that it would be necessary to organise boat transport in the Sweetwater Canal. Here the Navy lent vital assistance. Commander A. W. Moore, R.N., second-in-command of H.M.S. *Orion*, organised the Boat Transport Service. Two steam pinnaces and two naval cutters entered the Canal through the Ismailia locks, a dozen native boats were purchased, six horse boats and six naval launches were also in service by 25 August. In carrying supplies and in towing the boats of the hired transports, the Boat Service gave invaluable help to Wolseley in the period before he could make full use of his engines.[39]

While Arabi himself remained with the main Egyptian force at Kafr-ed-Dauar, General Ali Fehmy, a loyal supporter, had been given command of the Eastern Army which was based upon Tel-el-Kebir, thirty miles from Ismailia and which was responsible for the protection of the Canal flank. However, General Fehmy had been completely surprised by the capture of Ismailia as had Rashid Pasha, who commanded the Ismailia area and who had fallen back to Tel-el-Mahuta.[40]

So there was no immediate opposition to the advance upon Magfar that began at 4 a.m. on 24 August. General Drury Lowe with three squadrons of Household Cavalry, a detachment of the 19th Hussars, a small force of thirty-two mounted infantry under Captain R. R. Hutton (3/K.R.R.C.), together with the only two guns disembarked, led the way across the desert. Wolseley and Willis rode with them and Graham followed with the 2/York and Lancaster and some Marines along the railway embankment to avoid the heavy soft sand between Ismailia and Magfar. The cavalry reached the dam at Magfar at 7.30 a.m., easily dispersing enemy skirmishers. The dam itself was very solidly built and prisoners reported another one at Tel-el-Mahuta and also that Egyptian infantry were in force there.

After reconnaissance of the Tel-el-Mahuta position, Wolseley concluded that the enemy meant to make a serious stand, estimating them at over 8,000. Thereupon he boldly decided to try to keep the enemy in play until reinforcements could arrive to defeat them and allow him to secure the railway and Canal as far as Kassassin. Thus any danger to the water supply would be completely removed and a base could be established at Kassassin within striking distance of Tel-el-Kebir.

But Wolseley's hopes were disappointed. Graham was ordered to advance to Tel-el-Mahuta while the Guards Brigade and other available infantry at Ismailia and Nefiché were ordered to come up as quickly as possible. But the Egyptians did not come within effective range of the infantry. The action became an artillery duel that lasted until dusk, Wolseley himself having some narrow escapes. Fortunately although the Egyptians had a number of Krupp guns, most of their shells were fitted only with percussion fuses which buried themselves in the sand before bursting. The heat was very trying to the British troops. Willis collapsed and the Guards Brigade, arriving at 6.20 p.m. after a forced march, suffered severely. Wolseley had already protested to Childers about the unsuitability of summer campaigning in hot climates in the traditional red serge jackets, flannel shirts and woollen trousers, and his views were now echoed by the Duke of Connaught.[41]

The arrival of reinforcements encouraged Wolseley to plan an attack at dawn the next day. Returning to Ismailia for the night, he was back at Tel-el-Mahuta by 5.30 a.m. on 25 August. But the advance found the enemy works abandoned, and with great determination Wolseley sent the cavalry and horse artillery on to try to swing around the foe's left and cut him off.

The cavalry horses were not in good condition so soon after disembarking and, although the cavalry clashed with the enemy rearguard at Mahsama station, ten miles on, it was unable to cut it off. However, seven Krupp guns, seventy-five railway wagons and above all a great quantity of stores were captured, so that, although Wolseley had decided to halt at Tel-el-Mahuta, Willis, on his own responsibility, ordered infantry to support the cavalry at Mahsama. Not only did Wolseley confirm this order but at 8.0 p.m. ordered Willis to occupy Kassassin Lock, two and a half miles on. On 26 August it was occupied without resistance by Graham's brigade.

The total cost of the action on 24–25 August had been 5 killed, 28 wounded and 41 sunstroke cases, of which one died.[42] One important capture had been made on 25 August. General Mahmoud Fehmy Pasha, an engineer highly esteemed by Arabi, had succeeded General Ali Fehmy in command of the Eastern Army soon after the fall of Ismailia. Reconnoitring towards Mahsama, on the evening of the 25th, he was captured by a patrol of the Life Guards.[43]

Wolseley was now, as he wrote on 26 August, in a forward position, 'far in advance of what I expected to have occupied for at least a week hence'.[44] One or two engines at least must be working before he could advance again. He expected to resume the advance in ten to fourteen days and then hoped 'not to have to halt before Cairo and when I do reach that place I expect we shall have finished the war'.[45]

The encounter actions had strengthened his confidence and he reported that 'our infantry will have little to do during this war'. His only fear was that the Egyptians would bolt from Tel-el-Kebir before he could strike for he must build up enough supplies to be able to concentrate at Kassassin and pursue after the battle. He intended to bring Hamley with Alison's brigade up from Alexandria to reinforce him, leaving Wood for the time being in command of a garrison that would include his own brigade, marines and some garrison battalions.[46]

Inevitably the build-up of his forces took time. Even on 26 August the 1st Division had not been completely disembarked. Not until 28 August did the Indian contingent from Suez complete its concentration at Ismailia. On this day the impatient Hamley was ordered to embark for Ismailia, having been forbidden to use Alison's Highlanders for an attack on the Egyptian lines at Alexandria, before leaving.[47] A disgruntled Hamley arrived on 1 September at Ismailia. Meanwhile Drury Lowe now took over the Indian Cavalry Brigade under Colonel H. C. Wilkinson as his 2nd Brigade, while the English regiments formed the 1st Brigade under Baker Russell. Wolseley bestowed local rank of Brigadier-General upon both Wilkinson and Russell. But Wolseley had misgivings about the Indian contingent. Although Macpherson was an old friend, his appointment as commander had not been welcomed and his staff was, in Wolseley's view, 'ridiculous'. The Indian troops were only a 'tintip' compared with the 'steeltip' of the British soldiers. Wolseley had never been an enthusiast for the bombardment of Alexandria with the consequent need to occupy it, and he increasingly grudged the necessity to keep Wood's brigade there. However, his hopes that sufficient garrison battalions would arrive there to allow him to bring Wood up to him never materialised.[48]

Most worrying of all was the transport question. It was fortunate that the supplies and stores captured at Mahsama and Tel-el-Mahuta allowed the cavalry to stay at the former and the Guards at the latter station within supporting distance of Graham at Kassassin. Large working parties took several days to demolish the dams across the Sweetwater Canal and a large embankment across the railway at Tel-el-Mahuta. Until this was done the Boat Service could only work up to

Magfar. Not until 2 September could large boats come up beyond the latter, and because of the shallows they could never tow supply boats beyond Tel-el-Mahuta. From there mules, horses or pontoon rafts had to be used. Owing to pollution by bodies and animals here, all drinking water had to be boiled and filtered.

Then there was the inadequacy of the regimental wheeled transports. Firstly there was a serious shortage of mules to draw it. Adye, the Chief of Staff, had neglected properly to organise an efficient supply train as ordered. The Turks whom he hoped would provide mules had been maliciously unco-operative. Mules had indeed been purchased in large quantities—in America, Natal, Italy and Greece, some 10,000 in all. But most were sent out too late. It was fortunate that the Indian contingent had brought 2,500 mules. But the mule-drivers, said Wolseley, were 'the canaille of the Levantine towns and we really have no authority over them'. Moreover the regimental carts themselves were too weak, especially for the heavy going between Ismailia and Magfar. Some units suffered serious want of provisions as a result.

Then again, all the engines had had to go down to Suez and come up thence to Ismailia after the Suez–Ismailia line was repaired on 27 August. Also, two hundred yards of track between Ismailia and Magfar had been broken up. Not until the end of August was even one engine working on the line. This, combined with the obstructive dams, exposed some units to the glaring sun without tents or camp equipment for some days. Wolseley angrily commented that 'next time' he would 'insist upon having a full staff' of engine drivers and traffic managers.[49]

But thanks to the efforts of the commissariat and transport troops and fatigue parties directed by Major-General Earle, commanding the Lines of Communication and Base, combined with the Boat Service and temporary expedients—such as using mules to pull railway wagons up to Magfar whence horse- and mule-drawn regimental transport took over—no generally serious supply situation arose. Fresh meat and vegetables were supplied to the troops regularly—and despite the heat and unsuitable clothing their health was remarkably good, indeed much better than in England.[50]

While the build-up of the force was proceeding, Arabi Pasha himself arrived at Tel-el-Kebir. On 28 August he directed a sortie against Graham at Kassassin, whose force amounted to a weak brigade with only two guns carrying the ammunition in their limbers. Here again the Egyptian force made no real effort to attack. At 4.30 p.m., however, Graham requested by messenger and heliograph that the 1st Cavalry Brigade at Mahsama come up in support, and Willis at Tel-el-Mahuta moved the Guards Brigade towards Kassassin also. But, after some shelling, the Egyptians began to retire at about 7.15 p.m., when Graham advanced, just as the cavalry arrived, having been hurried on by a garbled message delivered by Graham's excited A.D.C. that he was only just able to hold his own. The Household Cavalry then delivered a brilliant charge which inflicted heavy loss on the retreating foe. The total British losses were 16 killed and 79 wounded.

Back at Ismailia, however, Wolseley had had 'a very bad quarter of an hour'. At 7 p.m. Willis had transmitted by letter the false news that Graham was in trouble, following at 8 p.m. with a telegram that 'Enemy advancing on Mahsama; fear Graham has been defeated'. Wolseley refused to credit this, and calmly went to bed for a rest, intending to set out at 2 a.m. on 29 August to find out the truth. However, about 1 a.m. the correspondent of the *Daily Telegraph* arrived with the excited Maurice to announce 'a brilliant victory'.[51]

This affair encouragingly demonstrated once again the low quality of the foe—the artillery was their only good arm, thought Wolseley. But the supply problem continued to vex him. The British Press was now severely criticising the delay in finishing Arabi off. *The Times*, to Childers' dismay, was especially critical of the transport situation.[52] At this period Wolseley constantly harped on the familar theme in his reports and letters home: he could not move until sufficient supplies—sufficient for at least ten days—were established at the forward base, Kassassin, so that he could concentrate there for a decisive blow with an annihilating pursuit. One grand coup, not little fights, was needed. The coup would necessarily mean some heavy losses but 'one cannot make omelettes without breaking eggs'.[53]

Although he realised that it would take time, the supply and transport situation depressed Wolseley at the beginning of September. On 3 September he wrote to Lady Wolseley: 'Despair seems to come over me at times.' Although he had no doubt of victory, he feared that Arabi's entrenchments at Tel-el-Kebir were very strong and would cause heavy losses. He then considered that 16 September, as previously prophesied, would be the decisive day.

Then by 5 September he began to see daylight in the transport situation. Several engines were at work and the railway was at last reported to be in good working order and able to carry enough stores for the whole army and build up a surplus. Wolseley now resolved to fight Arabi on Tuesday or Wednesday, 12 or 13 September, 'probably on both days as he has two lines of entrenchments', though, to avoid the danger that the foe might bolt after the first day, Wolseley considered 'making one day's work of it', which would provide a needed triumph over 'those who have striven to hunt me down for some years past'.[54]

On 8 September final orders were issued for the concentration of the whole army at Kassassin, where telephonic and telegraphic communications with Ismailia had been established. Then on the morning of 9 September, Generals Ali Fehmy and Rashid Pasha, with some 8,000 troops, advanced about 4 a.m. against Kassassin, encouraged by misleading Bedouin reports that it was weakly held. It was in fact strongly held by nearly 8,000 men, including the Cavalry Division and Graham's reinforced brigade. Once again the Egyptians, both their generals having been wounded, fell back when Willis, after despatching alarmist messages to Wolseley, ordered a general advance. The Egyptian retreat became a rout and Wolseley, arriving just before noon, called off the pursuit which was within 5,000 yards of the Tel-el-Kebir defences, and ordered a return to camp. He wrote soon after that if the attack had continued 'our losses would have been enormous' and we 'probably should have failed'. Even a success would have been unwelcome then, when he had little more than half the troops up with which he meant to crush Arabi, and was unable to make the decisive pursuit via Belbeis and Zagazig which would if possible 'save Cairo from the fate of Alexandria'.

Wolseley estimated Arabi's numbers—probably with some excess—as 30,000 troops, plus Bedouin and 60–70 guns, but, as he commented, 'many of the regulars are old men recalled who know nothing of rifles and new drill. We have taken some of these poor old creatures prisoners and they can be of no use to Arabi whatever.' Only the entrenchments, constructed since mid-August, would be a 'very hard nut' to crack. To avoid losses, Wolseley had decided by 10 September on the daring tactic of a night march. He was 'so weak that I cannot afford to indulge in any other plan'. Nor could he wait for reinforcements—'to do so would kill the spirit of my troops which at present is all I could wish it to be'.[55]

He planned to strike Arabi at dawn on Wednesday, 13 September, after a night march. The period 9–12 September was devoted to concentrating the whole force at Kassassin and to careful reconnaissance by Wolseley and his staff, each morning before dawn, of the enemy lines, nine miles from Kassassin, along the ridge of 'the big hill' Tel-el-Kebir, extending for nearly four miles from the Sweetwater Canal into the desert and about 120 feet high. About 20,000 troops held the lines, although only a small proportion were trained soldiers (armed mostly with Remington breech-loading rifles), with Bedouin irregulars and seventy-five guns, including a number of breech-loading Krupps, 6 and 8 cm. Behind a wide ditch along the ridge was a first line of large earthworks with gravelly-sand parapets and redoubts advanced at intervals from the line. Behind was a second line of shelter trenches and rifle pits.

Thanks to their reconnaissance, Wolseley's staff could estimate the time the foremost works would be reached, allowing for a night march at about one m.p.h. The start was fixed at 1.30 a.m., so that the troops would arrive just before dawn before the enemy's works, and there would be plenty of light for pursuit. Finally the reconnaissances clearly showed the lax watch of the enemy, who, relying on the unreliable Bedouins, only sent outposts out beyond their works at dawn.

Wolseley explained his plan on the morning of 12 September, at a conference on Ninth Hill outside Kassassin camp. On the left, north of the Sweetwater Canal, would be Hamley with Alison's Highland Brigade in front and a composite brigade behind. Willis would be on the right with Graham's Brigade leading and the Duke of Connaught's Guards Brigade behind. Wolseley had been very anxious over the Duke's safety, which may account for his positioning.

The forty-two 9- 13- and 16-pounders of Brigadier-General Goodenough, R.A., were put between the two divisions—to give support, and to act as a guide and as a rallying point.

South of the Canal would be the Indian infantry brigade and the Naval Brigade with an armoured train carrying a 40-pounder. This force would advance an hour after the main body to avoid alarming the villagers along the cultivated belt which began here.

On the extreme right flank was nearly all the cavalry, with batteries of Horse Artillery, with the role of outflanking (if possible cutting off) and pursuing the enemy. In all, 17,401 troops were present; 12,124 infantry, 2,785 cavalry and 2,492 artillery with sixty-one guns and six naval Gatlings. Wolseley recommended that the divisions should advance in half-battalion columns so that the order of march would be the order of action. However, Hamley's men advanced in double company columns at deploying intervals while Willis's started off in half-battalion columns, then after delays deployed into line, then into fours.

The troops were informed at 3 p.m. on 12 September of the forthcoming battle and prepared for action. One hundred rounds and two days' rations were issued to each man. Strict orders were issued for silence on the march. No smoking and no lights were permissible. To lull suspicion, tents were left up until dusk and camp fires were left burning. The troops were silently assembled at Ninth Hill, assisted by the line of telegraph poles running west for 1,000 yards that the Engineers had laid down, as directing posts. By 11 p.m. the troops were assembled on the start line at Ninth Hill and were inspected by Wolseley. The stars were to be the main aids to keeping direction and Wolseley assigned Lt Rawson, R.N., a skilled sidereal navigator, to Hamley, to direct the Highlanders. Rifles were unloaded to prevent chance shots. Only one drunken Highlander, quickly suppressed, disobeyed the orders for silence.

At 1.30 a.m. the main advance began. The stars were obscured by cloud and only the North Star and Great Bear remained nearly always visible. Halts were frequent to check direction and alignment. Thus at 3 a.m. the Highland Brigade halted for a short rest, but the order to halt did not reach the flanks at once. These lost direction and circled around so that the brigade halted in crescent formation and when it advanced again, the flank battalions advancing to their front nearly met in front of the centre!

Wolseley had followed the Highlanders and about 4.30 a.m. ordered the composite brigade to close up on Alison, believing the enemy works to be near. Then at 4.50 a.m. a deceptive light flashed from a comet in the east. A few minutes later the Highlanders neared the enemy's works. As they set, the stars had moved slightly northwest, and unwittingly the British columns had done the same. They closed obliquely on the earthworks, in echelon, with the Highland

Brigade forward. This helped the Highlanders to by-pass on the right an advanced redoubt, about 500 yards ahead of the main line.

The Egyptians were taken completely by surprise. About 4.55 a.m. Egyptian sentries saw the Highlanders and fired a few shots. Without halting, the Highlanders fixed bayonets and advanced. Willis was echeloned back 800–900 yards, and further delay was caused by his decision to deploy into attack formation before attacking. Thus for ten or fifteen minutes the Highlanders were unsupported. The sentries' shots were followed by a heavy rifle-fire which fortunately went high. The Highlanders then charged in two long waves, the half-battalion double columns having gradually merged. The loose sand of the enemy scarps made mounting the parapets difficult and the first line dissolved into groups in which the men helped each other up the parapet, forcing an entry at various points. Here the struggle was severe. Sudanese troops resisted fiercely. The left of the 1/Gordons and 1/Camerons was driven back and Alison himself forced back over the parapet. Here Hamley fully proved that he could command in the field. He rallied the groups that had retreated, brought up the second line of the Gordons and Camerons and, leading the advance to support the men in the front trench, drove the enemy out of it. On right and left, however, the other Highland battalions were temporarily checked and the Gordons and Camerons were met by heavy fire when they attempted to advance against the inner ring of entrenchments.

Meanwhile Graham's brigade, arriving later than Alison's, rushed the first line of entrenchments successfully. Then, on the extreme right, the cavalry had begun to advance about 4.40 a.m., and, at the start of the battle, were about 2,000 yards from the Egyptian lines. The Horse Artillery opened fire on the Egyptian left, while the cavalry with the Indian cavalry brigade leading, began to swing on to the enemy's left rear. Then also, about 5.20 a.m., Goodenough's guns opened fire against enemy holding out in the works. The defenders opposite Graham broke first. The artillery in front and flank and the cavalry now threatening their left rear demoralised them and they fled before Graham's renewed attack on the second line, but fell victim to the advancing cavalry, who cut down or transfixed many, pursuing them towards the bridge over the Sweetwater Canal. Graham's troops, followed by the Guards, advanced towards the bridge about 6 a.m.

The Highlanders, well supported by the artillery, were already getting the upper hand in a stubborn fight in the first and second lines, when the collapse of the resistance to Graham completed the demoralisation of the whole Egyptian line, and by 6 a.m. the whole force was in flight north of the Canal, attempting to escape south over the canal bridge.

South of the Canal the Indian contingent and Naval Brigade had no serious fighting; the enemy broke before them and the task was one of pursuit. Arabi himself fled on horseback to Belbeis and took a train for Cairo. By 7 a.m., the entrenchments, camp and railway station at Tel-el-Kebir were all in British hands. Wolseley had followed the Highlanders and took up a position at the canal bridge where he received reports. Having written a telegraphic despatch announcing his victory to the War Office, he ordered a sustained pursuit by the cavalry and Indian contingent—the former to Cairo, the latter to Zagazig to cut the connections between the various portions of the Egyptian Army left in the Delta.

The total cost had been 57 killed, 382 wounded and 30 missing. The Highland Brigade lost 45 killed, 182 wounded and 6 missing, although the Royal Marine Light Infantry battalion in Graham's brigade, with 80 casualties, was the worst-hit unit.

Wolseley might well congratulate himself on the daring of his night attack—'a new thing, I may say, in our military annals'. It was going too far, however, to claim, in his despatch, that the British infantry had never distinguished itself more. Once battle had actually been joined, the result was a foregone conclusion.[56]

Wolseley himself did not now believe further serious resistance possible,[57] nor was it. The pursuit was daring and successful. The Indian Cavalry reached Belbeis in the night of 13 September and the following evening, now led by Drury Lowe, Cairo itself fell to them, unresisting. Arabi, with his army in dissolution and his will to continue the struggle broken, gave himself up that night to Drury Lowe. The campaign had in fact ended at Tel-el-Kebir, for the Nationalist forces thereafter passively allowed themselves to be disarmed or simply demobilised themselves. On 15 September, Wolseley reached Cairo and telegraphed to Childers that the war was over. Tewfik was restored, Arabi exiled and the British Government was now, although this was not realised, committed to a very long occupation.

Disappointment awaited Wolseley in the end. He deemed the Queen's personal letter of congratulations 'as cold-blooded an effusion as you have ever read'. He decided that he would make no further efforts to mollify the Queen and would revert to 'the independent position I occupied before and all the Royalties may go to Old Scratch!!' Furthermore, much to his indignation, instead of being made a Viscount, he was made a Baron like Seymour, now Lord Alcester. Nor was he made a Field Marshal in compensation. He was promoted full general and received a grant of £30,000, not much below the £35,000 he had wanted.[58]

The campaign had been one of Wolseley's best. His only problem, the one big organisational weakness, was the transport and supply problem after Ismailia. Apart from this, Wolseley had always been in control of the situation and his stand at Tel-el-Mahuta and his night attack at Tel-el-Kebir were exceedingly bold operations. He was fortunate, however, in being opposed by antagonists of such low calibre. As a soldier, Arabi himself had neither judgement nor resolution and his lieutenants were no better. Their troops were for the most part raw conscripts with no heart in the struggle although some Sudanese units resisted gallantly. It is clear that the Egyptian peasantry from which they came were indifferent, as a class, to Arabi's downfall.[59]

From the British viewpoint as a whole, the misgivings about possible need for reinforcements aroused during a triumphant campaign showed how difficult it was for the small regular army to both guard the Empire and United Kingdom and send overseas a respectable-sized and efficient expeditionary force. The Egyptian campaign was, in this respect, another example of a recurrent Victorian military problem.

References

1   *All Sir Garnet: A Life of Field Marshal Lord Wolseley*, by Joseph Lehmann. London: Jonathan Cape, 1964: p. 338.

2   *Life of W. E. Gladstone*, by John Morley. London: Macmillan, 1903; vol. III, pp. 73–4.

3   The fullest account of the diplomatic and political background is to be found in *Africa and the Victorians: The Official Mind of Imperialism*, by Ronald Robinson and John Gallagher, with Alice Denny. London: Macmillan, 1961. The quotation from Milner is from p. 86.

4   Sympathetic portraits of Arabi Pasha and the Nationalists are given by

Wilfred Scawen Blunt. *Secret History of the English Occupation of Egypt.* London: T. Fisher and Unwin, 1907, and by his counsel, A. M. Broadley, *How we defended Arabi.* London: Chapman and Hall, 1884. Sir Edward Malet, the British Consul-General, is understandably hostile in his *Egypt, 1879–1883,* edited posthumously by Lord Sanderson. London: John Murray, 1909.

5 Robinson, Gallagher and Denny, op. cit., p. 98.

6 *The Military Life of the Duke of Cambridge,* by Colonel Willoughby Verner. John Murray, 1905; vol. II, pp. 232–3. *The Life of the Rt. Hon. Hugh C. E. Childers,* by Spencer Childers, John Murray 1901; vol. II, pp. 88–9.

7 Robinson, Gallagher and Denny, op. cit., pp. 110–11. *The Letters of Queen Victoria,* edited by G. E. Buckle, 1928; 2 series, vol. III, p. 305 and p. 308.

8 Spencer Childers, op. cit., II, pp. 94–5.

9 Verner, ibid., II, pp. 233–4.

10 Robinson, Gallagher and Denny, ibid., pp. 114–19.

11 Morley, III, p. 81; *Hansard* 3rd Series CCCXXII cols. 1590 and 1872–89; *The Letters of Queen Victoria,* p. 314; *A Political Memoir of Joseph Chamberlain,* ed. C. H. D. Howard, Batchworth Press, 1953, pp. 80–1.

12 Verner, ibid, II, pp. 223–8. See also 'Mr Gladstone's Invasion of Egypt, 1882'. *The Army Quarterly,* vol. LXXXI, no. 1, October 1960, pp. 87–91, and 'The Effect of the Cardwell Reforms in Army Organization 1874–1904' *Journal of the Royal United Service Institution,* vol. CV, November 1960, pp. 515–24, both by Brian Bond.

13 Blunt. *Secret History,* ibid., pp. 401–11. *The Military History of the Campaign of 1882 in Egypt,* by Colonel J. F. Maurice, R.A., H.M.S.O., 1887, p. 4 and p. 7, The Official History. Also 'Critics and Campaigns', J. F. Maurice, in the *Fortnightly Review,* XLIV NS 1888, pp. 112–14.

14 Maurice. *The Campaign of 1882 in Egypt,* ibid., pp. 4–5, 7–8 and 23–4. Spencer Childers, ibid., II, p. 90.

15 Maurice. *The Campaign of 1882 in Egypt,* ibid., p. 11.

16 Spencer Childers, ibid., II, pp. 96–7, Childers to the Queen, 20 July 1882. Verner, ibid., II. The Duke of Cambridge's Diary of the War, pp. 235–6.

17 *The Royal George,* by Giles St Aubyn. Constable, 1963; pp. 179 and 188–90. *The Life of Lord Wolseley,* by Sir F. Maurice and Sir George Arthur. William Heinemann Ltd., 1924; pp. 135–42.

18 *The Letters of Queen Victoria,* ibid., 2 series, III, p. 311. St Aubyn, *The Royal George,* pp. 191–2.

19 Lehmann, ibid., p. 301. Maurice. *Campaign of 1882 in Egypt,* ibid. Appendix II.

20 The Wolseley Correspondence, Royal United Service Institution. Wolseley to Lady Wolseley, 10 September 1882. For Hamley see *The Education of an Army: British Military Thought 1815–1940,* Jay Luvaas. London: Cassell, 1964; pp. 155–8.

21 The Wolseley Correspondence, R.U.S.I. Wolseley to Lady Wolseley, 17 August 1882, and 25 September 1882. *The Letters of Lord and Lady Wolseley, 1870–1911,* by Sir George Arthur. Heinemann, 1922—Lady Wolseley to Wolseley, 4 and 12 September 1882. Lehmann, *All Sir Garnet,* ibid., p. 302. *The Letters of Queen Victoria,* ibid., p. 315.

22 Wolseley Correspondence, R.U.S.I. Wolseley to Lady Wolseley, 18 August 1882. *The Letters of Queen Victoria*, ibid., p. 312.

23 Wolseley Correspondence, R.U.S.I. Wolseley to Lady Wolseley, 26 August 28 August and 7 September 1882.

24 Maurice. *The Campaign of 1882 in Egypt*, p. 20 and Appendix I. Lt-Commander Caspar F. Goodrich, U.S.N., *Report of the British Naval and Military Operations in Egypt in* 1882, Office of Naval Intelligence, U.S. Government Printing Office, 1883, pp. 165–77. *Recollections of a Military Life*, by General London: Sir John Adye: Smith, Elder, 1895; pp. 332–3.

25 Maurice. *Campaign of 1882 in Egypt*. Appendix I. Goodrich, ibid., pp. 99–104.

26 Spencer Childers, ibid., Childers to Wolseley, 18 August 1882, pp. 104–5; 25 August 1882, p. 113; and 1 September 1882, pp. 117–18. Maurice. *Campaign of 1882 in Egypt*, p. 28. Goodrich, ibid., pp. 99–104

27 Spencer Childers, pp. 104–5, op. cit., p. 113, op. cit., pp. 123–4, Childers to Wolseley, 8 September 1882. *The Letters of Queen Victoria*, ibid., pp. 321–2.

28 Maurice. *Campaign of 1882 in Egypt*, pp. 15–22 Goodrich, ibid., pp. 182–4. Spencer Childers, ibid., p. 99.

29 Wolseley Correspondence R.U.S.I. Wolseley to Lady Wolseley, 2 August 1882, and 3 September 1882.

30 Ibid., Wolseley to Lady Wolseley, 17 August 1882. Maurice. *Campaign of 1882 in Egypt*. Appendix I.

31 Wolseley Correspondence, R.U.S.I. Wolseley to Lady Wolseley, 11 August 1882. Lehmann ibid., pp, 306–7. Verner ibid., II, p. 241. Cambridge to Wolseley, 21 August 1882. Spencer Childers, II, pp. 104–5, Childers to Wolseley, 18 August 1882.

32 Wolseley Correspondence, R.U.S.I. Wolseley to Lady Wolseley, 18 August 1882. Blunt. *Secret History*, p. 397. Maurice. *Campaign of 1882 in Egypt*, p. 16.

33 Maurice, ibid., pp. 23–5, pp. 29–30. Goodrich, ibid., pp. 208–15.

34 Blunt. *Secret History*, pp. 397–8. Maurice. *Campaign of 1882 in Egypt*, pp. 29–32.

35 Spencer Childers, II, pp. 105–8. Maurice. *Campaign of 1882 in Egypt*, pp. 41–2. Blunt. *Secret History*, pp. 398–9, gives about 13,000 Egyptian Regulars in all.

36 Spencer Childers, II, ibid.

37 For Hamley see Luvaas, *Education of an Army*, p. 156. For Wood, see Wolseley Correspondence, R.U.S.I. Wolseley to Lady Wolseley, 26 August 1882, and 16 September 1882. Spencer Childers, II, p. 109— Wolseley to Childers, 26 August 1882.

38 Goodrich, ibid., pp. 208–15.

39 ibid., pp. 188–9. Spencer Childers, II, p. 109. Wolseley to Childers, 26 August 1882.

40 Blunt. *Secret History*, p. 396.

41 Spencer Childers, II, pp. 104–5. *The Letters of Queen Victoria*, pp. 342–3.

42 Maurice. *Campaign of 1882 in Egypt*. Appendix VII.

T

43　Maurice, ibid., p. 52. Blunt, *Secret History*, pp. 415–16.

44　Wolseley Papers, R.U.S.I. Wolseley to Lady Wolseley, 26 August 1882.

45　Ibid.

46　Spencer Childers, II, pp. 109–10. Wolseley to Childers, 26 August 1882.

47　Maurice. *Campaign of 1882 in Egypt*, pp. 54–8.

48　Spencer Childers, II, p. 112. Wolseley to Childers, 26 August 1882, pp. 212–3. Wolseley to Childers, 8 September 1882. Verner, II, pp. 242–3. Wolseley–Cambridge, 1 September 1882.

49　*The Life of Lord Wolseley*, Sir F. Maurice, pp. 152–3. Goodrich, *The Campaign of 1882 in Egypt*, pp. 217–21. Lehmann, p. 318. Maurice. *Campaign of 1882 in Egypt*, pp. 54–7.

50　Verner, II, p. 244. Wolseley to Cambridge, 7 September 1882. Goodrich, p. 219.

51　Wolseley Correspondence, R.U.S.I. Wolseley to Lady Wolseley, 31 August 1882.

52　Spencer Childers, II, pp. 114–15. Wolseley to Childers, 31 August 1882. Childers to Wolseley, 1 September 1882, pp. 117–18.

53　Spencer Childers, ibid., pp. 114–15. Wolseley to Childers, 31 August and 4 September 1882, pp. 115–17. Verner, II, pp. 243–4. Wolseley to Cambridge, 7 September 1882. Wolseley Correspondence, R.U.S.I. Wolseley to Lady Wolseley, 31 August 1882.

54　Wolseley Correspondence, R.U.S.I. Wolseley to Lady Wolseley, 7 September 1882.

55　Ibid. Wolseley to Lady Wolseley, 10 September 1882. Verner, II, pp. 242–4. Wolseley to Cambridge, 1 and 7 September 1882.

56　Maurice. *Campaign of 1882 in Egypt*, pp. 67–96 and Appendix VII. Goodrich, p. 152. Lehmann, op. cit., pp. 320–32. Wolseley Correspondence, R.U.S.I. Wolseley to Lady Wolseley, 14 September 1882.

57　Wolseley Correspondence, ibid.

58　Wolseley Correspondence, ibid. Wolseley to Lady Wolseley, 21, 25, and 28 September, 3 and 11 October 1882.

59　Arabi was put on trial, pleaded guilty to rebellion against the Khedive, and was exiled to Ceylon. Although he eventually returned to Egypt his political career ended in 1882.

The Reconquest of the Sudan
1896-9

The Reconquest of the Sudan 1896–9

Cyril Falls

Britain's roots in Egypt go back, it may be said, to the year 1798, when she successfully challenged the French occupation of the country. Nelson's victory in the Battle of the Nile had paved the way, but it was not until 1801 that another admiral, Lord Keith, put Sir Ralph Abercromby's force ashore in Alexandria harbour, and even then, despite the former's skill, there had been a measure of good luck. Bonaparte had gone; his capable successor Kléber had been murdered; and the latter's incompetent successor Menou had mustered to oppose the landing only about a quarter of the troops he could have made available, thus giving the landing party an opportunity without which it would almost certainly have failed.

Even then the genius of Bonaparte had left behind a scientific and cultural influence which certainly survived to the end of the nineteenth century. His band of experts, scientists, budding Egyptologists, which had accompanied him, has never been forgotten by the intellectuals of the country and its influence has been strengthened by the later work of brilliant Frenchmen in the same field. France, whether wisely or not, threw away a chance to recover her physical influence when her fleet might have joined the British in 1882 in the bombardment of Alexandria, or her troops in the subsequent campaign. In the following year Sir Evelyn Baring, the future Earl of Cromer, came on the scene as British Agent.

Gladstone's Government genuinely intended, and expected, that

British troops would be withdrawn as soon as order and a stable Egyptian government had been restored. It soon became apparent, however, that only continuing British occupation could safeguard these blessings, and Lord Cromer became the real ruler of Egypt.

In 1881, the year before Tel-el Kebir, which means that Britain had then no military hold on the country, there arose a native of Dongola, Mohammed Ahmed, a fanatic with a touch of genius, who assumed the title of Mahdi, 'the longed-for leader' or 'Messiah'.

He realised that the extortions of the Egyptian Government could be exploited to free the Sudan. The next year he captured El Obeid, the chief city of Kordofan, and massacred, as was to become his practice, men, women, and children. Encouraged by this success, he destroyed at the end of 1883 a miserably equipped and spiritless Egyptian force under the command of a British officer, Hicks Pasha.[1] This disaster was followed in 1884 by the rout of General Baker, who was trying to relieve Tokar, on the Red Sea south of Port Sudan.

What was to be done now? There were perhaps men in the British Government, Rosebery for example, who would have been prepared to take strong action, but the Prime Minister, Gladstone, was determined to avoid it. His reasons may have been high-minded, but one cannot help feeling that the middle course he adopted, that of continuing British rule in Egypt while letting the Sudan go its own way, was a grave mistake. The followers of the Mahdi, from now on led into deeper and deeper fanaticism, armed, and trained, believing that paradise which included the company of beautiful concubines would be the reward of those who gave their lives in battle, were certain to endanger Egypt and might well at least capture its most vital outposts; and this at a time when many powerful Egyptians were believed to be intriguing with the Sublime Porte in order to arouse the Sultan's suspicions of British intentions.[2]

The only serious action taken for some time to come may be described as fantastic and the results were feared by most people with any knowledge of the country. It was Gladstone's Government—Winston Churchill suggests on the advice of Mr Stead, not the most suitable adviser—which decided that Major-General Charles Gordon would be useful. Despite the doubts of Baring, who thought it a mistake to send a Christian, least of all one with his temperament, that strangest of strange soldiers was sent to Khartoum in late January 1884, with orders to bring back all the Egyptian garrison and such of the townspeople as had reason to fear the Dervishes. Just a month after Gordon's arrival General Graham defeated them at El Teb, but this was to be the last success for a long time to come and in any case did not seriously improve Gordon's situation. What might have been expected followed immediately: Khartoum was invested by the Mahdi and Gordon was trapped. This was only the beginning. In May 1884 Berber, roughly two hundred miles downstream, was

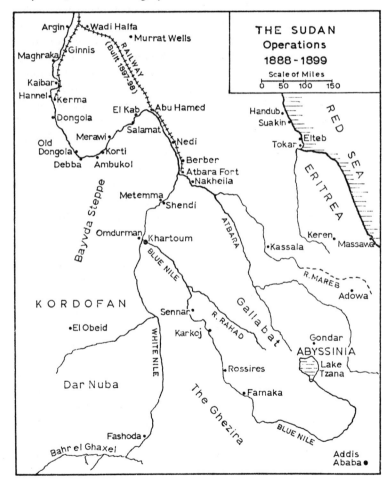

THE SUDAN
Operations
1888 – 1899

captured and the customary massacre took place. Still the British Government refused to allow any active operations for Gordon's relief.

Nevertheless, had fortune been on his side—and he never failed to deserve her favour—the curious experiment might have succeeded. The greatest English rhetorician since Gladstone, who was to see the final victory in the reconquest of the Sudan, wrote a tribute that is fully merited:

> 'The long and glorious defence of the town of Khartoum will always fascinate the historian. That one man, a European among Africans, a Christian among Mohammedans, should by his genius have inspired the efforts of 7,000 soldiers of inferior race, and by his courage have sustained the hearts of 30,000 inhabitants of notorious timidity, and with such materials and encumbrances have offered a vigorous resistance to the increasing attacks of an enemy who, though cruel, would yet accept surrender, during a period of 317 days is an event without parallel in history.'[3]

Yet Gordon too could be cruel when his religious feelings were outraged. When his friend, the charming Austrian Baron Rudolf Slatin, was defeated in Darfur and his Mohammedan troops attributed their ill fortune to his religion he proclaimed himself a Muslim in order to raise their spirits, and succeeded until the defeat of Hicks cancelled the effect. Gordon never forgave him and would not allow him to return to Khartoum, though grievously in need of a first-class subordinate, and it was the discovery by the Mahdi of their correspondence that led to his being put in chains. He had some consolation when, after his escape, he was received by the officials and officers in Egypt with sympathy and admiration for his courage. Thereafter his knowledge of men and matters in the Sudan proved invaluable.

We must hark back several years to bring upon the scene, in the person of Slatin, a character as curious as Gordon, to whom he had proposed in 1878 that he should serve in the Sudan because he was already aquainted with the country. His start had been promising and all the tasks he had undertaken, including that of Governor of Darfur, had been competently managed. To start with he got on well with the Mahdi and seems to have hoped that the latter would be brought into the right path, but if so the process proved illusory. He must have been as strong in body as in spirit, for he was to remain a captive for twelve years, long after his gaoler, the Mahdi, had died of typhus.[4]

At last an adequate force, under Wolseley, the most famous commander of his time, was mustered for the relief of Khartoum. Realising that his infantry, in boats, could not reach the town in time to save Gordon, he sent a little detachment across the desert along the base of the great bend of the Nile between Korti and Metemma; and also embarked a handful of men in steamers, hoping that they would stiffen the shaky Egyptians, so that resistance might be prolonged until the main body arrived. Then came the bloody action of Abu Klea. The heavily loaded camels caused the rear face of the square to bulge and the skirmishers running in masked its fire for a few minutes. The Dervish onrush fell on a corner where the pressure of the camels had made a small gap, into which yelling spearmen burst their way. The British force faced annihilation, but its response to the threat was magnificent. Every Arab who got in was killed by bullet or bayonet and the square closed again. This splendid victory was, however, fruitless. When two little steamers came in sight of Khartoum on 28 January 1885 they saw no flag on the palace flagstaff. Gordon had been hacked to death and all had to be begun over again.

The Mahdi died soon after Gordon, in June 1885, to be succeeded by the ablest of his followers, Abdullahi, an older man who had taken the title of Khalifa, *anglice* Caliph. The new chief had gathered a great deal of experience from his predecessor and had inherited his military machine: an enormous body of fighting men accepting death without question, trained to manoeuvre, and by now armed not only with rifles but with a certain amount of artillery. On the other hand, the Mahdi had never met brigaded British troops, a revitalised Egyptian contingent, or the less intelligent but more dashing Negro tribesmen of the Sudan, whom some British officers preferred, once they had undergone training, to the Egyptians, while all were led by Britons of high quality. We may take it that both Mahdi and Khalifa were as good leaders as savages could be in those days.

The foremost figure of this narrative was now to take over command. Horatio Herbert Kitchener had spent a great deal of his military career in the Middle East and had been appointed at the age of thirty-three to help train a new Egyptian Army. He had come to the conclusion that Wolseley's plan for the relief of Khartoum was 'fatuous', resigned his commission in the Egyptian Army in July 1885, six months after the action of Abu Klea, and returned to England. Next year he came back with the appointment of Governor of the Eastern Sudan and the Red Sea Littoral, with headquarters at Suakin, the last British outpost in the Sudan, but found his position useless. He met, in fact, with a rebuff: he sallied forth against one of the ablest of the Khalifa's lieutenants, Osman Digna, and stormed Handub, fifteen miles north of Suakin, but his irregular soldiers started to loot and were driven off in confusion. Severely wounded in neck and thigh, he brought his troops back to their fortifications.

*   *   *   *   *   *

Two steps were necessary if the rulers of the Sudan were to be over-thrown: first a British Government prepared to fight and to see that the Egyptian Army underwent a radical reform, and to make use of a strong British contingent; secondly, to arrange that communications should be established which would allow the biggest force required to penetrate into the heart of the country and reach the Khalifa's greatest fortress, Omdurman. Both needs were met when, in 1895, one of the greatest British statesmen of the nineteenth century, Lord Salisbury, took office as both Prime Minister and Foreign Secretary.

Between 1892 and 1896 several factors combined to cause Lord Salisbury's Government, with Lord Cromer's approval, to abandon its previously cautious attitude towards the reconquest of the Sudan. The remarkable resurgence of the Egyptian economy and finances under British control provided the means to mount an expedition with-out involving the British taxpayer. Next the security of the upper reaches of the Nile against French encroachment began to appear a crucial issue in imperial strategy, especially after the Italian defeat by the Abyssinians at Adowa on 1 March 1896. Lastly, the humiliation of the failure to relieve Gordon, or avenge his death, was not forgotten by soldiers such as Kitchener, and their determination was encouraged by the missionary zeal of books such as Alfred Milner's *England in Egypt*, published in 1893. Thus the Cabinet's decision to reconquer the Sudan was a deliberate act of policy and the campaign did not begin hap-hazardly like so many of Britain's small wars. Kitchener, the Com-mander-in-Chief, was placed under Foreign Office control and took his orders from Lord Cromer, whose constant theme was economy.[5]

The reconquest of the Sudan between 1896 and 1899 was to reveal how successfully the British had retrained the Egyptian Army after its humiliating defeat by Wolseley in 1882. The Egyptian Army was raised by conscription and the fellaheen were paid a subsistence wage of only one piastre or about $2\frac{1}{2}d$. a day. Less than 22,000 men out of a population of ten millions were called to the colours in time of peace, though this had recently been rare. Each infantry battalion, whether fellaheen or Sudanese blacks, mustered about seven hundred rifles. The cavalry was all Egyptian because the Sudanese could not be relied upon to groom and feed their horses. Two artillery batteries were armed with the modern Maxim-Nordenfeldt quick-firing 9-pounders, the horse batteries having 12-pounder Krupp guns. Some Egyptian battalions were officered by Britons, but four entirely by natives. However, in the final campaign for the recovery of the Sudan there were to be three British officers to an Egyptian and four to a Sudanese battalion. The seconded British officers included some sprung from the nobility, but the majority were professionals attracted by promotion, at least to the rank of *bimbashi*, the equivalent of major. The officer commanding a battalion, a *kaimakan* or lieutenant-colonel, was nearly always a captain in the British Army. It was therefore a young army, led in 1898 by a Sirdar, Major-General Sir Herbert Kitchener, aged forty-eight.

It might be said that there was a third need—for an engineer of genius with special knowledge of railway construction. This was also met in the person of a young French-Canadian, Lieutenant Percy Girouard, who had been trained on the Canadian-Pacific Railway and had been awarded the D.S.O. in the Dongola expedition. An anecdote shows that he was no respecter of persons: the formidable Kitchener, who was notable neither for patience nor good-temper, had forced the driver of a heavily-loaded train to drive at top speed and was obviously shaken by the time it reached its destination, in record time. Girouard merely remarked, 'You'll break the record and your own ruddy neck one day.'[6] Like all British officers attached to the Egyptian Army, Girouard was temporarily promoted, in his case to the rank of *bimbashi*.

Gordon might have been saved had he not stopped the projected extension of the railway, then in existence as far as Wadi Halfa. Now, despite warnings that a railway from Halfa could not be taken on to Abu Hamed across the waterless Nubian Desert, the Sirdar and Girouard were determined to lay it. Water was found after some abortive boring and good progress was made. Next work was begun on the stretch of some hundred and fifty miles to the Atbara, but before it could be reached the Khalifa's powerful force confronted the Anglo-Egyptian Army and had to be dealt with.

This, it seemed, might best be achieved by drawing him out, and was attempted by sending an Egyptian battalion in gunboats to Shendi, where he was known to have left the women of his force, including his own wives. The little garrison promptly fled, taking with it the Arab women but leaving behind those of the blacks. Next morning a Dervish force was seen, but it made off in the direction of Omdurman after a couple of rounds of shrapnel had burst over its head. Still, however, the exact position of the resolute young commander at Metemma, Emir Mahmud, remained unclear because the cavalry accompanying the battalion was only eight hundred strong and vastly outnumbered.

Finally, on 30 March 1898, Major-General Archibald Hunter moved out in force, with the cavalry, its horse-battery, and four maxims, while two infantry battalions and a field battery followed in support. This time the enemy's strong position was found, eighteen miles away, and closely observed. He was at Nakheila, some thirty miles as the crow flies from the confluence of the Atbara and the Nile. To the satisfaction of the observers and of the Sirdar when the news reached him, the enemy faced the open desert, so that the attack could be launched over the most suitable ground. The position was, however, strong, surrounded by a *zariba* (a hedged or palisaded enclosure) three miles in length and with high ground in the centre, where there were trenches affording three tiers of fire. Mahmud lay low and there was no reply to the fire of the horse-battery. G. W. Steevens, about the best of the correspondents who have written about the campaign, tells us that the prevailing view in the camp was that the Sirdar would wait until the enemy was forced by hunger to attack or disperse, especially as the white troops were beginning to feel the heat. They should have known their Kitchener better by this time.'

Yet he had no intention of attacking until he had acquired further information and worried the enemy with fighting patrols. Another eye-witness, in this case destined for immortality, has also left interesting notes on the preliminaries. The young Winston Churchill thought it likely that the Khalifa did not fully recognise the importance of the railway now closing upon him. He goes on to state what he cannot have heard until after the battle: that the clever Osman Digna had urged his superior, whom in his secret heart he detested and despised, to strike at the railway. Osman based the alternative which he put forward on the capacity of the Dervishes to endure privation greater than that of any of the Sirdar's army but the tireless Negro natives of the Sudan. After a full council had been called and the Emirs had agreed with Osman Digna, the Emir Mahmud gave way. This accounts for the fact that the hostile army had tried to reach the railway at Berber, and, when it failed, established the fortress camp in which the British reconnaissance had found it and where it was already beginning to dwindle.[8]

In the afternoon of 7 April 1898, the Anglo-Egyptian force left its bivouac. There were eight squadrons of Egyptian cavalry commanded by Lt-Colonel Broadwood and a company of Camel Corps under Captain King. The infantry consisted of a British brigade of four battalions under Major-General W. F. Gatacre and three Egyptian under General Hunter, whose brigadiers were Lt-Colonels Macdonald (the hard-fighting ex-ranker who was to play a decisive role at Omdurman), Maxwell (who was to defeat the Easter Week rising in Dublin in 1916), and Lewis. There were also an English maxim battery and four Egyptian mule batteries. Finally, there was a rocket party under a young naval officer who was to become famous in the First World War as commander of the battle-cruiser fleet at Jutland, and as Jellicoe's successor as naval commander-in-chief, and later First Sea Lord, namely Lieutenant David Beatty

The Dervish position, now well known as a result of reconnaissances, was roughly an oval resting on the river. It lay at the bottom of a kind of crater, of which the radius was about six hundred yards, so that it would be impossible to open fire at a greater range.

The force halted for about three hours' rest at 11 p.m., and at sunrise on the 8th reached a position within six hundred yards of the *zariba*; but the Dervishes were experts at taking cover and hardly a man was to be seen until some of their cavalry appeared and seemed to threaten an attack. The Sirdar drew up his force with artillery on the extreme right, then Maxwell's brigade with three battalions in line, Macdonald's in the centre in the same formation, then another battery, then Gatacre, with only the Cameron Highlanders in a long thin line and the remainder in three company columns, with another battery on the left. Lewis was in reserve, covering the transport, and the Camel Corps near his left. Finally, the Egyptian cavalry covered the extreme left, approximately three miles from it. Sir Clinton Dawkins, who wrote the penultimate chapter of Lord Milner's extremely successful book, *England in Egypt*, gives the total strength as twelve thousand, of which about two thousand were cavalry, and this strength must be near the mark, though some less reliable authorities put it at about two thousand or even four thousand more.

Still the enemy remained unexpectedly quiet and there is no mention of a single shot being fired by his artillery, though it is known that he had three rifled howitzers, the guns he used later at Omdurman.*[9] In fact, hardly a Dervish was seen, a remarkable tribute to the leaders who had trained these extremely unruly men. It was not until a little after 8 a.m., when the Sirdar ordered the infantry to advance and the artillery moved forward in support, that the enemy's heads appeared and he opened a hot musketry fire, fortunately high, as was generally the case. The assault burst into the *zariba* and the Dervishes bolted in every direction. The river bank was reached, which meant the end— an unexpectedly easy victory.

The Emir Mahmud was lucky to escape death. After making an inspection of his defences he had entered a specially constructed casemate which might charitably be called a command post and less charitably a refuge. He was dragged out of it by excited Sudanese and would undoubtedly have been killed if a British officer had not recognised him and called off these dogs of war. The scene was horrible, great numbers of women and children having been killed and Negroes in chains having met the same fate. When brought before the Sirdar, he told him that his much-detested second-in-command, Osman Digna, had ridden off the field with the Baggare horse, and it appeared that the latter had selected his position in the *zariba* for this purpose in case matters went wrong. Osman Digna was probably the most intellectual and ablest of the Dervish leaders, but he certainly deemed it wise to

* The guns in the earlier battle were in all probability Krupps. There would have been no difficulty whatever in taking munitions of war round the Cape, and in fact no very serious danger in using the Red Sea.

live in order to fight another day. Mahmud, the victor of Metemma, was at worst a capable fighting man and did not deserve the harsh treatment he received as Kitchener's prisoner.[10]

The Anglo-Egyptian casualties were approximately six hundred and fifty, including eighteen British and sixteen Egyptian officers. It may not seem a very heavy loss to those who think in terms of wars fought between highly developed peoples, and was certainly small by comparison with those of horrible fiascos such as that of Hicks Pasha, but it was high for this stage. The wounds inflicted by spears were terrible and, though the medical services had reached a level laudable for the times, the wounded had to face great discomfort and the risk of disease bred in the filth of every position occupied by the enemy. As a result of Kitchener's unavoidable parsimony there were only seven doctors in each brigade. The number of the enemy's losses is impossible to estimate, but well over 2,500 dead were found in or near the *zariba* and there must have been many more beyond the Atbara. Only a few hundred prisoners were taken and these for the most part Negroes, because few Sudanese would surrender.[11]

Except among students of the recovery of the Sudan, the battle of the Atbara is little known by comparison with the capture of Omdurman, but Kitchener held that it was the former which marked the turning-point of his career. He could not have been accorded more confidence than he had had from Lord Salisbury, but Cromer had been remarkably cautious, referring his telegraphed request for permission to attack to General Grenfell, the Commander-in-Chief in Egypt, who in turn referred it to the War Office. Not getting much practical aid from either, Cromer had suggested that he should not attack immediately but should await his most promising opportunity. Before this advice arrived, however, Kitchener had informed him that Hunter, who had been inclined to adopt this policy, had changed his mind and that Gatacre also favoured immediate action in the shape of an assault.[12] The incident reveals the Sirdar in 'an astonishing fit of indecision', but these two subordinates were experienced and had never shown themselves over-cautious. Wolseley had told the Government that it had a first-class commander and that the obvious thing was to trust him. He let down Kitchener very gently, writing: 'You must be a better judge than Lord Cromer or me, or anyone else can be. You have your thumb on the pulse of the army you command; and you can best know what it is capable of.'[13]

Now, however, it was desirable to give the troops, especially the British contingent, a rest, and even if it had not been there would have had to be a pause for the further development of the railway, which did not reach the army's position on the Atbara until the beginning of July 1898. The Sirdar actually took a month's leave in Cairo in June and told Cromer, as the latter reported to Salisbury, that he believed the enemy had been dealt a blow which would make it easier to deal with him in future.

Whether or not this was the case, he was going to take no risks. He had decided that before he moved on Omdurman his force must be increased by four British battalions, a regiment of cavalry, a field battery, one of the new 5-inch howitzers, two 40-pounders, a company of Engineers, with Army Service Corps and Royal Army Medical Corps in proportion. He got them all without question. He was now in fact in the position of Wolseley in the days when everything the latter attempted was 'all Sir Garnet' to his admirers. It is worth noting, too, that one of Kitchener's infantry battalions was the 1st Grenadier Guards and that in those days the troops of the Brigade seldom served abroad in what were known as 'bush-whacking' expeditions.[14]

Before the next move was undertaken the threat of various diseases, the legacy of the Dervishes, had to be surmounted, in particular the threat of bad water, which was virtually overcome within a few days and entirely so by the time the British reinforcements arrived. Now there were relaxations: shooting for officers, fishing for all ranks, and the various athletic sports which our troops improvise in all their campaigns. There was even a race meeting, with a rough stand. Winston Churchill remarks that modesty forbade him to describe the 'Atbara Derby', which was in fact won by an officer of his regiment, the 21st Lancers.[15]

By early July Kitchener had concentrated his considerable army at Wadi Hamed, some sixty miles north of Omdurman, but there was still much to be done in organising river transport, the flotilla of ten gunboats and five steamers for supply. He sent a message to the Khalifa to the effect that he would bombard the town and advised him to move the women and children into safety. If we could dig into the Khalifa's extraordinary and constantly flickering mind, our first impression would be that he was confident he could beat the British, but it was to become apparent that he was, in fact, uneasy and often changed his views.

'With the possible exception of the Maoris, more civilised and perhaps more chivalrous, the Dervishes were among the most formidable and dangerous savages the British ever had to face. Their tactics when on the attack were based on surrounding their enemy and assaulting him from two directions, as was to occur in the battle now under review, or suddenly laying an ambush on the lines of that used against the 21st Lancers. Mounted on hardy horses and camels, they made long marches at high speed and this mobility could be used to obtain surprise. They made best use of their traditional weapon the long spear, for when the greater proportion were armed with firearms their fire was nearly always too high and did little damage.

The advance on Khartoum began at an unlucky moment, the Nile being exceptionally high and continuing to rise. It was creating the well-known *khors*, which were depressions that took on the appearance of tributaries except that they ran in the opposite direction, that is, against the current of the river. Some became so big that quite a march was needed to get by them. At Metemma, the better part of halfway to their destination, the troops found the grisly remains of the battle which had been fought about the Emir Mahmud's camp. Little was seen of the enemy, such of his troops as appeared being small bodies out to mark the progress of the Anglo-Egyptian forces, which fell back whenever they were threatened by the cavalry. Steevens, usually so astute in his observation, went very far astray when he concluded that the decisive battle might be fought well north of Omdurman.[16]

On 1 September the infantry camped between the sprawling village of Kerreri and the Nile, while the cavalry drove in the enemy's outposts. From the little hills which dotted the plain it could be seen that the Dervish army had moved out of Khartoum and was drawn up in battle array. In the centre was the huge black banner of the Khalifa and others could be recognised, including that of Osman Sheikh ed Din, his son and the nominal commander-in-chief. It was realised that he must have returned to his father's favour, previously forfeited when he advised him to make peace with the Sirdar. Colonel Broadwood's Egyptian cavalry and Major Tudway's camelry made a wide detour close to the enemy's left, but his horse appeared in such strength that Broadwood fell back. Meanwhile gunboats had begun to shell the enemy's earthen forts along the river. Though they were strongly made and well sited, their great embrasures were badly constructed

U

and had only a limited arc of fire, with the consequence that the gunboats, bringing into action their quick-firers and maxims, passed them without being hit.

As darkness fell the cavalry retired, parties of Dervishes following it enterprisingly enough, so that it was judged necessary to keep the

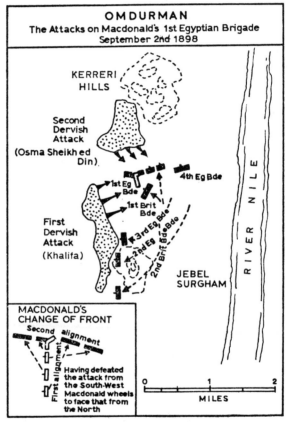

OMDURMAN
The Attacks on Macdonald's 1st Egyptian Brigade
September 2nd 1898

KERRERI HILLS

Second Dervish Attack

(Osma Sheikh ed Din)

4th Eg Bde

1st Eg Bde

1st Brit Bde

First Dervish Attack

(Khalifa)

3rd Eg Bde

2nd Eg Bde

2nd Brit Bde

JEBEL SURGHAM

RIVER NILE

MACDONALD'S CHANGE OF FRONT

Second alignment

First alignment

Having defeated the attack from the South-West Macdonald wheels to face that from the North

0   1   2
MILES

whole force under arms all night. The first howitzer shell was fired at half-past five on the morning of 2 September. The order from right to left ran: Collinson's 4th Egyptian Brigade lay on the right flank in reserve with Macdonald's 1st Egyptian Brigade to its left and Wauchope's 1st British Brigade moving up behind Macdonald; then came Lewis's 3rd Egyptian, Maxwell's 2nd Egyptian and Lyttelton's 2nd

THE RECONQUEST OF THE SUDAN, 1896-9

British Brigade (see sketch map). About a mile and a half from the river there was a height known as the Kerreri Hills and two miles south of it another, Jebel Surgham, less extensive but slightly higher at its crest. The greater part of the Anglo-Egyptian line faced the latter and took a roughly semicircular form with both flanks on the Nile, three gunboats to its right and two to its left. It looked likely that the battle would start with an assault on the fortifications of Omdurman, but it was in fact to take the form of a fierce struggle in the open and for Kitchener a defensive battle.

Enormous masses of Dervishes were installed on the two heights, on the northern under the command of Osman Sheikh ed Din, on the southern under that of the Khalifa himself. The capture of the latter position looked at first sight the easier, and indeed Maxwell was able to advance beyond its centre, with Lewis now on the lower ground to his right, Lyttleton on his left, and the 21st Lancers outside him. Meanwhile, however, the town was not left unscathed. The heavy guns, firing 50-lb. Lyddite shells, quickly found the range—about three thousand yards—hitting with the third round the base of the Mahdi's tomb and a little later the top. It could be seen that this success enraged the Khalifa's force, which leapt into activity. His horsemen quickly sallied out and drove in the British scouts, but three squadrons of the Lancers forced them back.

Then came the first phase of the most dramatic action of the campaign and one that is known to many who have otherwise little knowledge of the battle. The Khalifa set in motion the whole force under his direct command. Colonel Martin's Lancers could do no more than attempt to slow the enemy down and he was taking a bold step when he dismounted part of the regiment in the hope of checking the flood by rifle fire. A galloper was sent back to the Sirdar to tell him that the enemy was advancing his whole strength. His men had soon to fall back and the regiment moved down to the river so as to permit the artillery fire to be directed in full force against the Dervishes. By 3 p.m. the Sirdar had all his infantry and artillery in position awaiting the great clash which seemed certain to follow.

An anti-climax followed—the Khalifa changed his mind and to the surprise of the defenders halted his main body just out of range, and as the light failed withdrew them to their original position. Both sides ate their evening meal, the enemy, according to one observer, the better one. 'For supper', he writes, 'our men had stringy bully beef and biscuit or bread. The Dervishes had hunks of roasted mutton, goat, and cattle, done on the embers, and bannocks of dhura meal.'[17] It is clear that the Khalifa's best chance of success lay in a night assault carried out by men who not only knew the ground but had cat-like eyes in the dark. The Sirdar had done his best to encourage him not to move, sending Sudanese spies who were bidden to pretend that they were deserters and tell the Dervish leader that Kitchener was going to make a night attack. It is impossible to say whether they were able to slink away before he discovered the trick; the only certain feature of the affair is that Kitchener had plumbed the curious mind of his foe.[18]

In case the latter changed his mind at the last moment, the whole British force stood to arms at 3.30 next morning, but as daylight appeared the troops fell out to breakfast. The cavalry, camelry, and horse artillery moved out to regain touch with the enemy and were followed about 5.30 a.m. by the infantry, but the latter had hardly left its trench when news came in that he was moving forward to Jebel Surgham, but—yet another mystery—this body was moving alone and there was no sign of activity on the part of Osman Sheikh ed Din. It may be that his force was deliberately withheld in the hope that the Khalifa would get round the British left flank, in which case it would be launched to the attack. The way could not be left entirely open to him, but the task was assigned to Macdonald's Sudanese Brigade alone and it was posted on the right, somewhat in rear and about a quarter of a mile distant.

The shouting Dervishes came on fast. While six gunboats fired on them in enfilade the rest renewed the bombardment of Omdurman, where the strength of the enemy was, according to the Sirdar's information, about five thousand. The artillery, shortening its range as the enemy came on, fired with great effect. Finally the assault petered out, having progressed at a few points to within three hundred yards and, in the case of individuals, even closer.

The one serious set-back which now occurred—namely the charge of the 21st Lancers—was unnecessary, and if it had some defenders at the time it probably has none today. Burleigh went so far as to write that it had perhaps as good an effect on the enemy as a bigger victory of our arms, but admitted that it might be coupled with the Balaclava charge and recalled as 'magnificent but not war'. Colonel Broadwood's cavalry and camelry had played a fine part, though the latter had got into some trouble on rough ground. Now the Lancers came in contact with quite a small party and promptly charged without being able to see beyond a slight ridge. There were, in fact, some hundreds of men hidden in a dry river-bed. It was impossible to pull up and the regiment rode straight through the depression to the other side, but suffered terrible losses. It seems only fair, however, to note that arm-chair critics find it easy to tell us what ought to be done in such cases—in this case to push on a small patrol and then attack dismounted. In point of fact nobody had seen the *khor* until it was too late to pull up. One of the most vivid accounts of any incident of this sort is that of Winston Churchill, who took part in the charge. He writes that patrols were sent out and caught sight of about a thousand Dervishes in a slight depression, that the commanding officer, Colonel Martin, decided to attack, and that nobody was aware of the fact that the slight depression entered a much deeper extension of the so-called *khor*. Martin ordered 'right wheel' to be sounded. 'The pace was fast and the distance short. Yet, before it was half covered, the whole aspect of the affair changed. A deep crevasse . . . appeared where all had seemed smooth plain; and from it there sprang, with the suddenness of a pantomime effect and a high-pitched yell, a dense white mass of men nearly as long as our front and about twelve deep. . . . The riflemen, fighting bravely to the last, were swept head over heels into the *khor*, and jumping down with them at full gallop and in the closest order the British squadrons struck the fierce brigade with one long furious shout. . . . In 120 seconds, five officers, 65 men, and 119 horses out of less than 400 were killed or wounded.'[19] Three Victoria Crosses were awarded.

Elsewhere high courage combined with remarkable skill was being exhibited at about the same time. Macdonald's brigade had been formed up with all four battalions in line, that on the right having its right half bent back, nearly at right angles, in case Osman Sheikh ed Din got on the move. The Khalifa's men came on in enormous strength with their usual courage, but the combination of artillery fire and volleys from the infantry mowed them down. Just before the remnant dispersed, Osman's force swept forward in even greater strength. Macdonald had already ordered his left battalion to move across and deploy on the right of the part of the right battalion which he had already moved to face the new front, and it actually reached its position before the troops on the left had finished dealing with the southern attackers. Next he transferred another battalion to the new alignment, while the half battalion in the centre wheeled on it with the batteries and machine guns conforming. And finally the last battalion, having completed the rout of the first assailants, extended the new line to the left (see sketch of Macdonald's manœuvre p. 294).

He had even found time to summon to his side the officers of one of the regiments, the 9th Sudanese, and upbraid them with the rough tongue of a former N.C.O. for having wheeled into line in anticipation of his order. 'This was one of the occasions when the technicality of tactics was made clear to the general public, and the tactician became the idol of his country. The career of [the future] Major-General Sir Hector Macdonald, "Fighting Mac.", was to end in tragedy and suicide, but this crofter's son left behind him the record of one of the greatest masters in the conduct of small wars.'[20]

He was not left to stem the Dervish tide alone. Colonel Wauchope sent the 1st Lincolnshires to prolong his right and himself led the rest of the brigade to his left, but it was the Lincolns, arriving first, that played the greater part in holding the assault, shooting more steadily and effectively than the excited Sudanese, who were inclined to rush headlong on the enemy after getting the order to advance. Macdonald kept them in hand, but soon all were moving forward at his command in a long irregular line, enveloping the enemy and cutting him off from Omdurman and from the Khalifa, who had taken refuge in the town.[21]

This was the end. The Dervishes had suffered enormous losses and, as is generally the case with irregulars, these had been inflicted mainly on their most fanatical and enterprising men. They broke and fled. We may ask what would have happened had the two assaults been delivered simultaneously, but it is impossible to answer the question, though obviously the risks and trials of the Sirdar's troops would have been far heavier.

Kitchener now re-formed his troops and marched straight on Omdurman. While the march was in progress the Khalifa's black flag was brought to him by Captain Sir Henry Rawlinson—who was later to command the Fourth Army on the Somme in the First World War —and Major Lord Edward Cecil, the Prime Minister's son. The northern outskirts of the town were reached at midday and the troops halted for a meal and a rest. They did not move again until 4 p.m., and then as if on parade, Maxwell's brigade having the honour of leading the march and entering the place first. The filth and misery were as pathetic as they were disgusting, with men, women, children, and animals lying in heaps. Some shots were fired at the Sirdar as he approached the Khalifa's headquarters. The bird had flown at the last moment, but many leaders had fought until they had been killed on the battlefield and the invaluable Slatin had identified a number of them.

The losses in killed were only 48, including three British officers and 25 other ranks, and 434 wounded. Those of the enemy can be given approximately only, but some 11,000 corpses were counted on the battlefield and several hundreds in the town. In Britain victory celebrations were somewhat overclouded by controversy concerning the destruction of the Mahdi's tomb and the Sirdar's proposed treatment of his skull, which was to send it to the College of Surgeons in London—to the horror of Queen Victoria and many others. Some time later Cromer wrote to Salisbury that the destruction of the Mahdi's tomb was not only justified but necessary, but he did not defend Kitchener's absurd and repellent suggestion regarding the skull.

The affair merits a little more attention because it created an uproar at home and was exploited by a great number of people who were delighted to find Kitchener presenting such a target. It brought about angry questions in Parliament. He was also unpopular with the Army, though officers probably did no more than discuss the business in the military clubs. Most damaging of all was the fact that he had been unwise enough to set the Press against him, the only exceptions being *The Times*, represented by the Hon. Hubert Howard, unfortunately killed outside Omdurman by an unlucky shot from one of the gunboats, and the *Daily Mail*, represented by G. W. Steevens, so often quoted here, who was a close friend and a warm admirer. On 2 March 1899, Cromer, in reply to a telegram from Salisbury, wrote:

'The dead set made against Kitchener was sure to come, sooner or later. Apart from the natural reaction, he has not the faculty of making friends. The soldiers are furiously jealous of him, and many of the newspaper correspondents, whom he took no pains to conciliate, have long been waiting for an opportunity to attack him. He has his faults. No one is more aware of them than myself. But for all that, he is the most able of the English soldiers whom I have come across in my time.

'He was quite right in destroying the Mahdi's tomb, but the details of the destruction were obviously open to objection. . . .

'Kitchener is himself responsible for the rather unwise course of sending the skull to the College of Surgeons.'[22]

As regards the officers, there is little or no evidence that the more senior serving with him were jealous, while we know that most of the junior were his warm admirers. Cromer, in all probability, was speaking of administrative officers in Cairo.

Kitchener meanwhile returned to England, was raised to the peerage, made the guest of the Queen, and fêted wherever he went. It took just over a year to finish with the Khalifa, pursued and killed by Sir Reginald Wingate on 24 November 1899.

What was virtually a political mission to Fashoda, though Kitchener was accompanied by some hundreds of troops and a flotilla of five gunboats, had, however, been brought to a conclusion before this and had revealed in him statesmanlike qualities which he had not previously seemed to possess. Politics and armed intervention were closely linked over a vast district; for example as mentioned earlier, it was the annihilation of an Italian army at Adowa that had hastened the reconquest of the Sudan. The hoisting of the French tricolor at Fashoda, on the White Nile, may have been little more than a bluff but it was a gesture that the British Government could not ignore. The latter had informed the French that the Nile valley between the lakes and the southern frontier of Egypt must be considered to be within the British sphere of influence, their ultimate concern being to safeguard the line of communications with India.

On 7 September 1898 Kitchener was informed that 'a white force' had occupied Fashoda, four hundred miles south of Khartoum. Under the orders of the able French Foreign Secretary, Gabriel Hanotaux, it had penetrated the hinterland of British West African settlements and hoisted the tricolor over the little town. Tact may not have been Kitchener's strong quality, but he showed it now by deciding not to hoist the British flag, which would have been intolerably humiliating to the French commander, Major Marchand.

Kitchener and the Frenchman, who was to distinguish himself in the First World War until he was relieved on account of age, took to each other at once. To the former's revelation that he had authority to say that the advance of the little French force was considered by his Government to be a violation of the rights of both Britain and Egypt, Marchand replied that he was merely obeying his orders and was prepared to give his life if Kitchener used force. The Egyptian flag was finally hoisted to the accompaniment of a salute of twenty-one guns. It was a happy solution because Marchand had only about five hundred Senegalese troops and four white officers—one of them, Lieutenant Mangin, not mentioned in the British messages or documents, but destined to become more famous than his chief and one of the most successful of French army commanders in the First World War. Marchand had succeeded without difficulty in capturing Fashoda from the little Dervish garrison and later defeated a small force sent by the Khalifa to collect supplies, only to find the place occupied by foreigners.[23]

There followed a very serious crisis, even whispers of war between Britain and France. However, Hanotaux was forced to resign and his successor, Théophile Delcassé, gave way and in March 1899 agreed to a dividing line being drawn between French and British spheres of influence. His Government had been influenced by anxiety about the intentions of Germany and decided that, should she threaten danger, it would have been madness to have weakened France's good relations with Britain. It was not to be long before the British Foreign Secretary, Lord Lansdowne, established the Anglo-French *Entente*. The Sudan campaign is thus linked with the most important European problem of the time.[24]

*   *   *   *   *   *

While this victory without a battle was being won, further difficult work had to be faced by a subordinate. Gedaref, in the Western Sudan, about a hundred and thirty miles south-east of Kassala and about a hundred and eighty east of the Blue Nile, had been garrisoned by an Arab leader named Ahmed Fedil with a force of about five thousand. He had received an order to join the Khalifa at Omdurman, but for reasons unknown had not started for a considerable time, with the consequence that he arrived too late to help. The Sirdar, whose intelligence officers worked well and had a number of spies at their disposal, knowing that the place was now relatively lightly held, ordered the Kassala garrison under Colonel Parsons to take it, but he did not feel justified in drawing out more than about fourteen hundred men, and these a scratch force. It consisted of a recently raised Egyptian battalion, a local Arab battalion which had done good work in the cause of the Italians, a very small party of cavalry, and between three and four hundred Arab irregulars.

It crossed the Atbara at El Fasher in boats, the Egyptians running together the frames from timber and covering them with canvas. There was not much trouble in swimming horses and mules over, but the camels had to be supported in front by inflated skins and the business took six days. By this time the troops had certainly learnt to look after themselves and make do.

Next morning, 17 September, the march south began and on the following morning reached Mogatta on the river bank, from which it had been decided to strike out for Gedaref after establishing a post to cover the harvest. A hostile patrol appeared in the afternoon, but was driven off without difficulty. The advance was continued at daylight on the 20th, uneventfully, but hampered by the fact that the ground was so broken as to necessitate movement in single file from time to time. Next day the head of the column came in sight of a village some four and a half miles from Gedaref after adopting dispositions suitable for battle, but some villagers came to report that the enemy had cleared out and that news of the fall of Khartoum had at last reached Ahmed Fedil.

With only five days' food the march was resumed with the minimum of baggage, but 150 rounds of ammunition per man and water for two days were considerable items. On the 21st an outlying village of the Gedaref district was reached and some of the inhabitants came out to report that the enemy had just retired. Next day he was found, drawn up at the bottom of a deep valley and on the lower slopes of a southern ridge some three-quarters of a mile off—riflemen in lines and behind them bodies in squares, banners waving.

Colonel Parsons immediately ordered an advance towards the ridge, from which he could command the position of the Dervishes while blocking them from their stronghold. But the enemy was equally enterprising and moved up the hill in line, firing as he did so. It thus looked likely to be something rare and exciting, an encounter battle, though on a small scale. The Arab battalion on the right pressed forward and drove its opponents back, then occupied one hill with a company and an outlying village with another.

Meanwhile the baggage train had perforce followed the fighting troops at a slower pace and had early on been threatened by a strong force of Dervishes which wheeled round its flank. An attempt to check this advance failed and the enemy reached a position whence he could advance not only on the train but in rear of the fighting troops. However, the Egyptian battalion turned to meet the threat, while the irregulars moved down the slope to deal with the frontal attack. The Camel Corps, steady old soldiers, dismounted to help cover the train and met the enemy's advance gallantly, but he was not to be denied. He pressed on and got among the baggage animals, killing some and carrying off others. The situation now looked ugly in the extreme, but the Egyptian battalion took up a position from which its fire flanked the troops and simultaneously hit the advancing Dervishes.

From now on matters began to improve. The irregulars pushed back the enemy's force in the valley and then found themselves free to turn in order to afford further aid to the baggage train, accompanied by part of the Arab battalion. At last the rapid fire not only held the attack but soon drove the enemy back in confusion, pursued by all the available force. What had appeared an extremely dangerous situation turned into a well-deserved victory. The troops advanced to the old parade ground, which had been Ahmed Fedil's headquarters, to find his deputy Nur Angur, a leader of considerable reputation, waiting to surrender with some two hundred and fifty of his men. When we take into account the weakness of the Egyptian force, with only a small proportion of well-trained troops, this complex action was a credit to their leadership, their gallantry, and their skill. The Dervishes had manœuvred skilfully also, but their bad shooting had let them down. The Egyptian losses were heavy enough, about forty killed and seventy wounded, but those of the enemy were estimated at not far short of five hundred dead.

Nur Angur provided some valuable information about the intentions and movements of Ahmed Fedil and the possibility of his return to Gedaref. He had not reached Khartoum and his force was intact; the threat of steamers from it had made it impossible for him to cross the Nile; and he had therefore moved to Gebel Araing, about two and a half days' march from Gedaref. Nur Angur was an interesting and much-married man, said to have seventy wives and a hundred children. He was sufficiently educated and intelligent to realise that his cause was doomed now that Khartoum had fallen, and this had been his reason for remaining at Gedaref. He also informed his captors that Ahmed Fedil might return.

Preparations to meet this possibility were of course set in train, based on the fortifications. He had formerly lived in an enclosure on a low hill-top, strong in itself but depending for defence on the wells in the valley bottom, which also provided the supply of the whole region. This was rendered possible for him, as it had been for his victors, by a treasury, a square brick enclosure close at hand and well adapted for defence. It was allotted to the Arab battalion, while Beit Zeki was occupied by the Egyptian battalion, the Camel Corps, and the hospital. Work was set in train on pallisades from which the defenders could shoot over the walls or through loopholes.

Officers were beginning to wonder whether Ahmed Fedil would ever turn up, and a Camel Corps patrol sent out sixteen miles along the road which he must follow came back to report that there was no sign of him. An hour later, however, an infantry outpost, established about four miles out, saw and fired on half a dozen Baggare horsemen. Next morning, the 28th, a strong cavalry patrol was sent out and before it had covered three miles heard drums and the trumpets of horsemen. This was followed by swift action on the part of Fedil, who halted his baggage train a couple of miles from the defenders and at once advanced to the attack. If, as is possible, he had expected to find Gedaref as he had left it, he must have had an unpleasant surprise as his men came in contact with the new defences.

The Dervishes opened fire from south, west, and north, simultaneously engaging the western and northern faces of the fort held by the irregulars. Next the attack developed further east, while a frontal assault was launched against an outwork of the irregulars. The enemy kept up a hot fire at all points and showed skill in making the best use of any protection afforded by the ground. Finally, however, he found the fire of the defence too hot, and, calling up such reserves as had hitherto not been engaged, fell back everywhere. But he was not yet done with. Having rallied his troops, he launched them on another assault, directed in the main against the northern and western faces of the town. They could not, however, maintain their advance and were shortly afterwards withdrawn into the valley to the west of it. At one point his own arms were employed against him, two brass guns captured on the 22nd having been mounted and used with effect. A renewed assault was still deemed possible or even likely, but by the afternoon it was clear that the enemy had given up the struggle in face of his heavy losses, estimated at five hundred or more.

On the two following days his force, still numbering well over three thousand, remained encamped about two miles to the west. Colonel Parsons decided not to attack, in view of the fact that Fedil's force was amply big enough to hold and at the same time work round and occupy the place. The main object had been attained; the Egyptian flag had been hoisted over Gedaref; and an Egyptian garrison was firmly established in it. Officers found it curious that Fedil should remain where he was, with little ammunition left and aware that his master had long ago fled from Khartoum. However, on 1 October he moved off again, and this time put several days' march between himself and the victors. Meanwhile troops of his former subordinate were being used against him, given arms, and pushed forward to watch him closely. Nur Angur was in all probability even more capable than he, a master of Dervish warfare, and quite willing to serve in this new role.

The weight was now to be removed from the shoulders of Parsons' little force. On 11 October a man arrived from Kassala on a camel with a telegram from the Sirdar to the effect that General Leslie Rundle— incidentally the most disaffected and hostile to Kitchener of any senior officer in the theatre of war—was on his way with considerable strength. Kitchener had also sent Arab messengers to Fedil's troops, promising them their lives if they surrendered, but missed him because he was then attacking Gedaref. Rundle's march was not an easy one because he had to face the problem of water as soon as he quitted the Blue Nile. He pushed forward a battalion to reinforce Parsons, directing its commander, Colonel Collins, to report whether greater strength was needed, in which case he himself would follow. However, Ahmed Fedil's force was found to be in full retreat, apart from a number who deserted him and surrendered. The next step would be, if possible, to elbow him on to the Blue Nile, where it would be easy to track him with steamers.

He did try to cross the river, but was caught in an awkward situation, having got about a thousand men on the far side and about the same number on an island in mid-stream. It took some time to find his ford, after which the assault of the 10th Egyptian battalion suffered heavier loss than in any previous affair during the course of this little campaign, over a hundred out of about four hundred, including its commanding officer and six Egyptian officers, killed or wounded as they advanced under heavy fire. The whole Dervish force, apart from some troops that had already crossed the river, were killed or taken. Ahmed Fedil fled with the survivors and finally succeeded in reaching the White Nile. He contrived to cross it, but with only a few personal followers, all the rest being taken. Once more, however, the victors' losses were severe, eight Egyptian officers and 150 rank and file being killed or wounded. This action disposed of the last Dervish force in the Eastern Sudan.

The little campaign has appeared to be well worth recording at some length because it marks, perhaps even better than the Sirdar's victories on the Atbara and at Omdurman, the progress made since the days of the luckless Hicks Pasha. Here were a handful of Egyptians and irregulars completely isolated, burdened by a very large baggage train which could not be cut down, up against one of the most enterprising of the Dervish leaders. Parsons appears to have combined boldness with caution most brilliantly.[25]

*   *   *   *   *   *

In the autumn of 1899 Kitchener led an expedition into Kordofan, where the Khalifa had taken refuge. He failed to catch him and had to return early in November for discussions with Cromer. As mentioned earlier it was Sir Reginald Wingate who eventually administered the *coup de grâce*, surprising the Khalifa's force and killing him. Wingate was almost immediately afterwards appointed Governor-General of the Sudan in succession to Kitchener and, on 18 January of the following year, had to deal with the mutiny of a Sudanese battalion which had murdered its British officers. This affair was in Cromer's view brought about by British reverses in South Africa, by the hostile attitude of the Khedive, by the native press—and, not least, by the extremely harsh rule of the late Sirdar.

On 19 January 1899 an Anglo-Egyptian condominium was established over the Sudan. This meant in effect that Great Britain took on a trusteeship of that vast area as a consequence of Kitchener's military conquest. This makeshift arrangement was to last and work with remarkable success for more than half a century.

Considering the indecision he had occasionally shown in command, and the brutality which he had permitted, Kitchener did exceedingly well out of the campaign. He was raised to the peerage as Lord Kitchener of Khartoum, thanked by the votes of both Houses of Parliament, and awarded thirty thousand pounds. Mahdism was thus finally stamped out in the Sudan just six weeks after a great struggle commenced in South Africa.[26]

*   *   *   *   *   *

When we talk of 'imperialism' today we are too apt to confine the word to the British Empire, because we recoined the term in the nineteenth century. It was, of course, equally applicable to the contemporary policy of the French, Belgians, Germans, Russians, Japanese, and Italians. British imperialism in the Sudan hardly needs to be defended because—given our half-reluctant commitment in Egypt since 1882—the Mahdi and the Khalifa made reconquest inevitable sooner or later. Had the Sudan not been recovered, Egypt would have been in deadly peril at the outbreak of the First World War, the closure of the Suez Canal being only one of the possible consequences.

The essential characteristic of British imperialism was the demand for complete obedience in the regions it covered, in return for which all considered possible for the natives' betterment was done or at least promised. Its most successful sphere was India, as is warmly admitted by the majority of its people, from intelligentsia to peasants. The romantic side of British imperialism in its hey-day was rather childish, but probably had little to do with Britain's imperial decline, which was due much more to the upsurge of nationalist aspirations to self-government. Clearly when nations reach a certain standard of civilisation, welfare, and political consciousness they will soon cease to regard a foreign power with gratitude as the source of their wellbeing. Perpetual indebtedness to a paternalistic alien ruler, however benevolent, will sooner or later prove intolerable to any but the least spirited people. Britain clung too long perhaps to the glamorous Victorian tradition with the unfortunate result that the British themselves eventually sickened of 'imperialism' even to the extent of deriding its very real achievements.

The reconquest of the Sudan constituted the high-water mark both of imperial conquests and of public euphoria resting on the confident, uncritical assumption of Great Britain's civilising mission. In the harsh blows it dealt this imperialist complacency, as well as in its revelation of Britain's military weaknesses, the Second South African War truly indicated that an era was ending.

References

1 Viscount Milner. *England in Egypt*, 4th ed. London: Constable, 1921; pp. 30, 70.

2 G. W. Steevens. *With Kitchener to Khartum*, 5th ed. Edinburgh: Blackwood, 1898; p. 2.

3 Winston S. Churchill. *The River War*, 2 vols. London: Longmans, 1899; I, p. 81.

4 Colonel Sir R. Slatin Pasha (Trans. Sir F. R. Wingate). *Fire and Sword in the Sudan*. London: Arnold, 1905; pp. 5, 195.

5 P. Magnus. *Kitchener: Portrait of an Imperialist*. London: Murray, 1958; pp. 81–2, 90.

6 Ibid., p. 104.

7 Steevens, op. cit., p. 128.

8 Churchill, op. cit., I, p. 375.

9 Ibid., p. 443.

10 'An Officer'. *The Sudan Campaign, 1896–99*. London: Chapman and Hall, 1899, p. 157. For Kitchener's harsh treatment of Mahmud see Magnus, op. cit., p. 122.

11 Churchill, op. cit., I, pp. 435–7.

12 Magnus, op. cit., pp. 119–21.

13 Ibid., p. 122.

14 'An Officer', op. cit., p. 173.

15 Churchill, p. 454.

16 Steevens, p. 247.

17 B. Burleigh. *The Khartum Campaign*. London: Chapman and Hall, 1899; p. 134.

18 'An Officer', p. 188.

19 Churchill, II, pp. 132 ff. and 282–7.

20 Burleigh, op. cit., pp. 181–93, and C. Falls. *A Hundred Years of War*. London: Duckworth, 1953, p. 121.

21 'An Officer', pp. 213–14, and Lt-Col H. de Watteville. *Lord Kitchener*. London: Blackie, 1939; p. 58.

22 Magnus, op. cit., pp. 133–7.

23 *Kitchener Papers*, Public Record Office.

24 K. Feiling. *A History of England*. London: Macmillan, 1950; pp. 1006, 1043–6.

25 'An Officer', chapter XVI, passim.

26 Magnus, pp. 136–7, 153.

Victorian Wars and Punitive Expeditions

1837–39. Rebellion in Canada.
1838–39. Capture of Aden and Occupation of Karrack.
1838–42. First Afghan War.
1839–42. First Chinese War.
1843. Sind Campaign.
1843. Gwalior Campaign.
1844. Southern Mahratta Campaign.
1845. Campaign against Hill Tribes on Sind Frontier.
1845–46. First Sikh War.*
1846–47. Second Chinese War.
1846–47. First New Zealand War.
1846–47. Seventh Kaffir War.
1848–49. Second Sikh War.*
1849–50. Expedition against Affreedees.
1850–53. Eighth Kaffir War.
1851–53. Burmese War.
1851–54. Expeditions against Mohmands and Affreedees.
1854–55. Crimean War.
1856. Race Riots (British Guiana).
1856–57. Persian War.
1856–60. Third Chinese War.*
1857–59. Indian Mutiny.

1858.	Expeditions against Tribes on North-West Frontier of India.
1860–61.	Second New Zealand War.
1861.	Sikkim Campaign.
1861–62.	Expeditionary Force to Canada.
1863.	Campaign against Tribes on North-West Frontier of India.
1863–66.	Third New Zealand War.
1864–65.	Bhootan Campaign.
1865.	Insurrection in Jamaica.
1866 and 1870.	Fenian Raids (Canada).
1866–67 and 1872.	Expeditions against Indians of British Honduras.
1867–68.	Abyssinian War.*
1868.	Campaign against Tribes on North-West Frontier of India.
1870.	Red River Expedition (Canada).
1871–72.	Looshai Expedition.
1873–74.	Ashanti War.*
1874.	Duffla Expedition (Naga Hills).
1875–76.	Perak Campaign.
1875–76.	Race Riots (Barbados).
1877–78.	Jowakhi Campaign.
1877–78.	Ninth Kaffir War.
1878.	Dispatch of Indian troops to Malta (Eastern Question).
1878–79.	Zulu War.
1878–80.	Second Afghan War.
1880–81.	First South African War.*
1882.	Egyptian War.*
1884–85.	Suakin Expedition.
1884–85.	Sudanese War.
1885.	Suppression of Riel's Rebellion (North-West Canada).
1885–92.	The Conquest of Burma.
1888.	Sikkim War.
1888.	Hazara War (the Black Mountain Expedition).
1889–90.	Chin-Looshai War.
1891.	Samana or Miranzai Expedition.

1.

xpedition.

1.

ion.

of Chitral.

Ashanti.

1896–99. Reconquest of the Sudan.*
1896. Matabeleland War.
1896–97. Bechuanaland Expedition.
1897. Samana or Affreedee Campaign (North-West Frontier).†
1897. Benin Expedition.
1897. Malakand Field Force.
1899–1902. Second South African War.
1900. Fourth China War.

* Campaigns studied in this volume.

† A complete list of expeditions to the North-West Frontier is given by Captain H. L. Nevill, *Campaigns on the North West Frontier*. London: Murray, 1912; p. 404.

x*

APPENDIX TWO

Notes on Sources

THE SIKH WARS, 1845–9

For the political background to this period J. Mahajan's work—to which frequent reference has been made in the footnotes—and J. D. Cunningham's *History of the Sikhs* (London, ed. 1918) are essential. Bajwa Sinjh goes into the organisation of the Sikh Army in great detail; unfortunately most of the documentary sources on this subject are written in Persian and located in India. The relevant Parliamentary Papers are interesting, but the indexes of the Punjab Government Records at the India Office are incomplete for this period. For the warfare itself there are numerous memoirs and eye-witness accounts. Sir Herbert Edwardes' account of the operations before Multan (*The Punjab Frontier in 1848–1849*, 2 vols. London, 1851) is an excellent first-hand source for this period, and indeed his reputation was partly made by the book. By far the best published authority for the part of the Second Sikh War he experienced is Major Lawrence-Archer, who makes good use of his first-hand knowledge. Captain Mackinnon's book on the First Sikh War is rather ill-organised and difficult to follow in detail. The Reverend Coley's comments on the First War are amusing because of his intensely evangelical outlook, but he also provides some interesting sidelights on the manners and attitudes of the early Victorian Army in India. Generally speaking though the commentaries on the Second War are more numerous and more instructive; an aide-de-camp, Lieutenant E. J. Thackwell's *Narrative of the Second Sikh War* (London, 1851) and that of the anonymous subaltern in the 2nd Bengal Europeans are particularly good.

The most difficult and interesting problems however are those relating to the Sikh Army. For example, the communications from the Sikh generals to their British opponents, and the correspondence of Major George Broadfoot, the Resident at Lahore 1844–5 who was killed at the battle of Ferozeshah, are both in the Punjab Record Office. Thus although adequate material exists in this country for a study of British policy towards, and military actions in, the Punjab, the Sikhs' role cannot be fully understood without research in the Pakistani and Indian archives.

THE THIRD CHINA WAR, 1860

This war is extremely well covered as there are a number of published eye-witness accounts; notably by Wolseley, Rennie, Swinhoe and Loch. Wolseley's letters, which are in Hove Public Library, are easy to handle and so well written that they can be studied with pleasure. The authorities there are most helpful, and the letters filed carefully. The Hope Grant despatches in the British Museum are disappointing; they comprise only one file and are not numbered except for the first ones; they are, however, easy to deal with as they are in chronological order in the file. The Gordon Letters in the British Museum are difficult to deal with, consisting as they do of about forty files each containing many bundles. The most valuable file in the Public Record Office is the Confidential Print of Affairs in China 1859–60 (FO 405/5). This gives the correspondence between Lord Elgin and Lord John Russell, and from it a good account of the war can be arrived at, as well as the nature of the relationships of the principals involved.

THE EXPEDITION TO ABYSSINIA, 1867–8

The basic work is Holland (Major T. J.) and Hozier (Captain H. M.), *Record of the Expedition to Abyssinia; compiled by order of the Secretary of State for War.* 2 vols. London, 1870. This is an exhaustive work, an ancestor of future 'Official War Histories', containing a wealth of information on every aspect. Hozier also wrote a far shorter narrative account, *The British Expedition to Abyssinia*, London, 1869, which is more critical than the larger work. Interesting first-hand accounts of various stages of the campaign are to be found in Scott (Lieutenant W. W.), *Letters from Abyssinia during the Campaign of 1868*, London, 1868; Phayre (Colonel R.), *Abyssinian Expedition; official journal of the reconnoitring party of the British force in Abyssinia.* London, 1869; and in an article by Webb-Carter (Brigadier B. W.), 'A subaltern in Abyssinia' (Walter Andrew Wynter), *Journal of the S.A.H.R.*, Vol. XXXVIII, 1960. Further information can be culled from Cowper (Colonel L. L.), *The King's Own—the Story of a Royal Regiment*, Oxford, 1939, Vol. II; and Lee (A)., *History of the 33rd Foot*, Norwich, 1922.

The standard biography of the Commander-in-Chief is Napier (Lt-Colonel H. D.), *Field Marshal Lord Napier of Magdala*, London, 1927, which quotes extensively from Napier's private correspondence. Other letters, most particularly to and from the Duke of Cambridge, are printed in Napier (Field Marshal Sir R. C., First Baron), *Letters of Field Marshal Lord Napier of Magdala concerning Abyssinia etc.*, London, 1936. The bulk of the Napier Correspondence is to be found in the Old India Office Library.

More documentary evidence is included in War Office Papers, *Abyssinia, 1867–68: extracts from reports on field equipments etc.* (A.0400) 1869, and *Abyssinian Expeditionary Force Quartermaster-Generals' Journal from 19th January 1868 to 11th February, 1868,* (A.0349) 1868. Two interesting articles on the building of the railway are included in the Professional Papers of the Corps of Royal Engineers (New Series), namely Lt-Colonel Wilkins, R.E., *The Abyssinian Expedition* (Paper XI in Vol. XVII, Woolwich, 1870) and Lt Willans, R.E., *The Abyssinian Railway* (Paper XII in Vol. XVIII, Woolwich, 1871). An accurate description of the Magdala position by the same Lt Willans, R.E. appears in the same series (Paper XII, Vol. XVII, as above). Dealing with the financial aspects of the Expedition *in extenso* is the *Report* of the Select Committee on the Abyssinian War, London, 1869.

A colourful, though at times highly inaccurate, account of the expedition by a newspaper special correspondent is to be found in Stanley (H. M.), *Coomassie and Magdala*, London, 1874, while the pages of the *Illustrated London News* for 1867 and 1868 contain many sketches and descriptions. The best modern treatment of the subject (though a trifle thin on the military side) is included in Alan Moorehead, *The Blue Nile*, London, 1962.

THE ASHANTI CAMPAIGN, 1873-4

The best general history of the region is W. W. Claridge's *History of the Gold Coast and Ashanti* (Murray, 1915) though his pioneering work in African traditional history has been carried forward by R. S. Rattray, particularly in *Ashanti Law and Constitution* (Oxford, 1929) and by W. E. F. Ward in *A History of Ghana* (Allen and Unwin, 1958). E. Martin, *The British West African Settlements, 1750–1821*, (London, 1927) is useful for the history of the British presence. The fullest account of the immediate circumstances of the war and the most plausible explanation of the *casus belli* is advanced by Douglas Coombs in *The Gold Coast, Britain and the Netherlands, 1850–74* (Oxford, 1963), and the most scholarly account of the British response to the crisis of 1873 is by Dr W. D. McIntyre, 'British Policy in West Africa, 1873–4, in the *Historical Journal*, Vol. VI, 1962. Kimberley's Journal for 1868–74 is in the Camden Miscellany, Vol. XXI, 1958, ed. E. Drus, and throws some light on the launching of the expedition. The best account of the campaign is still that of Wolseley's private secretary, Henry Brackenbury, *The Ashanti War* (Blackwood, 1874), which reprints the most important instructions, despatches and correspondence. The regimental histories are very disappointing, except for the chapter in Sir John Cope's *The History of the Rifle Brigade* (Chatto, 1877). The papers of Captain Sir John Glover, R.N. at the Royal Commonwealth Society would be important had his march contributed significantly to Wolseley's success. Wolseley's own papers, at the Hove Public Library, add little to our knowledge of this passage in his career. But his autobiography, *The Story of a Soldier's Life* (Constable, 1903), is colourful, and there are two good biographies, Maurice and Arthur: *The Life of Lord Wolseley* (London, 1924) and Joseph H. Lehmann: *All Sir Garnet* (Cape, 1964). A good recent study which takes the history of the Ashanti wars down to 1900 is: Alan Lloyd, *The Drums of Kumasi* (London: Longmans, Green, 1964).

THE SOUTH AFRICAN WAR, 1880-1

The 'Blue Books' on South African Affairs for 1880, 1881 and 1882 print in full the official correspondence between the British Government and South Africa and constitute the most important source of information on both political and military developments. Little fresh evidence could be gleaned from the Cabinet Papers for 1880 and 1881 at the Public Record Office. Much more useful were the Gladstone Papers at the British Museum: the correspondence of all Cabinet ministers with the Prime Minister was checked, but the only volumes of real significance were 44129 (Childers), 44425–6 (Kimberley) and 44642 (Cabinet Minutes). Also at the British Museum, the Dilke Papers (vol. 43935) provided the best evidence of Radical opposition to the war within the Government.

For the crucial role of Sir George Colley I have been obliged to rely chiefly on the extremely well-written but somewhat partisan biography by Sir William Butler (1899). The manuscript of this book was kindly loaned to me by the biographer's son, Colonel P. R. Butler, D.S.O., but unfortunately it adds little to the published version. Colonel Butler recalls that his father was obliged to modify certain criticial sections at the insistence of Lady Colley, and fears that the Colley papers used by the biographer were subsequently lost. Should they come to light a reassessment of Colley would be a rewarding assignment. I was more successful in tracing the papers of Lieutenant (later General Sir Bruce Meade) Hamilton, Colley's brother-in-law who was present in Colley's force, though he did not take part in the action at Majuba. These are in the possession of General Hamilton's great-nephew, Major Bruce Hamilton, who has generously allowed me to borrow and quote from them. The bulk of a large box of papers relate to family matters, but there are a few letters to and from Sir George Colley, a fragment of an uncompleted biographical sketch of him by his widow, and her poignant diary written up shortly after Majuba. The collection also contains some fascinating military photographs, including a few of Majuba in 1881. The Wolseley Papers at Hove Public Library include only a few, but important, letters from Colley and Sir William Butler.

The private papers of Hugh C. E. Childers (Secretary of State for War 1880–2) are easily accessible in the library of the Royal Commonwealth Society, but they contain little of interest to military historians except on the controversy over military appointments involving Wolseley, Queen Victoria and the Duke of Cambridge. However, the biography by his son, Spencer Childers, is particularly good on the military aspect.

I sought in vain the papers of Field Marshal Sir Evelyn Wood, who succeeded Colley in the Natal Command. Wood, like Colley, merits a modern reassessment should the documentary material become available.

THE EGYPTIAN CAMPAIGN OF 1882

(1) *The Wolseley Correspondence*.
Royal United Service Institution. The letters of Lord and Lady Wolseley for 1882 are very important for the campaign and the personal relationships of Wolseley, his colleagues and subordinates.

(2) *Life of the Rt Hon Hugh C. E. Childers* by Lt-Col Spencer Childers. Vol. II.
Spencer Childers made very good use of the Childers papers when writing the section on the Egyptian campaign.

(3) *The Official History*.
Sir Frederick Maurice's *History of the Campaign of 1882 in Egypt* is generally thorough and reliable though tending to inflate Egyptian strength. It was heavily criticised in the *Edinburgh Review*, CLXVII, 1888, but Maurice made a vigorous and generally convincing defence in the *Fortnightly Review*, XLIV, 1888.
Also Lt-Commander Caspar F. Goodrich, U.S.N.'s account: *Report of the British Naval and Military Operations in Egypt in 1882'* has much detail on organisation omitted by Maurice.

(4) *Biographies*.
The official biography: *The Life of Lord Wolseley* by Sir Frederick Maurice (son of the Official Historian), Heinemann, 1924, has material of value. *All Sir Garnet* by Joseph H. Lehmann, Jonathan Cape, 1964, is journalistic but valuable.

THE RECONQUEST OF THE SUDAN, 1896-9

Documentary sources examined:
War Office Papers, Public Record Office.

Kitchener Papers, Public Record Office.

The following published works were found to be most useful in studying the campaign:

Burleigh, Bennet: *Sirdar and Khalifa*. London: Chapman & Hall, 1898; and *Khartum Campaign*. London: Chapman & Hall, 1899.

Callwell. C. E.: *Small Wars, their Principles and Practice*. London: H.M.S.O., 1906 ed.

Churchill, Winston Spencer: *The River War*. 2 vols. London: Longmans, 1899.

De Watteville, Lieut-Col H.: *Lord Kitchener*, London and Glasgow: Blackie, 1939.

Falls, Cyril: *A Hundred Years of War*. London: Duckworth, 1953.

Magnus, Sir Philip: *Kitchener, Portrait of an Imperialist*. London: Murray, 1958.

Martin, Percy F.: *The Sudan in Evolution*. London: Constable, 1921.

Milner, Viscount: *England in Egypt*. 4th ed. London: Arnold, 1907.

'An Officer': *Sudan Campaign, 1896–99*. London: Chapman & Hall, 1899.

Slatin Pasha, Colonel Sir R.: *Fire and Sword in the Sudan*. Translated by Lieut-Col Sir F. R. Wingate. London: Arnold, 1905.

Steevens, G. W.: *With Kitchener to Khartum*. 5th ed. Edinburgh: Blackwood, 1898.

Traill, H. D.: *England, Egypt, and the Suez Canal*. London: Constable, 1900.

Index